MW01673393

'This is an exceptionally well-written book, highly informative, well-articulated, and stands on its value of simplicity. With ageing people numbering high in our country, and their care becoming a constant priority for professionals comprising psychologists, social workers, caregivers, and family members alike, the book comes at an appropriate juncture to fill the gap for such a work. As a technical-cum-academic volume which will help guide both praxis and research, this is a must-add to libraries of institutions as well as organizations in the fields of gerontology and caregiving. Highly recommended for the interested reader or an individual caring for the aged!'

S. S. Nathawat, *Professor Emeritus and Ex-Head, Department of Psychology, University of Rajasthan, Jaipur and former Director, Amity Institute of Behavioural and Allied Sciences, Rajasthan, India*

'This book is a landscape of life in the twilight zone. The book infuses one with hope, optimism, and positivity by giving snapshots into authentic ageing, living with dignity, transpersonal gerontology, unity with nature, and ultimate transcendence. The activities prescribed direct one towards positivity and a celebration of life lived well until the very end. The book is not only a treasure trove on ageing; it gives a glimpse of the benefits of contemplation and introspection as tools for meaningfulness.'

Indranee Phookan Borooah, *Professor and Head, Guwahati University, Assam, India*

'This book is very interesting and informative. Given the increasing number of elderly people across countries, it is expected that the book will have a good market in India and globally too because of its valuable and relevant contents.'

Sibnath Deb, *Professor and Director, Rajiv Gandhi National Institute of Youth Development, Ministry of Youth Affairs and Sports, Government of India, Sriperumbudur, Tamil Nadu, India*

POSITIVE AGEING

This book presents a kaleidoscopic view of the positive layers of ageing as well as key interventions that can help generate and maintain positivity and well-being among the elderly. It explores the connections of ageing with spirituality, nature and existentialism, and leisure to encourage creativity, individuation, happiness, and emotional detachment. It further examines various interventions such as end-of-life care, mindfulness and yoga, retrospection, life review, and so on, which may improve the overall quality of life by promoting the health of the elderly individual.

The book focuses on authentic ageing, transpersonal gerontology, the concept of the elder child, geriatric interventions, and caregiving, and suggests practical improvements in health and facilities for the elderly. It also covers aspects of the inner life of the prolonged ailing or dying person from a mental health perspective and emphasizes the value of positive ageing. A guide to applied geriatrics and geriatric psychology, with its simple style and clear methods in end-to-end praxis, the book shows how mental well-being can be fostered in the elderly to help them find meaning and purpose in old age.

This book will interest students, teachers, and researchers of psychology, positive psychology, geropsychology and gerontological studies, sociology and social work, public health, medical education, and geriatric nursing. It will also be useful to practitioners including psychologists, counsellors, gerontologists, mental health professionals and NGOs working with the elderly, and the interested reader.

Nilanjana Sanyal is former Professor and Head, Department of Psychology, University of Calcutta, Kolkata, India, and a practising Psychoanalyst. She specializes in gerontology and ageing, psychoanalysis, psychodynamic psychotherapeutics, positive psychology, spiritual psychology, and counselling. She has published numerous books, journal and conference papers, and is the co-creator of an International Assessment Standard. She is associated with various apex bodies and has chaired many international conferences. She is also a columnist in national dailies and magazines and is involved in mass media programmes.

Manisha Dasgupta is Associate Professor, University of Calcutta, Kolkata, India. She has interests in gerontology, personality, clinical psychology, and projective psychology, and has several publications. She has been engaged in research and practises therapeutic interventions as a holistic mental health educator and professional. She is a co-developer of the Indian adaptation of an International Assessment Standard.

POSITIVE AGEING

An Approach Towards Transcendence

Nilanjana Sanyal and
Manisha Dasgupta

Routledge
Taylor & Francis Group
LONDON AND NEW YORK

First published 2021
by Routledge
2 Park Square, Milton Park, Abingdon, Oxon OX14 4RN

and by Routledge
52 Vanderbilt Avenue, New York, NY 10017

Routledge is an imprint of the Taylor & Francis Group, an informa business

© 2021 Nilanjana Sanyal and Manisha Dasgupta

The right of Nilanjana Sanyal and Manisha Dasgupta to be identified as authors of this work has been asserted by them in accordance with sections 77 and 78 of the Copyright, Designs and Patents Act 1988.

All rights reserved. No part of this book may be reprinted or reproduced or utilised in any form or by any electronic, mechanical, or other means, now known or hereafter invented, including photocopying and recording, or in any information storage or retrieval system, without permission in writing from the publishers.

Trademark notice: Product or corporate names may be trademarks or registered trademarks, and are used only for identification and explanation without intent to infringe.

British Library Cataloguing-in-Publication Data
A catalogue record for this book is available from the British Library

Library of Congress Cataloging-in-Publication Data
A catalog record has been requested for this book

ISBN: 978-0-367-62099-8 (hbk)
ISBN: 978-1-003-13414-5 (ebk)

Typeset in Sabon
by Deanta Global Publishing Services, Chennai, India

DEDICATED TO OUR PARENTS

CONTENTS

List of figures xi
List of abbreviations xiii
Foreword xiv
Preface by Nilanjana Sanyal xvi
Acknowledgements xx

PART I
Positive layers of ageing: A kaleidoscopic view 1

1 Ageing and spirituality: The entwined elements in life's journey 3

2 'Authentic ageing': Reflections from an existential perspective 23

3 A glimpse into the transpersonal gerontological canvas 38

4 Leisurely ways of attaining positive ageing 52

5 Positively empowered elders with creative 'chisels' in hand 67

6 Nature: The friend and philosopher of old age 80

7 Searching for individuation in retiree identity 94

8 Detachment: The positive end of the elderly mind 110

PART II
Intervention-orientation: Ways to initiate positivity in ageing **123**

9 The reflective mind of the dying person in old age 125

10 Geriatric interventions: The 'eraser' of dark emotionality in the elderly 137

11 End-of-life care in dementia: Geriatric burden or elderly blessing? 157

12 Mindfulness practices: The essential alchemy of meaningful ageing 178

13 The life-story matrix: The retrospective wisdom forum 194

14 Health promotion and well-being in ageing 210

15 Reflective ripples of geriatric life 226

Glossary 233
Index 239

FIGURES

1.1	Major spiritual tasks during the process of ageing	7
2.1	Understanding the finitude of life in terms of death anxiety	26
2.2	The mystery of the present	28
2.3	Inter-relationship of ageing in the context of existential crisis	30
2.4	The conception of the self in accordance with existential terminologies	34
3.1	The multi-faceted nature of ageing	41
3.2	Components of gero-transcendence	45
3.3	Transpersonality in gerontology	47
4.1	The implication of leisure activities in old age	62
5.1	Creativity and allied terms	68
5.2	The major benefits of elderly individuals in pursuing creative activities	72
6.1	Elderly well-being in relation to nature	86
7.1	Changes associated with the initial transition to retired life	99
7.2	Emotional changes in the psyche of the retiree	101
7.3	Guilt issues associated with retirement	102
7.4	Identity crisis in retirees	103
7.5	Personality disposition of generative retirees	105
7.6	Transition to retirement in accordance with Erikson's psychosocial stages	105
10.1	The use of animal-assisted therapy (A.A.T.) among the elderly	144
10.2	Music therapy for the elderly	146
10.3	The use of art therapy for the elderly	146
10.4	Different psychotherapeutic interventions for the elderly	148

11.1 The caring dilemma on the part of family caregivers 163
11.2 Themes of ageing associated with spirituality among caregivers of elderly individuals 171
12.1 Interactions among the different realms with regard to the self in accordance with intentional systemic mindfulness 180
12.2 Mindfulness meditation 185
12.3 Some mindfulness exercises for the elderly 188
13.1 Facilitator and client outcomes in accordance with the SolCos model 197
13.2 Schematic representation of wisdom 200
13.3 Balance theory of wisdom 201
13.4 H.E.R.O.(E) model of wisdom 203
13.5 Brown's wisdom development model 203
13.6 Reminiscence components in accordance with the heuristic model 204
14.1 Factors influencing health among the elderly 220

ABBREVIATIONS

A.A.	Alcoholic Anonymous
A.A.T.	Animal-assisted therapy
A.D.	Alzheimer's disease
C.A.	Conscious ageing
C.B.T.	Cognitive-behaviour therapy
D.D.S.	Dawn–dusk simulation
Gc	Crystallized intelligence
Gf	Fluid reasoning
Gs	Processing speed
H.D.L.	High-density lipoprotein
H.O.P.E.	Health for Privileged Elder
I.G.N.O.A.P.S.	Indira Gandhi National Old Age Pension Scheme
I.S.M.	Intentional systemic mindfulness
M.B.S.R.	Mindfulness-based stress reduction
N.D.A.	Near-death experiences
N.G.O.S	Non-government organizations
N.P.O.P.	The National Policy on Older Persons
N.P.S.	National Pension System
N.R.E.M.	Non-rapid eye movement
N.S.A.P.	National Social Assistance Programme
N.S.P.	Non-starch polysaccharides
O.A.W.I.	Older adults with insomnia
P.F.C.	Prefrontal orbital cortex
P.N.I.	Psychoneuroimmunology
P.R.	Progressive relaxation
S.A.	Successful ageing
S.A.D.	Seasonal affective disorder
S.C.	Stimulus control
S.C.T.	Sleep compression therapy
S.R.T.	Sleep restriction therapy
U.N.	United Nations
V.O.C.	Volatile organic compounds
W.H.O.	World Health Organization

FOREWORD

Positive Ageing: An Approach towards Transcendence by Professor Nilanjana Sanyal and Dr. Manisha Dasgupta presents a wonderfully elegant idea. They take up the challenge of addressing important questions about ageing from a refreshing perspective. They do so in a way that enables us to frame ageing in a graceful manner. The volume carefully and systematically presents an array of concepts, values, insights, and practices that allow conceptualizing old age as a part of growth. It is a laudable effort to advance our understanding that transcends various layers of the human psyche. By offering a comprehensive explication of the psychodynamics of ageing, it has become a compelling invitation to try it theoretically and practise it in daily life.

In this time of universal strife and distress, where the entire human species is rallying around to face disaster together, the foci, often, are getting blurred – vaccines, physical distancing, co-morbidities, lockdowns, and unlocks are the new buzzwords of the hour, and the world is moving one step at a time but decisively towards the New Normal. As is an inherent quality of such change, we tend, in embracing the new, to discard the Old. Yet the Old do not reflect the status quo alone, but old people, old human beings, sustained us, nurtured us, cared for us, and ensured that we are what all we are today.

Also, the need of the hour is to realize that there is a demographic shift in the population of India. The senior citizen today represents a very large portion of India's present population, and with increasing ecological and systemic constraints. These range from scarcity in healthcare and socio-economic and growth prospects. All of them cumulatively impact the aged and bring into the process of ageing a quantum of fear – for those undergoing the process, and those having to offer care from social, economic, or system perspectives. In this perspective, a book which focuses on caring for the old, nurturing the old, indeed looking at the old with new eyes, in a new light, is definitely a welcome breeze of fresh air, especially for practitioners of a developmental frame of mind. I appreciate the effort of the authors, coming from the practice areas that they do, to have deeply researched and created a very time-relevant manual of hope, based as strongly on needs as on values.

As a sourcebook for ageing people, it deconstructs the myths about ageing and offers profound insights to rediscover and construct the meaning of life during old age. The presentation is scholarly and incisive in its analysis. At the same time, the complex concepts are explained with remarkable clarity in elegant and vigorous prose. The need for such an understanding and appreciation of the phenomenon of ageing has never been greater. To the reader, whether they hail from related disciplines or not, I would recommend a read – it would not just provide information and knowledge (which has been captured and encapsulated scientifically), but a view, a vision of what we often tend to overlook, caring for our old, as just another chore or social duty, but an essential aspect of our values, of life itself. I have found its reading revelatory in many respects. This is a book that can change people's lives.

Girishwar Misra
Former Vice-Chancellor, Mahatma Gandhi Antarrashtriya Hindi Vishvavidyalaya, Wardha (Maharashtra) and Professor and Head, Department of Psychology, University of Delhi, Delhi, India

PREFACE

As an academic, author, and practitioner of some decades of standing, it has been a long journey – since the journey comprised movement back and forth between and among various developmental aspects of teaching, researching, guiding research, and designing both interventions and methodologies within the field of psychology, it has often been a realization that I had moved away from one of my primary loves in my chosen field, gerontology. I had, of course, had the opportunity to extensively work in the field of gerontology both in practice as well as research, but the 'creative bug' had bitten me and I had felt a strong urge, both as an educator as well as practitioner, to write a volume that focused on the entire spectrum, albeit in a simple and approachable manner. My erstwhile student and (I can proudly state) present co-author, Manisha, was matched, both in intent and enthusiasm to such a co-creation, and this is that work seeing the light of the day, finally.

For the students and researchers, this provides sequenced referential material to read, learn, and use in their creation of models, hypotheses, and other such academically oriented activities, offered in a simple manner and lucid language. I hope it serves to create enthusiasm among some of them to delve deeper and perhaps adopt this focus area as their own.

For the practitioner, this can act as a guide and workbook, offering some theoretical and practical tools and techniques, as well as the rationale behind them, to help streamline their practices better. We hope this serves the purpose; there would be more to come in the future this way.

For the interested reader and enthusiast, this book provides a simple yet holistic framework, a point of departure to begin serious studies – a straightforward yet valid representation of the discipline and its underlying protocols. We hope you are enthused to persist and pursue your studies further.

Structure of the book

This book provides an overview of the positive layers of ageing as well as the avenues to initiate them. It is designed to encourage readers to embrace ageing positively in their life-frames by deconstructing and demystifying the myths associated with the process. The book comprises two main sections. The first section introduces multiple layers of ageing from a positivistic perspective. It includes eight chapters. The second section has seven chapters and deals with major interventions that may be inculcated to foster positivity among the elderly.

Chapter 1 presents an introduction to the entwined components of ageing and spirituality. It elaborates on certain spiritual interventions in the form of prayers and religious rituals, yoga, meditation, and reminiscence as therapeutic modes to enable the development of the elder personality. The spiritual significance of utterance and pranayama among the elderly is highlighted. Chapter 2 delves into the existential perspective of ageing. Ageing is living in time and calls for an appreciation of the intricate interconnections between the past, the present, and the projected future. Such *lived* time in its changing configurations implies a different time perspective to the process. Developing an art of ageing for living life authentically is the call of the day. Acknowledging and gracefully accepting the dignity of *existential* limitations is essential for the quality of living. Chapter 3 locates processes to help elders to proceed happily and be able to interpret life-flows with a positive lens. Concepts of 'conscious ageing,' 'contemplative ageing,' 'spiritual practices,' and stepping into the realm of 'transcendence' are focused here. The specific arena of 'transpersonal gerontology' has also been touched on to offer a glimpse into the elderly psyche. Chapter 4 sheds light into a definite positive activity regimen in terms of leisure-time activities as per the ability and choice for the elderly so that they are far more contributory in their generative perspective. The implications of leisure activities are discussed. A kaleidoscopic six-tier body of leisure is addressed and its impact on ageing verified. In Chapter 5, the significance of engagement in creative pursuits among the elderly is shown by self-empowerment to improve their overall quality of life. By adopting two major strategies, first, using examples of certain illustrious individuals who have been/are currently internationally and nationally known for their creative endeavours, and, second, by elaborately discussing creativity in the latter half of life, the chapter offers a therapeutic view for individuals with illness(es). Chapter 6 comprehends ageing following the simple laws of nature. Nature serves as the genuine 'connector' with the universe *per se* and enables the elderly to be mindful of the present by providing a 'spiritual connect.' The mind becomes calm and tranquil and the elderly person basks in 'spiritual bliss' and transcendence by relaxing and healing one's mind-frame in the oxygenous rim of nature. Nature becomes the only companion in old age to be with, boosting the 'feel-good factor' and serves as the authentic philosopher of the senior individual. The following chapter (Chapter 7) deals with the inner topography of the retiree and his/her transition in terms of adjustment to the home and self to become a senior. The need for individuation for the retiree is palpably felt in overall contentment and purpose of life. The nuances of retirement from a developmental perspective have also been addressed such that senior individuals may engage in self-realization. Chapter 8 discusses the significance of detachment to attain the experience of 'bliss' along positive psychology. The person becomes liberated from worldly expectations and instead becomes emotionally content with the givens of life. Detachment seems to be the connector-point with higher spirits in the realm of transcendence and an unencumbered spontaneous self.

The second section of the book focuses on some intervention-orientation strategies to initiate positivity in ageing. Chapter 9 unfolds the 'inner topography' of dying individuals having prolonged ailment(s) to understand their basic purpose and meaning in life from the positivistic perspective. It is based on a literature review of individuals having near-death experiences (N.D.A.). The road to death often reveals deeper and novel experiences in a personal direction, positive purpose, and social intimacy. The developmental trajectory engaged in by a dying person is highlighted in this chapter. In Chapter 10, an in-depth discussion on different therapeutic interventions and policies at the societal level for elderly individuals to have an improved quality of life has been framed. They are expected to erase dark emotional patches as far as practicable to help them move along the path of unconditional acceptance of their selves with their limitations and to develop a positive regard to the self to attain stability in their remaining days in a graceful way. Chapter 11 looks into the nuances of end-of-life-care in dementia and asks whether to view it as a geriatric burden or an elderly blessing. The necessity of dementia-friendly communities as well as complementary and alternative interventions has been underscored. Caring for the caregivers of dementia is also mandatory. The spiritual realm of caring for such 'caged birds' is palpably felt where elderly individuals serve as 'magic mirrors' whereby they reflect their authentic selves and impart 'life lessons' to the caregivers as 'gifts.' In Chapter 12, the necessity of mindfulness practices for elders and their caregivers to embrace positivity in general is shown. The conceptual overview of such practices of body, mind, feelings, and mind-objects has been discussed in light of Buddhist philosophy. Realization of the impermanence of life, the practise of non-attachment, and tailoring such practices as per the needs of the elderly is highlighted. Chapter 13 discusses the efficacy of life review, especially for the aged. The benefits of reminiscence in finding meaning in life, improving problem-solving skills, assisting with grief process(es), and increasing emotional support, among others, which lead to retrospective wisdom are shown. The process is bound to provide the 'gift' of wisdom as a harvest. The art of positive living may thus be inculcated. In Chapter 14, the nitty-gritty of the health promotion of senior people from the psychosocial perspective is showcased. This includes strategies such as de-cluttering one's lifestyle and adopting different physical avenues as well as a few psychological methods like deep breathing, meditation, and so on. Intra- and interpersonal well-being may be fostered by developing a sense of gratitude and reflecting on positive events, inculcating a forgiving stance, developing self-care practices, honing one's social capital, and so on. The senior but decapacitated individual is thereby expected to enjoy life to its fullest. Finally, the last chapter (Chapter 15) enumerates different folds of realization in the context of ageing along positive psychological routes. These have been presented in the form of meditative notes to offer experiential richness. The psychological equation to attain positive ageing is thus inscribed; the truncated and egoistic self broadens to merge with the 'contemplative imagination.'

Nilanjana Sanyal

ACKNOWLEDGEMENTS

The authors take this opportunity to acknowledge the publishers, who helped this project reach fruition. In this era of commercialization, the creation of a book is often exactly mapped to how much there is a need for the specific publisher's perceived market – for books which combine the academic with the applicable, the case approach with the caselet, often the point in focus is only small and not the system view. If this book helps readers, students, and practitioners alike, indeed, if the praxis stands enriched because of it, the publishers need to be thanked for having gone ahead with the project.

It would also be an appropriate juncture to thank all those who silently worked in the background – students, co-researchers, academic colleagues abroad, and other members of any practice group who directly or indirectly helped the authors ideate, pick topics, look at different perceptual positions, and helped clarify various representational systems to help qualify and quantify the various problem statements and solution architectures that give this book its present shape. A big vote of thanks to all of you!

Last, the secondary and tertiary stakeholders, ranging from those who took time out to read the proof, to friends, associates, and members of the authors' respective ecologies who supported, in thought and action, the creation of this volume, and the ethos behind such creation, we thank you in all sincerity.

Had it not been for all of you, this book would not have seen the light of day.

Part I

POSITIVE LAYERS OF AGEING

A kaleidoscopic view

1

AGEING AND SPIRITUALITY

The entwined elements in life's journey

The glamour-clad 21st-century society has a prominent signpost: a significant percentage of the population is ageing. The advancements of biomedical science seem to be its initiator. Despite the fact of great mental strength in many elderly people, this stage commonly calls for physical and emotional frailty on the part of most of its members. The scientific enterprise has been probing solutions for an improved quality of life for aged individuals. The traditional Hindu view acknowledges the existence of four stages of life. These are:

1. *Brahmacharya Ashrama*: Childhood marked by character-building and learning the duty to others;
2. *Garhastha Ashrama*: A householder's stage of life that begins at marriage;
3. *Vanaprastha Ashrama*: Leaving home when children have reached adulthood;
4. *Sannyasa Ashrama*: The final stage of life when one mentally renounces worldly ties. The elderly person entering this stage spends her/his time in meditation and contemplation, pondering the mysteries of life.

Elderly people, upon reaching this fourth stage of life's journey, are expected to be physically dependent on others, in general, and mentally prompted by a renewed search for the meaning of life. The search seems to include a shift in life values and an increased openness to living with ambiguities and uncertainties. Adjustments of new varieties are required to the decrements of an ageing body and changed perspectives of the mind. They need to step into a new realm of life, either to look at it with a positive lens or to brood on the losses that are obvious at the time.

Ageing: The saga of loss and sadness

Traditionally, ageing tends to be described in terms of losses of a multiple nature, and for some of the oldest ones, it seems to be the sum of all those losses that can be catastrophic and could lead to significant depression. Ageing thus seems to be the saga of loss and sadness (Albans, 2013). The ageing journey, in fact, signifies that the different stages of life are marked by specific tasks or priorities and this also holds true for late-life. In Eriksonian et al.'s (1997) concept, the eighth or last stage of life demands the integration of all acumens of life to touch the fringe of the wisdom-flair. After Erikson's death, the possibility of a ninth stage of 'transcendence' was proposed by Joan Erikson to address the still-growing experience of the greater number of people approaching old age. Joan Erikson was under the influence of Tornstam's theory of gero-transcendence, claiming a shift in non-agerians from a materialistic and rational vision to a more cosmic and transcendent one is normally accompanied by an increase in life satisfaction (Tornstam, 1994). The theory predicts that a gero-transcendent person will experience feelings of communion with 'the spirit of the universe.' There is expected to be a redefinition of time, space, life, and death, a redefinition of the self, and a greater need for solitary reflection and meditation.

Erikson's eighth stage implies a capacity for reflection and self-review that brings experiences of both joys and sorrows, successes and failures, together holding them under the divine feelings of wisdom. This is the base for self-acceptance and viewing life as worthwhile. The outline of this eighth stage is reminiscent of Kierkegaard's (1996) important ideation that a review of life makes it understandable to look back, but the motion of life needs a forward thrust. Evidence pinpoints the process of sifting through memories and accrued paraphernalia for many older people is a helpful device that moves them through a process of de-cluttering and reviewing towards the acceptance of ageing along with a number of its obvious limitations.

Historically, the elders of a society are conceived to be the functional transmitters of sacred knowledge and rituals. They seem to establish an awareness of the culture and its roots that is necessary for the health and growth of the community (Moberg, 2001). With the expansion of older adults in the population, the role of elders in society is expected to be more beneficiary in providing meaning to the lives of its ageing members. Along the same lines, Jung (1970) regards the possibilities of later life as not only superior but 'constituting its true purpose and meaning.' He thus considers that it is the privilege of later life to reflect on and make sense of experience, not only for one's own benefit but to pass it on to others through the process of 'generativity.' Generative concern then becomes a strong drive for older people to live life meaningfully, keeping aside the personal stories of sadness.

Jacoby (2012) also coins the term 'emotional correctness,' wherein the word 'old' is conceived as an expression of prejudice rather than a factual description of this final stage of life. In fact, it seems impossible to keep an account of how many peoples' journeying into old age is marked by reasonable health and active participation in wider society and vice versa in terms of proving their frailty. Statistics are expected to offer double indicators of positivity and negativity. The idea results in a newer notion.

Old age: The autumn of life

Autumn is the time of endings: of days shortening and trees shedding their leaves as nature gets ready for winter. But autumn is equally the season of vivid colours and the season for harvesting fruits. The season is considered the crowning point of the year and in the midst of the dying back, the whole purpose of the year becomes obvious. Metaphorically, Goodman (1999) suggests that the experience of our later years from 'everybody expecting me just to wind down and disintegrate' to a place of joyful, conscious ripening, with a focus on self-worth, to harvest the fruits of a lifetime. Holding a similar sentiment, Newell (1999) expresses that old age is repeatedly devalued into an inferior state of being, regarded as a decline or fall from the fullness of life. In fact, the fruit that an old tree yields an abundance that outweighs the crop of the young.

The idea pinpoints that decay and diminishments are the rules in old age. But the positive perspective is to look at its silver lining and the positive attitude of offering means to live more happily in extended years and is the correct orientation in today's world. Facilitating true participation in the community, with a role appropriate to the aged person's ability, should be the vital point of helping them discover or rediscover a purpose in living. Hence the need for finding out avenues of revitalization – avenues located in spiritual practices to be adopted in the autumn stage of life to have a colour and smell impact of life.

Spirituality and ageing

The concept of spirituality is just not a mental flair available in the last lap of life. In the Eriksonian manner, Fowler (1991) recognizes six stages of faith, acknowledging that individual development may stop at any stage:

1. *Intuitive-projective faith (ages 2–7)*: A child tends to become aware of the concept of God;
2. *Mythic-literal faith (ages 7–12)*: When family-specified perspectives and meanings of morals are embedded in the self;
3. *Synthetic-conventional faith (adolescence onward)*: When faith is accepted without any criticality;
4. *Individuation-reflective stage*: When faith is critically examined and one's own belief system is reconstructed;
5. *Connective faith (midlife and beyond)*: When disillusionment with the belief system sets in and one develops conflict and openness to other religious traditions;

6. *Universalizing faith (late-life)*: Brings oneness with the divinity, willingness to promote justice in the world, and embracing others in fellowship disregarding their faith stage or belongingness to other religions.

Most psychologists emphasize faith development in later life as a mental element after the completion of all developmental cognitive stages. According to Moberg (2001), this late-life faith is a lifelong developmental task until death.

Dimensionally, ageing simply does not have chronological or biological progression in the developmental sequence. The two most important dimensions to be considered in late-age development are '*psychological ageing*' and '*spiritual ageing*.' The former one is defined in terms of both adaptability and attitude as follows:

- Psychological age refers to the adaptive capacities of an individual on the basis of learning, memory, intelligence, emotional control, motivational strength, coping styles, and so on (Rybash, Roodin, and Santrock, 1991).
- Spiritual age refers to developmental changes in the spiritual dimension. For example, Fowler (1991) has proposed that faith progresses through different developmental stages from simple childish faith to spirituality. Tornstam (1994) postulates seniors' attitude of adopting a spiritual dimension that includes a preoccupation with intergenerational relationships, the meaning of life, and death.

In Jung's (1971) terms, in old age, there is an increase in interiority and focus on achieving integrity (Erikson, 1963). Gutmann (1987) points out that increasing interiority is basically an age-related phenomenon. This involves the integration of past experiences with current situations into a meaningful story. This shift from 'doing' to 'being' and from 'outer attachments' to 'inner life' is the mark of spiritual growth. MacKinley (2001) delineates a helpful model of how spirituality interacts with ageing. Her proposal states that there are developmental tasks demanded by older age and the process of ageing that can be resolved are:

- *Self-sufficiency versus vulnerability*
- *Relationship versus isolation*
- *Hope versus fear*

The associated tasks are thus to transcend difficulty, disability, loss, and so on, to search for final meanings, to find intimacy with God and others, and ultimately to have hope. MacKinley's (2001, 2006) conception of a generic model of a spiritual model inclusive of spiritual tasks at a later age pinpoints the process of spiritual development in later life (Figure 1.1).

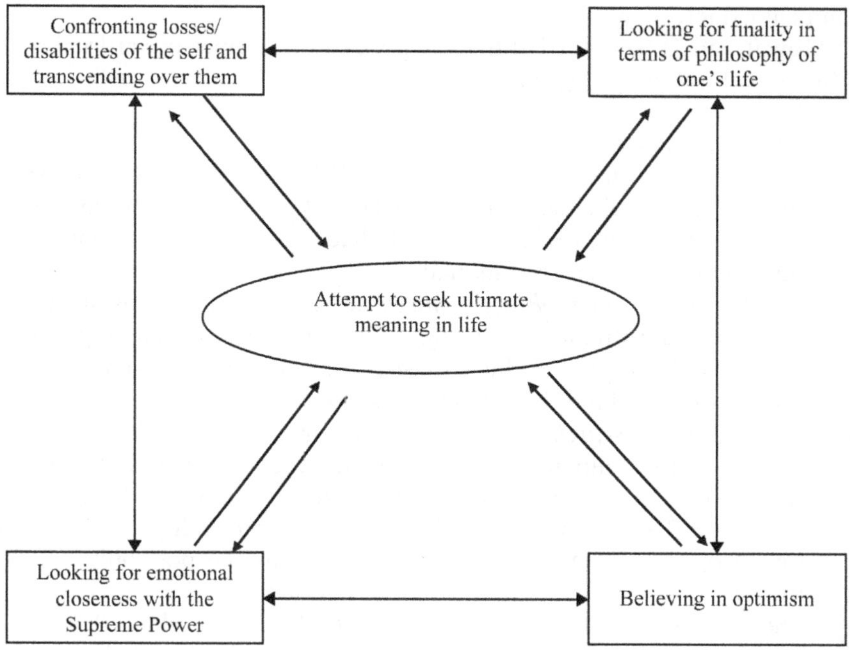

Figure 1.1 Major spiritual tasks during the process of ageing (source: modified from MacKinley, 2006).

In the last two decades, gerontologists and psychologists have become increasingly aware of the importance of spiritual orientation in ushering in and maintaining mental stability.

Spirituality: The theme

Karen et al. (2006) identified the word spirituality as originating from the Latin 'spiritus.' Spirituality was seen as having life beyond life. Mason, Singleton, and Webber (2007) view a person's spirituality as a life perspective reflecting one's set of values and practices. Erbe (2005) views spirituality as 'a person's internal sense of purpose, meaning and future' (p. 12). Others have defined the concept as the individual's existential relationship with a higher authority, a perceived transcendence or God (Goodmann, 1999). Coheman and O'Haulon (2004) opine that though spirituality is concerned with a higher level of meaning, value, and purpose in life, it is usually associated with belief in a force beyond the material world. It concentrates on '*existential meaning.*' Spirituality has both generic and specific dimensions. The generic wing encompasses meaning, transcendence, and relationships;

the specific wing encompasses religion, music, art, and response to the environment (MacKinley, 2001).

Mowat and O'Neill (2013) has categorized the themes of spirituality in different definitional categories:

- *Spirituality as related to religious belief*;
- *Spirituality as a secular concept*: King (2011, p. 21) believes that spiritualities are certain ideational points behind specific practices and commitments that nurture, sustain, and shape the fabric of human lives, individually as well as communally;
- *Spirituality as a metaphor for absence*: Swinton and Pattison (2010) view that in spirituality, by raising the importance of meaning, purpose, hope, love, God, or relatedness issues, resistance and protest against the absence of some kind of care is highlighted;
- *Spirituality is a search for meaning with or without God*: Spirituality recognizes the human need for the ultimate meaning in life being fulfilled through a relationship with God or otherwise (Mowat and O'Neill, 2013). Ferguson (2011) views that spirituality may or may not be open to ideas of transcendence and to the possibility of the divine;
- *The contemporary use of the word spirituality*: Sheldreke (2007, p. 2) conceives that spirituality implies some kind of vision of the human spirit which assists the individual in achieving his/her full potential.

Ageing and spirituality: The entwined elements in life

Research into ageing and spirituality has the basic assumption of ageing as a journey, as a search for meaning, balance, integration, and reconciliation (Mowat, 2004). There are a number of key theories available to establish the entwined interconnect of ageing and spirituality.

- *Socio-emotional selectivity theory (Carstensen, Issacowitz, and Charles, 1999)* proposes a greater emphasis on emotional goals as individuals become aware of the brevity of life;
- *Jung (1959)* conceptualized that increasing spiritual goals and pursuits accompanied by introspection from mid to later life are but a natural part of the maturational process;
- *The disengagement theory (Cummings and Henry, 1961)* assumes that a societal benefit is the result of adults' withdrawal from all roles and activities. Considered as an inevitable condition in life prior to death, this withdrawal is filled up by the youth generation and the older adults retire;
- *Binachi's (1984) activity theory*, on the other hand, emphasizes increased activities and taking active roles are needed to have healthy ageing;

- *Atchley (2009)* developed the *continuity theory* that states that individuals develop preferences to be spiritual as old age approaches. To him, spirituality is 'deep inner silence,' 'insight,' 'compassion,' 'connection with the ground of being,' 'transcendence of personal self,' 'wonder,' and 'transformation' to look for deeper meanings in personal experiences; he also emphasized the role of spiritual practices in the experiential process of dying;
- *Tornstam (1994)* introduced the *concept of gero-transcendence* and conceived spiritualistic practices as a transition from a materialistic and rationalistic perspective to a more cosmic and transcendent view of life that accompanies the process of ageing;
- *Hill and Pargament (2003)* are of the opinion that spirituality may be understood as an attempt to *search for the sacred*, which underlies a process of self-discovery essentially. A search for life meaning is conceived as a central aspect of spirituality by many (Aponte, 2002; MacKinley, 2001; Ortiz and Langer, 2002). Spirituality encompasses religiosity but widens one's perspective of understanding the transcendent.

Spirituality is a human awareness of heightened knowledge beyond sensory perceptions. Holmes (1982) also defined spirituality as a phenomenon which transcends sense experience in human capacity. A person perceives it as a heightened or expanded consciousness that prompts one to have awareness of the self, others, and the world in greater depth.

The core philosophy of life opines that spiritual well-being is the affirmation of life in a relationship with God or a supreme power; the self, community, and the environment that nurtures and celebrates wholeness, permeates and gives meaning to all life. The term *spiritual well-being* indicates wholeness in contrast to fragmentation and isolation (Brennan and Missinene, 1980). The markers of spiritual well-being include positive self-concept, unselfish giving, moral character, belief in an all-encompassing God, personal transcendence, and so on. Thus, 'being spiritual' involves an individual to provide complete 'holistic' care of that person's psychological and spiritual needs.

The commonality of the theories pinpoints that spirituality appears to play an important and adaptive role in ageing that prompts people to have a better quality of life, enhanced self-satisfaction, and confidence in the self even in the process of dying. The definite procedures of spiritual interventions need a brief review.

Spiritual interventions

Basic feature-wise spiritual interventions are found to be more cross-cultural, affective, transcendent, and definitionally experiential. Their proper durations are not quite stipulated, yet the impact on body and mind has been reported to be undoubtedly positive (Levretsky, 2014). Certain common spiritual practices are:

Prayers and religious rituals: Prayer is a powerful form of coping that helps people physically and mentally. The system acts as a communication or conversation with a divine power or a 'higher self.' Its various modes include:

- *Group prayer*: Being associated with generative good wishes for everyone;
- *Solitary prayer*: Generally is followed in depression and loneliness (Poloma and Pendleton, 1991).
- *Spiritual reading or bibliotherapy*: Worship and rituals are integral to most religions. Benson (1997) is of the opinion that potentially therapeutic elements of worship include music, aesthetic surroundings, rituals, prayers, contemplation, and opportunities to socialize with others. Bibliotherapy is the spiritual reading that involves the use of literature to help gain insight into feelings and behaviours and to assist with positive coping.
- *Practising forgiveness and repentance*: All major theistic world religions preach that everybody should accept and forgive those who had been the cause of harm in their lives and seek forgiveness from those they have harmed intentionally or unintentionally. In Alcoholic Anonymous (A.A.), such a mode of practice calls for 'confessions' and recounting of one's wrong-doings. In medical settings, the process of forgiveness and repentance are consistent with the client's needs and requests and are within the purview of a pastoral counsellor or clergy person (Latovich, 1995).

Yoga: The alchemy that generates systemic (mind-body) equilibrium

'Yoga' is derived from a Sanskrit word *yuj* that means union, to yoke, or to join, attach, or bind. It relates to the merging of the microcosm with the macrocosm as far as the existence of the body is concerned. Philosophically, it involves the individual self, or *jivatma*, to unite with the universal self, or *paramatma*. It produces a state of bliss where there is cosmic union, where feelings of egoism and narcissistic feelings do not emerge. It enables the union of the physique with the psyche and the psyche with the self at the level of consciousness. It means a poise of the soul which aids one to look at life in all its aspects evenly (Iyengar, 1976, 1993). Yoga is thus a dynamic, internal experience which integrates the body, the senses, the mind, and the intelligence, with the self (Iyengar, 2006).

The consequence is freeing the soul from the bondage of body, mind, power, and pride of success, where it reaches the state of *kaivalya* or freedom. 'It is then that the seasoned, mature mind transcends frontiers to reach beyond mundane observation' (Iyengar, 2006). It helps the system to reach the highest state of mind, being, *niruddha*, or the controlled, restrained mind. According to Patanjali, the persistent practice of yoga helps in the attainment of *niruddha*. This enables the individual to conquer greed, lust, and cravings of varied kinds and helps one to reach the peaks of self-realization (Deshpande, 1978). This is also in accordance with the preaching of the Bhagavad Gita to attain wisdom in one's personality (Shivananda, 2000).

It is during this condition that the individual immerses himself or herself completely in the absorption of self-consciousness, allowing no distraction of any kind to contaminate the serenity. It is during the quiet phase of the brain when the intellect is at peace, the individual is serene and balanced, and poised in pure consciousness. The yoga practices in the form of posture, breathing, and relaxation serve to quieten the mind for the contemplation of deeper issues, such as the roots of suffering, internal peace, and spiritual insight. Yoga then becomes a lifestyle. In time, one's behaviour is aimed towards balance and peace of mind, and this, in turn, enriches life (Mackenzie and Rakel, 2006; John, Sharma, Sharma, and Kankane, 2007).

Yoga among the elderly: An avenue to attain spiritual bliss

Yoga among the elderly is becoming a commonly practised, mind-body approach (Oken, Zajdel, Kishiyama, Flegal, Dehen, Haas, Kraemer, Lawrence, and Leyva, 2006). Yoga therapy appears to have a number of different benefits, some of them being increasing muscular strength along with flexibility, motility, and energy for the elderly individual. Such an individual is also expected to enjoy a greater sense of well-being, decreased pain, improved sleep quality, and a reduction in the perception of stress (Oken, Kishiyama, Zajdel, Bourdette, Carlsen, Haas, Hugos, Kraemer, Lawrence, and Mass, 2004; Raub, 2002; Tran, Holly, Lashbrook, and Amsterdam, 2001; Vempati and Telles, 2002). Yoga can address known fall risk factors (poor balance, impaired mobility, reduced strength, and flexibility) and improve balance in older adults (Schmid, Van Puymbroeck, and Koceja, 2010). Yoga has been increasingly used for therapeutic purposes although it has a spiritual inclination. It is often used in a variety of conditions like multiple sclerosis, rheumatoid arthritis, breast cancer, low back pain, migraine, and epilepsy (Alyson, Rosett, Harris, Patel, Hall, and Judith, 2007; Yardi, 2001).

Yoga has been found to have a therapeutic effect on body balance. Yogasanas range from simple to complex body postures, along with controlled breathing. The different *asanas* involved in yoga often require the stretching and relaxation of major muscle groups to assume a static posture (Oken, Zajdel, Kishiyama, Flegal, Dehen, Haas, Kraemer, Lawrence, and Leyva, 2006). Consequently, muscle strength, endurance, flexibility, motility, and cardiopulmonary endurance of the individual tend to increase because of an altered flow of blood leading to the optimal supply of oxygen to different parts of the body. Body-awareness and proprioception are increased, leading to improved balance in older adults as a result of yoga therapy (Iyengar, 1976). Moreover, the inner journey towards self-realization to enlighten oneself with the purpose of life becomes gradually enunciated through the help of the different gentle poses. Yoga brings into alignment values and lifestyle, which includes a healthy diet, exercise, yoga postures, breathing, meditation, study, and a positive attitude. Yoga teaches the elderly to remove ignorance by detachment and practice (Aranya, 1981, p. 35). As the mind is stabilized and an enlightened worldview dawns, a person is both undisturbed by pain and pleasure and becomes full of willpower that cultivates a healthy way of life. According to the Upanishads, India's earliest literature, one in the highest state of consciousness cannot suffer (Yogendra, 1993, p. 49). It enables the elderly to live in the present and be genuinely concerned about the same. This consequently results in developing a style enriched with gratitude, acceptance, and low sufferance, being wrapped up within the embraces of positive psychology.

To take an illustration of the success of internalizing yoga at the systemic level, Yogacharya B.K.S. Iyengar may be regarded as a legendary figure in this aspect. He took to yoga in 1934 with the hope to regain his health as he was afflicted with many diseases since his childhood. He did not know that yoga would become his style of life, teaching him to be punctual and disciplined despite different hardships. He is credited with bringing the ancient art of yoga into the modern world. His teachings spread over the West, winning numerous accolades internationally. He passed away at the ripe age of 95 years after a brief illness. However, even at such an advanced age, he continued to teach around the world until just prior to his illness. Iyengar is regarded as the 'Michelangelo of Yoga,' the 'King of Yogis,' and was enlisted in *Time* magazine's global list of the world's 100 most influential people. His pioneering works in the form of seminal books like 'Light on Yoga' and 'Light on Pranayama' are noteworthy amidst others. His life is regarded as a life of light and he is one of the most revered yoga practitioners in contemporary times.

Yoga for the elderly relates internally, working with our limits, both physical and emotional, attending to what is still available. Elder-care yoga involves consideration of the following (McBee, 2008):

- Stretching: Physical stretches help the elderly person to become more flexible. It allows them to explore their edges. It is also important not to push themselves too far or too fast;
- Balancing: Balancing is not something one can think about doing, it only happens when one lets go and lets it happen. It enables the elderly to be compassionate with themselves;
- Transitions: Transitions between yoga poses and *asanas* enable the elderly to inculcate the ability to experience transitions in our life gracefully;

- Letting go: Both effort and ease are practised in yoga. Effort gives individuals the strength to hold the pose, but they also need ease, a letting go. Yoga poses may remind the elderly of this duality. *Savasana*, the corpse pose, gives individuals a chance to practise letting go. It helps an individual to get to terms with issues of his/her mortality and enables the bringing in of a greater awareness regarding which part of the body is the person holding his/her tension;
- Flexing and extending the spine: It may be helpful to consider a series of movements, especially of the spine, and to adapt them to seated or prone positions to keep muscles supple and flexible in the elderly. Modifications of the cat and cow poses while lying down, seated, kneeling, or standing may be incorporated;
- Elders in wheelchairs need to be reminded to do only what feels right to them. Participants need to be encouraged to pay attention to body sensations and honour them. At the same time, physical exploration and stretching in new ways may be encouraged. Hands-on assistance may be provided, if needed. Progress needs to be slowly attempted by offering encouragement and praise;
- Yoga for bed-bound elders: Deep breathing may be practised by almost anyone who can follow simple instructions. For people having physical limitations, it may be modified. Bed-bound elders may be guided to engage in bed stretches gently and slowly and to pay attention to the process of moving as well as holding a position.

Meditation appears to be an essential yogic exercise with the primary focus on breath-control and regulation. The need is felt to understand its intricacies to recognize the importance of meditation among the elderly so that they may bask in the light of spirituality.

Meditation: Young and Taylor (2001) opine that meditation is a physiological state of reduced metabolic activity that leads to physical and mental relaxation and is reported to enhance psychological balance and emotional stability. Meditation brings in a sense of calm, limited thought, and attention. It involves deep concentration on internal events such as breathing, a mental object, one point in space or a mantra or in the mindfulness variety, the expanding of attention without judgement on moment-to-moment experience, and observing thoughts and feelings from a meta-cognitive aware state. Swami Vishwatmananda's (2016) view upholds that the great spiritual traditions of the world throughout the ages have promoted various forms of meditation as an important factor in fostering spiritual development and awakening. Citing its benefits, he mentions:

- First, it prevents stress from getting into the system;
- Second, it alleviates the already accumulated stress in the system.

Meditation is both an ancient spiritual practice as well as a contemporary mind-body technique for calming of the mind. The real purpose behind it is the liberation of the self. The mind is compared with a lake that is disturbed by agitating thoughts as waves or '*vrittis*.' The water in the lake becomes muddy and as a result the bottom of the lake – our 'self,' is not visible to us. Meditation and yoga are all about how to train and restrain the mind and not to have a disturbed mind with fleeting thoughts. Further, the spiritual entwining of the elderly self may be related to Zen Buddhism in that meditation (*zazen*) is the epitome of spirituality. It may be regarded as a mental ideal and has a therapeutic effect. The authentic self appears to be bathed in spiritual essence through meditation (Lloyd, 2012, Warner, 2010).

Hinduism believes that meditation is the continuous flow of the mind towards the Divine. It is a form of mental worship. In Maslow's (1971) conception of peak experience or a self-realizational fold, the yoga system prescribes the eightfold steps of meditative practice:

- *Yama*
- *Niyama*
- *Asana*
- *Pranayama*
- *Pratyahara*
- *Dharana*
- *Dhyana*
- *Samadhi*

The net result of all these is '*sunyata*'; the highest meditative state or experience.

In modern-day life, the concept of 'guided meditation' seems very helpful. A guide helps one to relax physically and mentally and in this relaxed state, he/she takes one on an inner journey to improve one or a number of aspects of one's life. The method seems the easiest way to enter into a state of deep relaxation and inner stillness. This is an enhancer of the sense of well-being and a transforming agent of bringing in positive perspectives in life. The guide gradually brings back one to a state of normal awareness with a very relaxed, refreshed, and rejuvenated mental state.

Meditation traditions generally primarily use one type of practice (concentrative, mindfulness, or directed), but most contain elements of all three. Transcendental meditation (T.M.) is often accompanied by *mantra*, which is repeated continuously and silently in the mind. However, sustained effortful focus is not emphasized here (Achterberg et al., 1994). *Breath meditation* seems to be one of the simplest and most fruitful primary meditation techniques. The breath and the body are interconnected – breath and emotions are entwined. In this method, one needs to keep the back straight and breathe normally to gradually attain calmness of mind. Being aware of this breathing sensation is the object of this meditation. With practice on a regular basis, breadth becomes refined and so does our inner awareness. The implications of meditation for the elderly are worthy of being noted, which is highlighted in the following section.

Meditation among the elderly in the backdrop of spiritual essence

Both elderly care recipients and their caregivers (inclusive of formal and informal members) have been found to benefit through meditation practices. They are found to address issues of impermanence, death, and dying, having the underlying notions from Buddhist and Hindu philosophy. It has been adopted primarily in hospice and palliative care settings where elderly individuals have to experience a number of challenges in life (Cason and Lindbergh, 2001; Ostateski, 1994).

Meditation has been found to be involved as a treatment modality to bring about improvement in the quality of life of individuals having chronic or debilitating ailments. It is often used as a therapeutic modality to help clients to cope better with their stresses of illnesses and treatment regimen (Achterberg et al., 1994), to develop an increased sense of control, and be adorned by spiritual experiences (Astin, 1997). Meditation is found to significantly decrease the number of somatic symptoms in patients and significantly increase their confidence level. They say that their relationships with others are improved and they experience more enjoyment and appreciation of life (Baime and Baime, 1996; Kabat-Zinn, 1996).

Such practices have been found to help elderly individuals in coping with distress and disability in their daily life, as well as addressing issues of depression, anxiety, and affective disorders. Besides, meditation also caters to deeper goals, some of them being liberating the spirit from the egocentric self, developing a sense of harmony within the universe, and nourishing the ability to increase compassion of the individual with life as a whole. These values may be increasingly important to elderly people as they work to understand physical declines, impending death, and the loss of friends (Helpard and Meagher-Stewart, 1998).

It is through the non-judgemental acknowledgement of thoughts, feelings, hopes, and fears that meditation provides a context where anxieties about physical and mental functioning may be faced, felt, and understood. Often, elderly individuals have to face problems of social isolation and consequent loneliness. Meditation practices in a group with a facilitator may optimally address such issues (Bishop and Scurlock, 1992).

Elders and their caregivers often face concerns of memory loss and an inability to concentrate, and integrative medicine may have the ability to prevent and even reverse memory loss (Branin, 2001). Institutionalized elders engaged in mindful learning have been shown to be more active, alert, and happy than their counterparts (McBee, 2004; McBee, Westreich, and Likourezos, 2004; Smith, 2004, 2006).

Elders may be engaged in guided meditations in the form of breath awareness and body scan, as well as forgiveness meditation (McBee, 2008). Elderly individuals are enabled to develop a wider perspective of life in general through meditation where they tend to overcome their inherent fear of loss of control and come to terms with death anxiety. Meditation in the elderly also concentrates around the phoneme *OM* along with breath meditation in the form of pranayama, both having therapeutic and spiritual impacts, which are illuminated in the following section.

The spiritual significance of OM utterance and pranayama among the elderly

Meditation on the phoneme *OM* connotes to symbolism found in Mândùkya Upanishad where the letter 'A' of '*A-U-M*' corresponds to the waking state of consciousness, 'U' to the dream state, and 'M' to the state of deep sleep (King, 1992). When one meditates upon these letters, the intrinsic connection associated with various states of consciousness helps the individual to gradually understand the fragmentary or transient state of each condition. This leads to the realization of the self in association with the whole universe or *turiya*. The 'measureless' and 'limitless' reality (*amàtra*) consequently has no pathway. The focusing of the mind on the syllable *OM* helps the person to confront all his/her fears since *OM* is related to the *Brahman* (the Eternal). A person who engages in exploring the depth of his/her consciousness layers through focusing on the syllable is expected to develop against all tides and has no fears whatsoever. *OM* is essentially the process through which one attains to that (*Brahman*) immediately (King, 1992).

During the regimented pattern of breathing in the form of *pranayam*, a sense of peace is enunciated within the body where it has to dip in the solace of quietude, which allows the nervous system to function more effectively. Inhalation involves receiving primaeval energy in the form of breathing and bringing the spiritual cosmic breath into contact with the individual breath. Exhalation relates to the removal of toxins from the system in the form of carbon dioxide.

Thus, *pranayam* brings about the linkage of the physiological and spiritual layers of the individual. At first, *pranayam* is difficult and requires great effort. Proficiency is achieved when pranayama becomes effortless. Just as the diaphragm is the meeting point of the physiological and spiritual body, the retention of energy or *kumbhaka* is realizing the very core of one's body (Iyengar, 2006). When the distractions of the body in the form of movements are controlled, inner silence prevails. It is then that there is no thought and the mind is crystal clear in its experiential richness. Then the individual comes to experience the elevated state of oneness with the self and can attain the level of spiritual bliss. This is of utmost significance for the elderly so that they may come to terms with life as a whole, deal with its challenges, and reap the essence in relation to the universe during the evening phase of their journey.

Reminiscence as therapy for elderly people

Reminiscence is but a natural part of ageing. Spiritual reminiscence involves personal storytelling sessions, finding the linkages between their story and God's story, and connecting with the story of their family and the wider community. The process effectively assists older people to reflect and reframe aspects of their life journey in the process of moving from provisional meaning to find meanings in life. The process demands the reminiscence to re-journey to earlier life episodes, re-examine chapters of the story, and to realize they had acted the best way they knew at that time. The reminiscer sees the event in a new light for the first time and with fresh insight, where the pain, guilt, and regret may be finally laid to rest – the event gets reframed in this new knowledge. This acts as a powerful and freeing experience for the individual from the stored guilt, regrets, or a sense of unforgiveness.

Gibson (2004) offers ten reasons for doing reminiscence work. To him, reminiscence:

- Provides the connection to a person's past, present, and future;
- Encourages sociability and offers new relationships;
- Confirms a sense of unique identity with feelings of self-worth;
- Assists the process of life review;
- Changes the perspectives of relationships;
- Alters others' perceptions and understanding;
- Aids in assessing the present functioning mode to improve on it;
- Reverses the gift of relationship;
- Retains and transmits cultural heritage;
- It seems enjoyable to most people.

Reminiscence is, therefore, extremely valuable if used appropriately, both as a natural phenomenon as well as an effective therapy in residential aged care.

The needed spiritual intervention for the aged in the future

With the advancements of neurological science, future spiritual interventions may encounter changes in their patterns. Fundamentally, the aim seems to be enhancing coping and reducing stress in such a population where a need is felt to consider spiritual diversity and develop targeted programmes to initiate further efficacy of the system. In addition, the future studies of the neurobiology of spiritual interventions and personalized spiritual treatment should include neuroimaging as well as assessment of individual genetic, psychosocial, and biological vulnerability factors. The integrated approaches of spiritual interventions (e.g., combining meditation, yoga, mindfulness, tai chi) are expected to offer greater promise for improving overall functioning and well-being in older adults.

Conclusion

Acquisition of knowledge is the rolling process of life dynamics. If it is true that with age and accumulated experiences, we become more ourselves, more rounded and connected to our faith, have generativity and warmth, and are more concerned regarding others, with a drive to transcend and integrate our life's experiential gains, then there is a huge potential to touch the fringes of divinity, which we neglect at our peril. With the freedom of mind and spirit, with glowing feelings of happiness, the frail body will perhaps salute life acknowledging its blessings on us. Spiritual practices engage the elderly in a mental disciplining regimen, whose harvest is reaped in their positive lifestyle. The sunset years of life are filled with the celebration of orange, red, and yellow leaves in the sunlight before they drop from trees and carpet the ground. The flavour of life reaches its epitome while bearing the fruits of wisdom, purpose, and transcendence among the aged. The flame of life thereby acquires meaning and purpose. The notion of positive ageing as the energy of all nature begins to draw inwards and down into the earth, preparing a safe place to rest and recoup for winter.

References

Achterberg, J., Dossey, L., Gordon, J.S. et al. (1994). Mind-body interventions. In *Alternative medicine: Expanding medical horizons. A report to the National Institutes of Health on alternative medical systems and practices in the United States* (pp. 03–43). Washington, DC: US Government Printing Office.

Albans, K. (2013). Supporting and learning from the oldest old: The spiritual journey of ageing. In Johnson, M. and Albans, K. (Eds.) *God, me and being very old*: Stories and spirituality in later life (pp. 20–36). London: SCM Press.

Alyson, B.M., Rosett, C.S., Harris, M.S., Patel, S.R., Hall, C.B., Judith, J., & Sparano, J.A. (2007). Randomized controlled trial of yoga among a multiethnic sample of breast cancer patients: Effects on quality of life. *Journal of Clinical Oncology*, *25*(28), 4387–4395.

Aponte, H. (2002). Spirituality: The heart of therapy. *Journal of Family Psychotherapy*, *13*(1–2), 13–27.

Aranya, S. (1981). *Yoga philosophy of Patanjali.* Calcutta: University of Calcutta Press.

Astin, J.A. (1997). Stress reduction through mindfulness meditation: Effects on psychological symptomatology, sense of control, and spiritual experiences. *Psychotherapy and Psychosomatics*, *66*(2), 97–106.

Atchley, R.C. (2009). *Spirituality and ageing*. Baltimore, MD: Johns Hopkins University Press.

Baime, M.J., & Baime, R.V. (1996). Stress management using mindfulness meditation in a primary care general internal medicine practice. *Journal of General Internal Medicine*, *11*(S1) (Suppl.1), 131.

Benson, H. (1997). *Timeless healing: The power and biology of belief*. New York: Gale.

Binachi, E.C. (1984). *Ageing as a spiritual journey*. New York: Crossroad.

Bishop, A., & Scurlock, N.D. (1992). A community health program for the elderly. *Caring*, *11*(12), 50–54.

Branin, J.J. (2001). The role of memory strategies in medication adherence among the elderly. *Home Health Care Services Quarterly*, *20*(2), 1–16.

Brennan, C.L., & Missinne, L.E. (1980). Personal and institutionalized religiousity of the elderly. In J.A. Thorson & T.C. Cook Jr. (Eds.), *Spiritual well-being of the elderly* (pp. 92–99). Springfield, IL: Charles C. Thomas

Carstensen, L.L., Issacowitz, D.M., & Charles, S.T. (1999). Taking time seriously: A theory of socio-emotional selectivity. *Annals of Psychology*, *54*(3), 165–181.

Cason, A., & Lindbergh, R. (2001). *Circles of care: How to set up quality home care for our elders*. Boston: Shambhala.

Coleman, P.G., & O' Haulon, A. (2004). *Ageing and development*. London: Arnold/ Hodder.

Cummings, E., & Henry, W.E. (1961). *Growing old: The process of disengagement*. New York: Basic Book Company.

Deshpande, P.Y. (1978). *The Authentic Yoga: A fresh look at Patañjali's Yoga-Sutras with a new translation, notes and comments*. London: Rider.

Erbe, R.C. (2005). Spirituality: A missing dimension in health education. *The Health Education Monographs*, *22*(2), 12–16.

Erikson, E.H. (1963). *Childhood and society*. New York: Norton.

Erikson, E.H., & Erikson, J.M. (1997). *The life cycle completed*. New York: W.W. Norton.

Ferguson, R. (2011). *George Mackay Brown: The wound and the gift*. Edinburgh: St. Andrew Press.

Fowler, J.W. (1991). *Weaving the new creation: Stages of faith and the public church*. San Francisco: Harper and Row.

Gibson, F. (2004). *The past in the present: Using Reminiscence in health and social care*. Baltimore: Health Professions Press.

Goodman, J. (1999). Harvesting a lifetime. In A. Jewell (Ed.), *Spirituality and ageing* (pp. 65–70). London: Jessica Kingsley Publishers.

Gutmann, A. (1987). *Democratic Education*. Princeton, NJ: Princeton University Press.

Helpard, H., & Meagher-Stewart, D. (1998). The 'kaleidoscope' experience for elderly women living with coronary artery disease. *Canadian Journal of Cardiovascular Nursing*, *9*(3), 11–23.

Hill, P.C., & Pargament, K.L. (2003). Advances in the conceptualization and measurement of religion and spirituality. Implications for physical and mental health research. *Annals of Psychology*, *58*(1), 64–74.

Holmes, U.T. (1982). *Spirituality for ministry*. San Francisco: Harper & Row.

Iyengar, B.K.S. (1976). *Light on yoga* (2nd ed.). New York: Schocken Books.

Iyengar, B.K.S. (1993). *Light on the yoga-Sütras of Patañjali*. London: Aquarian Press.

Iyengar, B.K.S. (2006). *Iyengar Yoga for beginners: An introduction to the classic poses*. London: Dorling Kindersley Limited.

Jacoby, S. (2012). *Never say die: The myth and marketing of the new old age* (p. 5). New York: Vintage Books.

John, P.J., Sharma, N., Sharma, C.M., & Kankane, A. (2007). Effectiveness of yoga therapy in treatment of migraine without aura: A randomized controlled trial. *Headache*, *47*(5), 654–661.

Jung, C.G. (1959). *The basic writings of Jung*. New York: Modern Library.

Jung, C.G. (1971). The stages of life. In R.F.C. Hull (Ed.), *The portable Jung* (pp. 3–22). New York: Viking Press.

Jung, C.G. (1970). The stages of life. In *The structure and dynamics of the psyche:* The *collected works of C.G. Jung* (2nd ed., pp. 387–403). Princeton, NJ: Princeton University Press.

Kabat-Zinn, J. (1996). Mindfulness meditation. In Y. Haruki, Y. Ishii, & M. Suzuki (Eds.), *Comparative and psychological study on meditation* (pp. 161–170). Amsterdam: Euboron.

Karen, K.J., Hafen, B.Q., Smith, N.L., & Frandsen, K.J. (2006). *Mind Body Health: The effects of attitudes, emotions and relationships* (3rd ed.). San Francisco: Pearson Benjamin Cummings.

Kierkegaard, S. (1996) *Papers and journals* (A. Hannay, trans., p. 161). London: Penguin.

King, R. (1992). Asparśa-yoga: Meditation and epistemology in the GauḌapādīya-kārikā. *Journal of Indian Philosophy*, *20*(1), 89–131.

King, U. (2011). Can spirituality transform our world? *The Journal for the Study of Spirituality*, *1*(1), 17–34.

Latovich, M.A. (1995). The clergyperson and the fifth step. In R.J. Kus (Ed.), *Spirituality and chemical dependency* (pp. 79–89). Binghamton, NY: Haworth Press.

Levretsky, H. (2014). Spirituality and ageing. In *Resilience and ageing: Research and practice* (p. 114). Baltimore: John Hopkins University Press.

Lloyd, G.E.R. (2012). *Being, humanity, and understanding: Studies in ancient and modern societies*. Oxford: Oxford University Press.

Mackenzie, E.R., & Rakel, B. (Eds.). (2006). Complementary and *alternative medicine for older adults a guide to holistic approaches to healthy aging*. New York: Springer Publishing company.

MacKinley, E. (2001). *The spiritual dimension of ageing*. London: Jessica Kingsley Publications.

MacKinley, E. (2006). *Spiritual growth and care in the fourth age of life* (pp. 11-29). . London: Jessica Kingsley Publishers.

Maslow, A. (1971). *The farther reaches of human nature*. New York: Viking Press.

Mason, M., Singleton, A., & Webber, R. (2007). *The spirit of generation Y: Young people's spirituality in a changing Australia* (p. 150). Melbourne: John Garratt Publishing.

McBee, L. (2004). Mindfulness practice with the frail elderly and their caregivers. Changing the practitioner-patient relationship. *Topics in Geriatric Rehabilitation*, *19*(4), 257–264.

McBee, L. (2008). *Mindfulness-based elder care: A CAM Model for frail elders and their caregivers*. New York: Springer Publishing Company.

McBee, L., Westreich, L., & Likourezos, A. (2004). A psycho-educational relational group for pain and stress management in the nursing home. *Journal of Social Work in Long-Term Care, 3*(1), 15–28.

Moberg, D.O. (2001). *Ageing and spirituality: Spiritual dimensions of ageing theory, research, practice and policy*. Binghamton, NY: Haworth Press.

Mowat, H. (2004). Successful ageing and the spiritual journey. In A. Jewell (Ed.), *Ageing, spirituality and well-being*. London: Jessica Kingsley Publishers.

Mowat, H. and O'Neill, M. (2013). Spirituality and ageing: Implications for the care and support of older people. *Insights: Evidence summaries to support social services in Scotland*, Institute for Research and Innovative in Social Services, Glasgow. .

Newell, J.P. (1999). *On foot in Eden: A Celtic view of the stages of life* (p. 76). Mahwah, NJ: Paulist Press.

Oken, B.S., Kishiyama, S., Zajdel, D., Bourdette, D., Carlsen, J., Haas, M., ... Mass, M. (2004). Randomized controlled trial of yoga and exercise in multiple sclerosis. *Neurology, 62*(11), 2058–2064.

Oken, B.S., Zajdel, D., Kishiyama, S., Flegal, K., Dehen, C., Haas, M., ... Leyva, J. (2006). Randomized, controlled, six-month trial of yoga in Healthy seniors: Effects on cognition and quality of life. *Alternative Therapies in Health and Medicine, 12*(1), 40–47.

Ortiz, L., & Langer, N. (2002). Assessment of spirituality and religion in later life: Acknowledging client's needs and personal resources. *Journal of Gerontological Social Work, 37*(2), 5–21.

Ostateski, F. (1994). Stories of lives lived and now ending. *Inquiring Mind, 10*(2), Retrieved from http://www.zenhospice.org/html/what/stories_0494.html

Poloma, M.M., & Pendleton, B.F. (1991). The effects of prayer and prayer experience on measures of general well-being. *Journal of Psychology and Theology, 19*(1), 71–83.

Raub, J.A. (2002). Psychophysiologic effects of Hatha Yoga on musculoskeletal and cardiopulmonary function: A literature review, *Journal of Alternative Complementary Medicines, 8*(6):797–812.

Rybash, J.W., Roodin, P.A., & Santrock, J.W. (1991). *Adult development and ageing* (2nd ed., p. 17). Dubuque, IA: Wm C. Brown Publishers.

Schmid, A.A., Van Puymbroeck, M., & Koceja, D.M. (2010). Effect of a 12-week yoga intervention on fear of falling and balance in older adults: A pilot study. *Archives of Physical Medicine and Rehabilitation, 91*(4), 576–583.

Sheldrake, P. (2007). *A brief history of spirituality*. Oxford: Blackwell Publishing.

Shivananda, S. (2000). *Bhagwad gita*. Uttar Pradesh: The Divine Life Society.

Smith, A. (2004). Clinical uses of mindfulness training for older people. *Behavioural and Cognitive Psychotherapy, 32*(4), 423–430.

Smith, A. (2006). 'Like waking up from a dream': Mindfulness training for older people with anxiety and depression. In R.A. Baer (Ed.), *Mindfulness-based treatment approaches* (pp. 191–212). Burlington, MA: Elsevier.

Swinton, J., & Pattison, S. (2010). Moving beyond clarity: Towards a thin, vague and useful understanding of spirituality in nursing care. *Nursing Philosophy, 11*(4), 226–237.

Tornstam, L. (1994). Gerotranscendence – A theoretical and empirical exploration. In L.E. Thomas & S.A. Eisenhandler (Eds.), *Ageing and the religious dimension* (pp. 203–226). Westport, CT: Auburn.

Tran, M.D., Holly, R.G., Lashbrook, J., & Amsterdam, E.A. (2001). Effects of Hatha yoga practice on the health-related aspects of physical fitness. *Preventive Cardiology*, *4*(4), 165–170.

Vempati, R.P., & Telles, S. (2002). Yoga-based guided relaxation reduces sympathetic activity judged from baseline levels. *Psychological Reports*, *90*(2), 487–494.

Vishwatmananda, Swami (2016). Meditation and spiritual life. *Bulletin of the Ramakrishna Mission Institute of Culture*, *LXVII*(9), 5–13.

Warner, B. (2010). *Sex, Sin, and Zen: A Buddhist exploration of sex from celibacy to polyamory and everything in between*. Novato: New World Library.

Yardi, N. (2001). Yoga for control of epilepsy. *Seizure*, *10*(1), 7–12.

Yogendra, J. (1993). *Cyclopedia yoga 1*. Santacruz: The Yoga Institute.

Young, J.D., & Taylor, E. (2001). Meditation as a voluntary hypo-metabolic state of biological estimation. *News in Physiological Sciences*, *13*, 149–153.

2

'AUTHENTIC AGEING'

Reflections from an existential perspective

The last century witnessed a remarkable surge in longevity in industrialized countries, with an average increase in life expectancy close to 40 years for women and up to 30 years for men (Houde, 2003; Dubé, 2003; Friedan, 1995). The new, so-called 'supplementary' December years of life (Houde, 1999) often present unique challenges for individuals and society at large. Elderly individuals increasingly face a number of losses (e.g., physical, relational, professional, or emotional) often associated with ageing and the mere cumulative passage of time. However, an increase in the quality, meaning, and purpose of life for older adults has not been guaranteed because of an extended lifespan (Cole, 1984; Gaillot, 1996; Wong, 2000). At this juncture, is it possible to develop an inspiring culture of ageing that neither belittles the exciting possibilities of enjoying a long and meaningful life nor hides the vulnerabilities of life – a culture that celebrates ageing but also remains realistic? The need is felt at this juncture to re-think *ageing* as an *extended part of life*.

Ageing, considered as being the chronometric art of life, needs researchers to acknowledge the vulnerability that is inherent in life which may increase as people live longer, although not in synchrony with their ages. Second, they also need to recognize that ageing is potentially a process of ongoing creativity and of deepening the uniqueness of individuals (Baars, 2012). Ageing thus becomes a process leading man out of distraction and diversification, wherein he could lose himself, and bring him back to reflect upon himself and his life. In a healthy mental frame, ageing essentially involves a *concentration of life*, wherein the elderly individual has relatively greater clarity and focus of consciousness, owing to experiential richness. More experienced than ever, the old person faces the basic questions of existence, regarding its limits, its transitoriness, its being beyond control, its being 'what for?' – and the fact that whether life succeeds or fails depends on oneself. Successful ageing allows a person to mature, as Rilke said, for a death that is *his or her death* (Langle, 2004). A necessity is perceived to probe into the current theoretical conceptions of ageing as a construct in the sunset years of life.

The notion of ageing amidst inter-human vulnerability

Just like fragile teardrops, ageing is part of the ever-vulnerable 'inter-human condition,' it is explained by social embeddedness offered by 'natality' – human beings being *born* into the world (Arendt, 1958; Baars, 2002; 2010a, 2010b). It belongs to the most basic characteristics of the so-called sophisticated inmates. Human beings are born, live, age, and die as unique individuals, being sensitive to vulnerability of different kinds (Baars, 1991).

To approach ageing from the perspective of a fundamental vulnerability of inter-human condition is to accept ageing with all its unknown possibilities, problems, and promises as an important part of human life. Ageing is basically the continuation of life beyond a number of years that indicates the ending of 'normal adulthood.' The vulnerability of an individual to senescing processes is also unpredictable, being dependent on individual chance and action as well as environmental and genetic characteristics (Baars, 2012; Kitzmuller, Clancy, Vaismoradi, Wegener and Bondas, 2018). Besides, the increasing vulnerability of life concerns not only one's own life but also the growing possibility of losing friends, partners, or even children and becoming deeply lonely. Thus, ageing is essentially a part of the inter-human condition, a social-existential, rather than a pathological process. To take the help of an illustration, the current world scenario is posing an increasing threat in the lives of people in the form of the new pandemic posed by Covid-19 virus. This has essentially brought forth the realizations of the uncertainty of life in the scientific forum. Elderly individuals appear to be more prone to infection, owing to their increased vulnerabilities of having a lower immunity frame. Hence, the art of ageing necessitates coming to terms with the very unpredictability of life so as to help individuals to age gracefully. This involves taking account of death anxiety to resolve the same as far as practicable. In fact, death anxiety may be referred to as the *universal human recognition and dread of the eventual personal demise* of an individual (Missler, Stroebe, Geurtsen, Mastenbroek, Chmoun, and Van Der Houwen, 2012). This may be regarded as essentially a human problem because human beings are endowed with intellectual and rational capacities and have the ability of language. It requires the recognition of the finitude of not only one's own life but also other living creatures. It may be noteworthy to mention that the *deeply repressed contents* of death anxiety tend to be of three kinds:

1. *Extremely threatening aspects of death-connected events that do not register consciously but are subliminally perceived and processed in the deep unconscious system.*

2. *An extremely traumatic death-related event that is consciously perceived and then shunted to the deep unconscious system, where it is kept under repression in a form that is no longer available to direct recall.*
3. *The death-related meanings of all non-death-related events that are unconsciously connected with death and evoke death anxiety.*

This may be further understood with the help of a diagrammatic representation (Figure 2.1).

Towards an art of ageing: Beyond conventional wisdom

A re-actualization of the connection between wisdom and ageing requires paying more attention to the subtle ways in which experiences are processed as people grow older. Nothing should be considered as waste in our experiential reservoir; the basic experience of the aged must convert them into 'essentials' to enjoy life in a different perspective. Ageing persons may be eminently able to tolerate and approach multi-dimensional and polyvalent situations or questions in a fruitful way. They tend to engage in 'post-formal rationality' for which they can enter into the thoughts and expressions of others, the capacity to deal with problems creatively by using various approaches, and adopt a flexible view of what is possible in difficult situations (Baltes and Staudinger, 2000; Baltes, Gluck and Kunzmann, 2002). Aged individuals are able to acquire, nourish, and deepen reflections due to their wisdom flare in the personality frame. Schaie (2005) has also elaborately demonstrated that learning processes are still possible among the elderly due to different kinds of neuronal associations.

Cohen (2005) elaborated his theory of 'developmental intelligence,' which is supported by evidence of the continuing interaction of myelin and axons in the brain that supports the more flexible and sophisticated thought process in the form of post-formal thought and wisdom in the second half of life. Besides, Goldberg (2006) gathered evidence of continuing neurogenesis in the ageing brain to combat outdated views that the brain could not renew its neurons and would be doomed to a progressive loss after full development in young adulthood.

Ageing gives an advantage over younger persons in what may be called '*deeper layers of change*.' Ageing persons have more opportunities than young people to decipher developments in a longer temporal perspective and to recognize patterns of continuity and discontinuity behind the surface of daily 'change' (Baars, 2012). Moreover, they have more experience in giving an adequate response to *specific* situations, which must come from reflective experience with conflicts that can be deepened through the years. In addition, ageing persons have an advantage in having a deepening awareness that life is finite. Ageing persons develop attitudes, qualities, and

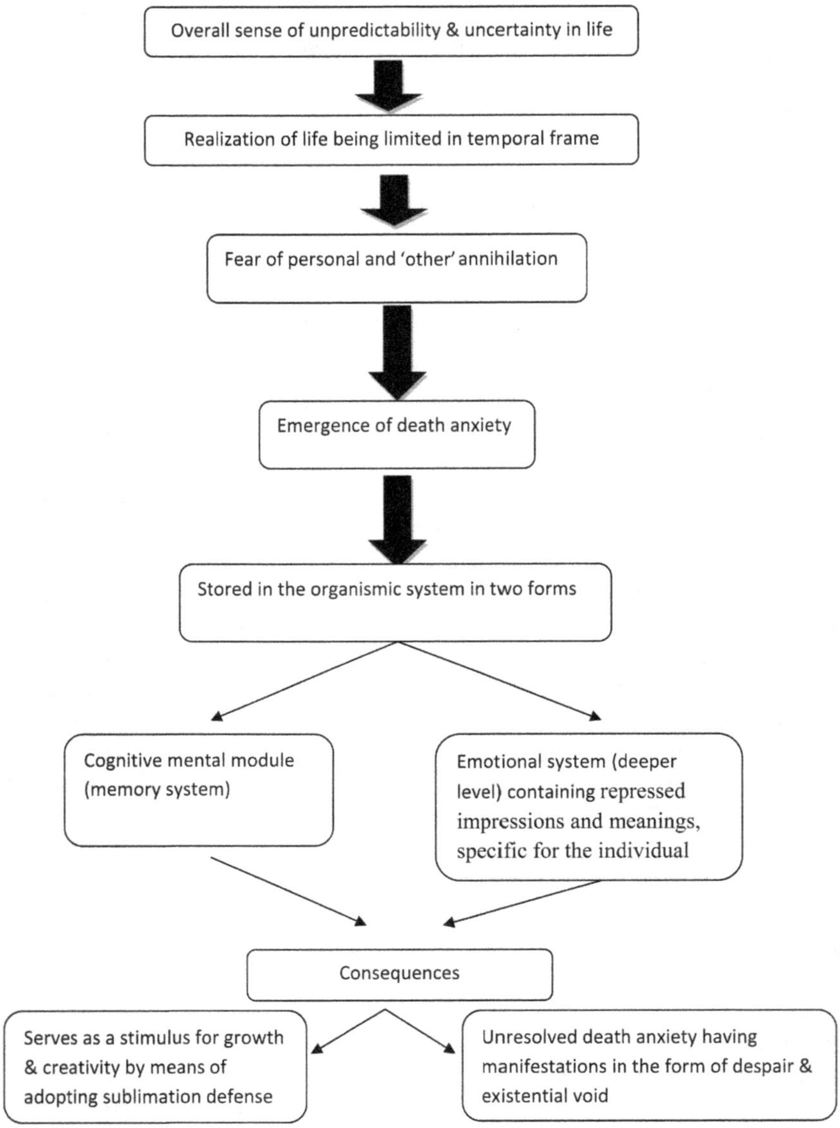

Figure 2.1 Understanding the finitude of life in terms of death anxiety (source: authors).

preferences that are different from those of young people because they live in time horizons that are different (Carstensen, Mikels, and Mather, 2006). At some point in their lives, ageing persons understand that their remaining time is limited, which lead to motivations that are different from those of younger people. The perception of the finitude of life leads to a deeper awareness of the intensity of finite lives. Nevertheless, the death of the *other* remains a painful horizon of life, even if one has complete peace with one's own death.

Ageing by living in different times

Ageing is living in time and calls for an appreciation of the intricate interconnections between the past, present, and projected future. Philosophers are of the opinion that lived time enables an awareness of the present, which entails an intense awareness of the preciousness and fullness of life (Raosaheb, 2016). However, the exclusive attention for the present as the only reality that would matter 'here and now' neglects an important temporal perspective: the interweaving and complexity of the three-dimensional present having its references to the past and the future constantly. This calls forth a multi-layered present (Baars, 2012). The three-fold present implies that the past is present in one's memories and the future in anticipations. Such *lived* time in its changing configurations of present, past, and future implies a different time perspective since there are no water-tight compartments between the three.

Hence, the present has deep temporal layers that are filled with references to the past and anticipations of the future. As Heidegger (1996) emphasized, the openness of the future is not an abstract openness in which 'everything is possible.' The specific qualities of one's existence can open a future that is different from the future of other individuals. This means that such individuals have already lived the past and are actually living in the present reality of a lifeworld. In that sense, the past is still present and the future is not completely unstructured or open; moreover, the projected future 'backfires' on the present since what one hopes and strives for also shapes what one does 'now' and experiences as the 'present.' The future that confronts one also influences the things he/she remembers for which memories tend to have their own times (Figure 2.2).

In addition, human actions and interactions play a major role in not only *taking* time (which can be measured) but also *constituting* time (Baars, 1997; Mittelstrass, 1992). Thus, different lifeworlds, situations, and actions have their respective temporal characteristics. An important part of understanding the process of ageing is to understand how life may change after major life events which are associated with specific experiential qualities and images. They not only require time to develop but they also qualify and colour times. Living and ageing do not follow chronometric time.

Philosophers related to the art of living have stressed not to emphasize the fear of death. Montaigne (1991) has repeated this message that fear of death can be avoided because death is unavoidable (Baars and Dohmen, in press; Seneca, 2005). Thus, the very *acceptance* of the inevitability of death forms the beginning of the Stoic art of life.

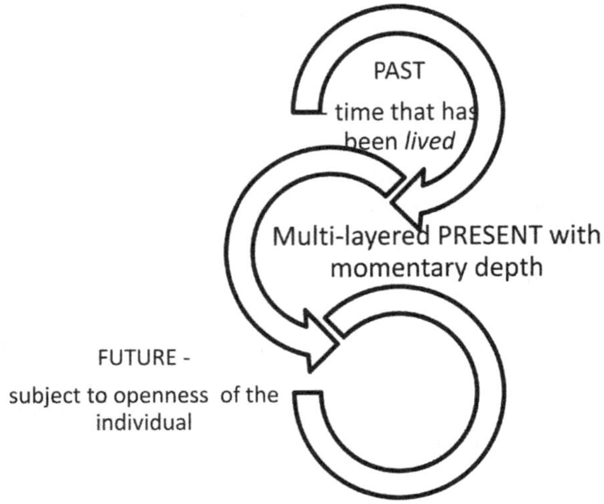

Figure 2.2 The mystery of the present (source: authors).

Epicurean philosophy stresses to *ignore* death since it is not a part of life. According to Epicurus, we will never meet death until the time we are living; death is absent there, and when death arrives, individuals no longer exist. This notion has also been supported by Wittgenstein (1974). This indicates that the awareness about the finitude of time has something important to say about life. However, the death of *others* dear to us will be fully experienced and remains a painful horizon of vulnerable life as it seeps into the experiential filter of the self unlike the death of the self (Baars, 2012).

Ageing involves a saturation of interior orientation as far as self-development of the psyche is concerned. It thereby calls forth concentration of unique subjectivity on the part of individuals. This, in turn, colours the elderly individual's experiential process resulting in 'wisdom' in personality fragrance. The need is felt to delve deeper into the ageing person's ideographic frame of personality at this crossroads.

Beyond longer lives: Ageing as finitization in its authenticity mode

Individuals remain essentially under the illusion that our activities and personal views really matter, but in reality, they rest on nothing more than an all-too-short breath of life. However, instead of concluding that mortal life is hardly important because after a while we will all be dead, Baars (2012) emphasizes that every moment gets a special depth and every life is unique *because* of its finitude. Even Heidegger's (1996) thought about 'Being to Death' is not just a death cult but intends to open Being for its authentic possibilities. When we realize that the times of our lives are limited, we become aware of *living* it wisely and facing the challenges and opportunities that are most essential to us.

Thus, the extension of finitude to the different times in which we live and age leads to the elaboration of the perspective of *finitization*: the underlying idea that the inevitability of change can inspire us to appreciate the uniqueness of persons and situations as they are changing over time (Baars, 1997; 2002; 2010a, 2010b). The easy association between ageing and finitude in the limited sense of mortality tends to occlude the finitude that pervades human life as we live it (Nussbaum, 2001). Ageing life may offer opportunities and unexpected exciting challenges that are foreseen in youth. Thus, other dimensions of time may open up so that life can remain an adventure. In other words, the adventure of life does not only unfold in youth but also in later life. It is the art of life to *discover missed opportunities*.

Human beings are often confronted with circumstances that support, frustrate, crush, or inspire them. Living implies a constant confrontation with situations that spontaneously 'present themselves' to people. In this permanent interweaving of passivity and activity, individuals are confronted with the finitude of life every day. In fact, unique sequences of situations and actions that lead to characteristic patterns in someone's life belong to the empirical reference of 'finitization.' As such, ageing implies an increasing individualization of experiences

This perspective on the life course calls individuals to acknowledge the uniqueness of each person's life and to develop an understanding of living life as such. It calls forth the necessity to live life attentively in the realization that finitude does not imply that life would be pointless or devoid of meaning. Karl Jaspers (cited in Baars, 2012) emphasizes that individuals should confront life events not through planning and calculation but through becoming *ourselves* in surrendering acceptance. Heidegger (1996) idealizes suffering as the only way to live authentically.

In ageing, uniqueness interacts with hope and transcendence. Arendt (1958) is of the opinion that the human condition is characterized by 'natality': we are not in the world to die but to be *born*. In his words, human beings are endowed with the capacity to begin afresh and to do the unexpected. Natality qualifies human lives from birth to death, inspiring life with hope, creativity, critique, rebirth, and the emergence of new horizons.

Ageing is thus not an individualistic project that remains isolated from other people; it is always situated in a life world and confronted with systemic structures and processes. Celebrating ageing as a vital part of life implies the acknowledgement of the potentials *and* limitations, the pleasures *and* sufferings, the continuity, vitality, competence, *and* vulnerability of ageing. Developing an art of ageing, therefore, involves developing meaningful ways of encountering situations in life that *cannot* be controlled. Acknowledging and gracefully accepting the dignity of *existential* limitations is essential for

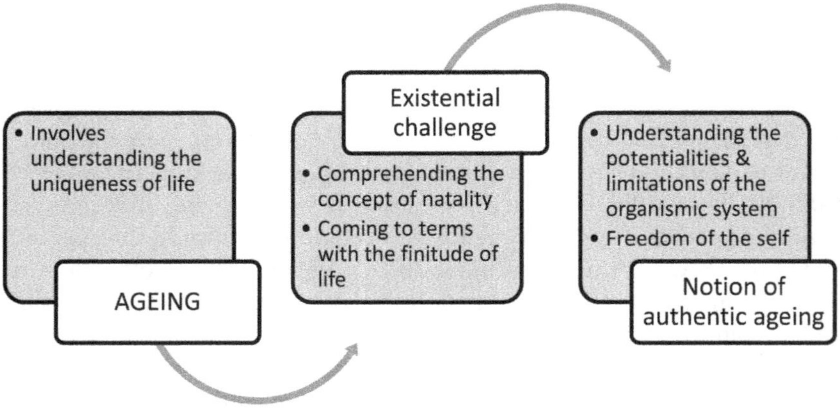

Figure 2.3 Inter-relationship of ageing in the context of existential crisis (source: authors).

the quality of living with them. Thus, discovering new bases for meaning is one of the major tasks of ageing (Brat, 2000; Kimble and Ellor, 2000; Leclerc, Couture, and Roy, 2003). In tune with this notion, Längle (2001, 2004) speaks of ageing as an existential challenge in which one has the choice to redefine one's being-in-the-world by attributing meanings to different events of one's life. Even conditions that we cannot change or did not choose should at least be *dignified* and, if possible, meaningfully intertwined in our lives and in society. Otherwise, the meaninglessness of life as 'a fact' or as 'something that occurs' stares us in the face. It may be schematically represented as in Figure 2.3.

It is at this juncture that meaningful existence calls forth 'authentic living.' As such, authenticity is essentially a life-dictum of graceful ageing.

Art of ageing through authenticity

Authenticity revolves around issues to be human, what it means to be happy, and what it means to be oneself (Hegel, 1977, 1991; Heidegger, 1996; Kant, 1929; Kierkegaard, 1985; Nehemas, 1999; Rousseau, 1979; Sartre, 1992). Self-identity, individuality, meaning-making, and anxiety are some terms that are often used in the associated field. It relates to being in touch with one's inner self, knowing one's self, having a sense of one's own identity, and then living by one's sense of self (Kierkegaard, 1985). To be authentic, people must assert their will in the choices made when confronted by possibilities (Sartre, 1992; Maslow, 1968; Heidegger, 1996). Reality itself is meaningless and people must make meaning by means of selectively perceiving events as such. This is how authentic existence is experienced by individuals (Sartre, 1992; Tillich, 1952). Meaning is created through experiencing love, through acting creatively, and through suffering according to Frankl (1984). It is only one's own direct experience that yields truth (May, 1953; Rogers, 1961). The meaninglessness of existence creates anxiety which is deeply ingrained in the self and people need courage to face it (Heidegger, 1996; May, 1953).

Authenticity thereby indicates a certain kind of integrity – an identity waiting to be discovered. The measure of an authentic life gets reflected in the integrity of a *narrative*, that to be a self is to constitute a story in which a kind of wholeness prevails, to be the author of oneself as a unique individual (Nehamas, 1999; Ricoeur, 1991). Authenticity in ageing enables the elderly to engage in tasks in a committed fashion selectively through situations where meaning in life can be deciphered so that one feels contented and fulfilled at the end, unlike the inauthentic self, which is mainly dictated by different 'dictums' of the world.

The possibility of authenticity is a mark of '*my freedom*' and it is through freedom that existentialism approaches questions of value to many of its most recognizable doctrines (Crowell, 2010). The attainment of authenticity entails risks, setbacks, and suffering, especially when it is contrary to social norms. Thus, the quest for authenticity to carve one's niche and find meaning in one's existence requires one to often meet different challenges in life (King and Napa, 1998). Hence, from an existential perspective, authentic happiness flows from an authentic mode of living. This can help fetch happiness among the elderly in the long run to have overall harmony and contentment in life (Schumaker, 2007). Existentialists have emphasized a willingness to 'stand naked in the storm of life' to face all kinds of oddities, consequently becoming emotionally resilient and mature (Becker, 1973). To Sartre, freedom is the fountain of hope, the foundation of all human values which defines the existential dictum (Sartre, 1946). Here, *transcendence* refers to the capacity to transcend time and space of the present world by transporting oneself to the future. Authenticity does not automatically mean self-actualization because the project of becoming authentic is fraught with multiple difficulties. Instead, it involves graceful acceptance of reality amidst all its oddities and moving forward in time by adopting an optimistic stance towards life in general.

Heidegger (1996) opines that to be oneself existentially means to exist according to one's nature or essence, which transcends day-to-day behaviour or activities or thinking about self. Existential authenticity is experience-oriented and accounts for the rich repertoire of an elderly individual's experiential treasure. Heidegger's (1996) idea is that to be human is to have possibilities sourced in one's individual and communal past called 'heritage' and the capacity to choose among them. There is also the pole of 'destiny' as well. This distinction is also supported by Boorstin (1961) and MacCannell (1973). Heidegger (1996) believes the world exists in the form of a network of related things. Everything in the world is connected in some way with other things, with the connections being preserved in the form of memories, books, education, socialization, culture, art, myths, and sense of places. Heidegger (1996) says people experience the connectedness of the world as possibilities for doing things, for taking action, and for behaving in certain ways to etch their imprints. This has been referred by Heidegger as *dwelling*. These form the bases for authenticity in Heidegger's framework. According to Heidegger, whether people are authentic or inauthentic is determined by how individuals project themselves. The necessity of weaving an entity in the life-space among the elderly by means of authenticity accounts for positive ageing. This requires delving into the meaning of one's existence.

Etching existential/personal meaning among the elderly

The answer to the question, why individuals age, has often been explored by different theorists (Kirkwood, 1991). Ageing provides individuals with the opportunity to attain some distance from our earlier lives so that they can appreciate what they have been trying to achieve with all their energy or what they failed to do. At a cultural level, the meaning of ageing could be that it allows individuals to appreciate that the inter-human condition is deeply characterized by and dependent on intergenerational bonds, which require an active, meaningful commitment on the part of individuals to maintain them.

In fact, Frankl (1963) and Maslow (1968) saw existential meaning, or personal meaning, as a universal human need. According to Frankl (1963, 1988), there are three major sources of meaning which include:

- Meaningful work or good deeds;
- Authentic encounters with others; and
- The overall attitude that one adopts when faced with an uncontrollable situation.

Hocking (1957) has pointed out the two-fold nature of personal meaning, namely, the *specific* events that give rise to meaning and satisfaction, and the ultimate or *total* meaning from which specific aspects of life derive their meaning. Yalom (1980) distinguished between terrestrial meaning and cosmic meaning. According to Brat (2000), life review (L.R.) can facilitate the finding of such sources of meaning. Related to this, Blanchard de Ravinel and de Ravinel (2003), Hogue-Charlebois and Paré (1998), and Missinne (2000) suggest that the most fundamental sources of meaning pertain to how to love oneself and others. They also suggest that L.R. can help the older adult in his/her search for existential meaning.

Wong (1999) defines personal meaning as 'an individually constructed cognitive system, which is grounded in values and is capable of endowing life with personal significance and satisfaction.' Numerous sources of personal meaning were identified by him, including work, social status, and activity. When these sources begin to decline and are no longer available, many older people become sceptical about the quest to live life. This is also expected to influence their overall health and life satisfaction. According to Erikson (1963), *ego-integrity*, being characterized by the feeling that one's life is worth living, is the major developmental task in old age. An individual who has achieved ego-integrity is described as 'having a balanced investment in self as well as in others, and as having moved from concerns with things to ideas, from actions to meanings' (Birren and Renner, 1980).

Butler (1963) observes that as the older person frequently feels a lessening of personal control, the search for meaning becomes crucial for adaptation. Schulz (1986) also points out that personal meaning becomes a major source of life satisfaction and personal growth among the elderly when they face disability and the losses of advancing age. He said that existential acceptance and acknowledging them gracefully may be more adaptive for the elderly at the juncture.

Thus, if the elderly can reap the fruits of their work or see their children grow up (Williams and Loeb, 1968), there can be intense satisfaction in becoming older. Moreover, if life has pleasures to offer, enjoying them and acknowledging them graciously is the key to having a satisfied life. Nevertheless, contemporary problems regarding a meaningful and dignified integration of aged persons in society will not be solved by extending their lives; instead, focus must be given to its *quality*. This is schematically represented in Figure 2.4.

Conclusion: Ageing as a personal challenge

Ageing can succeed and lead to final personal maturity, which is expected to depend on a balanced amount of interest, involvement, and participation in the world (Langle, 2001, 2004). The success of this step will depend on retirement and disengagement being more than the resignation of giving up work or social functions being torn out of one's hands. Successful retirement and disengagement will mean an active letting go as a resolute and thereby voluntary farewell. Whoever can do this active letting go is 'ripe' enough for old age.

The words of Bertrand Russell (1951) paint an interesting picture by comparing individual human existence to a river – which is small at first, narrowly contained within its banks, and increasingly rushing passionately across boulders and over waterfalls. Ageing essentially involves the variation of old cultural images about a transcendence of individualism as individual lives participate like finite drops in the infinite oceans of life beyond the scope of different activist agendas.

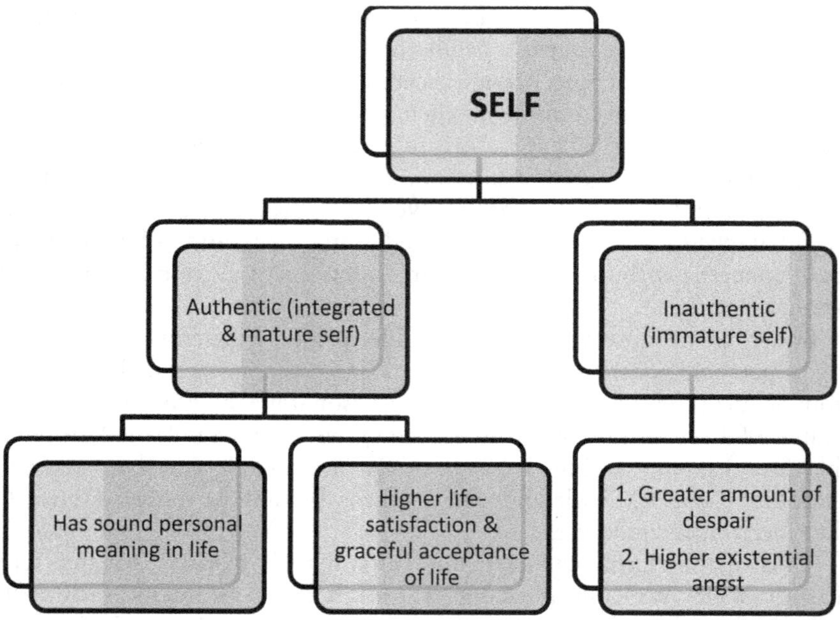

Figure 2.4 The conception of the self in accordance with existential terminologies (source: authors).

Similarly, ageing can also be an invitation to embrace goals that extend further than one's own life so that a meaningful participation is possible until the end. Death is the end of life but not its goal. Thus, ageing is not only a matter of projects but also of a deeper receptivity to a new openness of experiencing, giving, and receiving from the continuum of life. It is then that the elderly can accept the existential limitations and vulnerability of advanced age gracefully and become ripe for embracing life in its complete umbra. The meaning of life can then be inscribed by the person to enable him or her to enjoy and accept a life worth living. The art of authentic living can then be weaved successfully.

References

Arendt, H. (1958). *The human condition*. Chicago: University of Chicago Press.

Baars, J. (1991). The challenge of critical gerontology: The problem of social constitution. *Journal of Aging Studies*, *5*(3), 219–243.

Baars, J. (1997). Concepts of time and narrative temporality in the study of aging. *Journal of Aging Studies*, *11*(4), 283–296.

Baars, J. (2002). *Ouder worden en de fragiliteit van de intermenselijke conditie*. Utrecht: Inaugural Lecture, University for Humanistics.

Baars, J. (2010a). Ageing as increasing vulnerability and complexity: Towards a philosophy of the life course. In J. Bouwer (Ed.), *Successful ageing, spirituality, and meaning* (pp. 39–52). Leuven: Peeters.

Baars, J. (2010b). Philosophy of aging, time, and finitude. In T.R. Cole, R. Ray, & R. Kastenbaum (Eds.), *A guide to humanistic studies in aging* (pp. 105–120). Baltimore: Johns Hopkins University Press.

Baars, J. (2012). *Ageing and the art of living*. Baltimore: The Johns Hopkins University Press.

Baars, J., & Dohmen, J. (in press). *Towards an art of aging: A rediscovery of Forgotten texts*.

Baltes, P.B., Gluck, J., & Kunzmann, U. (2002). Wisdom: Its structure and function in regulating successful life-span development. In C.R. Snyder & S.J. Lopez (Eds.), *Handbook of positive psychology* (pp. 327–347). Oxford: Oxford University Press.

Baltes, P.B., & Staudinger, U.M. (2000). Wisdom: A metaheuristic (pragmatic) to orchestrate mind and virtue toward excellence. *American Psychologist*, *55*(1), 122–136.

Becker, E. (1973). *The denial of death*. New York: Free Press Paperbacks.

Birren, J.E., & Renner, V.J. (1980). Concepts and issues of mental health and aging. In J.E. Birren & R.B. Sloane (Eds.), *Handbook of mental health and aging* (pp. 3–33). Englewood Cliffs, NJ: Prentice-Hall.

Blanchard de Ravinel, C., & de Ravinel, H. (2003). *Le temps libéré: Dialogue sur la retraite*. Ottawa: Novalis. Freed time: Dialogue on retirement.

Boorstin, D. (1961). *The image: A guide to pseudo-events in America*. New York: Harper & Row.

Brat, P.T. (2000). Logotherapy in the care of the terminally ill. *Journal of Religious Gerontology*, *11*, 103–117.

Butler, R.N. (1963). Life review: An interpretation of reminiscence in the aged. *Psychiatry*, *4*, 1–18.

Carstensen, L.L., Mikels, J.A., & Mather, M. (2006). Aging and the intersection of cognition, motivation, and emotion. In J. Birren & K.W. Schaie (Eds.), *Handbook of the psychology of aging* (pp. 343–362). San Diego: Academic Press.

Cohen, G.D. (2005). *The mature mind. The positive power of the aging brain*. Chicago: University of Chicago.

Cole, T.R. (1984). Aging, meaning, and well-being: Musings of a cultural historian. *International Journal of Aging and Human Development*, *19*(4), 329–336.

Crowell, S. (2010). Existentialism. In *The Stanford Encyclopedia of Philosophy* (Spring Edition), Edward N. Zalta ed. URL=http://plato.stanford.edu/archives/spr2010/entries/ existentialism/

Dubé, M. (2003). Le vieillissement réussi. *Revue québécoise de psychologie*, *24*, 15–22. Successful Ageing.

Erikson, E.H. (1963). *Childhood and society*. New York: W.W. Norton.

Frankl, V.E. (1963). *Man's search for meaning*. New York: Washington Square Press.

Frankl, V.E. (1984). *Man's search for meaning*. New York: Simon and Schuster.

Frankl, V.E. (1988). Découvrir un sens à sa vie avec la logothérapie. In C.J. Bacon & L. Drolet (Trans.), *Man's search for meaning*. Montréal: Les Éditions de l'Homme.

Friedan, B. (1995). *La révolte du troisième âge: Pour en finir avec le tabou de la vieillesse* (J. Lehana, Trans.). [Fountain of Age]. Paris: Albin Michel.

Gaillot, J. (1996). *Ce que je crois*. Paris: Desclée de Brouwer. What I believe.

Goldberg, E. (2006). *The wisdom paradox: How your mind can grow stronger as your brain grows older*. New York: Gotham Books.

Hegel, G. (1977). *Phenomenology of spirit*. Oxford: Clarendon Press.

Hegel, G.W.F. (1991). *Elements of the philosophy of right*. Cambridge: Cambridge University Press.

Heidegger, M. (1996). *Being and time*. Albeny: State University of New York Press.

Hocking, W.E. (1957). *The meaning of immortality in human experience*. New York: Harper & Brothers.

Hogue-Charlebois, M., & Paré, R. (1998). *Les nouveaux retraités*. Montréal: Fides. The new retirees.

Houde, R. (1999). *Le temps de la vie: Le développement psycho-social de l'adulte*. Montréal: Gaëtan Morin. Time of life: Adult psycho-social development.

Houde, R. (2003). Comment habiter sa vieillesse? *Revue québécoise de psychologie, 24*, 95–105. How to live out one's old age?

Kant, I. (1929). *Critique of pure reason*. New York: Macmillan.

Kierkegaard, S. (1985). *Fear and trembling*. Harmondsworth: Penguin.

Kimble, M.A., & Ellor, J.W. (2000). Logotherapy: An overview. *Journal of Religious Gerontology, 11*(3–4), 9–24.

King, L.A., & Napa, C.K. (1998). What makes a life good? *Journal of Personality and Social Psychology, 11*(1), 156–165.

Kirkwood,T.B.L. (1991). Genetic basis of limited cell proliferation. *Mutation Research, 256*, 323–328.

Kitzmuller, G., Clancy, A., Vaismoradi, M., Wegener, C., & Bondas, T. (2018). 'Trapped in an Empty Waiting Room' – The existential human core of loneliness in old age: A meta-synthesis. *Qualitative Health Research, 28*(2), 213–230.

Längle, A. (2001). Old age from an existential-analytical perspective. *Psychological Reports, 89*(2), 211–215.

Längle, A. (2004). *Transforming loss, suffering and death by finding existential attitudes and meaning*. Paper presented at the Second Biannual International Conference on Personal Meaning, Vancouver, Canada.

Leclerc, G., Couture, M., & Roy, J. (2003). Une théorie de l'adaptation à la retraite par l'ajustement des sources de sens. *Revue québécoise de psychologie, 24*, 53–70. Adjusting sources of meaning: A theory of adaptation to retirement.

MacCannell, D. (1973). Staged authenticity: Arrangements of social space in tourist settings. *American Journal of Sociology, 79*(3), 589–603.

Maslow, A. (1968). *Toward a psychology of being* (2nd ed.). Princeton: Van Nostrand.

May, R. (1953). *Man's search for himself*. New York: Dell Publishing.

Missinne, L.E. (2000). The meaning of life in old age. In J.A. Thorson (Ed.), *Perspective on spiritual well-being and aging* (pp. 126–133), Springfield: Charles C. Thomas Publishers Ltd.

Missler, M., Stroebe, M., Geurtsen, L., Mastenbroek, M., Chmoun, S., & Van Der Houwen, K. (2012). Exploring death anxiety among elderly people: A literature review and empirical investigation. *Journal of Death and Dying, 64*(4), 357–379.

Mittelstrass, J. (1992). Zeitformen des Lebens. Philosophische Unterscheidungen. In P.Baltes & J.Mittelstrass (Eds.), *Zukunft des Alterns und gesellschaftliche Entwicklung* (pp. 386–407). Berlin: De Gruyter.

Montaigne, M. de (1991). *The complete essays*. Harmondsworth: Penguin.

Nehamas, A. (1999). *Virtues of authenticity: Essays on plato and socrates*. Princeton: Princeton University Press.

Nussbaum, M. (2001). *The fragility of goodness: Luck and ethics in Greek tragedy and philosophy*. Cambridge: Cambridge University Press.

Raosaheb, M.V. (2016). Existentialism: A philosophic stand point to existence over essence.*The South Asian Academic Research Chronicle, III*(1), 13–20.

Ricoeur, P. (1991). Narrative identity. *Philosophy Today*, *35*(1), 73–81.

Rogers, C. (1961). *On becoming a person*. New York: Houghton Mifflin.

Rousseau, J.-J. (1979). *Emile or on education*. Alan Bloom: Basic Books.

Russell, B. (1951). The future of man. *The Atlantic*. Retrieved from https://www.theatlantic.com/magazine/archive/1951/03/the-future-of-man/305193/

Sartre, J.-P. (1946). *Existentialism is a humanism* (P. Mairet, Trans.). Public lecture. Retrieved from homepages.wmich.edu/~baldner/existentialism.pdf

Satre, J.P. (1992). *Being and nothingness*. New York: Simon and Schuster.

Schaie, K.W. (2005). *Developmental influences on adult intelligence: The Seattle longitudinal study*. New York: Cambridge University Press.

Schulz, R. (1986). Successful aging: Balancing primary and secondary control. *Adult Development and Aging News*, *13*, 2–4.

Schumaker, J.F. (2007). *In search of happiness: Understanding an endangered state of mind*. United Kingdom: Prager Paperback.

Seneca, S. (2005). *On the shortness of life*. New York: Penguin Books.

Tilich, P. (1952). *The courage to be*. New Haven: Yale University Press.

Williams, R.H., & Loeb, M.B. (1968). The adult's social life space and successful aging. Some suggestions for a conceptual framework. In B.L. Neugarten (Ed.), *Middle age and aging* (pp. 79–81). Chicago: University of Chicago Press.

Wittgenstein, L. (1974). *Tractatus logico-Philosophicus*. New York: Routledge.

Wong, P.T.P. (1999). *A brief outline of meaning centered counseling and therapy*. Retrieved August, 23, 2003 from Trinity University, International Network on Personal Meaning Web site http://www.meaning.ca/articles

Wong, P.T.P. (2000). Meaning in life and meaning in death in successful aging. In A. Tomer (Ed.), *Death attitudes and the older adult* (pp.23–35). New York: Brunner/Mazel Publisher.

Yalom, I.D. (1980). *Existential psychotherapy*. New York: Basic Books.

3

A GLIMPSE INTO THE TRANSPERSONAL GERONTOLOGICAL CANVAS

The current world is witnessing a sensational surge of human longevity resulting in conceptualizations of ageing. Within its folds, ageing has sets of fulfilments as well as sufferance of myriad qualities. Old age is an experience-ripe matured state. In its existential frame, the supplementary years confront the decay, diminishments, and deteriorations in multi-dimensional life contexts. In healthy ageing, the scientific probe is there to locate conditions and processes to help elderly people proceed happily and be able to interpret life-flows with a positive lens. Several concepts and theories colour the canvas of gerontology. Concepts of 'conscious ageing,' 'contemplative ageing,' 'spiritual practices,' and ultimately stepping into the realm of 'transcendence' seem to be a brighter avenue to tread on during the extended years of life. The philosophy of believing in spirituality and overcoming the limitations of the 'self' to trudge on 'beyond self' realizations of transcendence seems to be the target of 'transpersonal gerontology.' Practising these processes are expected to yield greater will power and strength to cope with inevitable diminishments, prompt interiority in attaining detachment, accept sufferance as a spiritualistic guide in the family, feel the importance of '*presence*,' and develop wisdom and compassion as life armour.

The change in increasing longevity has resulted in conceptualizations of ageing. Old age, the last chapter of life, is not a uniform experience for everybody (Elder, 1991). In the sunset years, some elderly persons achieve a sense of fulfilment and satisfaction, while others stay bitter and bewail the decline of their physical abilities and the glare of social significance (Ardelt, 1997). No doubt, old age is the period of decline and deterioration. But life shows its span to be at least one-fourth of one's total life and it seems hard to imagine this span as being marginalized, unlike its earlier periods of childhood, adolescence, and early adulthood, especially when the late period signifies that during this we finally know who we are, what is really important, how we can contribute, and may be even how life works and what is the cause of our existence on Earth (Wacks, 2011). Honde (1999) felt that these 'supplementary' years obviously have a consequent number of losses like physical, professional, relational, cognitive, or emotional in the passage of time. Consistent with this research, evidence has proved that an extended life span has not guaranteed an increase in the quality, meaning, and purpose of life for older generations (Cole, 1984; Gailott, 1996; Wong, 2000). Hence, the current search for mental elements or orientations to erode the effects of so many ailments – physical, mental, social, financial – in the advanced years of life. Transpersonal gerontology, wrapping spirituality in its umbra, seems to be one of the ways.

Conscious ageing: The cry of the day

Conceptualizations of ageing have evolved significantly over a few decades. Varied modes of conceptual notions pinpoint the important dimensions of late life. Jung (1933) and Moody (1976) seemed to be the possible voice for the potentials of life's second half. Jung spoke of a religious perspective beyond religion as the essential problem his clients encountered in their second half of life, whereas Moody (1976), having a great regard for older people, proposed four model patterns to be adopted in treatment procedure – rejection, social services, participation, and self-actualization and transcendence. To him, old age is either an invisible void in one's psychological life-frame or it is to be filled up with activities in common with previous roles and responsibilities (Moody, 1976, p. 9).

Cumming and Henry's (1961) *theory of disengagement* claimed that a good adjustment to ageing involved self-renunciation and acceptance of one's helplessness. They posited that older people naturally withdraw from society and the roles of earlier life. Declaiming such theories as self-abnegation in old age people, Rosow (1974) and Williamson (2002) both emphasized the active role of adults in old age in paving the way for their newly designed successful ageing by adopting a new set of activities and role-playing that seemed to be satisfying to them. To provide anecdotal evidence in favour of this, an elderly retired lady was reported to say that she had disengaged herself from 'work' ever since her retirement but was selective in choosing ventures as she wanted to opt for remaining active in the last quarter of her life. She wanted to have a 'feel' of remaining connected with life through her selectivity.

Atchley (2003) spoke of the basic attitude-value-belief orientations together with the previous lifestyle as the infrastructure of the continuity of adaptation to the personal and professional changes inherent in retirement and ageing. The controversial content seems to exist between the concepts of successful ageing and conscious ageing. Rowe and Kahn's (1987) theory of successful ageing (S.A.) defined S.A. as involving:

a. The ability to maintain a low risk of disease and disease-related disability;
b. Intact mental and physical function; and
c. Active engagement with life.

Wong (2000) argued that personal meaning was the best predictor of happiness, perceived well-being, absence of psychopathology, and depression in older adults. Aguerre and Bouffard (2003) argued that the concept of S.A. should be multi-faceted and include spirituality, sexuality, and emotional openness. They tended to include forgiveness towards oneself and others as an essential element of S.A. Authors like them and Moody (2003) proposed the concept of conscious ageing (C.A.). There, they conceived of ageing as a developmental phase somewhat akin to a rite of passage or a personal journey in the line of transformation. Old age, as necessary conditions for spiritual practice and growth, is demonstrated in the '*conscious ageing*' movement. In Jung's '*individualization*' orientation, conscious ageing means to integrate divergent elements of the self into increased awareness and living consciously in later life. Supporting the C.A. concept, Bianchi (1986) expressed that a fuller spirituality of ageing is a precursor of social making, the fullest expansion of the inner potentials of the older adult. This newer concept, C.A., supports values of autonomy, individuality, expressiveness, and self-transcendence. Moody inscribed, 'Conscious ageing is a spiritual process that draws its inspiration from religion, art, lifelong learning… reflected in the field of transpersonal psychology and wisdom traditions in the great world religions' (p. 139). In the light of the C.A. concept, Tornstam (1996) coined the term 'gero-transcendence' – connecting the self with the universe implying re-defining time, death, and the self. To him, 'gero-transcendence' is developmental and intrinsic in nature. Older adults are generally predisposed to consider the cosmic or transcendent dimension of life. In his attempt to establish C.A.'s greater implication in old age, Moody (2003) suggested that the increased spiritual awareness involved in C.A. resembles the Jungian concept of individuation and a path towards wisdom. In his conceptual frame of individuation or in late life, the 'integration' of youthful as well as elderly layouts of mind, the indication is obvious that the process calls for further development of a spiritual need to attain wholeness of character. Similarly, Heard's (1963) evolutionary model is found to advocate a '*second maturity*' in the additional span of life where one possibly develops an extended consciousness moving beyond one's individuality. Atchley (2011) reported the contemplative mystical experience as part of an '*everyday mysticism*' in late adulthood. Thus, C.A. seems to hold greater potential for growth in old age than S.A. The concepts dealt with so far are illustrated schematically in Figure 3.1.

Late-life developmental tasks as a precursor of conscious ageing and spirituality

Moberg (1990) stated, 'Among all domains for change in human lives, the one that provides the most opportunity for continuing growth in the later years is the spiritual.' Jones (1984) felt ageing as a spiritualizing process.

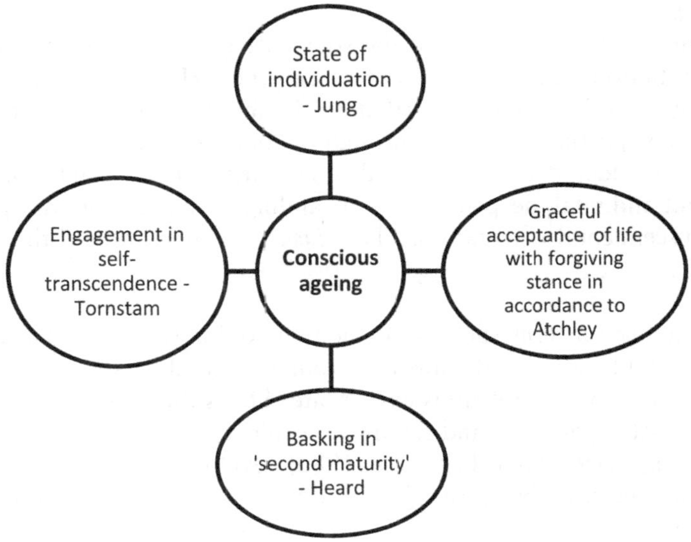

Figure 3.1 The multi-faceted nature of ageing (source: authors).

Erikson (1982) identified that the typical style, or 'ritualization' of old age, can be called '*philo-sophical*' in the sense of maintaining some order and meaning in the dis-integration of body and mind that can also advocate a durable hope in wisdom. Bringing a similar context into consideration, Jaspers (1967) claimed, like Erikson, that a philosophical faith is one which relies on reason and experiential insight rather than revelation, prophecy, or doctrine. In his notion, such a faith could move one in maturity towards the Ground of Being, 'the incomprehensible, inconceivable, the all-encompassing.' The theme of Being is considered central to '*Contemplative Ageing*.' In contemplation on breadth, full awareness is generated regarding mundane activities like walking, eating, thinking, etc. with a certain aura and sanctity. Atchley (2011) called this 'the everyday' mysticism of old age. According to Moody (2003), in the spiritual quest of contemplative ageing, people are commonly challenged by feelings of regret, disillusionment, depression, and often cynicism that are the result of past events and behaviours to a great extent. In the mould of contemplative ageing, older persons attempt to:

i. Resolve the troubling past issues
ii. Arrive at a better understanding of one's self
iii. Determine the meaning of one's life

The spiritual nature of this everyday mysticism seems to belong to the gero-transcendence experience. The theory of gero-transcendence, thus, claims that if elders spend more time in meditation, they develop '*cosmic consciousness.*'

Wuthnow (1998) considered the study of ageing centred in journeying and negotiation called '*spirituality of seeking.*' He mentioned about an emerging '*practice-oriented spirituality*' in the present era, wherein people develop spirituality by and through ongoing practices. Hence, the later years are considered as a time period when spiritual needs can become more important and vital, deepening and expanding to include the transpersonal and transcendental orientations. The '*tasks*' of later lifespan thus get re-oriented as:

i. Involving concerns such as loss, letting go, life review, and acceptance being understood and addressed from a spiritual perspective;
ii. The major world religions expect later life as the time for having deep spiritual experiences and serving as a spiritual guide;
iii. In Jung's (1933) and Erikson's (1982) developmental theories, old age is characterized by spirituality in terms of transcendence and wisdom flairs;
iv. As a process of ego integration or transcendence (Wacks, 1987), many adults search for answers of an existential and spiritual nature in the form of a life review; and
v. Erikson (1997) spoke of a ninth stage of development, in addition to Erikson's eight stages, that is expected to occur in old age with increased spirituality from middle age to a transcendent spiritual perspective in later old age crossing 70 years.

Two broad models for spiritual growth in later life have been proposed by Wink and Dillon (2002). The first counts spiritual growth as the positive bearing of the maturational process supporting the Jungian post-formal stages of cognitive development being conductive to spiritual questing. The second considers spiritual growth as tackling avenues to the constrains and adversities of late life. Hence, having a spiritual perspective and practising conscious ageing seems to be the pillar of strength for the decaying days of late life.

Ageing: The yacht in the spiritual journey

Atchley (2011) considered spirituality as a great potential for continued psychological growth throughout adulthood. Definitionally, spirituality refers to an inner mental layer of human experience which is commonly found in healthy adult beings. Most adults report having experiences of spiritualistic nature and consider their life as a spiritual journey in itself. This concept of a spiritual journey is a reference to one's personal narrative, about her or his spiritual life, and development indicating ebbs and tides. Such narratives usually depict a history of experiences, actions, and insights connected with a search for spiritual meaning and understanding. The undertone of the spiritual journey is an intentional process of seeking spiritual experiences, using values and insights being prompted by spiritual experiences to make life choices and learning from the process itself. Atchley (2011) indicated that through experience, the spiritual journeys of the elderly are strongly belief-based and hence persistent, yet they are an imperfectly known journey into the unknown, an untravelled territory of life where traces of insight are not expected to be adequate. Thus, spirituality seems to be a region of experience. It serves as a backdrop to all our experiences, especially in the advanced years of life.

The essential features of spiritual journeys are elements of commitment, self-discipline, and regular spiritual practice. The regularity in spiritual practices leads to the development of habits of both mind and body and the habit of 'being' that comes naturally. In the open quest of spirituality, such practice-bound habits become enlivening. Such practices are adopted on a regular basis to celebrate, appreciate, invite, or act on experiences of presence, transcending the personal self and ascertaining the ground of 'being.' Many types of meditation and prayer, inspirational reading and reflection, and movement-oriented spiritual disciplines can be followed to support a contemplative, practice-oriented spirituality (Atchley, 2011). The spiritual journey can be conceived as a quest for balance between being and doing. It is mostly about learning to bring '*being*' back into the consciousness. This process seems to introduce a healthy distance from, and perspective on, social roles and serves as an element of creativity and spontaneity to one's lived experience. The general assumption is that as fully awakened spiritual beings, people feel their interconnectedness with everything. These are transcendent, contemplative experiences that open up the understanding of a plethora of spiritual intricacies. The system has mysticism at the heart of it that leads to such insights. Spiritual traditions hold mysticism as the center of spirituality and mysticism refers to transcendent, contemplative experiences that enhance spiritual understanding.

Spirituality: An expected tune in ageing

In the opinion of Hill and Pargement (2003), 'Spirituality can be understood as a search for the sacred, a process through which people seek to discover, hold on to.' The belief system leads to a positivistic orientation to whatever life experiences they have. In Dalby's (2006) conceptualization, spirituality refers to God, the divine, ultimate reality, and the transcendent, as beyond or outside the individual human life or material realm. In McFadden's (1996) term, spirituality can be seen as 'the motivational and emotional foundation of the long quest for meaning' (p. 164)

Old age usually confronts issues of loss, change, physical illness, decay, and mortality. Development of spiritual perspective offers a direct support system in these late periods. A number of psychological theories lend support to the view and offer different dimensional explanations of how spiritual orientation serves as positive reference points in life. In the psychoanalytic frame, Jung (1959) proposed that increased spiritual goals and pursuits, and an increase in introspection, are but a natural part of the maturational process from mid to later life. In socio-emotional selectivity theory, Carstensen et al. (1999) emphasize emotion-related goals in late life, especially when individuals become aware of the likely shortness of life remaining.

Erikson's (1982) model of psychosocial development seems to be an attempt to combine psychological and spiritual development. In 1989, Erikson revisited the later stages of his theory by trying to further understand older people's engagement with their lives and developmental tasks (Sacco, 2013). He developed this notion that spiritual development begins in middle age with a development of 'generative concerns' for younger generations which balances one's self-absorption. The later hood thus gets enveloped with 'wisdom,' that the sense of self transcends a time-bound identity maintaining a detached concern with life in the face of death. Erikson said that the lack of this pattern of development could lead one to develop despair, disdain, and dogmatism. Joan Erikson (1997) advocated a ninth stage – the task of developing an attitude of retreat and retirement in relation to the world. She considered this as an increased development of spiritual perspective. To Erikson, Erikson, and Kivnick (1986), spirituality leads to a gradual emergence of a type of consciousness that results in a 'heightened awareness that can by no means be claimed by the usual "ego"' (p. 51). This defined the specially oriented 'I' which could be called a transpersonal 'I am.' This, in turn, leads to a higher awareness of the self. It is expected to bring about greater witnessing of the mind with spontaneous non-doing and 'flow' conditions (Cziksentmihalyi, 1990). The self becomes a witness/*Sakshi* of the non-doing state, becomes tranquil and, in turn, basks in bliss.

Tornstam (1996) in his theory of gero-transcendence suggested a paradigm shift as people age that calls for a move from a materialistic and rational perspective on life to an increased '*cosmic and transcendent*' one. This is a shift towards the sacred in spiritualistic terms. Gero-transcendence, he conceived, manifests on three levels:

i. The cosmic level where the perception of time and space changes, a sense of connection with earlier generation develops, fear of death disappears, a mysterious dimension of life is accepted, and one experiences the rejoicings of subtle aspects of life;
ii. At the self-level, there is less self-centredness, less body concern, increased altruism, and the experience of ego-integrity;

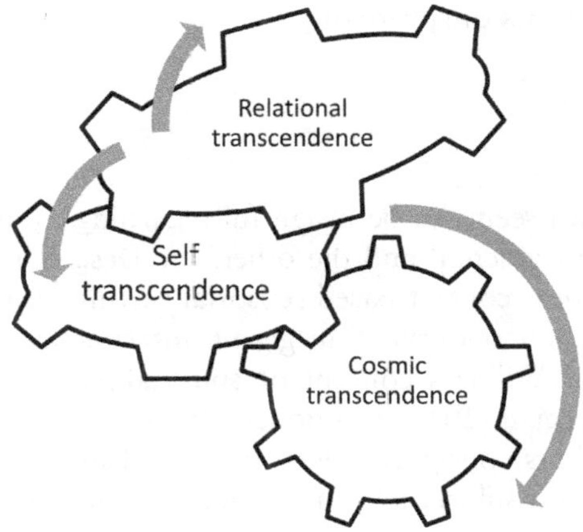

Figure 3.2 Components of gero-transcendence (source: authors).

ii. In terms of social and individual relations, the pattern changes with an increased need for solitude and an urge to abandon roles.

This is schematically illustrated in Figure 3.2.

Tornstam (2005) understood gero-transcendence as 'intrinsic and culture-free' (p. 59). His theory also has a resemblance to the earlier 'theory of disengagement' (Cumming and Henry, 1961), which posited that older people naturally withdraw from society and its earlier social roles. Tornstam's theory emphasized re-orientation towards spiritual perspectives in old age, rather than simple withdrawal from the mainstreams of life. Thus, in the final stage of life development, in Erikson, Erikson, and Kivnic's (1986) term, 'the successive increases in capacity to stand outside one's own self-centred agendas and feel connection and concern for things larger than oneself develops' (p. 53) This capacity is rooted in *existential spirituality* as an outcome of older people's concern for *transcendent wisdom*.

Transpersonality in the gerontology canvas

Gerontology is the scientific study of ageing and old age. Transpersonal psychology embraces as its primary mission the attempt to better understand and experience the part of the person that lies beyond personality, individuality, ego, acculturation, and social beliefs that envelop the totality of the whole person in terms of mind, body, soul, and spirit (Wacks, 2011). This has semblance with Maslow's (1971) reference of the need for self-transcendence. Transpersonal is also named as the highest tier of

Wilber's (2006) integral model of development. Wilber (1996) differentiated between two types of spirituality:

a. Ascending; and
b. Descending.

The Ascending path seems to be insightful regarding meanings of life, and hence, purely transcendental and the other, the Descending path, seems to celebrate the concrete, contact-based sensorial earthly pleasures in life.' The concept of 'cosmic consciousness' in gero-transcendence is the merging of these two types of Wilber's concept of spirituality. In explaining cosmic consciousness, Sherman (2011) mentioned about Eliade's (2009) concept of 'Ecstasy.' The authors conceived this as a form of meditative absorption, a state experienced as a subject-less envelopment or immersion. According to Atchley (2011), transcendence in Tornstam's explanation includes an inexorable inner magnet as a mental element that in the absence of socio-cultural or personal hindrance, draws people to it more and more as they move into the linings of later life. The concept of 'transpersonal' also includes what has historically been called the '*mystical experience*,' considered either as a state or stage of consciousness. Thus, in transpersonal, '*personal*' has a '*psycho-spiritual*' model of growth and development, implying that it both includes and transcends human '*bio-psychosocial*' selves (Wacks, 2011). This seems to be the composite content of realization of the unity of all experiences, detachment in the form of a let-go attitude, reflective living to find and learn meaning from daily experiences, seeing and accepting things and happenings as it is, acceptance of and learning from loss, finding an appropriate balance between human and seeking the at-one-ment with God, personalized wisdom, self-transcendence, meaning in being an elder, and accepting life in the totality spectrum (Blazer, 1991; Howe, 1983; Jones, 1984). This expanded consciousness, thus, seems to be constituted of a deep sense of a sacred, greater meaning-making capacity, an extended role and practised spirituality, conception or widened awareness of something more or greater than the self, and so on. This inner potential and realization of expanded consciousness in later years is framed as '*transpersonal gerontology*.' The attainment of this growth and development is expected to gift human beings certain positive contents in mental flairs that mould the personality contours in attitudinal contents and bring out the practised behavioural frame with grace and grace only. The concepts ingrained in transpersonal gerontology are represented by Figure 3.3. Such gifts of transpersonal psychology need a conceptual review.

Gifts of transpersonal gerontology

Late-life years are usually seen as waning periods for beings. Decay and deteriorations are obvious. But that does not mean that these extended years

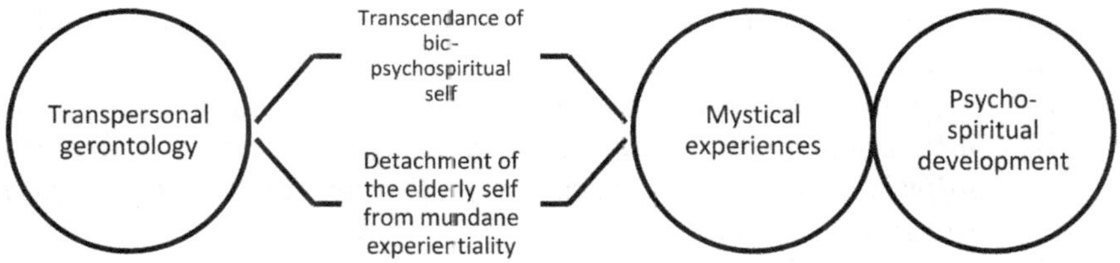

Figure 3.3 Transpersonality in gerontology (source: authors).

are totally devoid of any attainments. This is the ripe old stage of life; hence maximum maturity is expected in terms of extended flexibility to accept and accommodate all types of life experiences. Enjoying life to its fullest, the period is expected to mould the personality with layers of satisfaction, enriched experientiality, caring concern for others in generative tunes, spontaneous empathy, and serenity. The orientation to the transpersonal mode specifically gifts the aged the following traits or qualities in behaviour.

Spirituality to cope with diminishments

i. The reduction in ability of very senior people is inevitable. Life demands the courage of these people to take these adversities in their stride and accept the limitations as a natural phenomenon. Fisher (1985) opined that 'A spirituality of ageing must help us find a way to turn losses into gains, and to learn how the stripping process which often accompanies ageing can be a gradual entrance into freedom and new life' (p. 4). Diminishments are natural ways of turning people's mind from earlier priorities to a more complete and perhaps ultimate experience of ourselves. In old age, diminishments seem to be the spiritual curriculum that stimulates full human hood and teaches us the art of humility and self-acceptance. The transcendence of diminishments places one in front of life's greatest truths, removing the veil of deception and shocks us into the truths of ourselves and of life (Bianchi, 1986).
ii. ***A shift towards interiority to practice disengagements and detachment.*** Disengagement and withdrawal from previous societal roles are inevitable sequences in old age. Within the periphery of transpersonal gerontology, late-life disengagement is reframed as a spiritual practice of detachment or non-attachment Peck (1968) described this as 'transcendence' of work, body, and self. Jung's (1955/1970) concept of later life 'individuation' reflects the same disengagement of the transcendent from the person or social mask of living through one's societal roles. In Groeschel's (1984) conception, the spiritual seeker achieves *freedom* in detachment in later years.

iii. ***Acceptance of suffering as a shaper of life.*** Wacks (2011) pinpointed the positive role of sufferance in life as a developer of resilience in late life. He conceived:
   a. *In personal suffering, lies the possibility of redemption;*
   b. *Suffering provides a training forum to be prepared as the healer;*
   c. *Suffering indicates the need for further growth through a non-attachment attitude;*
   d. *Suffering as letting go prepares one to Eternality;*
   e. *Suffering serves as a hero's journey that transforms consciousness;*
   f. *In Campbell's (1988) view, suffering evokes and teaches compassion, the soothing behavioural streak in late life.*

   Seifer and Vieweg (2009) expressed that the pains in life are also resources. It demands concentration on the body condition as an immediate experience and detaches our true self from the higher spiritual self. The suffering-self cries in pain by the illusion of losing self-identity's core point of spirituality.

iv. ***Equanimity and the feel of presence.*** Late life calls for a new sense of immediacy of life and a corresponding ability to live in the present moment. Practising spirituality in late life ushers in a capacity to flow in the moment, feeling lost in an experience beyond time and place which consequently achieves transcendence. Myerhoff (1980) specified that the secret of ageing well is to have the capacity to live every aspect of life fully. In maturity, the aged seem to become authentic in self-acceptance and develop the true knowledge of how to live life. Spirituality teaches us to accept the self and transcend the self. Roberts (1982) thus concluded, 'This journey is the final process of our life span, wherein self-consciousness is gradually relinquished as we come upon *'that'* which lied beyond the self' (p. 196). The final process is the transpersonal or transcendent.

v. ***Wisdom and compassion.*** Hart (1987) felt that in later life, the transcendence of one's basic subjectivity and projections are likely to decrease one's ego-centredness and allow one to have a clear vision regarding life. Consequently, a greater acceptance evolves of limitations, contradictions, and negative aspects of human existence together with the knowledge of impermanence. This seems to be our wisdom-framed mind. Wisdom is characterized by an ironic stance on life that has its roots in awareness of the perpetual re-interpretability of one's existence. Nelson (1994) spoke of wisdom as a searching and savouring process of the stories that we are, a journey of '*autobiographical learning*' of self-discovery, of transformation: a journey with no predetermined end. This seems to be inseparable from the process of spiritual growth in late life. Wisdom is conceived as a prompt to spiritual growth. Self-transcendence is thus an essential component of wisdom. Wisdom offers a timeless knowledge of a universal nature and identity.

> Chinen (1985) therefore spoke about a new image of maturity that is centred around wisdom, self-knowledge, and transcendence.

The wisdom-rimmed behaviour element is compassion. This is genuine care and concern for others in a selfless attitude of mind. Compassion comes from a clear understanding offered by wisdom.

Conclusion

Hence, wise elders are able to accept life in its true colours and flavours. Conditions are not always congenial, yet spirituality in belief and practice-frame holds them in silence. Transcendence offers them the soothing layers to bear adversities. Taranto (1989) opined that:

> with acceptance, detachment, and humour about failing physical and social potential, aged people may still take charge of their lives and develop a new level of self-designed personal control taking into consideration all limitations of advanced age, yet having a deep positive orientation towards tidbits of life experiences that is ahead as pearls of attainments within life boundary.

With transcendence of ego-self and with the spiritual and unitive dimensions of human existence, transpersonal gerontology seems to be just not possible, but inevitable. The reliance on transpersonal gerontology is expected to offer the elders the *peace and harmony frills* of 'existential feels.'

The elderly, then, enjoy their remaining days of life with grace, witnessing every moment with awe (Chesterton, 1986).

References

Aguerre, C., & Bouffard, L. (2003). Le vieillissement reussi: Theories, recherché et applications cliniques. *Revue quibecoise de psychologie*, *24*, 107–129. Successful ageing: Theories, research and clinical applications.

Ardelt, M. (1997). Wisdom and life satisfaction in old age. *Journal of Gerontology: Psychological Sciences*, *52B*(1), 15–27.

Atchley, R.C. (2003). Why most people cope well with retirement. In J.L. Ronch & J.A. Goldfield (Eds.), *Mental wellness in ageing: Strengths-based approaches* (pp. 123–138). Winnipeg: Health Professions Press.

Atchley, R.C. (2011). How spiritual experience and development interact with ageing. *The Journal of Transpersonal Psychology*, *43*(2), 156–165.

Bianchi, E. (1986). *Ageing as a spiritual journey*. New York: Crossroad.

Blazer, D. (1991). Spirituality and ageing well. *Generations*, *15*(1), 61–65.

Campbell, J. (1988). *The power of myth*. New York: Doubleday Publishing.

Carstensen, I.L., Issacowitz, D.M., & Charles, S.T. (1999). Taking time seriously: A theory of socio-emotional selectivity. *American Psychologist*, *54*(3), 165–181.

Chesterton, G.K. (1986). *A second childhood.* In the collected poems, 81.
Chinen, A. (1985). *In the ever after: Fairy tales and the second half of life.* Wilmette, II. Chiron Publications.
Cole, T.R. (1984). Ageing, meaning and well-being.: Musings of a cultural historian. *Journal of Ageing and Human Development, 19*(4), 329–336.
Cumming, E., & Henry, W.E. (1961). *Growing old: The process of disengagement.* New York: Basic Books.
Czikzentmihalyi, M. (1990). *Flow: The Psychology of optimal experience.* New York: Harper and Row.
Dalby, P. (2006). Is there a process of spiritual change or development associated with ageing? A critical review of research. *Ageing and Mental Health, 10*(1), 04–12.
Elder, G.H. Jr. (1991). Making the best of life: Perspectives on lives, times and ageing. *Generations, 15*(1), 12–17.
Eliade, M. (2009). *Yoga: Immortality and freedom* (W.R. Trask, Trans.). Princeton, NJ: Princeton University Press.
Erikson, E. (1982). *The life cycle completed.* New York: Norton.
Erikson, E.H., Erikson, J.M., & Kivnic, J. (1986). *Vital involvement in old age.* New York: W.W. Norton and Company.
Erikson, J.M. (1997). *The life cycle completed.* New York: W.W. Norton.
Fischer, K. (1985). *Winter grace: Spirituality for the later years.* New York: Paulist Press.
Gailott, J. (1996). *Ce que je crois.* Paris: Desclee de Brohwer. What I believe.
Groeschel, B.J. (1984). *Spiritual passages.* New York: Crossroads.
Hart, W. (1987). *The art of living Vipasana meditation as taught by S. N. Goenka.* San Francisco: Harper.
Heard, G. (1963). *The five ages of man.* New York: Crossroads.
Hill, P.C., & Pargement, K.L. (2003). Advances in the conceptualizations and measurement of religion and spirituality: Implications for physical and mental health research. *American Psychologist, 58*(1), 64–74.
Honde, R. (1999). *Le temps de la vie: Le development psycho-social de l'adulte.* Montreal: Gaetan Morin. Time of life: Adult psycho-social development.
Howe, R.L. (1983). Spiritual dimensions of ageing. *Generations, 8*(1), 38–41.
Jaspers, K. (1967). *Philosophical faith and revelation.* New York: Harper and Row.
Jones, W.P. (1984). Ageing as a spiritualizing process. *Journal of Religion and Ageing, 1*(1), 3–16.
Jung, C.G. (1933). *Modern man in search of a soul.* New York: Harcourt Publishers Braces and World.
Jung, C.G. (1959). *The basic writings of Jung.* Oxford: Modern Library.
Jung, C.G. (1970). *Mysticism conjunctions: An inquiry into the separation and synthesis of psychic opposites in alchemy.* Princeton, NJ: Princeton University Press (Original published in 1955).
Maslow, A. (1971). *The farther reaches of human nature.* New York: NY: Viking Press.
McFadden, S.H. (1996). Religion, spirituality and ageing. In J.E. Birren & K.W. Schaie, R.P. Abeles, M. Gatz, & T.A. Salthouse (Eds.), *The handbook of the psychology of ageing* (4th edition, pp. 162-177). San Diego: CA: Academic Press. .

Moberg, D.O. (1990). Spiritual maturity and wholeness in the later years. *Journal of Religion and Ageing*, *7*(1/2), 5–24.

Moody, H.R. (1976). Philosophical pre-supposition of education for old age. *Educational Gerontology: An International Quarterly*, *1*(1), 1–16.

Moody, H.R. (2003). Conscious ageing: A strategy for positive change in later life. In J.L. Ronch & J.A. Goldfield (Eds.), *Mental wellness in ageing: Strength-based approaches* (pp. 139–160). Winnipeg: Health Professions Press.

Myerhoff, B. (1980). *Number our days*. Clearwater, FL: Touchstone Blocks.

Nelson, A. (1994). Researching adult transformation as autobiography. *International Journal of Lifelong Education*, *13*(5), 389–403.

Peck, R.C. (1968). Psychological developments in the second half of life. In B.L. Neugarten (Ed.), *Middle age and ageing* (pp. 441–463). Chicago, IL: University of Chicago Press.

Roberts, B. (1982). *The experience of no self*. Boston, MA: Shambhala.

Rosow, I. (1974). *Socializing to old age*. Berkeley: University of California Press.

Rowe, J.W., & Khan, R.L. (1987). Human ageing: Usual and successful. *Science*, *237*(4811), 143–149.

Sacco, R.G. (2013). Re-envisaging the eight developmental stages of Erik Erikson: The Fibonacci Life-Chart Method (FLCM). *Journal of Educational and Developmental Psychology*, *3*(1), 140–146.

Seifer, N., & Vieweg, M. (2009). *When the soul awakens*. Reston, VA: Gathering Wave Press.

Sherman, E. (2011). Transpersonal gerontology from a contemplative perspective. *The Journal of Transpersonal Psychology*, *43*(2), 253–286.

Taranto, M.A. (1989). Facets of wisdom: A theoretical synthesis. *International Journal of Ageing and Human Development*, *29*(1), 1–21.

Tornstam, L. (1996). Gero-transcendence – A theory about maturing into old age. *Journal of Ageing and Identity*, *1*, 55–63.

Tornstam, L. (2005). *Gero-transcendence: A developmental theory of positive ageing*. New York: Springer.

Wacks, V.B. (2011). The elder as sage, old age as spiritual path: Towards a transpersonal gerontology. *The Journal of Transpersonal Psychology*, *43*(2), 127–155.

Wacks, V.Q. (1987). A case for self-transcendence as a purpose of adult education. *Adult Education Quarterly*, *38*(1), 46–55.

Wilber, K. (1996). *A brief history of everything*. Boston, MA: Shambala Publications, Inc.

Wilber, K. (2006). *Integral spirituality*. Boston, MA: Integral Books.

Williamson, G.H. (2002). Ageing well. Outlook for the 21st century. In C.R. Snyden & S.J.Lopez (Eds.), *Handbook of positive psychology* (pp. 676–686). New York: Oxford University Press.

Wink, P., & Dillon, M. (2002). Spiritual development across the adult life course: Findings from a longitudinal study. *Journal of Adult Development*, *9*(1), 79–94.

Wong, P.T.P. (2000). Meaning in life and meaning in death in successful ageing. In A. Tomer (Ed.), *Death attitudes and the older adult* (pp. 23–55). New York: Brunner/Mazel Publisher.

Wuthnow, R. (1998). *After heaven: Spirituality in America since the 1950s*. Berkeley, CA: University of California Press.

4

LEISURELY WAYS OF ATTAINING POSITIVE AGEING

Adulthood in the human context calls for cognitive awareness of how to utilize our time and energy so that the interior and exterior decorations of life become meaningful to us. Primitive desires opt for instant materialistic pleasures, while impulse-controlled maturity drives us to look for deeper meanings in life. Life without purpose and meaning is an existential void that surfaces insecurity, anxiety, and ultimately, deep depression in life. To overcome the undesirable mental states and land on pleasure-painted life engagements calls for planning in life, in terms of activities – be it for livelihood or spending retirement with pleasurable hobbies. The main theme is to remain engaged in life before death with palliative layers of happiness and contentment. The signature philosophy of gerontologists is that 'it is better to wear out than to rust out.' Leisure seems to be the key ingredient in improving the quality of life among ageing adults owing to its mental engagement facilities (Dube and Choyal, 2012).

The concept of positivism

As per the dictum of the primitive frame of mind, sensuality and materialistic leanings are an obvious phenomenon in a human behaviour context. The desire for fulfilment is mostly concrete and material-based. The attitude of the mind is more towards exteriority and not to the interiority of searching soul-specific calmness and happiness. The practised modes create frustration of various kinds, leading to aggression, which can even result in terrorism and cruelty. This vicious circle produces enormous pain to human beings. The shackles need to be broken with positivism as a mind-frame philosophy. The quest of human beings should not just be material-based happiness, but lifting bare objective reality to inner subjective reality to initiate a quality of being, the crater of deep emotions embracing trust and positivity to reach the layers of ultimate security, peace, and harmony and to have happiness and well-being. The quest should be positivism – the most essential philosophy of life. To alter our experience quality, the whole world seems to be in the grip of a positivistic movement at present. Positivism is a system of philosophy based on things that can be seen or proved rather than speculation. It gives one absolute, complete meaning of being 'positive.' It has to be all-pervading. It is existence *per se* and the substratum for the entire ephemeral cosmos. It is knowledge *per se* and not the knowledge of something. It is uncontaminated by any desire, it is serene and an ocean of 'Bliss' (Singh, 2011). Positivism admits into the mind, thoughts, words, and images that are conducive to growth, expression, and success from which good and favourable results are expected. Conceptually, positivism encompasses all possible dimensions of life and aims at achieving enduring happiness and a better quality of life. Positivism demands one to get rid of all negative thoughts and practices and urges one to create a new belief system to step into a positive realm to usher in a positive lifestyle.

The panorama of ageing

Ageing is a receding lifeline of human beings. The decline in strength and resources are a natural phenomenon. But ageing is not just a total void of energy and ability. The better side of ageing is maturity, integrity, and a whole-life-unlimited knowledge point. If a positivistic mind-frame gets embedded into an aged person's system and there is found to be a definite positive activity schedule as per ability and choice, they would be expected to have a soothing fragrance of life and be far more contributory in their generative perspective. Life would offer them a station of 'blissful existence' despite numerous oddities; a smiling face will portray their well-being to others. A complete circle of life with its obvious negativities and practised positivities would become evidenced and marked. Their life will proceed on a meaningful track, the sense of meaning will add flavour to the diminishing light of their life.

As a branch of the social sciences, gerontology attempts to depict issues regarding old age as a means of comprehending the meaning of ageing. According to Erikson, Erikson, and Kivnick (1986), elders have both less and more ability in the canvas of their mind-frames. Unlike infants, the elderly have a reservoir of strength in their history and storytelling. They have rich resources of life experiences that they can creatively give to enrich their successors' experientiality. Their intellectual plane is full of self-earned experiences that prompt them to have a liberated self, being free of so many false notions that pervade our earlier stages of life. The clarity of mind is often accompanied by disillusionment. From childhood to midlife, the notion of upward progress generally persists in an ageing perspective, a man discovers to his dismay that his path now leads only to the grave. Possible helplessness and hopelessness may surface as a prominent emotion, but life shows itself that aged people with a positivistic frame of mind try to delve into some meaningful activities to touch upon the notion that things decay but the process of decaying can also be filled with natural meaning and happiness. The issue raises the question of remaining active and participatory in life to touch and feel the fragrance of transcendence in the life beyond. The extended life platter also contains so many positive elements to ponder on and relish. If we have suffered defeat, we are somewhere beyond the battle ... Here comes the positivistic mind-frame's utility of being involved in life in so many different directions that brings meaning-reservoirs for us as colourful facets to observe and feel the sunset days of our lifespans. The psychologist Jung (1965a, 1965b) believed that the psychological goal of later life is to become more and more oneself as an individual. To have this individualistic identity with experience-rich wrinkles on your face, one should have specific life-meaning deriving endeavours and utilize time and energy resources in a way that is fulfilling and, at the same time, providing meaning to oneself. Here will be the silver lining of our sunset days. When their experience clarifies the disillusionments with utter bitterness, their emotions should try to look for a meaningful anchor to still have faith in life and its flows and should look forward to having fulfilment and happiness.

Leisure in relation to ageing

Nowadays, an ageing society is more and more common. An ageing population is considered to be a reflection of human appreciation and the tryst with nature. Yet the population has concerns about possibly suffering from diseases and disabilities (Prohoska et al., 2006). Significantly, many health problems experienced in later life are preventable as they are often associated with the onset of a more sedentary lifestyle (World Health Organization, 1998). Increasingly, older adults' participation in 'leisure time/physical activity' offers an opportunity to reduce the prevalence of morbidity in later life and offset a potential burden of ageing on the public health sector (Fries, 1996). The highlights of Ejaz et al.'s (1997) research programme state that older people's quality of life is not solely dependent on the providence of quality medical and physical care but is also dependent on the involvement in appropriate leisure programs that are conducive to aged people's social, creative, emotional, psychological, spiritual, and cognitive well-being. Ingle and Nath (2008) added that the growth of individualism on account of increased urbanization, industrialization, and globalization has affected the status of the elderly. The problematic dimensions of their lives are due to a lack of social security and inadequate facilities for health care, rehabilitation, recreation, and leisure. The topic of leisure services for elders is thus one of growing importance. One reason for this increased concern is the continuous growth of elders in the population. The other such concern for elders is that they tend to have more free time than other adult age groups and that research has demonstrated the strong influence of satisfaction with leisure activities on quality of life. Elderly people have recently taken a greater interest in being more active and living more fully.

In Canada, for instance, the proportion of people over 65 enjoying physical activity regularly (at least once a month) rose from 50% to 63% between 1976 and 1981 (Statistics Canada, 1986). Because leisure activities often include social interactions (Crandall, 1979; Kelly, Steinkamp, and Kelly, 1986), leisure participation may be particularly beneficial to the elderly, as social involvement is considered a key factor in successful ageing (Atchley, 1976). Regular leisure participation has been shown to lead to psychological benefits among the elderly (Iso-Ahola, 1980; Tinsle, Colbs, Teaff, and Kaufman, 1987).

The benefits of leisure are multivariate – enhanced social skills, improved physical fitness, and intellectual alertness. It promotes stimulation and interest in life and offers pleasure and fun (Brown, 1994). The findings of the Department of the Arts, Sport, the Environment, Tourism and Territories (1990) of the Australian Government indicated that leisure induces a sense of belongingness, security, mental stimulation, happiness, improved decision making, independence, relaxation, socialization, escapism, opportunities to express ideas and be creative, and increased self-esteem and personal growth and decreased boredom and frustration. The reports also mentioned that the benefits included maintenance of fitness, improved sleep patterns, reduction in digestive complaints, and general improvement in physical-mental health. Juarbe et al. (2002) supplemented these health benefits with better management of disease, illness prevention, and promotion of mental health, indicating an overall improvement in quality of life. Leisure is expected to be a guard to physical-mental deterioration. Leisure activities stand as an identity after retirement and act as a dynamic force behind positive and exhilarating later years (McGuire et al., 1996).

Studies have shown that participation in active types of recreation pursuits generally declines with age. Leisure activities tend to become more passive, with media leisure activities such as reading, television, and radio among the main types of leisure interests for older adults (Levy, 1981). Levy found that people are socialized or develop attitudes to expect a decline in participation in active forms of leisure; only a few start any new active activities. Almost one-half of the seniors starting new activities chose pursuits in the creative, cultural, social, and passive category. This included activities such as handicrafts and hobbies, reading, and table games. Such interest showed a marked increase for people over 65 years of age or older. Relaxation, enjoyment of nature, keeping busy, using skills and talents, and meeting new people were important to a greater proportion of seniors than any other age category. Common observations also indicate their interest in various leisure activities. Regularity in such activities is expected to maintain equilibrium in body functioning and promote self-recognition. Once seniors are into regular recreational activities, they will gain more self-esteem and such activities could calm their moods, increase physical capability, slow down the ageing process, improve quality of life, and reduce medical expenditure.

The advantages of participation in such activities include promoting brain functioning, preventing memory loss, fighting off disease-induced disability, and improving nerve conduction (Lien, 2002; Devil et al. 1993).

Leisure activities among the elderly are not only restricted to any single social class or strata. Leisure-time activities for senior individuals belonging to the affluent class include attending clubs regularly, playing cards, billiards, golf, and so on (Badami and Yenagi, 2015; Yadav, 2010). They may also engage themselves in regular walks during a specific time of the day. Those hailing from the middle socio-economic class may develop culinary skills, engage themselves in embroidery activities, participate in morning/evening walks, and even engage in regular chats with their cohort group. Similarly, senior individuals belonging to the lower class may also be involved with their cohort groups, engage in conversation, physically help each other, and in bodily pleasurable activities such as massaging and haircuts (Demakakos, Hamer, Stamatakis, and Steptoe, 2010; Motl and McAuley, 2010). Birdwatching, photography, and gardening may be inculcated as leisure-time activities among senior individuals irrespective of social class or strata. These are especially true for nature lovers. Taking up old favourites, volunteering, and engaging in community centred recreational services may also be some other meaningful avenues (Singh and Kiran, 2013, 2014; Ueshima, Ishikawa-Takata, Yorifuji, Suzuki, Kashima, Takao, Sugiyama, Ohta, and Doi, 2010).

Leisure and recreation in the conceptual frame

Since the days of ancient Greece, philosophers and social writers had shown their intense concern regarding the importance of leisure in human life. At one point, they found that it served chiefly to identify the upper classes in society as a unique possession of social identity. More recently, leisure has been defined by economists and sociologists in simple frames of 'non-work time.' It is also regarded as a way of life marked by a sense of freedom and independent choice and as an opportunity for earning self-actualization. Leisure is simply not 'free time' to be considered as leisure; the time must be spent in pursuit of significant and worthwhile experiences. It is considered to be a time when people want to do things away from work and other commitments. Both leisure and recreation enrich people with a sense of identity and personal autonomy, thereby adding meaning to life and encouraging personal growth and self-expression (Van dar Par and Koopman-Boyden, 2009; Adams, Leibbrandt, and Moon, 2011). Roberts (2006) is of the opinion that despite the complexities of later life, leisure can provide the 'freedom to be.' Lee and Singleton (2000) opine that leisure is the occasion for the development of broader and deeper perspectives in life to enrich our body, mind, and spirit. Leisure provides the opportunity for learning and freedom for growth and self-expression, for rest and restoration, and for rediscovering life in the entirety, hence, leisure is free of one's work-connected responsibilities or obligated forms of self-care maintenance. Leisure means the independent and free choice of beings that meet one's personal needs for reflection, self-enrichment, relaxation, or pleasure. In this time, leisure may be regarded as one's holistic state of being having flairs of spiritual experiences. Thus, the term leisure refers to free and unbounded time where chosen activities are adopted to feel good rather than doing perfunctory activities as a daily routine (Leitner and Leitner, 2011; Mamatha and Lata, 2014). Recreation is a set of activities conducted during leisure, usually for the purpose of enjoyment. According to Zhan (2001), leisure activities mean that individuals willingly go for certain activity regimes that usher in mental, physical, and social health during free time. In such activities, individuals could be satisfied and happy being self-enriched in a leisure state. Mannel and Kleiber (1997) opine that leisure is both objective and subjective in dimension. It is objective when participating in one or multiple activities – meaning being engaged for a significant length of time, while subjective leisure means individuals obtaining inner satisfaction through activities.

Hence, leisure experiences are expected to have the underlying dynamism of motivation. Motivation is considered an integral part of the leisure experience (Iso-Ahola, 1979; Neulinger, 1974; Neelankavil and Chirappanath, 2012), and is defined as the force that initiates, directs, and sustains behaviour (Petri, 1981). Leisure motivation can be referred to as the energy that initiates, directs, and sustains leisure involvement. The literature reveals (Kraus, 1997) a six-tier leisure concept, which can be conceived as follows:

1. The classical view of leisure
   It has the following functionalities:
   - Leisure is activity, the basis of culture, and the source of a good life;
   - Leisure includes music, art, community involvement, physical fitness, and contemplation;
   - Moderation is a prerequisite for leisure and a good life;
   - Peace is a requisite for leisure;
   - People must be taught the correct use of leisure.
2. A symbol of social class being reflected through leisure
   The 19th-century eminent sociologist Veblen's (1912) research shows that patterns of old age leisure activities are social class-based. The spending pattern and chains of activities are related to one's own social class as the baseline of experience patterns in life. But in modern society, leisure is conceived to be a privilege for all, the affluent or the poor. The word, 'leisure' implies attaining a calm, quiet, contemplative, and unhurried state of mind involved in a chosen set of activities.
3. Leisure as unobligated time
   The *Dictionary of Sociology* states that *leisure is the free time after the practical necessities of life have been attended to by an individual.* It is devoid of a sense of obligation or compulsion. It is a personal choice to usher in a sense of happiness and well-being.

4. Leisure as an activity
   Leisure is an activity in which people engage during their free time. Dumazedier (1960) conceives leisure as a set of activities that are for relaxation, diversion, broadening of one's knowledge extent, spontaneous social participation, and the free exercise of one's own creative capacity.
5. Leisure as a state of being
   Neulinger (1974) pinpoints that leisure means looking for pleasure and satisfaction through one's expressed talents and potentialities and thereby seeking 'self-actualization' using one's degree of creativity and expressive ability.
6. Leisure as a spiritual expression
   The leisure experience is conceived to be wrapped up with the feeling of being connected with oneself and a sense of oneness with the universe. It may also facilitate spiritual experiences through 'peak experiences' of self-actualization or the 'flow' experience pattern of Csikzentmihalyi (1990).

Leisure may take its place as a way of being connected in life and setting a meaning-platform in the process. Leisure can simply be thought of as a 'discretionary time' which becomes more readily available during one's retirement years. Leisure is not simply what we do with 'leftover time.' But it definitely is a multi-dimensional quality of life different from paid employment, household maintenance, or other instrumental activities. It calls for an urge to be specifically involved in it. It seems to be a path to deeper meaning and having some dimension of growth or personal development. It is just not the available time in the post-retirement stage. Individual differences are prominent in the choice of leisure activities and age cannot be a lone factor in deciding leisure activities in later life.

- Sedentary activities appear to be the most popular leisure past-times;
- Most leisure activities occur within the boundary of home or close to home;
- Physically active leisure pattern is relatively low;
- More meaningful leisure activities are needed that place increased emphasis on cognitive and physical abilities (Leitner and Leitner, 2011).

Dimensional importance of leisure and recreation for the elderly: A survey of important literature

There is ample documentation of the general benefits of recreation in the elder-life function. Nimrod (2007) examined six activity factors that were found to contribute significantly to life satisfaction:

- High culture;
- Free out-of-home activities;
- Spirituality and enrichment;
- Popular culture;
- Following generation;
- Independent home activities.

Nimrod and Adoni (2006) found that older adults who were more involved in active forms of leisure had higher levels of satisfaction with their leisure and their life as well. Riddick (1993) found that for older females, the three types of activities found to be highly correlated were informal activity–friendship interaction, participation in community and volunteer organizations, and solitary activity. Greater leisure satisfaction and leisure participation were found to be associated with lower levels of anxiety (Kaufman, 1988). Positive leisure participation patterns increase happiness and lead to possible greater longevity. Duenwald (2002) correlated longevity with positive thinking and optimism – traits that are enhanced by positive leisure behaviour. Healthy lifestyles having daily recreational exercise and strong relationship bonds through social recreational activities have a greater impact on how well people age than heredity (Selland, 1999). Research cited by Pollak (1999) also seems to indicate that even non-strenuous recreational activities like playing cards, going to the movies, or visiting friends can help older adults live longer.

Volunteering seems to be a platform for leisure activity that can provide the opportunity to help others. Leisure activity participation can have a 'snowball effect,' in that participation can lead to enhanced psychological well-being and life satisfaction, which, in turn, can lead to greater involvement in other activities. The study implies that the more people are socially engaged, the better off they are cognitively and that in addition to social activities, recreational activities such as cards and checkers, which are mentally stimulating, could reduce the risk of Alzheimer's disease (Nagourney, 2002). Playing a musical instrument or dancing seems to be emotionally very satisfying (Johns Hopkins University, 2006).

Schafer (1991) cites a study implying that elderly bridge players were found to have better memory and reasoning abilities than non-players. According to Schafer (1991), activities such as crossword puzzles, chess, stimulating conversations, and challenging hobbies do have cognitive improvements like bridge playing.

The problems of loneliness and depression can be alleviated through specific recreational activities. Pennix et al. (2002) found that aerobic exercise significantly lowered depressive symptoms in elderly individuals. Riddick and Keller (1992) state that dance/movement is effective in reducing loneliness and that pet therapy seems to have its efficacy in providing a companion to elderly individuals. Winslow (2002) and Lindsey (2002) stated that a consistent light exercise programme in later life, as well as resistive exercise, can reduce bone loss.

General benefits of recreation

- High life satisfaction
- Significant spirituality through extended generative mood patterns and enrichment
- Informal activity–friendship bond
- Self-engrossment
- Sense of discipline
- Feeling happily engaged
- Lower levels of anxiety
- Enhanced happiness and well-being
- Better self-esteem
- Positive thinking and optimism
- A feeling of non-strenuous engagement
- Enhanced life span with better resilience
- Developing skills or talents in abilities (like cards, checkers)
- Ameliorating the possibility of Alzheimer's disease
- Sharpened memory orientation, owing to a keen interest in something
- Developing mental interest, stimulating conversations
- Taking up chattering hobbies;
- Alleviating depression and loneliness.

Leisure activities leading to further meaning paths in advanced years

In fact, human beings live in a symbolic world of shared meaning and the power of meaning can be a matter of life and death. Outliving the self – in Erik Erikson's coinage of 'generativity' is not limited to acts of sacrifice (Kotre, 1984). Transcendence and the search for meaning are the ulterior motives in human life to earn the name of 'humans.' In the last phase of life, human souls look for the meaning of existence. This quest for meaning creates a void where humans lose the basic motive to continue with life. In fact, it has only been since the 20th century that a sizable proportion of the population survived to experience real old age, establishing the fact that the meaning of old age has become an issue of scientific investigation. Kaufman (1986) states that the issue of whether old age has meaning is central to what is understood as life satisfaction or morale in old age. Old age is characteristically a time with fewer work role constrictions in life. In the debilitating state of health and personal resources, leisure seems to be a significant avenue of being actively engaged and involved with life as a result of having a positivistic flair that can possibly curve the newer paths and draw meaning in later life. A study of leisure found that the number of people starting new activities diminishes with age (Iso, Jackson, and Dunn, 1994). Movie-going drops from 38% in midlife to 17% after the age of 65, travel diminishes significantly among people over age 75, and outdoor gardening shows a modest decline, while others, such as watching television, sports, and engaging in informal discussion, show no age-related decline at all.

Implications of leisure in the late-life context

Patterns of late-life leisure seem to have important implications for the economy in an ageing society. Old age leisure is also a means of affirming one's identity, a vital dimension of the phenomenological 'lifeworld' at a time when other roles may be lost (Hendricks and Cutler, 1990). Leisure-time activities are an important part of our personal world of meaning and also a part of a shared horizon of socio-economic and socio-cultural transactions. Most people do not simply disengage altogether from meaningful activities because such activities bring some facets of life involvement. Habits of religiosity, like other behaviours, tend to remain stable as people move into later life, but faith can take on new meanings with age. Religious orientations are found to help people, especially in old age to cope with life in a variety of ways.

Often the personal search for meaning leads to a deeper insight into religious faith. Further, successful ageing is preserving through activity – be it for work life or to arrange leisure for oneself. Simone de Beauvoir (1972) offers the view of a philosopher rejecting traditional ideals of old age as a time of tranquillity or disengagement but believes in continuous activity engagement in the earlier stages of life to come to a point of calmness in old age. Erikson (1963) sees old age as different from other stages because it offers a kind of culmination to life as a whole. He believes that through concern for the welfare of future generations, older people find a sense of meaning in later life. Jung's (1965a, 1965b) belief is that advanced age is a time for turning inward for deeper reflexing. Berman (1986) opines that even when outer activity is cut off, it is still possible to find deep meaning in the last stage of life. If unresolved conflicts and fears are successfully reintegrated at this stage, they can give new significance and meaning to an individual's life (Butler, 1974). Butler's view has resemblance with that of Erikson's who sees the psychological task of late-life as achieving ego-integrity, a reintegration of all aspects of the individual's life that leads to having a solid set of life-embracing meaning. The implications of leisure activities in late-life are schematically represented in Figure 4.1.

The gamut of old age

On the whole, old age is a culmination point of life experiences. The life story of everyone has both the dimensions of happiness and sadness, satisfaction

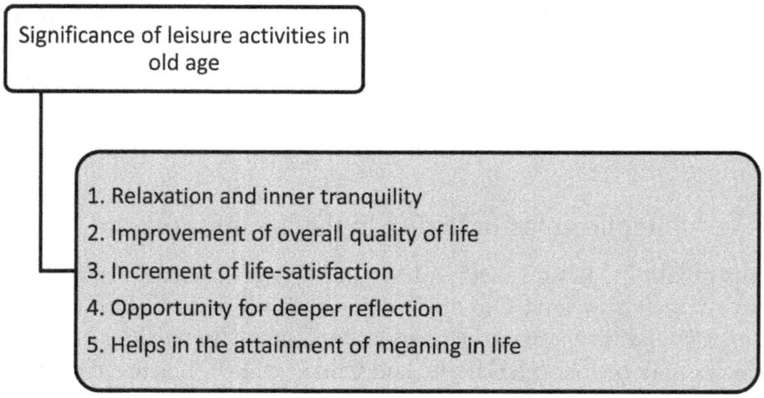

Figure 4.1 The implication of leisure activities in old age (source: authors).

and frustration. The late stage of life, owing to its declining orientation in the reservoir of resources, seems to be filled with basic disengagement and mental sufferings of various kinds. The maturity component, especially in the emotional parlance, signifies that the accounts of life, even at this advanced stage, can be rescheduled, redesigned, and reframed with positive beliefs in life and habits, as well as sufficient leisure-driven engagements in life. A lifespan offers many oddities, yet personalized resources with a deep philosophical bent of a positivistic mind can paint the lines of happiness with derived meanings.

Conclusion

Without meaning and purpose, life loses its dynamicity. The motion-less state of mind receives negativity that brings to the fore dread, fear, insecurity, and, at times, persecutory notions. The staggering gait of the lifeline even loses the positive reminiscences and gets engrossed in the pathos of the darker shades of life. The earthly existence becomes a drudgery, the eternal bliss of transcendence seems unreality. Helplessness, hopelessness, and haplessness engulf the self-system, they stand at the abyss of disdain and dismay. The appeal, since avenues of positivities are numerous, is that playful leisure activities are within the available reach of mental orientation – why not avail them to have meaningful satisfaction in the present life and in life reflections?

To end, we must consider Jung's (1965a, 1965b) saying that the afternoon of human life must also have a significance of its own and cannot be merely a pitiful appendage to life's mourning. Our saying should be 'Let there be meaningful leisure activities for aged ones… let them enjoy this opportunity of enjoying life to its brim.'

References

Adams, K.B., Leibbrandt, S., & Moon, H. (2011). A critical review of the literature on social and leisure activity and wellbeing in later life. *Ageing and Society*, *31*(4), 683–712.

Atchley, R.C. (1976). *The sociology of retirement*. Cambridge, MA: Schenkman.

Badami, S., & Yenagi, G.V. (2015). Leisure time activities: A boost for elderly health. *Adv. Research Journal of Social Sciences*, 6(2), 191–197.

Berman, E. (1986). In *Africa with Schweitzer*. Far Hills, NJ: New Horizon Press.

Brown, P. (1994). *Health care and the aged* (2nd ed.). Sydney: McLennan and Petty.

Beauvoir, Simone de (1972). *The coming of age*. Putnam Publishing Group.

Butler (1974). Retrieved from www.sagepub.in/upm-data/61106_Controversy_1.pdf, p. 534

Crandall, R.C. (1979). Social interaction, affect and leisure. *Journal of Leisure Research*, *11*(4), 165–181.

Czikzentmihalyi, M. (1990). *Flow: The psychology of optimal experience*. New York: Harper and Row.

Demakakos, P., Hamer, M., Stamatakis, E., & Steptoe, A. (2010). Low-intensity physical activity is associated with reduced risk of incident type 2 diabetes in older adults: Evidence from the English longitudinal study of ageing. *Diabetologia*, *53*(9), 1877–1885

Department of the Arts, Sport. the Environment, Tourism and Territories (1990). *Recreation in nursing homes. S A guide for recreation workers in nursing homes*. Canberra: Australian Government Publishing Services.

Devil, C.A., O'Connor, P.C., & Mattoon, P.M. (1993). Leisure activity, life satisfaction, and perceived health status in older adults. *Gerontology and Geriatric Education*, *14*(2), 3–19.

Dube, S., & Choyal, T. (2012). Leisure: Effect on healthy ageing. *Indian Journal of Gerontology*, *26*(3), 410–423.

Duenwald, M. (2002). Power of positive thinking extends, it seems, to aging. *The New York Times*, 6, D1.

Dumazedier, J. (1960). Current problems of the sociology of leisure. *International Social Science Journal*, *4*(4), 522–531.

Ejaz, F.K., Schur, D., & Noelkar, L.S. (1997). The effect of activity involvement and social relationships on boredom among nursing home residents. *Activities, Adaptation and Ageing*, *21*(4), 53–66.

Erikson, E.H. (1963). *Childhood and society* (2nd ed.). New York: Norton.

Erikson, E.H., Erikson, J.M., & Kivnick, H.B. (1986). *Vital involvement in old age: The experience of old age in our time*. New York: W.W. Norton and Company, Inc.

Fries, J.F. (1996). Physical activity, the compression of morbidity and the health of the elderly. *Journal of the Royal Society of Medicine*, *89*(2), 64–68.

Hendricks, J., & Cutler, S.C. (1990). Leisure and the structure of our life worlds. *Ageing and Society*, *10*, 854–894.

Ingle, G.K., & Nath, A. (2008). Geriatric health in India: Concerns and solutions. *Indian Journal of Community Medicine*, *33*(4), 214–228.

Iso-Ahola, S.E. (1979). Basic dimensions of definition of leisure. *Journal of Leisure Research*, *15*(1), 28–39.

Iso-Ahola, S.E. (1980). *Social psychological perspectives on leisure and recreation.* Springfield, IL: Charles C. Thomas.

Iso-Ahola, S.E., Jackson, E.L., & Dunn, E. (1994). Starting, ceasing, and replacing leisure activities over the human life span. *Journal of Leisure Research, 26*(3), 227–249.

Johns Hopkins University (2006). *Johns Hopkins 2006 white paper on memory.* Retrieved from www.hopkinsmemory.com

Juarbe, T., Turok, X.P., & Perez-Stable, J.E. (2002). Perceived benefits and barriers to physical activity among older Latin women. *Western Journal of Nursing Research, 24*(8), 868–886.

Jung, C.G. (1965a). *Memories, dreams, reflections.* New York: Vintage Book Company. Jung's autobiography, filled with dream accounts; essential to understanding his life and theories.

Jung, C.G. (1965b). *Psychology of the unconscious: A study of the transformations and symbolisms of the libido; a contribution to the history of the evolution of thought* (B.M. Hinkle, Trans.). New York: Dodd, Mead.

Kaufman, J.E. (1988). Leisure and anxiety: A study of retirees. *Activities, Adaptation, and Aging, 11*(1), 1–10.

Kaufman, S.R. (1986). Activities and well-being among older New Zealanders. In P. Koopman-Boyden & C. Waldegrave (Eds.), *Enhancing well-being in an Ageing Society*: 65–84 year old New Zealanders in 2007 (pp. 117–132). Retrieved from University of Waikato, website jhp.sagepub.com/content/39/4/30.refs

Kelly, J.R., Steinkamp, M.W., & Kelly, J.R. (1986). Later life leisure. How they play in Peoria. *Gerontologist, 26*(5), 531–537.

Kotre, J.N. (1984). *Psychology.* Baltimore: John Hopkins University Press.

Kraus, R. (1997). *Recreation and leisure in modern society.* Santa-Monica, CA: Addison-Wesley Educational Publishers Inc.

Lee, H., & Singleton, J.F. (2000). The meaning and concept of 'leisure': Older Chinese women's perspectives. In D.M. Samdahl & M.H. Havitz (Eds.). *National recreation and parks. Abstracts of the from the symposium on Leisure Research* (p. 42). Ashburn, VA: National Parks and Recreation Association.

Leitner, M.J., & Leitner, S.F. (2011). *Leisure enhancement* (4th edn.). Urbana. IL: Sagamore Publishing.

Levy, J. (1981, December). Leisure and retirement in Canada Part I: Leisure activities preferences of participants in a pre-retirement planning seminar: A longitudinal approach. *Recreation Research Review*, 28–33.

Lien, C.-M. (2002). Unpublished dissertation. Taiwan: Gerontological Research Centre, Yuan Ze University.

Lindsey, C. (2002). Fighting frailty in the elderly. *Biomechanics, 9*(7), 20–30.

Mamatha, S., & Lata, P. (2014). *Mental ability and adjustment among retired senior citizens.* Thesis, The University of Agricultural Sciences, Dharwad, Karnataka, India.

Mannel, R.C., & Kleiber, D.A. (1997). *A social psychology of leisure.* Pennsylvania: Venture Publishing Publishing Inc.

McGuire, F.A., Boyd, R.K., & Tendrick, R.T. (1996). *Leisure and ageing: Living in later life.* Champaign, IL: Sagamore Publishing.

Motl, R.W., & McAuley, E. (2010). Physical activity, disability, and quality of life in older adults. *Physical Medicine and Rehabilitation Clinics of North America, 21*(2), 299–308.

Nagourney, E. (2002). Social whirl may help keep the mind dancing. *The New York Times*, 7.

Neelankavil, M.F., & Chirappanath, A.K. (2012). *Contemporary geriatric problems of Kerala. A socio-medical.* Analysis Thesis. Mahatma Gandhi University, Kottayam, Kerala, India.

Neulinger, J. (1974). *The psychology of leisure: Research approaches to the study of leisure.* Springfield, IL: Charles C. Thomas.

Nimrod, G. (2007). Retirees' Leisure: Activities, benefits, and their contribution to life satisfaction. *Leisure Studies*, *26*(1), 65–80.

Nimrod, G., & Adoni, H. (2006). Leisure-styles and life satisfaction among recent retirees in Israel. *Aging and Society*, *26*(4), 607–630.

Pennix, B.W.J.H., Rejeski, W.J., Pandya, J., Miller, M.E., DiBari, M., Applegate, W.B., & Pahor, M. (2002). Exercise and depressive symptoms: A comparison of aerobic and resistance exercise effects on emotional and physical function in older persons with high and low depressive symptomology. *Journal of Gerontology*, *57B*(2), 124–132.

Petri, H.L. (1981). *Motivation: Theory and research.* Belmont, CA: Wadsworth.

Pollak, M. (1999). Stay busy, live longer, experts suggest. *The New York Times*, D8.

Prohaska, T., Belansky, E., Belza, B., Buchner, D., Marshall, V., McTigue, K. ... Wilcox, S. (2006). Physical activity, public health and ageing: Critical issues and research priorities. *The Journal of Gerontology*, *61*, 267–273.

Riddick, C.C. (1993). Older women's leisure activity and quality of life. In J.R. Kelly (Ed.), *Activity and aging: Staying involved in later life* (pp. 86–98). Newbury Park, CA: Sage.

Riddick, C.C., & Keller, M.J. (1992). Efficacy of recreation on influencing the social psychological health of elders. *Parks and Recreation*, *20–24*, 161.

Roberts, K. (2006). *Leisure in contemporary society* (2nd ed.). Oxon: CABI Publishing.

Schafer, W. (1991). Use it or lose it. *Stress & Health Report* (p. 1). Chico, CA: Enloe Hospital Stress & Health Center.

Selland, K. (1999). In aging, author says, genes aren't everything. *The Boston Globe*, A12.

Singh, S. (2011). Positivism in relation to health. In A.K. Chauhan & S.S. Nathawat (Eds.), *New facets in positivism* (p. 201). London: Macmillan.

Singh, B., & Kiran, U.V. (2013). Loneliness among elderly women. *International Journal of Humanities and Social Sciences*, *2*(2), 10–14.

Singh, B., & Kiran, U.V. (2014). Recreational activities for senior citizens. *IOSR Journal of Humanities and Social Science (IOSR-JHSS)*, *19*(4), 24–30.

Statistics Canada (1986). *The serious boom: Dramatic increases in longevity and prospects for better healthy.* By L.O. Stone and S. Fletcher (Catalogue number 89–515E). Ottawa: Health and Welfare Canada.

Tinsley, H.E., Colbs, S.L., Teaff, J.D., & Kaufamn, N. (1987). The relationship of age, gender, health, and economic status to the psychological benefit of older persons report from participation in leisure activities. *Leisure Sciences*, 53–65.

Ueshima, K., Ishikawa-Takata, K., Yorifuji, T., Suzuki, E., Kashima, S., Takao, S., ... Doi, H. (2010). Physical activity and mortality risk in the Japanese elderly: A cohort study. *American Journal of Preventive Medicine*, *38*(4), 410–418.

Van dar Par, S., & Koopman-Boyden, P. (2009). *Leisure and recreation*. New York: BW Huebsch.

Veblen, T. (1912). *The theory of the social class: An economic study of institutions*. New York: BW Huebsch.

Winslow, R. (2002). Yes, you can turn back the clock. *The Wall Street Journal*, *3*, D1.

World Health Organization (1998). *Growing older staying well: Ageing and physical activity in everyday life*. Geneva: World Health Organization.

Yadav, L.V. (2010). Depression in advanced age. *Indian Psychological Review*, *74*(3), 175–180.

Zhan, Z.R. (Eds.) (2001). *Urban sociology*. Shanghai: Shanghai University Press.

5

POSITIVELY EMPOWERED ELDERS WITH CREATIVE 'CHISELS' IN HAND

The notion of ageing, being associated with stereotypes of various kinds, and a decline in different spheres, has vehemently been challenged by the positivistic view of ageing, which recognizes that ageing can be accompanied by potential beyond problems. This perspective began emerging by the end of the 20th century and reflected a major conceptual transition in ageing (Cohen, 2000a). In fact, the focus on psychological growth and development in the last lap of one's life has prompted a newer understanding of the capacity for positive change and creative expression (Cohen, 2005). It acknowledges the humane and productive aspects of human life and also considers individual differences. This is expected to bring forth improved levels of personal empowerment in the elderly (Formosa, 2011). There is a need to delve into the creative fervour of elderly individuals to understand the process of ageing from the positivistic paradigm and to realize its implications along multiple layers of personal empowerment. The present chapter adopts two major strategies, namely, taking the help of some illustrious people in the country who have been/are currently internationally and nationally known for their creative endeavours, and, second, by prescribing certain creative activities for the senior inhabitants to be empowered in varied spheres. Several other renowned names may be mentioned, but this will naturally be a limited list of examples in keeping with the scope of the chapter.

Creativity in the latter half of life

Creativity may be regarded as the ability to innovate and change the environment rather than merely adjusting to it in a more passive sense (Simonton, 1994). It involves one to remain open to new ideas and approaches and engage in divergent thinking to seek an original solution for a problem or challenge at hand (Fisher and Specht, 1999). It is through such activities that an individual deepens an understanding of the self and cultivates purposeful or meaningful involvements (Fisher and Specht, 1999). It offers a channel to

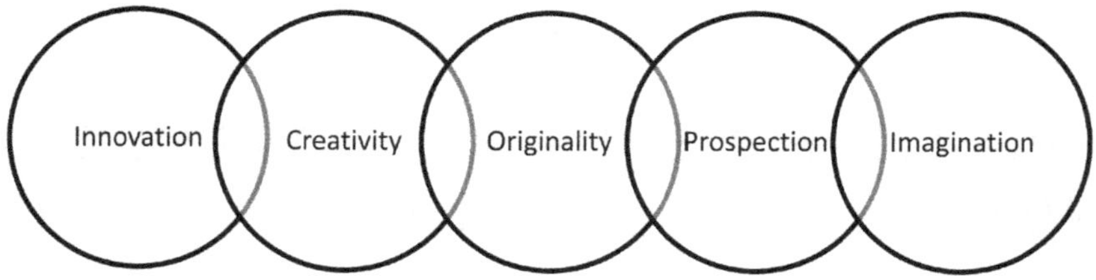

Figure 5.1 Creativity and allied terms (source: authors).

respond to the limits and uncertainties of existence (Hickson and Housley, 1997). Creativity requires the use of originality, which, in turn, requires prospection and imagination. Moreover, it requires usefulness and a good sense of the 'audience' who tend to make use of the idea (Amabile, 1988; Sawyer, 2012). The inter-relationships of creativity with the allied terms may be understood by the diagrammatic representation in Figure 5.1.

It is to be noted that innovation relates to original and useful mental representations of the future implemented on a large scale while creativity involves original and useful mental representations of the future. At the same time, originality refers to original mental representations of the future while prospection relates to mental representations of the future. Further, imagination denotes mental representations of events that are not present.

From the psychoanalytic perspective, Anthony (1987) argued that creativity is related to ego autonomy, which is, in turn, related to mental health. Creative activities involve not only features of openness to new ideas, but also problem-solving abilities, thereby creating novel, meaningful products, solutions, or outcomes, and apply both convergent and divergent thinking as mentioned earlier. However, many elderly individuals may be reluctant in engaging with specific creative activities and may not describe themselves as creative. Kerka (1999) opines that older adults may experience a decrease in the ability to generate many novel and authentic ideas. Nevertheless, the second half of life may provide a relatively better time for reflecting; therefore, creative pursuits aimed at the construction of one's life story aid in this process. In this context, it is worth noting that Addams-Price (1998) commented that late-life creativity reflects aspects of late-life thinking involving the phases of synthesis, reflection, and wisdom. This is essentially true for creative stalwarts like Rabindranath Tagore, whose literary and artistic contributions are a product of all the different phases. They are the result of sublimation *per se* of the instinctual drives present in the great poet, philosopher, writer, and artist. In fact, Adler is of the opinion that all human beings are essentially creative by nature and that they have 'striving toward superiority' as a compensatory mechanism with regard to their different ingrained inferior pockets of the self. Besides, fluid reasoning

(*Gf)* and processing speed (*Gs)* are extremely vulnerable to ageing, whereas crystallized intelligence (*Gc)* – knowledge – is maintained throughout most of the adult life (Cattell and Horn, 1978; Salthouse, 1985, 1996, 2004). Thus, while many cognitive abilities tend to decline with age, knowledge and expertise increase, and these factors play a major, necessary role in creativity. In fact, increased knowledge may compensate for decreased mental speed, decreased short-term memory, poorer reasoning, and less originality as individuals age.

There are ample benefits of creativity for older individuals. Creative activities have been found to improve problem-solving ability, self-esteem, coping skills, anxiety, life satisfaction, and depressive symptoms. Such interventions have generally elicited positive anecdotal feedback from older adult participants and stimulated their involvement and responsiveness (Lamdin and Fugate, 1997). Some of the key benefits of creativity to elder health include increased mental clarity, increased awareness as a means for expressing the elusive, such as the divine or spiritual experiences of life, enabling the resolution of long-standing conflicts, helping in continued adaptation, improved emotional states, and physical healing (Beck, 2005). To provide a few illustrations for this, the clarity and sharpness of the mental functioning of Pandit Ravi Shankar, Ustad Vilayat Khan, Pandit Hariprasad Chaurasia, and Ustad Amzad Ali Khan, just to name a few, have no bounds, as reflected in their unique and creative pieces of music. It is through their illustrious performances that music transcends the eternal and has a spiritual connotation for the 'mindful' listeners; the melodious vocal tone of the *Nightingale of India*. Ms Lata Mangeshkar is also an example of creativity *per excellence* even during her advanced age.

Nobel Laureate, poet, writer, and novelist, Rabindranath Tagore (May 7, 1861–August 7, 1941), is an international figure for his creative pursuits which continued even during his ripe years. His enormous contributions to humanity in the form of his philosophy, preaching, and literary works know no boundaries. He may also be regarded as a legendary spiritualistic torchbearer of the 20th century. In addition, the literary contributions of Nirad C. Chaudhuri (November 23, 1897–August 1, 1999) are also revered internationally. He was crowned with an honorary doctorate from the University of Oxford in 1990 and an honorary Commander of the Order of the British Empire in 1992. His literary works like *The Autobiography of an Unknown Indian; Thy Hand, Great Anarch; Three Horsemen of the New Apocalypse* and many others won international recognition.

Nobel Laureate Amartya Sen (born on November 3, 1933–) is considered as one of the greatest stalwarts in economics and his academic contributions to the world are acknowledged by different institutes internationally. His contributions to welfare economics are globally acclaimed. It may also be noted that Professor Sen has received several other awards in addition to the Nobel Prize, including the Mahalanobis Memorial Prize from the

Indian Econometric Society, the Indira Gandhi Gold Medal from the Asiatic Society, Bharat Ratna (the highest Civilian Award in India), the Companion of Honour from the U.K., the Eisenhower Medal from the U.S.A., the International Humanist Award from the International Humanist and Ethical Union, and the Lifetime Achievement Award from the prestigious Indian Chamber of Commerce.

The director Satyajit Ray (May 2, 1921–April 23, 1992) is acknowledged for his insightful contributions to the field of cinema in the country, which continued even in his ripe and golden years of life. He may be regarded as a pioneer who brought Indian cinema to world recognition with *The Song of the Road* (*Pather Panchali*), followed by its sequels known as the *Apu Trilogy*. Ray was extremely versatile and may be considered as one of the greatest filmmakers of the 20th century. He not only had his expertise in being a great motion-picture director but was also an extremely good writer and illustrator, mostly for young children.

Finally, President A.P.J. Abdul Kalam (October 15, 1931–July 27, 2015) is internationally revered for not only his scientific visions but also his positivistic and spiritualistic messages for the citizens of the Indian subcontinent. Bharat Ratna, Dr Kalam, was a great rocket and missile scientist who rose to such heights of professional excellence from a humble background. His entire life is an inspiration and a learning lesson for all of us to realize the inner potentials of beings. His preaching and philosophical orientation reached all strata of individuals, leaving behind a deep mark of his existence. The stalwart finally passed away suddenly when he collapsed while delivering a speech at the Indian Institute of Management, Shillong, Meghalaya, India.

Other stalwarts in the film industry in India are noteworthy as well, who have continued to remain stars despite their advanced ages. Amitabh Bachchan (October 11, 1942–) appears in the limelight of the Indian film industry even at an advanced age. He has been adorned by numerous awards ranging from the Filmfare awards to the Civilian Award of India. He has won National Film Awards, a Filmfare Lifetime Achievement Award, India's and France's highest civilian award, the Knight of the Legion of Honour, and the actor of the century award, among others. Other examples include Soumitra Chattopadhyay, Sharmila Tagore, and Jaya Bachchan. These examples are just a few glimpses of how creativity ushers itself in full expression and fervour even in the advanced years of life to add to the well-being of individuals in society. Generativity is in full swing for such personalities. However, if elderly individuals refrain from such generative orientations, stagnation is likely to result, thereby impeding the process of positive ageing towards transcendence.

Creative activity has been found to contribute to successful ageing by encouraging the development of problem-solving skills that translate into practical creativity in older adults' daily life (Fisher and Specht, 1999). Their social-adaptive functioning is also expected to improve owing to their engagement in such endeavours. Creativity fosters a sense of competence, purpose, and emotional growth. Further, at the physiological level, when the brain engages in creative work, it alerts the parasympathetic nervous system; heart rate and breathing slow down, blood pressure decreases, blood circulation to the intestines increases, and the body shifts into relaxation (Samuels and Lane, 1998). Such activities also have been found to stimulate the hypothalamus to activate the autonomic nervous system, thereby stabilizing and maintaining blood flow, heart rate, and hormone levels (Lane, 2005). They are also likely to stimulate the release of endorphins from specific areas of the brain, thus affecting brain cells and the immune system and improving their function. Kreitzer and Snyder (2002) reported that the placement of art sessions in intensive care functioned to help clients relax, use less pain medication, and be discharged earlier than peers who did not have any artwork in their rooms. Creative arts can also provide an avenue of catharsis to allow elderly people to communicate with others. This can take the form of different means like painting, crafting, moulding, creating art, music, and so on, which enables such people to etch a mark of themselves in the life canvas. These art forms can have a tremendous healing impact, especially for those who have some disabilities. Thus, it is seen that arts and creative expression appear to promote health with ageing. To give some anecdotal illustrations, an elderly housewife reported that she felt a sense of meaning in life after becoming gradually engaged in creative activities. She used to look forward to spending some part of the day in such exercises and reported 'feeling rejuvenated.' Another elderly retired gentleman was observed to spend a significant amount of time gardening in his terrace garden and having quality time amidst nature. He told his family members that he did not miss his professional life much because he spent substantial time with plants and remained connected with nature. This was also a means of staying healthy both physically and mentally for him. He used to even stay connected with others by organizing regular 'family meets' of his acquaintances where he used to show them his newly developed 'craft' of nurturing flower plants. Another senior adult was observed developing his culinary skills to such an extent during his golden years that he started supervising chefs in a nearby restaurant in preparing different dishes and thereby started deriving meaning in the later years of his life. The different benefits of engaging in creative activities among elderly individuals are schematically represented in Figure 5.2.

This is brought about by the help of a number of interacting mechanisms as follows:

Sense-of-control mechanism

Positive health outcomes have been increasingly associated with the engagement of older people in activities where they experience a sense of proficiency

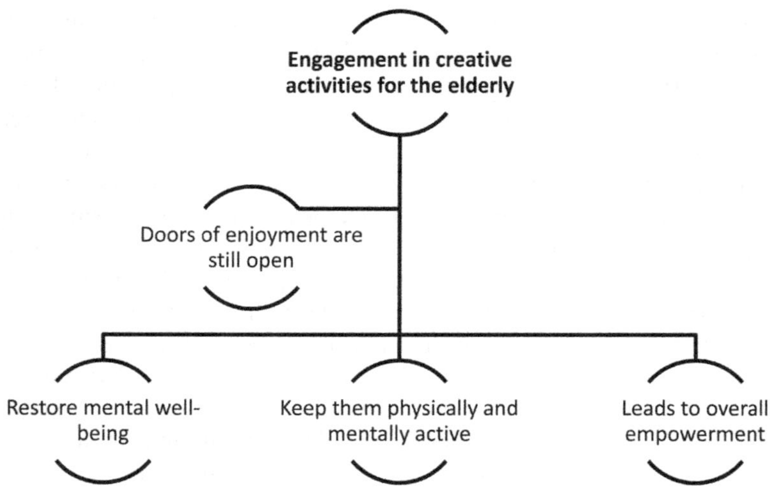

Figure 5.2 The major benefits of elderly individuals in pursuing creative activities (source: authors).

(Rodin, 1986, 1989). This experience of a sense of proficiency also leads to increased feelings of empowerment which enable elderly individuals to increase the levels of comfort, confidence, and esteem by exploring new challenges. It is also in different forms of arts that opportunities to create something new and beautiful are endless, which offer an enormous sense of satisfaction and empowerment in the long run (Cohen, 2006). The sense of control that is gained by the elderly individual tends to increase satisfaction in general.

Studies in the field of psychoneuroimmunology (P.N.I.) suggest that positive feelings associated with a sense of control tend to trigger responses in the brain that send signals to the immune system to produce more beneficial immune system cells. This consequently stimulates a boost in immune system cells, including T cells and natural killer (N.K.) cells (Cohen, 2006).

Social engagement

Studies have shown that social engagement accompanied by creative activities has a positive influence on general health and reduced mortality (Avlund, Damsgaard, and Holstein, 1998; Glass et al., 1999). Social relationships in the second half of life have been associated with reduced blood pressure as well as reduced stress levels. In fact, many forms of art tend to provide a significant opportunity for social engagement including chorales, poetry groups, bands and other instrumental groups, and groups that engage in painting, writing, drama, and dance.

Poetry was found to offer many benefits such as provoking insight, promoting life reviews, and encouraging the resolution of unresolved conflicts (Sluder, 1990; Edwards, 1990). It is not only a catalyst for creative expression of individuals *per se*, but triggers reminiscences and allows the transmission of different values and stories to others. Brady and Sky (2003) suggested that journal writing may benefit elderly individuals by increasing their ability to cope, engaging in the joy of discovery, and by nurturing their voice and spirit, as well as building confidence. This is reflected in the works of William Carlos Williams, who took to writing poetry to get out of the shell of depression following a cerebral stroke that prevented him from continuing practising medicine. It was his work in the form of *Pictures from Brueghel and Other Collected Poems* (Williams, 1962) that was awarded a Pulitzer Prize. It was by means of his creative expression in the form of poetry that he was able to add to his life despite ageing and mellowing. Journal writing helps people to reflect on and analyse their lives and the events and people surrounding them in a non-judgemental manner as much as possible (Snyder and Lindquist, 2002). It is through journaling that a person gradually possesses the power to deal with life and assumes responsibility for his/her own growth (Baldwin, 1990). It is expected to expand one's consciousness and deepen spiritual awareness and growth leading to the enhancement of wholeness in the long run (Cameron, 1992; Rainer, 1997). Reminiscence, as a creative activity, is associated with more positive meaning and being less negative about the self and social relationships (Westerhof, Bohlmeijer, and Valenkamp, 2004). It has features of creativity by entailing cognitive and emotional processes involved in the conception of meaningful solutions to past problems. It has been found to be related to improved levels of intrapersonal empowerment, having its repercussions in the form of domain-specific perceived control and self-efficacy, motivation to control, perceived competence, and proficiency (Zimmerman, 1995). Past conflicts may be transformed into more stable and creative products by the means of reminiscence. Further, McGarry and Prince (1998) focused on creative expression in a non-competitive, supportive environment by means of art forms comprising individual and group poetry, storytelling, drawing, painting, and music. At the interpersonal level, creative endeavours also tend to bring about changes in elderly individuals. Engagement in reminiscence pursuits bring about changes in attitudes and skills in interacting with other people, such as an appreciation of other people's merits, willingness to seek help from others, and eagerness to care for others.

Certain creative activities may be tailored for elderly individuals by their specific needs and abilities. For instance, some individuals may be encouraged to participate in group activities like salad making (e.g., fruit salad, smoothies), decorating interiors and consequently their 'inner selves' in a reciprocal manner, engaging in gardening flower pots in well-lit areas of their homes such as the veranda or an open balcony, and so on. They may also be reinforced by engaging in certain art groups by splashing paint on a canvas and experiencing an expression of their emotions therapeutically. Certain group sessions may also be organized such that elderly individuals get the opportunity to socialize as much as possible in the cohort group and enjoy the presence of others' company in a neutral, non-judgemental manner. Moreover, creative psycho-educational groups for elderly individuals may be conducted regularly to address different emotional issues as well as to encourage them to remain engaged in creative pursuit(s) as much as possible taking into consideration their different limitations (Phoenix, Irvine, and Kohr, 1997). Such groups may essentially tailor the specific needs of the elderly individuals as discussed earlier. This may be used to prevent social isolation, enhance positive health behaviours, and offer resources for older adults to maintain independence despite the ageing process (Gerson and Berg, 2004). The internet may also be used to organize certain online creative sessions for the elderly to engage in such that their well-being is maintained in the comfort of their home.

Elderly individuals pursuing creative activities are expected to have a boost in terms of self-esteem, coping skills, social support, internal locus of control, and an improved state of mind to tackle depressive and hypochondriacal symptoms (Singh and Kiran, 2013, 2014; Treffinger et al., 2012; Price and Tinker, 2014). Their involvement and responsiveness in terms of such activities are consequently stimulated. Senior individuals are better able to adapt to the different challenges of late-life by means of developing creative coping strategies (Flood and Phillips, 2007; Flood and Scharer, 2006; Westerhof and Bohlmeijer, 2014). At the physiological level, newer neuronal connections start developing owing to environmental stimulation in the brain. This may further bring about changes at the level of neurotransmitters which, in turn, influence cognitive and executive functioning (Flood and Coleman, 1990; Flood et al., 1985). As such, age-related neurological decline may be hindered to some extent through encouraging elderly individuals to engage in creative endeavours. Creative activities may have a therapeutic impact on the senior person by not only bringing about some amount of physical activity in his/her routine but also increasing the opportunity for social interactions with others. Senior individuals may also form cohort groups based on their preferences for creative activities and enjoy improved social support.

Findings suggest that creative activities can improve problem-solving abilities, self-esteem, coping skills, anxiety, internal locus of control, life satisfaction, depressive symptoms, and hypochondriasis. Moreover, creative interventions have generally elicited positive anecdotal feedback from older adult participants and stimulated their involvement and responsiveness.

Brain plasticity

It has been observed that challenging activities in the form of engaging in creative endeavours and new experiences induce the sprouting of new dendrites, thereby enhancing brain reserves at the physiological level. Art activities are especially good since they are more likely to be sustained and the benefits of challenges for the brain increase when they are ongoing (Verghese et al., 2003; Cohen, 2005). This is expected to rejuvenate the spirit of elderly individuals and keep them mentally as well as physically healthy.

Creative activities against the backdrop of alleviating illness(es) in later life

Cohen (2000a) has researched the impact of art and art therapy on debilitating illness in late life. Studies on patients with different forms of dementia revealed that such clients suffer significant intellectual impairment while, at the same time, show newly acquired or enhanced artistic skills. Thus, it may be inferred indirectly that the damage done by the unwanted deterioration also destroys some other areas which cause a blockage of activity in the artistic arena (Miller et al., 1998). Therefore, it reinforces the instillation of *skills* (*strength points*) that are preserved to varying degrees and also *satisfactions* (areas, activities, actions that bring a satisfying or pleasurable feeling) among elderly individuals (Cohen, 2000b). It is at this juncture where art and creative opportunities merge in a strength-based comprehensive intervention that has a remarkable effect among clients suffering from different degenerative disorders. Such exercises provide therapeutic implications for elderly individuals with such disorders. Basting (2011) engaged such individuals with creative storytelling projects, where she poignantly demonstrated that even as memory fails, imagination persists (Sierpina and Cole, 2004; Basting, 2003). Thus, creative opportunities enable ongoing meaningful interpersonal engagement which tends to contribute to the overall quality of life for both the client and the caregiver. Hence, it is desirable that individuals develop some creative endeavours during young and middle adulthood such that they can be further practised in late life and elderly individuals can enjoy the benefits.

Outcomes of creative engagement among the elderly

It may be noted that creative pursuits lead older adults towards improved levels of active, successful, and productive ageing. The myriad physiological and psychosocial benefits reaped by elderly individuals essentially engage in empowering them. Such individuals are now more adept at acquiring knowledge and skills for coping with problems and stress, have better control over the different uncertainties of life, are able to comprehend social and political realities, and cultivate resources and strategies to help achieve goals (Cheung, Mok, and Cheung, 2005). Empowerment in the elderly individuals occurs at the individual level in terms of personal qualities, which may include their specific outlook on life, personal ability, emotional control, and knowledge about society, all of which are conducive to more effective decision making and handling of problems. It is creativity which bolsters elderly individuals to become competent and efficacious, thereby becoming more 'agentic' in the process. The close links between creativity and empowerment are also because creative individuals are open to different paths to the same goal and hence are more adaptive. This stance of openness brings in them greater tolerance to frustrations of different kinds, thereby instilling patience as a consequence. Any kind of barrier serves as a creative challenge for the elderly individual to work with the tools available to find another means to achieve the same goal (Fisher and Specht, 1999).

Thus, creativity has the potential to aid elderly participants to achieve their developmental tasks of generativity and integrity (Erikson, 1982), and thereby, achieve gero-transcendence along Tornstam's (1989) terminology. The meta-perspective of the elderly individuals is shifted from a material and rational vision to a more cosmic and transcendent one, which is usually associated with an increase in life satisfaction. Such activities have the potential to trigger the process of integrating one's life experiences into a more cohesive whole, and thereby, allowing people to grapple with their vulnerability and mortality as they reassess the meanings of their lives. Landau and Moaz (1978) are of the opinion that it is through creative decision making that self-actualization is possible. This is because the creative personality becomes emotionally free, responsive, and flexible in its approaches, yielding a plethora of possibilities for creative activities in older individuals (Flood and Phillips, 2007).

Conclusion

Developing and inculcating creative coping strategies necessarily enable older adults to adapt more effectively to physical, psychological, and psychosocial changes that occur in later life. It looks into what they can still 'make' with what they have 'left.' It is only when challenges of individuals are considered against the pedestal of their specific potentials that mental health is best promoted and illness is best cared for. The ultimate art and creativity of medicine and healthcare rest there, bringing in hope and clarity to situations that might otherwise be challenged by despair and confusion. The aged individual experiences spiritual growth and enrichment, exercises creativity, and works towards integration through the process of reflecting on and spending time in such engagements. Fostering creativity thus leads to the promotion of self-realization in the long run. The time is ripe to provide a congenial and facilitating ambience for our elderly inhabitants so that their quality of life is significantly enhanced.

References

Addams-Price, C. (1998). *Creativity and successful aging*. New York: Springer.

Amabile, T.M. (1988). A model of creativity and innovation in organizations. *Research in Organizational Behavior*, *10*, 123–167.

Anthony, E.J. (1987). Risk, vulnerability and resilience: An overview. In E.J. Anthony & B.J. Cohen (Eds.), *The invulnerable child* (pp. 3–48). New York: Guilford Press.

Avlund, K., Damsgaard, M.T., & Holstein, E.E. (1998). Social relations and mortality: An eleven year follow-up study of 70-year-old men and women in Denmark. *Social Science and Medicine*, *47*(5), 635–643.

Baldwin, C. (1990). *Life's companion: Journal writing as a spiritual quest*. New York: Bantam.

Basting, A. (2003). Dare to imagine: Exploring the creative potential of people with Alzheimer's disease and related dementia. In J. Ronch & J. Goldfield (Eds.), *Mental wellness and ageing: Strength-based approaches*. (pp. 353–367). Baltimore, MD: Health Professions Press.

Basting, A. D. (2011). *TimeSlips Training Manual: Creative Storytelling with People with Dementia*. Milwaukee, WI: University of Wisconsin Milwaukee Centre on Age and Community.

Beck, C. (2005). *Creative elderhood, What's art got to do with it?* Retrieved from http://www.imagineaging.com/generic.html?pid=1

Brady, E., & Sky, H. (2003). Journal writing among older learners. *Educational Gerontology*, *29*(2), 34–40.

Cameron, J. (1992). *The artist's way: A spiritual path to higher creativity*. Los Angeles: Jeremy P. Tarcher.

Cattell, R.B., & Horn, J.L. (1978). A check on the theory of fluid and crystallized intelligence with description of new subtest designs. *Journal of Educational Measurement*, *15*(3), 139– 164.

Cheung, Y.W., Mok, B.-H., & Cheung, T.-S. (2005). Personal empowerment and life satisfaction among self-help group members in Hong Kong. *Small Group Research*, *36*(3), 33–40.

Cohen, G. (2000a). *The creative age: Awakening human potential in the second half of life*. New York: Avon Books.

Cohen, G. (2000b). Two new inter-generational interventions for Alzheimer's disease patients and families. *American Journal of Alzheimer's Disease*, *15*(3), 1–6.

Cohen, G. (2005). *The mature mind: The positive power of the ageing brain*. New York: Basic Books.

Cohen, G.D. (2006). Research on creativity and ageing: The positive impact of the arts on health and illness. *Generations, XXX*(1), 7–15.

Edwards, M. (1990). Poetry: Vehicle for retrospection and delight. *Generations, Winter*, 61–62.

Erikson, E. (1982). *The life cycle completed: A review*. New York: Norton.

Fisher, B., & Specht, D. (1999). Successful aging and creativity later in life. *Journal of Aging Studies*, *13*(4), 457–472.

Flood, D., Buell, S., Defiore, C., Horwits, G., & Coleman, P. (1985). Age-related dendritic growth in dentate gyrus of human brain is followed by regression in the 'oldest old.' *Brain Research*, *345*(2), 366–368.

Flood, D., & Coleman, P. (1990). Hippocampal plasticity in normal aging and decreased plasticity in Alzheimer's disease. *Progressive Brain Research*, *83*, 435–443.

Flood, M., & Philips, K.D. (2007). Creativity in older adults: A plethora of possibilities. *Issues in Mental Health Nursing*, *28*(4), 389–411.

Flood, M., & Scharer, K. (2006). Creativity enhancement: Possibilities for successful aging. *Issues in Mental Health Nursing*, *27*(9), 939–959.

Formosa, M. (2011). Re-thinking empowerment: A post-modern appraisal of critical educational gerontology. In E. Veloso, P. Guimarães, F. Martins, D. Silva, & M. Maria (Eds.), *Elderly, education, intergenerational relationships and social development. Proceedings of the 2nd conference of education and learning of older adults (Eloa)* (pp. 84–87). Braga, Portugal: CIED – Centro de Investigação em Educação Instituto de Educação, Universidade do Minho.

Gerson, L., Berg, J., Berg, J., & Rose, L.E. (2004). Enhancing self-care in community-dwelling older adults. *Geriatric Nursing*, *25*(5), 272–276.

Glass, T.A., de Leon, C.M., Marottoli, R.A., & Berkman, L.F. (1999). Population-based study of social and productive activities as predictors of survival among elderly Americans. *British Medical Journal*, *319*(7208), 478–483.

Hickson, J., & Housley, W. (1997). Creativity in later life. *Educational Gerontology*, *23*(6), 539–546.

Kerka, S. (1999). Creativity in adulthood. *ERIC Digest.*, *204*, 1–7.

Kreitzer, M., & Snyder, M. (2002). Healing the heart: Integrating complimentary therapies and healing practices into the care of cardiovascular patients. *Progressive Cardiovascular Nursing*, *17*(1), 15–23.

Lamdin, L., & Fugate, M. (1997). *Elder learning: New frontier in an ageing society*(p. 63). Phoenix, AZ: American Council on Education & the Oryx Press.

Landau, E., & Moaz, B. (1978). Creativity and self-actualization in the aging personality. *American Journal of Psychotherapy*, *329*(1), 117–127.

Lane, M. (2005). Creativity and spirituality in nursing. *Holistic Nursing Practice*, *19*(3), 24–32.

McGarry, T., & Prince, M. (1998). Implementation of groups for creative expression on a psychiatric inpatient unit. *Journal of Psychosocial Nursing*, *36*(3), 19–24.

Miller, B.L., Cummings, J., Mishkin, F., Boone, K., Prince, F., Ponton, M., & Cotman, C. (1998). Emergence of artistic talent in fronto-temporal dementia. *Neurology*, *51*(4), 978–982.

Phoenix, E., Irvine, Y., & Kohr, R. (1997). Sharing stories. *Journal of Gerontological Nursing*, *23*(4), 10–15.

Price, K.A., & Tinker, A.M. (2014). Creativity in later life. *Maturitas*, *78*(4), 281–286.

Rainer, T. (1997). *Your life as a story*. Los Angeles: Jeremy P. Tarcher.

Rodin, J. (1986). Ageing and health: Effects of the sense of control. *Science*, *233*(4770), 1271–1276.

Rodin, J. (1989). Sense of control: Potentials for intervention. *Annals Publishing of the American Academy of Policy and Social Science*, *503*(503), 20–42.

Salthouse, T. (1985). *A theory of cognitive aging*. New York: Elsevier.

Salthouse, T.A. (1996). The processing- speed theory of adult age differences in cognition. *Psychological Review*, *103*(3), 403– 428.

Salthouse, T.A. (2004). What and when of cognitive aging. *Current Directions in Psychological Science*, *13*(4), 140– 144.

Samuels, M., & Lane, M. (1998). *Creative healing*. San Francisco: Harper Collins.

Sawyer, R.K. (2012). *Explaining creativity: The science of human innovation* (2nd edn.). New York: Oxford University Press.

Sierpina, M., & Cole, T.R. (2004). Stimulating creativity in all elders: A continuum of interventions. *Care Management Journal*, *5*(3), 175–182.

Simonton, D.K. (1994). Creativity and wisdom in ageing. In A. Monk (Ed.), *Columbia retirement handbook*. (pp. 320–329). New York: Columbia University Press.

Singh, B., & Kiran, U.V. (2013). Loneliness among elderly women. *International Journal of Humanities and Social Sciences*, 2(2), 10–14.

Singh, B., & Kiran, U.V. (2014). Recreational activities for senior citizens. *IOSR Journal of Humanities and Social Science (IOSR-JHSS)*, *19*(4), 24–30.

Sluder, H. (1990). The write way: Using poetry for self-disclosure. *Journal of Psychosocial Nursing*, *28*(7), 12–20.

Snyder, M., & Lindquist, R. (2002). *Complementary/ alternative therapies in nursing*. New York: Springer.

Tornstam, L. (1989). Gero-transcendence: A reformulation of the disengagement theory. *Ageing: Clinical and Experimental Research*, *1*(1), 60.

Treffinger, D.J., Selby, E.C., & Schoonover, P.F. (2012). Creativity in the person: Contemporary perspectives. *Learning Landscapes*, *6*(1), 409–419.

Verghese, J., Lipton, R.B., Katz, M.J., Hall, C.B., Derby, C.A., Kuslansky, G., ... Buschke, H. (2003). Leisure activities and the risk of dementia in the elderly. *New England Journal of Medicine*, *348*(25), 2508–2516.

Westerhof, G.J., & Bohlmeijer, E.T. (2014). Celebrating fifty years of research and applications in reminiscence and life review: State of the art and new directions. *Journal of Aging Studies*, *29*, 107–114.

Westerhof, G., Bohlmeijer, E., & Valenkamp, M. (2004). In search of meaning: A reminiscence programme for older persons. *Educational Gerontology*, *30*(9), 51–57.

Williams, W.C. (1962). *Pictures from Breughel and other collected poems*. New York City: New Directions.

Zimmermann, M.A. (1995). Psychological empowerment: Issues and illustrations. *American Journal of Community Psychology*, *23*(5), 588.

6

NATURE

The friend and philosopher of old age

Human existence, physically, is etched on Mother Earth's canvas – the forum of human life in a natural set-up. Hence, nature and human life are entwined with each other. In fact, the rules of nature, the spontaneous norms of 'nature-flow' dictate the smooth or rough conditions of life in general. But human mental orientation today is drawn more towards concrete contacts and less to nature. We fail to understand and follow the natural dictates of life that result in enormous mental suffering of which we are not aware. The din and bustle of city life, sporadic visits to nature, the unbearable physical-mental stresses, the strains from interpersonal relations, and the financial stresses of various kinds have robbed us of peaceful mental states that are possible to attain in a calm and quiet environmental ambience. People try to attain such peace by travelling to places with an abundance of natural surroundings. Such experiences are neither frequent nor affordable by everybody with regard to time and money. The younger days of life are always busy with achievement targets. But the sunset serene days of life have the time to look at nature and observe its flow and rules so that individuals can attain heavenly peace at times. Gerontology is ready with its lenses and paintbrushes to offer pictures of soothing mental states. Let us have a look at this point.

The aesthetic beauty of nature in terms of its colour, fragrance, diversity, texture, growth pattern, and so on is surely open to everyone, provided we are mindfully observing them. Flowers, trees, plants, creepers, and weeds – even the textures and colour of a blade of grass – are attractive and soothing for human nerves and the stressful mind. The world seems truly beautiful and can prompt our strivings to live longer if our understanding and love for nature deepen. Nature not only carries the instructions of the cosmos to assemble the flowers and plants; it also contains fragments of the story of the origin and evolution of all life on Earth. Hence, the Earth has become the grandest possible expression of the laws of nature (Cox and Cohen, 2013).

The passion to observe nature and care for it cannot come during the late-age phase of life. People having a great passion for gardening, travelling to see nature, engaging themselves in photography, birdwatching, and finding time to observe trees and plants uninterruptedly and introducing these habits to very young boys and girls are the passions of young or middle-aged people (Sanyal, 2017). The suggestion of inculcating them in the daily routine of very old people does not seem to be a sound one, owing to the possibilities of limitations of various kinds. Despite the fact that even if such habits were there earlier, physical capabilities may appear to be debilitating factors for being actively involved with nature. As such, physically less able elderly people can be made aware of the presence of Nature's grace and motherly touch on our body and mind by explaining and bringing them in close interaction with nature regularly. The 'touch and feel' experiences of earth, air, and smell, and the soothing sights of greenery in different shades will make one extra energetic in body and mind. Nature and living things, it seems, tend to boost the 'feel-good factor' in most people (Kellert and Wilson, 1993; Maller et al., 2002). In fact, the efficacy of 'green-exercise' in achieving good physical and mental health has been ascertained in research by Pretty et al (2005). Botanical science explains in detail how nature-interaction processes heal us in a true sense. Belief in naturopathy treatment for various ailments of body and mind claims the same attention and recognition. The openness of nature, its basic cosiness, the wind rustling through the leaves and making a faint soothing sound, dried leaves falling, and greenery creating a true and authentic ambience carries a tune of a soothing lullaby for everyone – provided one has a trained, interested mind of being mindful of them. Nature's beneficial effects are not only restricted to a mere restoration to baseline after negative periods of stress, anxiety, or depression but also help to positively increase the true mental health and well-being of individuals. This helps to enter into an additive state of thriving and flourishing (Keyes, 2005; Parsmore, 2011). Many psychologists recognize that exposure to green space is useful as a means of boosting well-being, especially in elderly individuals (Gable and Haidt, 2005). Fredrickson (2009) specifically lists that finding oneself nearby nature appears to increase one's level of positivity as proven by earlier studies. American naturalist and writer John Burroughs (1837–1921) commented, 'I go to nature to be soothed and healed, and to have my senses put in tune once more' (Payne and Burroughs, 1993; Eliades, 2013).

Nature seems to be a habit for us. The change of seasons and their impact on us are accustomed features in our lives. But looking at nature, the touch and feel of nature, even in the form of having a few flower pots at home or in the next door neighbour's terrace, enjoying its intricacies should be developed as a personal habit. In later life, when people commonly suffer from loneliness of various kinds, nature is around to offer a soothing sense of support to the aged individual. This can be attempted by keeping plants in the vicinity to change the ambience of a particular room. A flower vase, with different flowers, kept on the table nearby can bring colour to one's mind and can serve as a token of life or simply make an elderly person feel pleasant and happy (Simson and Straus, 2003). Horticulture therapy has been found to play an important role in elderly individuals (Trellis, 2013; Rice and Reny, 1998). Burls (2007) depicted some of the benefits of eco-therapy being associated with the relationship between a healthy environment and the person. Johnson (1999) showed its efficacy in elderly care as a well-proven fact. Thus, introducing elderly people to nature in a nearby physical context and taking them out in open natural spaces to show them the beauties of mountains, fountains, rains, rivers, skies, parks, gardens, or forests through projections or photographs, seems to bring a layer of positivity in their otherwise dull and stereotyped patterns of life. Being engaged in nature, the mind stops thinking, obsessing, and worrying. People feel calm and safe in the natural space and they leave with a sense of well-being. Adequate research has evidenced the crucial role played by nature in varied aspects of our mental health and well-being (Joye, 2007).

Elderly individuals in the Indian subcontinent

The population of India is showing signs of having an unaccountable number of elderly people. A century of advancement in biomedical sciences and technology has dramatically lengthened the human life span (Balaram, 2000; Yanker, 2000; Oeppen, and Vaupel, 2002). Anecdotal evidence suggests that a large number of such people are showing decay in their neurological functionalities, taking the form of different ailments like Alzheimer's disease, Parkinson's disease, and other brain-related illnesses, therefore, what can a social scientist comment about their overall quality of life? All of these are related to poor motor functionalities and memory capacities, with certain psychotic features like delusions, hallucinations, and so on, making life overall just a stretched length of sufferance (Hoehn and Yarh, 1967). In fact, Alzheimer's disease, also known as 'multi-factorial syndrome' is accompanied by the formation of neurotic plaques and neurofibrillary tangles (Ben-Shlomo, Whitehead and Smith, 1996). It, accompanied by Parkinson's disease and ischaemic brain injury in strokes, serves as one of the greatest threats to the well-being of elderly individuals (Balaram, 2000; Calne, McGeer, Eisen, Spencer, 1986). Thus, the major risk factor associated with ageing involves taking note of different killer diseases, some of them being cardiovascular disease, cancer, and neurodegeneration, with the major burden of ill-health falling on senior individuals of the population (Riggs and Schochet, 1992). Psychological science looks for relieving pain and a cure if possible. In the decaying state, curing of ailments is not expected but relief is possible. Other than chemical dependence and surgical interventions, the natural conditions of help seem to be nature-based.

Nature as a means of connection in the era of digitalization

The present generation increasingly functions digitally (Carr, 2010; Comin, and Hobijn, 2010). At home and in other social spheres, the constant use of smartphones and smart technology such as the 'internet-of-things' (IoT) is creating negativity for everybody including elderly individuals (Gubbi, Buyya, Marusic, and Palaniswami, 2013; Li, Xu, and Zhao, 2015). Increased digitalization is affecting health and too much of a dependence on smartphones is considered to be bad for psychological health. Exposure to nature, observing nature, or being amidst nature seem to be soothing for the elderly. Looking at a flowing river or the dancing waves of the sea, being in the vast openness of mountains, or the close affinity with nature in a forest context takes people into the laws of nature. This is because the natural flow of a river resembles the biological network of veins in our body. If we channel our energy with flowing rivers, it could have a positive impact as the river systems and its surroundings can mellow out the agitated, aggravated nerves of the senior citizens. Observing rivers, seas, mountains, or forests cannot be accepted as a common event for everybody for a significant amount of time, and our ordinary lives can look at nature ordinarily. In any social set-up, the trees and plants are there. The grass is green on every patch of earth we come across. The elderly need to develop the habit of looking at them, looking at them mindfully – that these elements are also our natural parts of existence – we need to acknowledge. Because of our unawareness, we pollute our nature. It becomes necessary to understand that demographic issues, environmental factors, and people are all interdependent (Boote, 1990). Human survival is necessarily dependent on different factors, some being the maintenance of the natural, ecological, and life support resources of the planet. More immediately, quality of life is particularly linked to population size, growth or diminution, and composition. It is often because of the ignorance and exploitation of nature by humans that water and trees are mishandled, misleading life-flow, which results in physical and mental sufferance. A small garden or a balcony corner filled up with flowerpots can also serve as a rectifier for us. A garden or arranged pot in the open veranda or terrace reminds us that we should respect nature. Acknowledging its contributions in our life and developing care and concern towards nature with our stretched longevity, we can stand as a human relic – a great contributor towards nature.

It is also to be noted that the population explosion is the driving force behind so many of the global environmental and related economic problems and potential catastrophes of the current world. In many countries, its effects are immediately obvious and felt through air and water pollution, transport congestion, faulty or inadequate infrastructure, litter, overcrowding, loss of wildlife and amenity sites, and general deterioration of the environment of Man and Nature. Members of less developed countries suffer much from the above and even more from fundamental factors such as soil exhaustion, lack of cultivable land, and inadequate water supplies (Chopra, 2016). An increasing level of environmental degradation tends to affect people's health and longevity in the long run (Boote, 1990). The most vulnerable victims are the poor, the young, and the elderly. It is through man's activities and domestic animals that the radiation balance of the earth is affected by the emission of 'greenhouse gases.' This has potent far-reaching implications for the climate and oceans – and for Man. The main gases involved in this process are carbon dioxide, methane, and nitrous oxide, emitted from farming, burning fossil fuels, and animal and human wastes.

New impetus has arisen from research into the biological basis of ageing to address the underlying causes of many age-associated diseases and disabilities (Holliday, 1996). Studies have reflected that the process of ageing has evolved to provide a mechanism to guard against overcrowding (Wynne-Edwards 1962; Beutler, 1986). It implies that genetic control plays a key role in the programmed process of ageing (Kenyon, 1996). Despite the popularity of this view, this is highly debated on a number of grounds.

Nature: A spiritual connection for the elderly

In the recent era, the basic trend is to move away from nature and be engulfed with shining materialism and, instead, develop materialistic greed. Unknowingly, unmindfully, most of us remain insensitive to nature. It is only when we move away from nature that we start polluting our planet. Mass industrialization has led to large-scale deforestation, the exploitation of natural resources, and pollution of air and water (Chopra, 2016; Gogoi, 2013). The sensitivity regarding nature needs to be regained for our own benefit. An intimate relationship with nature seems to develop in the human psyche. Historically, mountains, rivers, trees, the sun, and the moon have always been honoured. The moment we are disconnected with these, we not only destroy our physical environment, but the destruction creates grooves in our mind too. A clean and positive environment affects our existence positively. When there is harmony with nature and our lives, we are exposed to a greater sense of peace and connectedness. Remaining connected with nature brings in spiritual senses. This helps to engage all our senses, sights, sounds, smells around us, touch where the textures of the soil tell a story, the emotional satisfaction of a harvest or a successful cutting, and the sense of belonging or a realization of a spiritual connection or transcendental peace (Schultz, 2010). Taking the present-day scenario into consideration, it needs to be realized at this hour that the increasing disconnectedness of *Homo sapiens* with nature has taken its toll in the form of different pandemics like Covid-19 (Galaverni, Bologna and Danovaro, 2020; Van Vliet et al., 2017). The loss of habitats, the modification of natural environments by means of deforestation, increased pollution, and so on, and more generally, the decline in biodiversity appear to be key determinants in the spread of emerging infectious diseases (Di Marco et al., 2020; WWF, 2018; McMahon, Morand, and Gray, 2018). Humans are increasingly exposed to newer forms of contact with microbes and wild species that host them through the destruction and degradation of forests. It is necessary to understand the roots of our existence and to acknowledge the same so that humanity can cohabit with other living organisms. In this context, it is to be noted that the spiritual and holistic side of horticulture therapy sees value in gardening as meditation. The practitioners of horticulture think that such contact with nature helps to quieten the conscious and usually restless mind, allowing the subconscious mind to discover solutions to problems in a proactive manner and counter a negative thinking pattern in the long run. Briefly, those who are attracted to gardening seem to be reflective and 'inside-mind' oriented. Such spirituality has the power to check greed. One's level of consciousness is elevated as a consequence. This leads to instilling a sense of caring and commitment for the whole planet. Such spiritual flow within our mind opens our eyes to the beauties of nature, encourages us to revere nature and life, and helps bring more joy and celebration into our lives, which is 'authentic' in nature. Elderly life is experienced and is matured to understand all these features – it is the awareness, acknowledgement, and acceptance of the planetary elements for the sake of arranging our life and mind to experience the bliss of nature's grace. There is a dire necessity for age-friendly environments, where elderly individuals can feel connected to the environment. The interrelations of the well-being of elderly individuals in relation to one's natural environment are shown schematically in Figure 6.1.

In fact, the World Health Organization (WHO, 2007) produced the seminal document of 'Global Age-friendly Cities: A Guide' as part of its ongoing work to support and promote active ageing among the world's increasingly urban, older population (Plouffe and Kalache, 2010; WHO, 2010). It is worth noting at this juncture that geographers have long been interested in the intrinsic connections between ageing and the environment (Rudzitis, 1984; Rogers and Woodward, 1988; Rogerson, 1998; Moore and Rosenberg, 2001). However, explicit attention has recently been paid in the way that urban built environments affect the health and quality of the life of the elderly. Called 'geographical gerontology' (Andrews et al., 2007), it is important to understand not only the nature of how and where people age (Dahms, 1996; McHugh and Ming, 1996; Rosenberg et al., 1989), but also the qualitative nuances of the same process taking into consideration diversity (Moore and Rosenberg, 2001), access to supportive care (Nemet and Bailey, 2000; Andrews, 2003), especially in rural and remote areas (Everitt and Gfellner, 1996; Hanlon and Halseth, 2005), and so on.

The World Health Organization has launched its age-friendly cities at the global level considering the growing importance of the ageing population on

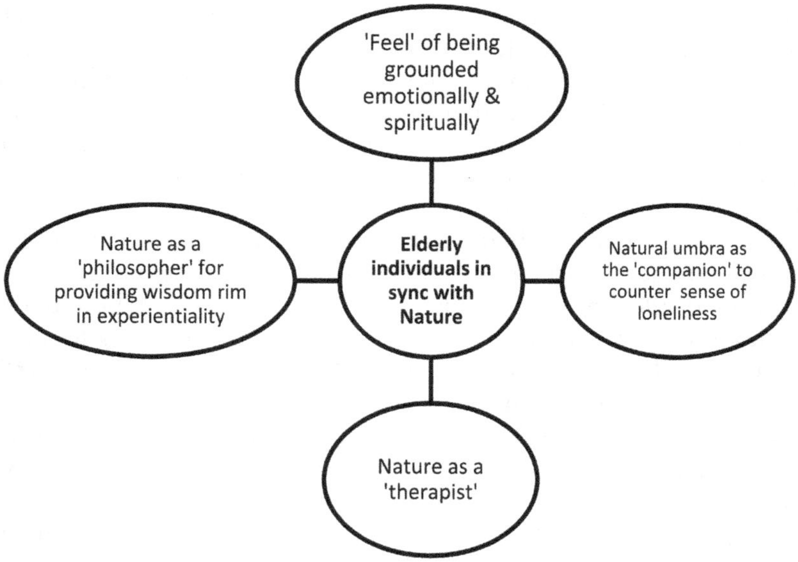

Figure 6.1 Elderly well-being in relation to nature (source: authors).

world demographics (Plouffe and Kalache, 2010). Its goal was to identify those elements that support ageing in the urban environment (WHO, 2010). The results found that there are eight 'areas of urban living' (WHO, 2007) that appear to characterize the degree to which a city can be considered age-friendly (Lui et al., 2009; Menec et al., 2011). It was found that a summer photography exercise identified six different concerns of elderly individuals, namely, ramps, stairs, railings, and curbs; fear of others; obstacles and broken pathways; seating; public transit; and aesthetics and cleanliness (Garvin, Nykiforuk, and Johnson, 2012; Garvin et al., 2010). Quiet, controlled, and peaceful environments fostered a sense of safety and belongingness as they were found to feel connected with 'Mother' Nature. Pleasing environments seemed to show respect for the neighbourhood. These results show that the participating seniors discussed at length two of the WHO domains: outdoor spaces and buildings and transportation. To a lesser extent, participants also discussed three other domains: social participation; respect and social inclusion; and communication and information as important factors that need to be considered during positive ageing. Outdoor spaces included the presence of aesthetics, safety, green space, availability of places to stop and rest, accessibility, and secure environments as key components of the built environment for seniors (Keizer et al., 2008). Maintaining built environments and fostering safe social environments are not only characteristics of age-friendly neighbourhoods, but they promote positive health outcomes for healthier behaviours (Nettle, 2011). In fact, home décor, especially the rooms of the elderly, should also be easily accessible, friendly, and clutter-free.

Nature: The oxygenous friend of ours

Nature in the form of trees, plants, herbs, shrubs, and the like serve as 'friends' of *Homo sapiens*, as they are essentially engaged in the process of oxygenating the environment and restoring the intricate balance of the different gases. They help to purify the atmosphere by silently serving as 'natural cleansers.' Nature enables humans to 'feel grounded' in many respects – emotionally and spiritually being pertinent ones. This oxygenous ally of our species essentially helps to maintain homeostatic balance in the long run and thereby protect all forms of life against ultimate destruction. The entire horizon of human existence is reflected in tree lore through the ages signifying the quest for beauty, truth, and enlightenment. Our ancestors celebrated the forces of nature by offering their gifts, songs, and prayers to revitalize the natural world, the world they felt themselves to be an intimate part. Trees and humankind have thus always had a symbiotic relationship. Trees continuously offer a multitude of benefits to humanity. Trees and plants seem to be man's strongest allies (Hageneder, 2005). These natural resources should be introduced to children to develop a familiarity with nature from a physical as well as a mental health point. At the end, when the business of human life is reduced significantly, the 'natural world' once again can stand as a close friend. In the geriatric phase, a habit of reaching out to nature seems like a helpful embrace for an old friend that assures one with positive vibrations. Hence, is this not the time to pay reverence to these 'natural connects' of ourselves by acknowledging their presence?

Nature: The relaxer and healer in life

Nature offers us multi-faceted benefits to keep us fit physically, mentally, socially, and spiritually. A garden though a created social-physical space for us is a sample representation of Mother Nature. Natural elements are 'givens' in the existential mode of life and the creation of nature through gardens, flowers, and varied forms of greenery is part of positive healing. Gardens appear as 'models' in the environment as a paradise to soothe our stained minds. Our existence amidst the green lushes, the hanging twigs, the multicoloured flowers, aromatic plants, soothing, soft grass, or leaning against the trunk of a big tree – all seem creative artefacts of heavenly beauty on earth. Modern living involves sensory deprivation and information overload – a piece of 'natural carpet' serves the restorative function. Because in general:

- Nature restores;
- Nature facilitates competence building;

- Symbols are carried by nature that tends to affirm one's culture or self;
- Nature offers a pleasing diversion.

Good quality green spaces are expected to encourage people to walk, run, cycle, or play, which provide opportunities for healthy physical activity and the relief of stress. Overall, air quality is improved through the addition of green spaces, noise is reduced substantially, and trees and shrubbery help to filter out dust and pollutants and serve to cleanse the environment.

On the whole, the calm and quiet green patch of land is our healer of stress wounds, the source of oxygen to the body and mind, a soothing emotional cushion, and the silence to take a plunge 'within' the self, touching nature to connect the self-spirit to transcendence. Being in a green garden, enjoying the fresh air and the natural aroma is an existential 'bliss' and not just a fantasy.

Nature: The only companion in old age

There are many changes in old age. The most significant ones are less ability and fewer available relational bonds. The resultant feature is a dependence on caregivers who, despite their best effort, overall, cannot be accepted as dear friends, therefore, loneliness results. The mind loses its flexibility and cannot easily accommodate changes, while acceptance range lowers to a great extent so no new engagement finds the time to shine in this phase of life. Hence, one feels lonely and dejected. Studies show old people who are close to nature feel engaged more than those who stay away from nature. Observing the day- and night-natural context and attempting to feel it from the heart, makes one feel more embedded in life and prompts a positive appreciative feeling of being alive. As such, nature is our closest companion, provided we train our mind to observe it. If the elderly individual can perceive himself/herself to be a small unit within the umbra of Mother Nature, the senior individual is likely to overcome his/her emotional pangs of loneliness and sense of inner void. He/she would then feel 'contented' and would have an all-embracing 'sense of social support' around him/her (Sanyal, 2017). The person is then expected to be less fearful of the different uncertainties of life, and instead, would accept the 'givens' of life gracefully. Death anxiety would consequently mellow on the part of the individual, who would look at life from a much more realistic and wiser perspective.

Nature: The philosopher in old age

Old age, being the last chapter of life, calls forth summation and reflection on life events as a major mental activity (Bluck, and Levine, 1998; Boylin, Gordon, and Nehrke, 1976). The wisdom-laden mind looks back at the rising rays of sun-filled activities. The reminiscence makes the elderly person happy over fulfilments, sad over losses, prompting him/her to laugh at so many immature attempts in life and make him/her cry over life defeats. This is but life. One has to take everything in his/her stride. That is the demand of life in motion. The only healer, the only consistent teacher in the whole life context is 'Nature.' Often, we look at nature with true curiosity and maintain this habit regularly and we would find that everything that happens in life is being reflected in natural changes. The marks of seasonal changes, the growth and perishing of trees and plants, the evidence of natural disasters – all are predictors of the laws of life. The encore philosophy of life is only embedded in nature. If our understanding regarding nature deepens, the existential queries in the form of 'why' would be fewer. People assimilate life's teaching as a normal happening and as an unalterable state just as nature reflects it (Baers, 2010; Baltes and Staudinger, 2000). The losses in nature temporarily create voids. They are soon replaced by other natural elements. The same is true for human life. The contents and commands are not in our grip. Everything is the display of cosmic energy and conditions. If the motions of human life bear a resemblance with nature so very significantly, is it not a fact that nature is the ultimate philosopher to summate life at the end phase?

Conclusion

Human life moves on a roller coaster; inconsistencies in life are the only consistent features. To understand life, to assess the spatial sketch of one's personal life, one needs to go through rumination and self-reflective processes. Adoption of such processes at the late age of life clearly pinpoints our cravings for happiness and fulfilment from one's younger days. To be happy, we need friends and relatives in a close bond. To be fulfilled, we need to have dreams to move and be engaged with activities. Old age cannot call for new friends and relatives. It is the chapter for closure in life. Losing physical abilities, mental clarity, things, friends, dear ones, and personal assets of various kinds are the common stories of late-life. Dreams are lost; however, wisdom remains an attainment point. To be happy at this juncture means depending less on materials and people and more on developing the attitude of being happy with an attachment to surrounding nature. This will lead to peace and contentment at heart, while stretching our arms towards nature to make it a friend and offering our deep respect and reverence, joining it as a restful boarder.

References

Andrews, G.J. (2003). Placing the consumption of private complementary medicine: Everyday geographies of older peoples' use. *Health and Place*, 9(4), 337–349.

Andrews, G.J., Cutchin, M., McCracken, K., Phillips, D.R., & Wiles, J. (2007). Geographical gerontology: The constitution of a discipline. *Social Science and Medicine*, 65(1), 151–168.

Baars, J. (2010). Philosophy of aging, time, and finitude. In T.R.Cole, R.Ray, & R.Kastenbaum (Eds.), *A guide to humanistic studies in aging* (pp. 105–120). Baltimore: Johns Hopkins University Press.

Balaram, P. (2000). Ageing. *Current Science*, *78*(7), 765–766.

Baltes, P.B., & Staudinger, U.M. (2000). Wisdom: A meta-heuristic (pragmatic) to orchestrate mind and virtue toward excellence. *American Psychologist*, *55*(1), 122–136.

Ben-Shlomo, Y., Whitehead, A.S., & Smith, G.D. (1996). Parkinson's, Alzheimer's and motor neurone disease: Clinical and pathological overlap may suggest common genetic and environmental factors. *British Medical Journal*, *312*(7033), 724.

Beutler, E. (1986). Planned obsolescence in humans and other bio-systems. *Perspectives in Biology and Medicine*, *29*(2), 175–179.

Bluck, S., & Levine, L.J. (1998). Reminiscence as autobiographical memory: A catalyst for reminiscence theory development. *Ageing and Society*, *18*(2), 185–208.

Boote, R.E. (1990). Ageing and environment: A resource approach. *Environmental Conservation*, *17*(4), 297–301

Boylin, W., Gordon, S.K., & Nehrke, M.F. (1976). Reminiscing and ego integrity in institutionalized elderly males. *Gerontologist*, *16*(2), 118–124.

Burls, A. (2007). People and green spaces: Promoting public health and mental well-being through eco-therapy. *Journal of Public Mental Health*, *6*(3), 24–39.

Calne, D.B., McGeer, E., Eisen, A., & Spencer, P. (1986). Alzheimer's disease, Parkinson's disease, and motor neurone disease: Abiotrophic interactions between ageing and environment. *Lancet*, 1067–1070.

Carr, N.G. (2010). *The shallows: What the internet is doing to our brains?* New York: W. W. Norton & Company.

Chopra, R. (2016). Environmental degradation in India: Causes and consequences. *International Journal of Applied Environmental Sciences*, *11*(6), 1593–1601.

Comin, D., & Hobijn, B. (2010). An exploration of technology diffusion. *American Economic Review*, *100*(5), 2031–2059.

Cox, B., & Cohen, A. (2013). *Wonders of life*. London: HarperCollins Publisher.

Dahms, F. (1996). The greying of South Georgian Bay. *Canadian Geographer/le Géographe Canadien*, *40*(2), 148–163.

Di Marco et al. (2020). Sustainable development must account for pandemic risk. *PNAS*, *117*(8), 3888–3892. doi:10.1073/pnas.2001655117.

Eliades, A. (2013). *Well-being gardening. Gardening for the body, mind and spirit.* Posted June 5, filed under General Health and Disease.

Everitt, J., & Gfellner, B. (1996). Elderly mobility in a rural area: The example of southwest Manitoba. *Canadian Geographer/le Géographe Canadien*, *40*(4), 338–351.

Fredrickson, B. (2009). *Positivity*. New York: Random House Inc.

Gable, S.L., & Haidt, J. (2005). What (and why) is positive psychology? *Review of General Psychology*, *9*(2), 103–110.

Galaverni, M., Bologna, G., & Danovaro, R. (2020). *The loss of nature and the rise of pandemics: Protecting human and planetary health*. Italy: WWF International.

Garvin, T., Johnson, S., Nykiforuk, C.I.J., Frost, L., & MacDonald, J. (2010). *Can we get old here? Aging and built environments in Edmonton*. Paper presented at the Annual General Meeting of the Western Division of the Canadian Association of Geographers, Edmonton, AB, 25–27 March.

Garvin, T., Nykiforuk, C.I.J., & Johnson, S. (2012, December). Can we get old here? Seniors' perceptions of seasonal constrains of neighbourhood built environments in a northern, winter city. *Human Geography*, *94*(4), 369–389.

Gogoi, L. (2013). Degradation of natural resources and its impact on environment: A study in Guwahati city, Assam, India. *International Journal of Scientific and Research Publications*, *3*(12), 10–15.

Gubbi, J., Buyya, R., Marusic, S., & Palaniswami, M. (2013). Internet of Things (IoT): A vision, architectural elements, and future directions. *Future Generation Computer Systems*, *29*(7), 1645–1660.

Hageneder, F. (2005). *The living wisdom of trees*. London: Duncan Baird Publishers.

Hanlon, N., & Halseth, G. (2005). The greying of resource communities in northern British Columbia: Implications for health care delivery in already-underserviced communities. *Canadian Geographer/le Géographe Canadien*, *49*(1), 1–24.

Hoehn, M.M., & Yarh, M.D. (1967). Parkinsonism: Onset, progression and mortality. *Neurology*, *17*(5), 427–442.

Holliday, R. (1996). The urgency of research on ageing. *BioEssays*, *18*(2), 89–90.

Johnson, W.T. (1999). Horticulture therapy: A bibliographic essay for today's health care practitioner. *Complementary Health Practice Review*, *5*(3), 225–232.

Joye, Y. (2007). Architectural lessons from environmental psychology: The case of biophilic architecture. *Review of General Psychology*, *11*(4), 305–328.

Keizer, K., Lindenberg, S., & Steg, L. (2008). The spreading of disorder. *Science*, *322*(5908), 1681–1685.

Kellert, S.R., & Wilson, S.O. (Eds.) (1993). *The Biophilia hypothesis*. Washington DC: Island Press.

Kenyon, C. (1996). Ponce d'elegans: Genetic quest for the fountain of youth. *Cell*, *84*(4), 501–504.

Keyes, C.L.M. (2005). Mental illness and or mental health? Investigating the axioms of the complete state model of health. *Journal of Consulting and Clinical Psychology*, *73*(3), 539–548.

Li, S., Da Xu, L., & Zhao, S. (2015). The internet of things: A survey. *Information Systems Frontiers*, *17*(2), 243–259.

Lui, C.-W., Everingham, J.-A., Warburton, J., Cuthill, M., & Barlett, H. (2009). What makes a community age-friendly: A review of international literature. *Australasian Journal on Ageing*, *28*(3), 116–121.

Maller, C., Townsend, M., Brown, P., & St. Leger, L. (2002). *Healthy parks healthy people*. Melbourne: Deakin University and Parks Victoria.

McHugh, K.E., & Mings, R.C. (1996). The circle of migration: Attachment to place in aging. *Annals of the Association of American Geographers*, *86*(3), 530–550.

McMahon, B.J., Morand, S., & Gray, J.S. (2018). Ecosystem change and zoonoses in the Anthropocene. *Zoonoses and Public Health*, *65*(7), 755–765

Menec, V.H., Means, R., Keating, N., Parkhurst, G., & Eales, J. (2011). Conceptualizing age-friendly communities. *Canadian Journal on Aging! La revue canadienne du vieillissement*, *30*(3), 479–493.

Moore, E.G., & Rosenberg, M.W. (2001). Canada's elderly population: The challenges of diversity. *Canadian Geographer/le Géographe Canadien*, *45*(1), 145–150.

Nemet, G.F., & Bailey, A.J. (2000). Distance and health care utilization among the rural elderly. *Social Science and Medicine*, *50*(9), 1197–1208.

Nettle, D. (2011). Large differences in publicly visible health behaviours across two neighbourhoods of the same city. *PLOS ONE*, *6*(6), 5–12.

Oeppen, J., & Vaupel, J.W. (2002). Demography. Broken limits to life expectancy. *Science*, *296*(5570), 1029–1031. doi:10.1126/science. 1069675

Parsmore, H.A. (2011). Feeling blue – Get green: The benefits of nature on our mental health and well-being. *Earth Common Journal*, *1*(1), 23–34.

Payne, D.G., & Burroughs, J. (1993). An American naturalist. *ISLE: Interdisciplinary Studies in Literature and Environment*, *1*(1), 193–194. doi:10.1093/isle/1.1.193

Ploffe, L., & Kalache, A. (2010). Towards global age friendly cities: Determining urban features that promote active aging. *Journal of Urban Health*, *87*(5), 733–739.

Pretty, J., Peacock, J., Sellens, M., & Griffin, M. (2005). The mental and physical outcomes of green exercise. *International Journal of Environmental Health Research*, *15*(5), 319–337.

Rice, J.S., & Reny, L.L. (1988). Impact of horticulture therapy on psychological functioning among urban jail inmates. *Journal of Offender Rehabilitation*, *26*, 169–191.

Riggs, J.E., & Schochet, S.S. (1992). Rising mortality due to Parkinson's disease and amyotrophic lateral sclerosis: A manifestation of the competitive nature of human mortality. *Journal of Clinical Epidemiology*, *45*(9), 1007–1012.

Rogers, A., & Woodward, J.A. (1988). The sources of regional elderly population growth: Migration and aging-in place. *Professional Geographer*, *40*(4), 450–459.

Rogerson, P.A. (1998). The geography of elderly minority populations in the United States. *International Journal of Geographical Information Science*, *12*(7), 687–698

Rosenberg, M.W., Moore, E.G., & Ball, S.B. (1989). Components of change in the spatial distribution of the elderly population in Ontario, 1976–1986. *Canadian Geographer/le Géographe Canadien*, *33*(3), 218–229.

Rudzitis, G. (1984). Geographical research and gerontology: An overview. *Gerontologist*, *24*(5), 536–542.

Sanyal, N. (2017). *Pebbles of Positivism, Positive Psychology and spirituality: Contents and approaches*. Kolkata: Ramakrishna Mission Institute of Culture, Golpark.

Schultz, N. (2010). Nurture nature. *New Scientist*, *208*(2785), 35–37.

Simson, S.P., & Straus, M.C. (2003). *Horticulture as therapy: Principles and practice*. Binghamton, NY: The Haworth Press.

Trellis, S. (2013). *Therapeutic horticulture: Theory and evidence*. Retrieved from www.trellisscotland.org.uk

Van Vliet, Moreno, J., Gómez, J., Zhou, W., Fa, J.E., Golden, C., … Nasi, R. (2017). Bushmeat and human health: Assessing the Evidence in tropical and subtropical forests. *Ethnobiology and Conservation*, *6*(3). doi:10.15451/ec2017-04-6.3-1-45

World Health Organization (2007). *Global age-friendly cities: A guide*. Geneva: World Health Organization.

World Health Organization (2010). *WHO global network of age-friendly cities and communities*. World Health Organization. Retrieved July 2, 2010, from www. who.int /ageing/ age_friendly_cities_network/ en/index.html

World Wildlife Fund (2018). *Living planet report 2018: Aiming higher*. Gland, Switzerland: World Wildlife Fund.

Wynne-Edwards, V.C. (1962). *Animal dispersion in relation to social behaviour*. Edinburgh: Oliver & Boyd.

Yanker, B. (2000). Horticulture. *Nature*, *404*(6774), 125.

7

SEARCHING FOR INDIVIDUATION IN RETIREE IDENTITY

Fifteen years before his death in 1939, Freud wrote to his friend and colleague Max Eitingon that he was no longer the same man as before and he was tired and in need of rest. He reported that he could hardly engage in six hours of analytic work effectively, and yet could not think of any other alternative. He felt that the correct solution was to give up all work and obligations and wait in a quiet corner for his natural end (Schur, 1972). In sync with this, the French author, Simone de Beauvoir (1996), regarded retirement as a stage, which could be looked upon either as a *prolonged holiday* or as a *rejection*, with an inherent sense of being thrown on the scrapheap. Though de Beauvoir is attempting to describe the two extremes of how some people experience retirement, the factual reality is that our identity is usually connected more to work than any other aspect of life (Schlossberg, 2009). The experiential realm of retirement calls forth heightened ambivalence and ambiguity as individuals struggle to maintain their autonomy, integration, and humanity.

Late-life transition tends to put forward different developmental tasks for the elderly, one of them being a most crucial challenge, that is, the transition to retirement. It is associated with a number of psychological effects owing to disengagement from work life, leading to associated alterations in lifestyle, finance, and time management. The identity of individuals often becomes partially disrupted, leading to paralysis in taking decisions, lowered self-confidence and trust, a sense of loneliness and having an emotional void, searching for a purpose and meaning in life while accompanied by death anxiety, and feelings of despair and associated issues (Osborne, 2012). Self-identity issues crop up as retirees may often experience a sudden void in their identity after many years of being engaged in a particular profession (Teuscher, 2010; Whitbourne, 1996; Antonovsky and Sagy, 1990). Consequently, the retiree's sense of identity appears to be 'stalled' owing to the transition. The need is thus felt to look for the imprints of individuation among the elderly so that the transition to retirement is experienced smoothly and gracefully. The present chapter will be an attempt on the part of the authors to understand the nuances of retirement from a developmental perspective so that senior individuals may engage in self-realizations leading to actualization by adopting a sound philosophy in life. Retirement involves certain concepts within its boundaries.

Routinization

At an advanced age, retirement demands prominent changes in this new developmental phase of life. It becomes necessary to abandon or modify old roles and bring about changes in habits and routines on the part of retirees which are needed to keep the dynamicity of life intact. In fact, routinization has been regarded by Giddens (1984) as a habitual, taken-for-granted character of the vast bulk of the activities of daily social living. Routines usually foster a sense of autonomy and integration, which brings about an underlying sense of control. There is a deep generalized affective involvement associated with routinization. It also minimizes unconscious sources of anxiety and has underlying 'meanings' for the individual (Marcus, 1999). When this systematized format of life is altered owing to retirement, it initially becomes difficult for the senior individual as he/she needs to find new sources of identity to replace the ones lost in retirement. It involves the use of both *identity assimilation* and *accommodation* to contribute to a balanced identity over time (Whitbourne, 1986). This is because although retirees may have developed an identity during adolescence and young adulthood as described by Erikson (1963), retirement can cause individuals to once again struggle with identity issues. However, the nature of identity issues experienced as people enter retirement is qualitatively different from those experienced earlier. In fact, Milne (2013) has found that more than 60 per cent of retirees 'un-retire' and carry on in some type of paid employment, and then 're-retire' or 'semi-retire' in the future, because of heightened ambivalence and ambiguity in maintaining autonomy, integration, and ties with humanity in general. As such, retirement involves significant re-fashioning of one's identity, relationships, and sense of purpose (Schlossberg, 2009). The inflexible attitude of the non-acceptance of joblessness causes serious dents in some mindsets, making individuals attempt to have a part-time job to keep them engaged, which can cause disrespectful attitudes from others. The scenario becomes that of mental suffering to a great extent, owing to rigid routinization in life that one cannot or will not alter. People, rather than appreciating the vigour of the elderly to utilize his/her expertise in doing something, look down upon their attempts as greed for more 'income.'

Impact bias

In addition, retirement is also associated with 'impact bias,' as it is an emotionally tinged event for the individual (Gilbert et al., 1998). These researchers have focused on the issue whereby people, in general, tend to look down upon senior individuals who have retired and have distressing feelings brought on by ego-bruising setbacks. The underlying essence of 'impact bias' in consideration of retirement is that one should re-think when reflecting on potential emotional responses to retirement and remember that the senior individual is likely to be better able to psychologically manage the transition better than expected. It is high time that we come out of such stereotypical thought patterns. For many individuals nearing retirement, real and symbolic losses of different kinds make them embrace a 'head-in-the-sand' approach to the most challenging stage of their life (Marcus, 2017).

Victor (1994) has identified five stages in the transition to retirement within the fold of impact bias:

i. *A growing interest as retirement approaches*;
ii. *Initial euphoria*;
iii. *Some stress*;
iv. *Dealing with adjustments to a new lifestyle*;
v. *Settling down slowly*.

It is to be noted that deciding when to retire is undoubtedly one of the most important decisions one makes during a lifetime (Knoll, 2011). It is dependent on a number of different factors like financial autonomy, sense of independence, emotional maturity, generative concern, and the outlook towards life in general. Besides, it is further important how one constructs a flourishing existence during this psychologically challenging life- and identity-altering transition. Debates over retirement as a phase or a separate stage continue within the mental frame of retirees. There are also controversies regarding it being either one single event or a process. Perspectives appear to differ in relation to the meaning of the term 'retirement' as 'being retired,' or at least being 'redefined' (Schlossberg, 2009; Milne, 2013; Marcus, 2017). Hence, what appears to be the underlying essence is that a successful transition out of full-time work demands the capacity to adapt to change. This is often accompanied by creative and skilful improvisation on the part of the senior individual.

The narcissistic injury feeling in retirement

Many retirees are challenged by the demand to replace their earlier work routine with a new structure in retirement (Van Solinge and Henkens, 2008). This is because the identity structure of an individual comprising of their personal and social identity can be severely traumatized by the loss of a work role. Some elderly individuals may experience an emotional void and sink into depression as time progresses (Kim and Moen, 2002). For most people, retirement is experienced as a 'narcissistic injury,' at least to some degree, for it evokes painful feelings of being non-valued, disrespected, unwanted, and unloved (Mendelson, 1974). The infantile wish to be at the centre stage is threatened by the transition to retirement. This may be equated with the loss of parental love and adoration, for which pangs of self-idealization are common for many individuals (Schlossberg, 2009). The traces of these feelings may be there in the subconscious, yet the conscious mind suffers because of its shadow effects which they cannot decipher.

To solve these issues, Erikson's (1963) model can be seen in terms of a repetitive process whereby one revisits earlier stages when challenged by circumstances that re-test retirees' prior resolutions of those stages. Logan (1986) reconceptualized Erikson's developmental model and considered the identity versus role diffusion stage to be pivotal. It colours the way an individual enters into their advanced years of life, taking into perspective the qualitative angle to view life and adopt a philosophy of one's own. Logan (1986) is of the opinion that identity is subject to existential issues throughout life.

Looking back and looking forward

Retirement often prompts a life review. It enables the individual to adopt a perspective as well as a retrospective view towards life in general. Some adopt a nostalgic perspective to life in general; others may develop a self-critical and repenting outlook, while others may adopt an indifferent attitude, with a few being content and satisfied with the way life has been for them. The person is likely to develop a deeper understanding of the continuity of one's life as well as its different transitions. Other existential issues that may emerge include whether or not retirees have fulfilled the goals related to their careers, family lives, and social relationships. Issues regarding the finitude of life and one's mortality come to the surface of one's awareness. This is especially true of retirees who outlive their contemporaries. Some suffer from pangs of death anxiety along with the fear of the unknown accompanied by guilt for having lived life in a less satisfactory manner (Tillich, 1952).

Retirement involves 'having a world,' or after one's pre-retirement way of life, 'losing a world,' owing to one's withdrawal from the full-time workforce, and 'replacing a world' of creating a satisfying way of life (Marcus, 1999). It is a process which involves a phase of maximizing growth, development, and learning amidst a wide range of personal loss and hence is a continuing and self-containing journey for the senior individual.

Choice dilemma and grieving

Retirees often experience choice dilemma in the fact that they may not trust their ability to make appropriate decisions and end up in decision paralysis. Retirees may experience a phase of grieving once the initial excitement of the transition is over if such individuals were more or less satisfied with their work life. This is similar to 'empty nest syndrome,' which female retirees often face, at least temporarily. The painful self-awareness of irreversibility of lived time and the sorrow over life's transience is the psychological context for an individual to grieve and mourn (Teising, 2013). On the contrary, the wise retiree-to-be and the elderly retiree believe in the 'art of living' the 'good life' which supports the notion that there is always a proper time to grow a sapling and a time to uproot the plant when needed to give space for other vegetation to take its place (Marcus, 2003). This means enduring intense separation anxiety in the best possible manner.

Becoming a senior

The transition to retirement often involves becoming a senior. Industrious retirees may still engage in different missions like part-time employment, hobbies, recreational activities, coaching, teaching, and mentoring to keep themselves occupied. However, occupying oneself excessively with work rather than any meaningful engagement during the transitive days of the elderly individual may indicate a tendency of avoidance and a fear of acknowledging the change. It thus becomes significant to note that meaningful engagement for retirees may be through relaxation and extracting contentment in some 'meaningful' activities like hobbies, doing some selective academic and professional work, and so on, thereby engaging in self-realization and gaining a deeper spiritualistic frame of mind to ultimately look for transcendence.

At home

Retirees need to engage in re-negotiation of domestic responsibilities as they need to spend more time alone or with a partner at home. This can lead to insecurity and anxiety unless the retiree is able to find meaningful engagement with others in a shared activity (Barnes and Parry, 2004; Davey and Szinovacz, 2004).

Individuation

Elderly individuals in their retirement phase have the opportunity to pursue individuation in a relatively less constrained manner by engaging themselves in interests and other allied activities that inculcate various forms of self-actualization. These activities can help the individual to move forward towards another developmental layer of identity formation added to the earlier Eriksonian model's stage of 'identity versus role confusion' (Erikson, 1963). Jung (1933) opines that individuation results in personal development by expanding one's sense of self-awareness. This can occur both unconsciously as well as with conscious effort. The self gets integrated as a result.

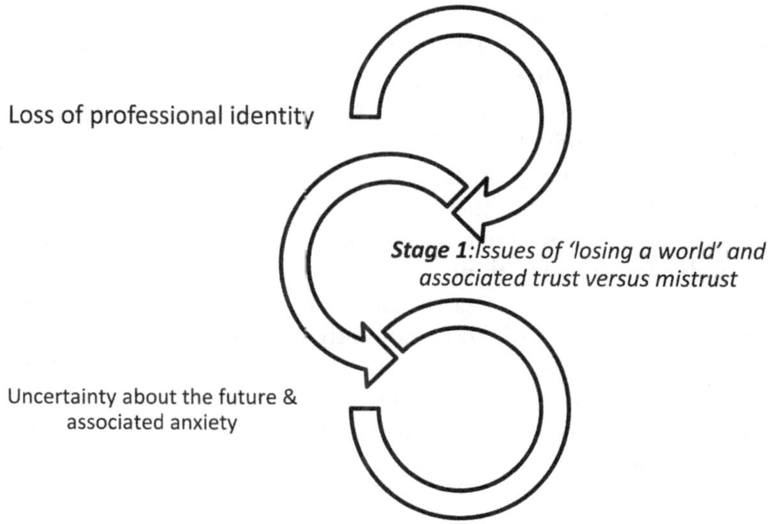

Figure 7.1 Changes associated with the initial transition to retired life (source: authors).

In fact, retirement involves a revisit to the earlier developmental stages of Erikson and a resolution for every crisis in each stage in a different manner. The present attempt is there to probe into the developmental model of Erikson to understand retirement issues from a holistic perspective.

Stage one: Issues of 'losing a world' and associated trust versus mistrust

The transition to retirement is primarily concerned with adequately coming to terms with one's real and imagined losses, such as one's identity, relationships, and purpose (Marcus, 2017). These losses often trigger feelings of uncertainty about the future, leaving behind an emotional void in many people regarding how life will turn out in post-retirement. This reflects a pathogenic perspective of retirement. Many individuals have difficulty in optimally relating to time. There are often 'fantasies of immortal objects and the hunt for an ideal object' (Teising, 2013). Retirees might feel wobbly about taking the 'right' decision, resulting in decision paralysis. They might even ask themselves, 'Am I adequate enough to take major decisions?' Feelings of self-doubt may trigger anxiety, avoidance, and delay. Many people do not retire when they plan to do so, mainly because of financial problems or because of decision paralysis (Anderson, Burkhauser, and Quinn, 1986) (Figure 7.1).

Some individuals may even engage in *bridge employment* or *encore career* options, owing to such issues. *Bridge employment* has been used to describe transitional work of a shorter duration that occurs between full-time employment in a career and complete labour force withdrawal (Wang, Zhan, Liu and Schultz, 2008; Feldman, 1994). *Encore career options* involve pursuing a 'new phase of work' after the departure from career employment. It is usually deeply personal and characterized by purpose, passion, and meaningful contribution (Cunningham, 2010; Freedman, 2011). Senior citizens may plan meticulously to engage in an encore career, which appeals to them as a meaningful option now that they have ample time and opportunity.

Thus, anxiety in relation to trusting oneself to take the correct decision to retire may be associated with procrastination and ruminative tendencies in some instances while it may urge the elderly to take an impulsive decision to retire in other instances. It is to be noted that Erikson's first stage is associated with the infant's experience with the primary caregiver. Similarly, for retirees, possible trust or mistrust emerges from themselves, i.e., the manner of how such senior individuals relate to themselves. Mistrust can lead to identity diffusion for the elderly individual.

Stage two: Autonomy versus shame and doubt

Many retirees often go through feelings of shame and doubt for no longer serving the role of a breadwinner which they had been habitually doing for a long time. They also perceive themselves as becoming dependent on the partner/offspring/other caretaker and feel ashamed because of this. Besides, being unable to take proper care of one's self and increasingly becoming dependent on others, both physically and emotionally, may also trigger feelings of shame and guilt. Physical dependency can also threaten personal autonomy, following which, a sense of helplessness emerges. As such, the stage of autonomy versus shame and doubt comes to the forefront. The issue of personal autonomy and competence in all the years of one's professional life is retrospectively revisited against the background of the fear of losing one's independence due to one's physical and psychological vulnerability in the later years of life. The fear of not being able to carry out basic physical activities (due to possible ailing conditions) for a 'dignified stay' at home calls forth a sense of shame and increasing doubt regarding their own capabilities (Figure 7.2).

Stage three: Initiative versus guilt

Elderly individuals may appear to realize after the initial excitement of being retired that being engaged with a schedule of pre-conceived recreational activities refrains them from becoming enriched completely regarding their quest for finding meaning and purpose of their lives. Instead, they often seem to search for other activities apart from recreations, hobbies, and travel to etch some meaning. Accompanied by this are feelings of powerlessness and isolation, which make it difficult for the elderly to overcome their desperate effort

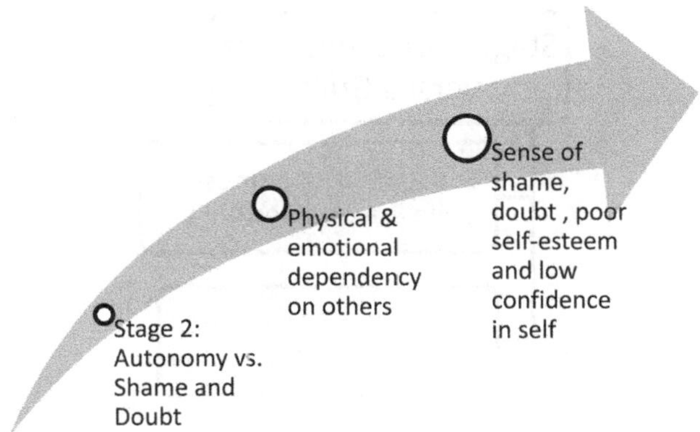

Figure 7.2 Emotional changes in the psyche of the retiree (source: authors).

to engage in some kind of project(s). These feelings make it more difficult for a retired person to look for projects and activities that are not a re-run of what they have already accomplished. The loss of the stimulation and meaning provided by their former employment, however, may draw some retirees back to their former work role, either in a part- or full-time capacity.

The senior individual is faced with the basic question of 'What do I do with my retirement?' and the answer may be difficult to cope with. The initiatives once adopted by the individual in his/her earlier days are naturally expected to be not feasible in the afternoon of life, having expended much energy and enthusiasm in earlier life. It often becomes difficult and, at times, impracticable for the elderly to pursue such initiatives in their twilight years. They may be filled with nostalgic moments and grief for the end of a career. Some of them still keep alive a burning and faint hope that they might become useful. The inability to spontaneously find initiatives in the current activities of one's prior work life often gives birth to feelings of guilt in the elderly (Figure 7.3).

The senior may confine him/herself to lives centred on recreation, relaxation, and travel. If, however, retirees' finances are adequate, meaning of life and life satisfaction – rather than economic necessity and ambition – are more likely to be the criteria that influence their choice of activities, projects, or employment. Engaging in spiritual activities may often take an upper hand at this juncture, providing meaning to the elderly and replenishing the 'meaning' component of the self.

Stage four: Industry versus inferiority

Retirement is a time when industriousness is optional. This is because many senior people seek part-time work, engage in volunteering, recreational

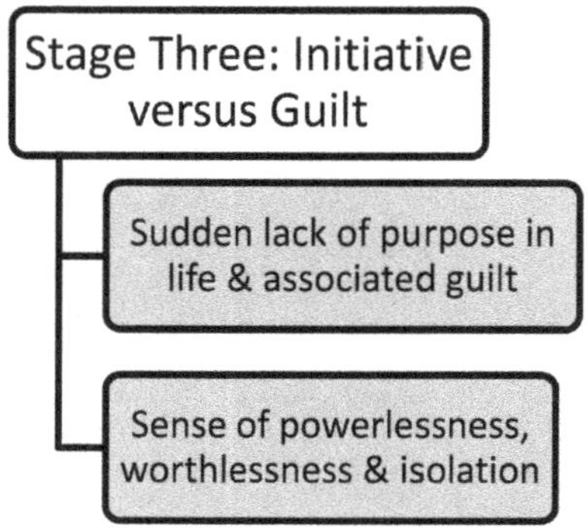

Figure 7.3 Guilt issues associated with retirement (source: authors).

activities, and travel where the extent of industriousness is less than earlier days of full-time work. Industriousness serves as a source of meaning in retirement; otherwise, a sense of inferiority may develop. Success in Erikson's stage of industry is almost a prerequisite for the emergence of generative concern in the following stage. The feeling that one's activity is instrumental in the retirees' contribution to the welfare of society and future generations is dependent on one's sense of industriousness. Many activities like teaching, volunteering, and so on appear to be desirable forms of engagement for the senior individual. Issues of competence and associated self-worth often crop up during retirement. Moreover, retirees can experience ageism and stereotypes when they become seniors which can create doubts for retirees about their competence as well as lead to feelings of inferiority.

Stage five: Identity versus role confusion

The stage of identity versus role confusion which was relevant during adolescence no longer has relevance to that extent in late-life as the individual's identity had already been developed and nurtured through the adult years. However, being an authentic member of society, even in late-life, it calls forth some degree of identity, even for a senior individual. For those retirees whose identity was defined almost exclusively by their jobs, there can be an identity crisis as discussed before. They do no longer belong to the workplace community where they had etched their identities all along the years of work. A typical void generally overtakes their mind. This can lead to feelings of uncertainty, anxiety, and even depression in some senior individuals. It then becomes essential to modify one's priorities and work/life structure. The challenge to find meaningful engagement in retirement and consequent life satisfaction can become the key to post-retirement life. The elderly individual engages in different roles that tend to help form and sustain

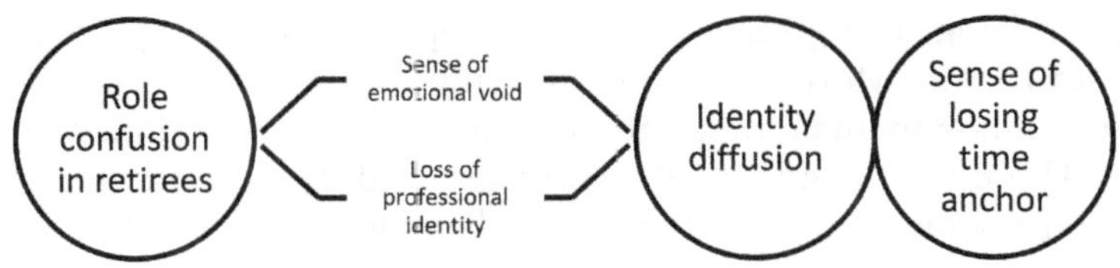

Figure 7.4 Identity crisis in retirees (source: authors).

post-retirement identity, some of which are a continuation of activities that the individual used to pursue before retirement. Nonetheless, responding to the challenge of adjusting one's identity in retirement sometimes leads to a sort of crisis described by Willing (1981). Consequently, there is the experience of identity diffusion in most elderly individuals. There is often an underlying feeling of time running out for the individual (Civitarese and Ferro, 2013; Junkers, 2013) (Figure 7.4).

However, if the senior person can find meaning in life even in his/her post-retirement phase, he/she is likely to get over the crisis and resolve the issue successfully. This meaning is mostly embedded in a spiritualistic orientation to embrace peace and unison, and ultimately, with divinity.

Stage six: Intimacy versus isolation

Logan (1986) is of the opinion that when revisited by retirees, this stage occurs within the context of retirement rather than young adulthood. Issues of intimacy continue in old age as well, but they tend to have qualitative changes in the nature of interpersonal relationships. Relationships appear to gain greater depth, meaning, and a sense of selfless satisfaction where each partner extends beyond their egoistic selves to accommodate the needs of the other significant person. Feelings of bliss are expected to accompany old age.

In families where a significant age difference exists between a couple, one person might be retired unlike the other. Women may be reluctant to retire as they feel that it is the ripe time to pursue their engagements, now that they are relatively freer in comparison to the early years of life. For retired older male partners of such women, issues related to 'cabin fever' or having to stay 'all alone' may result. In addition, women who have stayed at home so long may have developed a life apart from their partner in the form of other engagements, which they may wish to continue even when their partner retires. Thus, the balance between intimacy and isolation is important for a variety of living arrangements. A couple perhaps needs to increase mutual independence and respect for each other in late-life if their retirements are not concurrent.

Research based upon socio-emotional selectivity theory (Carstensen, Gross, and Fung, 1997) suggests that as people age, they may prefer fewer but closer friends whose company they enjoy most. More time is usually spent in solitude by the retirees unless retirees spend more time with fewer friends. Those senior individuals who shift to distant places do not tend to share the same quality of friendship that they had in earlier locations where they spent a significant period of time interacting with others. This is because the 'social convoy' (Kahn and Antonucci, 1980) of which they were a part in their previous community is left behind. This loss of 'good friends' often makes the elderly person experience pangs of isolation and feelings of being alienated from society. Thus, the dangers of co-dependency may also emerge in later life (Bayley, 1999).

Stage seven: Generativity versus stagnation

This stage may be understood in terms of the attempts of the elderly to leave behind a legacy for children and society as a whole. This generative concern of the senior individual is selfless and not egoistic in nature. Instead, it may be described in terms of investment by the individual to develop a well-adjusted society in the long run. There is a noticeable shift from an existential orientation of 'being for oneself' being the epitome of self-indulgence and self-satisfaction to a stance of 'being for the other.' It incorporates a productive and creative way of 'being' which is directed towards others to serve them selflessly. This is also a stage where initiative and industry of earlier stages can recur. The effectiveness of this stage depends on the extent of virtues acquired by the individual in earlier stages, leading to the emergence of the virtue of 'care' – it being a widening concern for everything that has been generated by love, necessity, or accident (Erikson, 1964). Care includes the development of self-awareness that one is needed, and maturity requires guidance and encouragement from what has been produced and must be taken care of (Erikson, 1963). Many retirees have already been heavily invested in the welfare of their children and grandchildren and find such issues to be applicable to them (Figure 7.5).

However, some other retirees may feel contented by raising their own children and that nothing else needs to be done for the younger generations because of their rigid and stringent outlook, whereas others look to volunteer for organizations that are focused on the well-being of citizens in an attempt to add some meaning in their lives. Such activities tend to increase their sense of generative concern for members of the younger generations. The challenge for elderly individuals depends on finding a unique balance between their commitments and their search for finding meaning in life. Some individuals may find volunteering fulfilling while others may find it disappointing. This depends on their different value profiles. Otherwise, feelings of incompetence may result in the development of feelings of

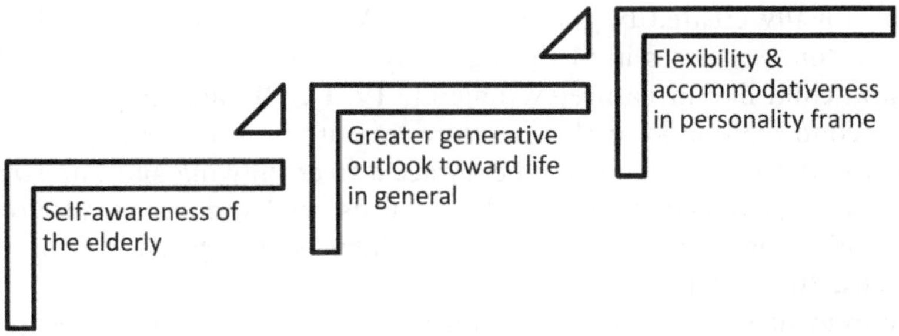

Figure 7.5 Personality disposition of generative retirees (source: authors).

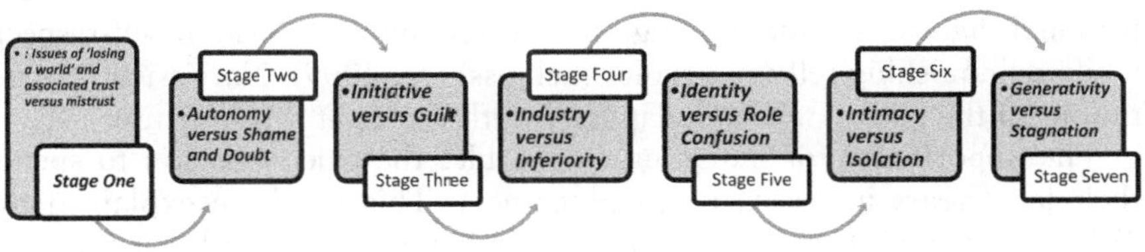

Figure 7.6 Transition to retirement in accordance with Erikson's psychosocial stages (source: authors).

stagnation in the elderly, a common indication being the emergence of death anxiety.

Thus, the relevance of the crises expressed in the stages of Erikson's model continues beyond the lifespan period in which they first occur. Logan's (1986) emphasis on the pivotal importance of the identity versus role diffusion stage of Erikson's model, and on the recurrent importance of the first two stages of psychosocial development, runs parallel to the experiences of retirees. When an old-aged person has acquired the capacity to face vulnerability, finitude, and mortality with courage and integrity, he/she acquires the ego strength or virtue called 'wisdom' – it being the 'detached concern with life itself, in the face of death.' Such a person has the ability to embrace harsh reality with an attitude of resignation without despair but with grace (Erikson, 1964). The different stages of Erikson are schematically represented along the lines of the retirement of individuals in Figure 7.6.

Summarily, wisdom is the awareness that gives the old-aged person a 'glimpse of immortality' (Marcus, 2015), where he/she believes that his/her creations in the realms of love and work will live on after him/her to the benefit of future generations. 'Death loses its sting,' with such a final synthesis and consolidation of the self (Erikson, 1963). Such an individual attains the ability to embrace harsh reality with an attitude of resignation without despair (Erikson, 1964). New ideas, meanings, stories, and persons are personally created by the wise elder (Monte, 1980). It is at this time that wisdom expresses itself through playful creativity which is spontaneous and child-like in nature (Winnicott, 1971). Old age may be regarded as a second childhood at this juncture, essentially because it provides an opportunity to 'travel lighter, to embrace a freer, flowing and unrestrained way of being associated with childhood at its best' and not because of failing health issues which make the person increasingly dependent on others (Marcus, 2003, 2017).

Retirement ensures the development of a capacity of the elderly individual to endure sufferings of various kinds, owing to multiple losses, and transforming that suffering into practical wisdom. This involves the adoption of the defence mechanism of sublimation. One can then climb up the stairs towards transcendence. This requires the use of adaptive defences, personal dignity, and developing an internal ability to sustain self-respect while relinquishing self-importance (Schlossberg, 2009). Narcissistic orientations of the person take an adaptive/healthy place at this juncture.

The opportunity for individuation enables the elderly person to spend their later years in search of enlightenment. This has been explained by Tillich (1952) as the 'freedom to be an individual,' to search for the ultimate. This may be explained through Heidegger's original concept of 'thrownness,' where he says that human beings are thrown into an abyss by means of their birth where they cannot determine or choose their parents or the environment into which they are born. They need to accept whatever is provided by destiny. This runs in parallel to retirement where the retiree may conceive it to be analogous to a prolonged holiday or as being thrown into an abyss once again as he/she had originally been exposed to, which apparently has no meaning for the person and it is the individual himself/herself who has to look out for finding some clues to decipher the meaning at this time of their life (de Beauvoir, 1996).

Search for enlightenment usually involves systematic self-observation as one way for people to learn who and what they are. Meditation, yoga, Tai Chi, counselling, personal growth workshops, group therapy, and philosophy are some of the types of practices and agencies available for delving deeper into the self-system of the psyche and for finding avenues of self-realization and gradual enlightenment. The ripened stage of post-retirement living is expected to engage the senior individual in the quest for detoxifying the psychic system, thereby making the system open to acknowledging the different 'givens' of life and inculcating a forgiving stance towards others and the self in general. The myriad fold of life experiences is essentially 'reflected upon' and 'basked on in the stillness' by the 'mature experiencer' who consequentially enjoys a calming effect. The individual becomes empowered with the virtues of basic trust leading to hope, will power, purpose (seeking meaning of life), competency (understanding the limitations and strength points of the individual self), mature identity, love towards life in general, care and generative attitude towards members of younger generations, and ultimate wisdom to understand the philosophy of life and its basic existence. This is expected to usher basic trust and contentment in life for the mature retiree who has overcome anxieties of a varied nature and is looking forward to embracing death in the last chapter of life with grace.

Conclusion

Retirement is a crucial life transition which needs to be cautiously dealt with as far as crises are concerned. It re-shuffles an individual to engage in re-visiting the Eriksonian psychosocial stages of life. The quality by which the retiree resolves each of the earlier crises determines the quality of matured life. The mature retiree engages in the final voyage of seeking the purpose of his/her life along an existential paradigm. The individual identity of the senior becomes ripened with a number of virtues so that his/her imprint is left behind after the soul departs. A coherent narrative of self-identity is likely to be the expected result which, in turn, leads to a sense of integration and personhood (Giddens, 1991). It results in a 'replacement world,' which comprises a set of routines, both attitudinal as well as behavioural, and a new set of roles that enables one to provide a degree of order and direction along healthy perfectionistic avenues in one's life. It not only results in the contentment of the senior psychic system but also the purpose of life is addressed along with generative terms for society at large. The matured retiree thereby seeks individualization along such lines and engages in the enjoyment of overall bliss and dips oneself in ultimate happiness.

Retirement truly is not an identity-loss, it is no pain to bear. Owing to extended longevity in the current century, it should be accepted as a new platform of life to relax, relish, and change the psychic energy in the integration of life experiences. It should come as a wisdom-loaded state of existence where one is still enjoying the benefits of concrete reality as well as getting prepared to detach oneself from the concreteness of life to the self-transcendent bliss experience. There should not be any hankering for identity; the basic faith and hope of life is expected to settle the senior mind to enjoy only the happiness and acknowledgement of life conditions that one has enjoyed. One needs to use ego strengths or virtues in the service of creating a world of meanings that will include a new sense of personal effectiveness and significance. This is going to be the positive frame of mind of any retiree. Looking at the morning sun and taking deep breaths of life, one says, 'Thank you life for giving me another day,' and be prepared for the sunset day of a thriving life.

References

Anderson, K.H., Burkhauser, R.W., & Quinn, J.F. (1986). Do retirement dreams come true? The effect of unanticipated events on retirement plans. *Industrial and Labour Relations Revue*, *39*, 518–526.

Antonovsky, A., & Sagy, S. (1990). Confronting developmental tasks in the retirement transition. *Gerontologist*, *30*(3), 362–368.

Barnes, H., & Parry, J. (2004). Renegotiating identity and relationships: Men and women's adjustments to retirement. *Aging and Society*, *24*(2), 213–233. doi:10.1017/S0144686X0300148X

Bayley, J. (1999). *Iris*. London: Duckworth.

Carstensen, L.L., Gross, J., & Fung, H. (1997). The social context of emotional experience. *The Annual Review of Gerontology and Geriatrics*, *17*, 325–352.

Civatarese, G., & Ferro, A. (2013). Prologue: Mourning and the empty couch: A conversation between analysts. In G. Junkers (Ed.), *The empty couch: The taboo of ageing and retirement in psychoanalysis* (pp. xv–xxv). London: Routledge.

Cunningham, D.H. (2010). Baby boomers and community college: A study of motivations. *Dissertation Abstracts International, Section A*, *71*(2), 421.

Davey, A., & Szinovacz, M.E. (2004). Dimensions of marital quality and retirement. *Journal of Family Issues*, *25*(4), 431–464. doi:10.1177/0192513X03257698

de Beauvoir, S. (1996). *The coming of age* (P.O.Brien, Trans.). New York: Norton.

Erikson, E.H. (1963). *Childhood and society* (2nd ed.). New York: W.W. Norton & Company.

Erikson, E.H. (1964). *Insight and responsibility*. New York: W.W. Norton & Company.

Feldman, D.C. (1994). The decision to retire early: A review and conceptualization. *Academy of Management Review*, *19*(2), 285–311.

Freedman, M. (2011). *The big shift: Navigating the new stage behind midlife*. New York: Public Affairs.

Giddens, A. (1984). *The constitution of society*. Berkeley, CA: University of California Press.

Giddens, A. (1991). *Mortality and self-identity*. Stanford, CA: Standford University Press.

Gilbert, D.T., Pinel, E.C., Wilson, T.D., Blumberg, S.J., & Wheatley, T.P. (1998). Immune neglect: A source of durability bias in affective forecasting. *Journal of Personality and Social Psychology*, *175*(3), 617–638.

Jung, C.G. (1933). *Modern man in search of a soul*. New York: Harcourt Publishers & Brace.

Junkers, G. (2013). Later, perhaps...transience and its significance for the psychoanalyst. In G. Junkers (Ed.), *The empty couch: The taboo of ageing and retirement in psychoanalysis* (pp. 17–31). London: Routledge.

Kahn, R.L., & Antonucci, T.C. (1980). Convoys over the life course: Attachment, roles and social support. In P.B. Baltes & O.G. Brim, Jr. (Eds.), *Lifespan development and behavior* (pp. 253–286). New York: Academic Press.

Kim, J.E., & Moen, P. (2002). Retirement transitions, gender, and psychological well-being: A life-course ecological model. *Journal of Gerontology: Psychological Sciences*, *57B*(3), 212–222. doi:10.1093/geronb/57.3.p212

Knoll, M.A.Z. (2011). Behavioural and psychological aspects of the retirement decision. *Social Security Bulletin*, *71*(4), 1–13.

Logan, R.D. (1986). A re-conceptualization of Erikson's theory: The repetition of existential and instrumental themes. *Human Development*, *29*(3), 125–136.

Marcus, P. (1999). *Autonomy in the extreme situation: Bruno Bettelheim, the nazi concentration camps and the mass society*. Westport, CT: Praeger.

Marcus, P. (2003). *Ancient religious wisdom, spirituality and psychoanalysis*. Westport, CT: Praeger.

Marcus, P. (2015). *Creating heaven on earth: The psychology of experiencing immortality in everyday life*. London: Karnac.

Marcus, P. (2017). *The psychoanalysis of career choice, job performance, and satisfaction: How to flourish in the workplace*. London: Routledge: Taylor and Francis Group.

Mendelson, M. (1974). *Psychoanalytic concepts of depression* (2nd ed.). Flushing, NY: Spectrum Publications.

Milne, D. (2013). *The psychology of retirement: Coping with the transition from work*. West Sussex: Wiley-Blackwell.

Monte, C.F. (1980). *Beneath the mask: An introduction to theories of personality* (2nd ed.). New York: Holt, Rinehart and Winston.

Osborne, J.W. (2012). Psychological effects of the transition to retirement. *Canadian Journal of Counseling and Psychotherapy*, *46*(1), 45–58.

Schlossberg, N.K. (2009). *A critical dictionary of psychoanalysis* (2nd ed.). London: Penguin.

Schur, M. (1972). *Freud living and dying*. London: Hogarth Press.

Teising, M. (2013). Narcissistic challenges for ageing analysts. In G. Junkers (Ed.), *The empty coach: The taboo of ageing and retirement in psychoanalysis* (pp. 46–52). London: Routledge.

Teuscher, U. (2010). Change and persistence of personal identities after the transition to retirement. *International Journal of Ageing and Human Development*, *70*(1), 89–106.

Tilich, P. (1952). *The courage to be*. New Haven, CT: Yale University Press.

Van Solinge, H., & Henkens, K. (2008). Adjustment to and satisfaction with retirement: Two of a kind. *Psychology and Aging*, *23*(2), 422–434. doi:10.1037/0882-7974.23.2.422

Victor, C. (1994). *Old age in modern society: A textbook of social gerontology*. London: Chapman & Hall.

Wang, M., Zhan, Y., Liu, S., & Shultz, K.S. (2008). Antecedents of bridge employment: A longitudinal investigation. *Journal of Applied Psychology*, *93*(4), 818–830.

Whitbourne, S.K. (1986). *The me I know: A study of adult identity*. New York: Springer-Verlag.

Whitbourne, S.K. (1996). *The ageing individual*. New York: Springer-Verlag.

Willing, J.Z. (1981). *The reality of retirement*. New York: William Morrow.

Winnicott, D.W. (1971). *Playing and reality*. London: Tavistock Publications.

8

DETACHMENT

The positive end of the elderly mind

The moment of birth and the process of life are attachment-based. Without this string of attachment, human beings cannot run their self-systems to be ready for experiences. The differentiation of pleasure and pain and attempts to attain more pleasure, achievements, successes, and pride are all stories of emotional and social attachments. The attachment spree seems to be the mental designer of life. This motivational spirit keeps the life-ball rolling and is wrapped up by emotional entanglements of various kinds. Life proceeds and phases get over one after another – we all experience a basic fact that attachments are obvious in life, but that seems to be the point of greatest trouble. Hence, with age, after experiencing life in multi-directions, there should be kept a 'mind,' a 'psyche,' ready to practise detachment. This new idea and practice would be the ultimate strength to remain calm and peaceful in old age and this mode helps us leave this life context having a positive mindset. This is expected to be the result of the attainment of wisdom on the part of the senior person. The current chapter attempts to help the elderly adopt this mode of practice in their daily life through small steps.

It is to be noted that the benefits of engagement with social activities and hence life are widely reported by gerontologists. They have been reported to be good for health and well-being so as to contribute to successful ageing. In fact, the effect of social engagement on successful ageing has its foundations in activity theory. The active lifestyle fostered by well-being is expected to provide an antidote to the loss of productive roles that are relinquished after retirement (Adams, Leibbrandt, and Moon 2010; Silverstein and Parker 2002; Thanakwang and Isaramalai 2013). Theorists favouring activity theory are of the opinion that activity is usually associated with happiness or, in other words, individuals need to be active in order to be happy in old age. According to them, if existing roles or relationships are lost, it is important to replace them, because if activity drops, there is a corresponding drop in life satisfaction (Maddox and Eisdorfer, 1962; Maddox, 1965). Activity theory assumes that participation in social activities tends to fulfil basic human needs for social interaction and affiliation (Jang and Chiriboga, 2011). Subjective well-being has been reported to be significantly higher in socially active older adults (Balboa-Castillo, León-Muñoz, Graciani, Rodríguez-Artalejo, and Guallar-Castillón 2011; Hawkins, Foose, Binkley, and Binkley. 2004; Jenkins 2011; Nimrod 2007; Simone and Haas, 2013). This may be because of the likely fact that psychological, physiological, and behavioural pathways appear to be interrelated and that the type of social activity engaged in plays a crucial role in the same. The individual feels 'engaged' by the set of different activities which keep him/her busy.

However, less is known regarding what drives people to withdraw from social activities in later life; they probably are physical ailments leading to physical disability, lack of basic physical energy, generalized inertia, and dealing with many emotional losses which appear to be important cornerstones. Social detachment has been found to have a detrimental effect on physical and mental health in later life, wrapping up the mind with loneliness and a sense of deprivation. Older people who withdraw from social activities have been found to suffer from a greater risk of mortality, disability, and depression as well as cognitive decline (Agahi and Parker 2008; Saito, Kondo, Kondo, Ojima, and Hirai 2012; Steptoe, Shankar, Demakakos, and Wardle 2013; James, Boyle, Buchman, and Bennett 2011; Lund, Nilsson, and Avlund, 2010; Mendes de Leon 2003; Chiao, Weng, and Botticello 2011; Andrew and Rockwood, 2010; Bassuk, Glass, and Berkman 1999; James, Wilson, Barnes, and Bennett 2011). Such reactions may be the outcome of greater expectations in life, clinging to materialism and concrete experiences and not having an open mind to accommodate the idea of life beyond. However, to have an uplift mentally, individuals need to be ready to absorb the idea of emotional detachment in order to be connected with higher spirits in the realm of transcendence. It essentially involves the elderly being flexible emotionally and open-ended in nature. Because there resides the ultimate peace, and the 'being,' who is fulfilled with blissful experiences. This demands 'Nature' and 'Life' connect in a wider perspective rather than having a narrow connection of a 'personal' life context and gross sensorial or factual attainments of the basic life.

Emotional detachment: The key to gero-transcendence

Emotional detachment helps the senior individual to free himself/herself from the clutches of emotionality and underlying attachment. This is essentially a gradual process and is extensively satisfying for the individual (Crandall, 1980). It enables the person to gradually engage in a qualitative shift by embracing transcendental flares of life (Tornstam, 1994, 1997; 1999a, 1999b). In fact, the gero-transcendent individual experiences a redefinition of time, space, life, death, and the self, being engaged in the process of emotional detachment. Gero-transcendence involves a change in the perspective of looking at life from a materialistic and pragmatic view to a much broader, more cosmic, and transcendent one in perceiving the world at large (Tornstam, 1997). Tornstam derives some assumptions from Zen Buddhism, whereby the chief focus is the union of the past, present, and future, enabling the individual to attain a state of cosmic transcendence. It further runs parallel to Jung's concept of the 'collective unconscious' where the individual reaches affinity with universal psychological structures having racial connotations. An intrinsic and culture-free transcendental process in old age is hinted upon which can be the product of normal living.

It is noteworthy at this juncture that the *Bhagavad Gita,* or 'Sacred Song,' essentially deals with man's relationship with divine power and the underlying intense joy of divine power. It is a tale in the form of a dialogue between Arjuna and Lord Krishna on the eve of the battle of Kurukshetra. Krishna teaches the fearful, ambiguous, and hesitant Arjuna the need for action and the requirement that it is only through the search for the Divine and the Absolute that the true self will be discovered. This can be gradually made feasible through detaching oneself from different worldly pleasures. The process is made feasible by the experiential processing of the being who adorns the wisdom-rim in his/her personality (Radhakrishnan, 2010). It may be said along the same lines that in a healthy frame of life experiences and consequential wisdom-laden temperamental pattern, emotional detachment in the elderly individual is expected to be manifested in the following orientations:

- ***A sense of increased communion with the 'spirit of the universe'***: A feeling of flowing energy is sensed by the individual coursing through the universe, making him/her feel in oneness with nature (Reed, 1991). The being increasingly has a sense of being an elemental aspect of the universe, acknowledging itself with grace, and feeling 'connected' with the cosmic energy.
- ***Perception of time, space, and objects – being redefined***: There is a decreased sense of self-centredness as the borders of past, present, and future become blurred and are diffused, leading to the development of a more cosmic self (Coles, 1990). One begins to realize gradually the ubiquity of time and space and understand every stimulus to be relative.
- ***Decreased fear of death with a redefinition of the concepts of life and death***: Life and death acquire different meaning for the individual, consequentially yielding less death anxiety (Rusnak, 2006). The philosophy of the individual towards life is altered.
- ***Increased acceptance of death with the alteration of affinity towards past and coming generations***: Elderly individuals are now more accepting of death, owing to increased feelings of affinity with the past and the upcoming generations in accordance with Erikson's notions.
- ***A decrease in interest in superfluous social interaction***: The individual loses his/her interest in establishing new acquaintances. There is an increased bent of selective social interaction which seems to be more desirable for

the elderly individual – e.g., with those old friends and/or acquaintances that confirm the identity of the person. This is in accordance with the theory of age-related socio-emotional selectivity (Singer, 2000).

- ***A decrease in interest in material things:*** Older persons realize that material goods do not necessarily open up the road to happiness. Many elderly individuals may be observed to give away personal belongings like books, precious possessions, larger heirlooms, money, or assets to their younger relatives or for some charitable purpose. Instead, the focus increases in the realm of experiential richness and associated realizations.
- ***A decrease in egocentrism with emotional maturity***: There is a gradual decrease of self-centrism with the attainment of emotional maturity in old age. This enables the development of generative concern in the elderly individual. The senior person has a resultantly greater extent of emotional insight about the personal self as well as life-realization contents.
- ***An increase in the time spent in meditation***: Pondering on life and the self as part of the psychological processes of old age is also considered a sign of gero-transcendence. There is a development to a greater extent of 'interiority' in old age (Gutmann, 1987). The elderly individual prefers spending more time in solitude and enjoys the bliss by being a hermit amidst the 'silence' (Maitland, 2009).

Old age detachment phenomenon in theoretical contentions

Gero-transcendence describes an altered state of consciousness in old age, brought forth by emotional detachment, and having different dimensions as follows:

1. Cosmic;
2. Self;
3. Relationships.

The cosmic dimension is reflected by means of the gradual shift from egoism to altruism which is noteworthy at this juncture along with the development of a generative self. Besides, genuine acceptance of the self is brought about unconditionally. Relationships that the individual enjoys are perceived from a different perspective and consequent meaning deciphered. The quality of interpersonal relationships deepens along with an increasing need for solitude as mentioned earlier. The elderly person enjoys the bliss of solitude without being lonely. There is also the emerging freedom of 'asceticism' in the senior person. Transcendence of right/wrong duality ensues with a gradual withdrawal of the judgemental nature of the emotionally mature being. This leads to a much more broadminded understanding of others

(Tornstam, 1997). A cosmic self develops, indicating prominent signs of gero-transcendence. The individual becomes 'body-transcendent' in accordance with Tornstam. It is a sign of maturity in old age not to put one's self or the body in focus. It is to be noted that the awareness of different bodily changes does not become obsessive with the emergence of body-transcendence, which is also a form of detachment.

Avenues for emotional disengagement for the elderly

Agahi et al. (2006) believe that engagement in leisure activities in middle age has a strong effect on engagement in older age. In fact, *continuity theory* emphasizes that individuals in their later-lives tend to make adaptations to enable them to continue the same style of life, personality, and habits that they developed in earlier years (Bowling, 2005). This continuity helps them in being better satisfied. Change is associated with the person's perceived past leading to alterations in inner psychological characteristics, social behaviour, and social circumstances. Continuity thus appears to be a sound adaptive strategy (Atchley, 1989).

Some activities which may engage in emotional disengagement include learning to play the piano, gardening, cooking, painting, baking, even re-arranging the room, tailoring, crafting, and engaging in any other creative activities. All of them are momentary in nature, resulting in creation and enjoying the activity with others. This calls for temporary emotion and positive engagement, but no deep attachment or expectations from any of such activities. It involves engaging in aesthetic activities for the time being. Consequentially, the psyche looks for options for 'beautification of the mind.' The existential experience of each and every moment is to be noted at this juncture. This is enjoying life for the sake of it, but practising detachment unknowingly, unmindfully.

The grace of 'awakening': The result of the detached being

Any conversation about awakening is expected to be fruitful. Aged individuals can engage in the journey towards awakening by means of detachment. In fact, the *dharma* of the aged should be to reflect on the truth underlying all wisdom traditions. The attainment of this state of mind demands detachment from materialistic reality and the absorption into realizational folds of experiences. The outcome is expected to bring about a generative frame of mind with positive layers of the following features (Singh, 2014):

The meditative mind having full concentration on titbits of the 'present'

The elderly individual is helped to become mindful of the present by encouraging him/her to observe momentary titbits, thereby noticing a shift in the state of his/her own awareness, concentration, and distraction (Kabat-Zinn, 2013). He/she engages in a meditative process whereby subtle changes in psychological functioning are 'sensed' by the self-system. This is done in a non-judgemental and non-striving manner, with genuine acceptance of the self without any associated expectations. It prompts the individual to remain unattached to the outcome(s) or achievement(s). The individual is thus expected to have an increased level of patience and consequently learns to listen to and trust his/her own being. He/she remains open to different instances and lets go of events to forgive himself/herself and others. There is an underlying sense of empathy, generosity, and gratitude for the 'givens' of life. The self of the detached elderly person embodies benevolence, compassion, and cherishes the present moment to bring about a merging of forgiveness with unconditional love. This becomes a virtue of the wise elderly person.

Withdrawal: Liberation from habits

The emotionally mature and detached elderly individual withdraws himself/herself from the fringes of different habits and thereby becomes 'free' as far as emotionality is concerned. He/she becomes liberated from mundane expectations of daily living from both himself/herself as well as other acquaintances and accepts life as it is. The senior person appears to enjoy each and every moment in his/her life and acknowledges the very fact that he/she is fortunate enough for having lived life for so many years. There is a gradual awakening of his/her consciousness which is by itself graceful. It opens the elderly person to be accommodative and flexible to the members of younger generations.

Silence: Liberation from expectations and fantasy

Silence enables the elderly individual's active mind to gradually move towards a non-active state in the form of transcendence. This helps him/her to be peaceful, calm, and quiet, to keep at bay the sharp splashes of the material world, and to reach to the fringes of fulfilment and well-being. It is to be noted that thoughts and the tendency to follow the senses outwards, towards sense objects, are the impediments to seeing the bright inner light. It is only when the 'emotional' fog disappears that vision becomes clearer. In fact, it is only when the lake is wave-free that its bottom can be seen. Making the mind quiet is the route to reach its deeper base, the inner world of *pure consciousness* that defines the grace of an awakening state. Anything that stops thought for a while, like watching a beautiful painting or listening to a wonderful piece of music, gives us glimpses of the quiet inner world. In this relaxed state, left without demanding thoughts and senses, the mind dives deeper in silence to touch the ultimate bliss in consciousness. Such 'inner silence' is just not the absence of worldly sound; instead, it is a means of connecting the self with the divine – the ultimate reality or one's own true self, one's own divine nature (Palmquist, 2006). The being becomes a witness of the divine love which is in abundance. In silence there is power, life, and light – the basic elements of the positive frame of mind. This helps the senior individual to experience a fuller, greater consciousness and awareness to finally result in a spiritual awakening that robs the sorrows of outer life. The result is increased emotional maturity of the system, leading to improved resilience and wisdom-rimmed experiential processes.

Solitude: Liberation from attachment and dependence on sufficiency

The senior detached self enjoys the bliss of solitude, being liberated from the strings of attachment. He/she consequently becomes emotionally self-sufficient and frees himself/herself from frustrations of unfulfilled expectations and desires. The materialistic needs of the individual come to a bare minimum, and instead, the person is contended with whatever that he/she has – considering them to be the grace of his/her fortitude.

Practising solitude enables the achievement of self-knowledge and, at the same time, is the result of knowledge itself. This seems to be the initial step in the total spiritualistic endeavour of a self. Silence, being of an introspective orientation, does not only blur the sharp intellectual activities of Ego, at the same time, it also tries to *silence* the emotions of oneself. The suspension of clear ego orientations then leads one to take a deep dip to its original self-layers (Zielinski and Bassuk, 2005). It is similar to the process of obtaining crystal-clear water after a pinch of limestone is used for removing the different impurities. Solitude is thus enjoyed by the emotionally mature individual. This sense of solitude, having its dimensions of physical, intellectual, and emotional nature, seems to be the only path to self-realization in search of true happiness or 'bliss' for the detached elderly individual.

Forgiveness: Freedom from anger and judgement

Such a detached elderly person is expected to liberate himself/herself from aversion and enjoy freedom from anger and judgemental notions as he/she accepts everybody unconditionally. The act of forgiveness belongs to the divine (Dooling, 1987). In other words, for a person to forgive, there is a distinct transcendent experience where the individual makes an intentional effort to forgive. When individuals have a personal 'turnabout' and begin to forgive others, rather than holding on to resentful emotions, they create stronger interpersonal relationships (Fincham, 2000; Fincham and Beach, 2002; McCullough et al., 1997). In order to effectively forgive others, people must at the outset be able to forgive themselves (Wright, 2000). Therefore, if we are paralysed by our past actions because of the fear of failure, we cannot lead. Failure must be forgiven and learned from, and there is no one harder to forgive than oneself. Forgiveness of the self is defined as a willingness to abandon self-blame and guilt following one's transgressions while cultivating benevolence and compassion towards oneself (Ingersoll-Dayton and Krause, 2005). The ability of the individual to forgive oneself eliminates feelings of anger, hurt, shame, and guilt, and releases emotional burdens that have created the incapacity to love others. This ability to forgive ourselves leads us towards freedom. Forgiveness is about freedom, the freedom to 'hold on' and 'let go' at will (Binau, 2007).

Humility: Liberation from pride

Inculcating the virtue of humility helps the elderly individual to bask in the glory of healthy narcissism and thereby gets himself/herself liberated from the 'strings' of pride, vanity, and entitlement. This helps him/her to feel contented with life in all spheres. The material splendour of achievements mellows and the person instead feels humble for all that has been reaped across the lifetime. He/she develops a generative outlook towards everybody and becomes a 'giver' in life by embracing the 'universal mother' role irrespective of sex. The person becomes a real contributor to society at large owing to his/her mothering role.

Life review: Stepping into complete emotional freedom

Life review helps the elderly individual to obtain realizations about time and past events through storytelling leading to alterations in his/her sense of place. He/she naturally gets a forum for personal introspection to assess, understand, and change health-related behaviours (Banks-Wallace, 2002; Hodge, Pasqua, Marquez, and Geishirt-Cantrell, 2002). It helps elderly individuals to look at life events in a non-judgemental and mindful manner. The senior person unknowingly frees themself from the tangentiality of emotions associated with the said events and consequently engages in the process of detachment. This is because he/she gradually surrenders to the needs of control by gracefully accepting the lived experiences. This releases the pain associated with it, if any, and detoxifying them and facilitating a powerful transformation. Life review helps the individual to become one with himself/herself which furthers his/her ability to become one with the universe at large. As such, the elderly individual becomes their own best friend and realizes that he/she is a child of the universe, as much as other elements like stars and trees. He/she feels protected and supported amidst the canopy of the universe, enjoying blissful experiences and ultimate peace.

The elderly individual thereby deserves to be mindfully present in the momentary basis to become the *spiritual elder* and *sage* in this regard. Wisdom and calm judgement are then manifested by the individual. The spiritual elder becomes a sage in the role of the elder in the context of family, community, and society at large. It is also to be noted that the process of *becoming* a sage involves the capacity to *bring into being in any moment* depending on the demands of the situation. It essentiates the ability to be intensely present along with simultaneously transcending purely personal perspectives on the part of the individual. This involves the stages of *sage-in-training*, *actualized sage*, and *transcendent sage* (Atchley, 2009). Thus, on the placard of the detached aged, would be written:

May we all grow in the beauty, peace, and grace of awakening.

Conclusion

Detachment is a form of wisdom-content. The enjoyment of life at a point of advanced age starts receding in number and content. The end section of life, being fulfilled, contended, or dissatisfied and frustrated, loses the vigour of sensorial pleasures of various kinds. It is a phase of life-reminiscence, the evaluation of rights and wrongs we have done, a phase of giving, generativeness, rather than receiving from others. The feelings of having enough, spending a pleasurable length of time with so many people as associates, and receiving so many gifts from life can mean that elderly people reach a stage of realization. To be engulfed into this and be prepared for transcendental orientation, emotional detachment from worldly affairs, or withdrawing mental energy from concrete matters to the abstraction or illusion of transcendence – the detached mind seems to be the wisdom-borne asset of our mind. It involves transcending at the *intrapersonal level* of the personal self, resulting in the expanded, transcendent concept of the self – the less distorted self-concept and less self-centred motives for action. Transcendence at the *interpersonal level* helps in the development of capacities of empathy, understanding, and compassion, as well as other virtues. Wisdom involves the integration of different types of perspectives, namely, affective/emotional, cognitive, and reflective or contemplative in nature (Ardert, 2003). Detachment is no frustration, no anger, no pain, and no reaction but the absorption of knowledge from the experientialities of life. It is no withdrawal from life; it is the submergence into the depth of life. Hence, detachment should be the main theme of the elderly, the practice mode – the belief pattern of the experienced self. Life at its end will shine with a different glow of surrendered acceptance.

The next section of the book will focus on certain strategies of intervention-orientations to reinforce positivity in ageing.

References

Adams, K.B., Leibbrandt, S., & Moon, H. (2010). A critical review of the literature on social and leisure activity and wellbeing in later life. *Ageing and Society*, *31*(4), 683–712.

Agahi, N., Ahacic, K., & Parker, M.G. (2006). Continuity of leisure participation from middle age to old age. *The Journals of Gerontology. Series B, Psychological Sciences and Social Sciences*, *61*(6), 340–346.

Agahi, N., & Parker, M.G. (2008). Leisure activities and mortality: Does gender matter? *Journal of Aging and Health*, *20*(7), 855–871.

Andrew, M.K., & Rockwood, K. (2010). Social vulnerability predicts cognitive decline in a prospective cohort of older Canadians. *Alzheimer's and Dementia: the Journal of the Alzheimer's Association*, *6*(4), 319–325.

Ardert, M. (2003). Empirical assessment of a three-dimensional wisdom scale. *Research on Aging*, *25*(3), 275–324.

Atchley, R.C. (1989). A continuity theory of normal aging. *Gerontologist*, *29*(2), 183–190.

Atchley, R.C. (2009). *Spirituality and aging*. Baltimore: Johns Hopkins University Press.

Balboa-Castillo, T., León-Muñoz, L.M., Graciani, A., Rodríguez-Artalejo, F., & Guallar-Castillón, P. (2011). Longitudinal association of physical activity and sedentary behavior during leisure time with health-related quality of life in community-dwelling older adults. *Health and Quality of Life; Outcomes*, *9*(47), 1–10.

Banks-Wallace, J. (2002). Talk that talk: Storytelling and analysis rooted in African American oral tradition. *Qualitative Health Research*, *12*(3), 410–426.

Bassuk, S., Glass, T., & Berkman, F. (1999). Social disengagement and incident cognitive decline in community-dwelling elderly persons. *Annals of Internal Medicine*, *131*(3), 165–173.

Binau, B.A. (2007). 'Holding On' and 'letting go': The dynamics of forgiveness. *Word and World*, *27*(1), 23–31.

Bowling, A. (2005). *Ageing well: Quality of life in old age*. Maidenhead: Open University Press.

Chiao, C., Weng, L.J., & Botticello, A.L. (2011). Social participation reduces depressive symptoms among older adults: An 18-year longitudinal analysis in Taiwan. *BMC Public Health*, *11*, 292, 119.

Coles, R. (1990). *The spiritual life of children*. Boston: Houghton Mifflin.

Crandall, R.C. (1980). *Gerontology: A behavioral science approach*. Reading, MA: Addison-Wesley Publishing Company.

Dooling, D.M. (1987). Forgiveness belongs to the divine. 'This word forgiveness.' *Parabola*, *12*(3), 6–9.

Fincham, F.D. (2000). The kiss of the porcupines: From attributing responsibility to forgiving. *Personal Relationships*, *7*(1), 1–23.

Fincham, F.D., & Beach, S.R.H. (2002). Forgiveness in marriage: Implications for psychological aggression and constructive communication. *Personal Relationships*, *9*(3), 239–251.

Gutmann, A. (1987). *Democratic education*. Princeton, NJ: Princeton University Press.

Hawkins, B., Foose, A.K., & Binkley, A.L. (2004). Contribution of leisure to the life satisfaction of older adults in Australia and the United States. *World Leisure Journal*, *46*(2), 4–12.

Hodge, F.S., Pasqua, A., Marquez, C.A., & Geishirt-Cantrell, B. (2002).Utilizing traditional storytelling to promote wellness in American Indian communities. *Journal of Transcultural Nursing*, *13*(1), 6–11.

Ingersoll-Dayton, B., & Krause, N. (2005). Self-forgiveness: A component of mental health in later life. *Research on Aging*, *27*(3), 267–289.

James, B.D., Boyle, P.A., Buchman, A.S., & Bennett, D.A. (2011). Relation of late-life social activity with incident disability among community-dwelling older adults. *The Journals of Gerontology. Series A, Biological Sciences and Medical Sciences*, *66*(4), 467–473.

James, B.D., Wilson, R.S., Barnes, L.L., & Bennett, D.A. (2011). Late-life social activity and cognitive decline in old age. *Journal of the International Neuropsychological Society*, *17*(6), 998–1005.

Jang, Y., & Chiriboga, D.A. (2011). Social activity and depressive symptoms in Korean American older adults: The conditioning role of acculturation. *Journal of Aging and Health*, *23*(5), 767–781.

Jenkins, A. (2011). Participation in learning and wellbeing among older adults. *International Journal of Lifelong Education*, *30*(3), 403–420.

Kabat-Zinn, J. (2013). *Full catastrophe living, revisited edition: How to cope with stress, pain and illness using mindfulness meditation*. New York: Bantam Press Books.

Lund, R., Nilsson, C.J., & Avlund, K. (2010). Can the higher risk of disability onset among older people who live alone be alleviated by strong social relations? A longitudinal study of non-disabled men and women. *Age and Ageing*, *39*(3), 319–326.

Maddox, G.I. (1965). Fact and artifact: Evidence bearing on the disengagement theory. *Human Development*, *8*, 117–130.

Maddox, G.I., & Eisdorfer, C. (1962). Some correlates of activity and morale among the elderly. *Social Forces*, *40*(3), 254–260.

Maitland, S. (2009). *A book of silence: A journey in search of the pleasures and powers of silence*. London: Granta Publications.

McCullough, M.E., Worthington, E.L., Jr., & Rachal, K.C. (1997). Interpersonal forgiving in close relationships. *Journal of Personality and Social Psychology*, *73*(2), 321–336.

Mendes de Leon, C.F., Glass, T.A., & Berkman, L.F. (2003). Social engagement and disability in a community population of older adults: The New Haven EPESE. *American Journal of Epidemiology*, *157*(7), 633–642.

Nimrod, G. (2007). Retirees' leisure: Activities, benefits and their contribution to life satisfaction. *Leisure Studies*, *26*(1), 65–80.

Palmquist, S. (2006). Ontology and the wonder of silence. *Journal of Wisdom and Philosophy*, *6*, 67–76.

Radhakrishnan, S. (2010). *The Bhagwadgita*. Uttar Pradesh: HarperCollins Publishers.

Reed, P. (1991). Toward a theory of self-transcendence: Deductive reformulation using developmental theories. *Advances in Nursing Science*, *13*(4), 64–77.

Rusnak, K.J. (2006). *The world of the dying*. Retrieved from www.thebrickwall2.com/twotd.htm

Saito, M., Kondo, N., Kondo, K., Ojima, T., & Hirai, H. (2012). Gender differences on the impacts of social exclusion on mortality among older Japanese: AGES cohort study. *Social Science and Medicine*, *75*(5), 940–945.

Silverstein, M., & Parker, M.G. (2002). Leisure activities and quality of life among the oldest old in Sweden. *Research on Aging*, *24*(5), 528–547.

Simone, P.M., & Haas, A.L. (2013). Frailty, leisure activity and functional status in older adults: Relationship with subjective well being. *Clinical Gerontologist*, *36*(4), 275–293.

Singer, W. (2000). Response synchronization: A universal coding strategy for the definition of relations. In M.S. Gazzaniga (Ed.), *The new cognitive neurosciences* (2nd ed., pp. 325–338). Cambridge, MA: MIT Press.

Singh, K.D. (2014). *The grace in ageing: Awaken as you grow older*. Boston: Wisdom Publications.

Steptoe, A., Shankar, A., Demakakos, P., & Wardle, J. (2013). Social isolation, loneliness and all-cause mortality in older men and women. *Proceedings of the National Academy of Sciences of the United States of America*, *110*(15), 5797–5801.

Thanakwang, K., & Isaramalai, S.A. (2013). Productive engagement in older adults: A concept analysis. *Nursing and Health Sciences*, *15*(1), 124–130.

Tornstam, L. (1994). Gerotranscendence: A theoretical and empirical exploration. In L.E. Thomas & S.A. Eisenhandler (Eds.), *Ageing and the religious dimension*. (pp. 203–225) Westport, CT: Auburn House.

Tornstam, L. (1997). Gero-transcendence: The contemplative dimension of aging. *Journal of Ageing Studies*, *11*(2), 143–154.

Tornstam, L. (1999a). Late life transcendence: A new developmental perspective on ageing. In L.E. Thomas & S.A. Eisendandler (Eds.), *Religion, belief and spirituality in late life* (pp. 178–202). New York: Springer.

Tornstam, L. (1999b). Gero-transcendence – A theory about maturing into old age. *Journal of Ageing and Identity*, *1*, 37–50.

Wright, W.C. (2000). *Leadership and forgiveness: An extract from 'Relational Leadership.'* Paternoster Press.

Zielinski, S., & Bassuk, D. (Eds.) (2005). *Psychology and silence*. Wallingford, PA: Pendle Hill Publications.

Part II

INTERVENTION-ORIENTATION

Ways to initiate positivity in ageing

9

THE REFLECTIVE MIND OF THE DYING PERSON IN OLD AGE

Death is an integral part of life. From times immemorial, nature has used dying and death as an essential constituent of its different compositions. It is both construction and destruction ingrained in living and dying which run parallel to each other as seamless processes. The purpose of this continual process is regarded as positive in the food chain of organisms. From a biological perspective, all living things have a positive purpose. Living forms use dying and death in cellular processes to enhance their life by being part of self-building and self-designing endeavours and in reinforcing other life functions (Allan, 2014; Greenberg, 1996. Dhabar, 2009). The modern technology-driven affluent world of today results in a major proportion of deaths being the outcome of chronic illnesses, for which dying appears to take time for many individuals. Modern medical science and technology also ensure most individuals know about any serious life-threatening or life-limiting ailment before they are symptomatic (Allan, 2014). As such, dying is multi-faceted in nature. It usually takes time and is not restricted to the last few minutes of a person's life. Instead, the experience of dying may be prolonged due to serious and advanced diseases, bringing forth re-orientation and alterations in a person's cognitive, affective, and conative platter. Besides, the imminence of an individual's death may arise from experiences of execution, death camps, suicide, or other reasons. Ageing and dying may also get blurred into one's experience of other contexts. Dying is thus a *process* and not an *event per se* (Allan, 2014). The present chapter probes into the psychological nuances and 'inner topography' of the dying process of individuals associated with prolonged ailment(s) to have a glimpse of the basic purpose and meaning in the life of such individuals and to understand the same from the positivistic perspective. This has been done on the basis of a literature review obtained in the context of individuals having near-death experiences (N.D.E.) since individuals in the dying process are normally non-vocal about their own experiences.

The challenge(s) of understanding the life stories of individuals help to shape the dying experience of individuals. Dying always seems to have a purpose that is surprisingly positive in the sense that it is commonly life-affirming, life-building, and life-enhancing as specified earlier. The road to death tends to erode habit, pretence, preconceptions, and even fear in one's usual character to reveal deeper and novel experiences in personal direction, positive purpose, and social intimacy. It is also to be noted that the unique blend of culture, family history, religious tradition, personality, and physical and spiritual characteristics appear to mould people in who they are in life as well as who they will be in death. The one who is dying must lead the way (Holder and Aldredge-Clanton, 2014).

Dying as a process of transition

Dying essentially involves a transformation of the perception of individuals. All egoism and ego-centred-perception along with ego-based needs now appear to fade into the background. Another world condition of consciousness, sensitivity, and hence another way of experiencing being, relationships, connectedness, and dignity comes to the forefront with the awareness of the notion that one's life is numbered (Monika, 2015). Grof and Grof (1984) have termed this '*Ich-Tod*,' meaning the death of the ego, which they claim to precede death. It is often observed among individuals suffering from chronic illnesses of various kinds and having the realization that their days are limited. This is usually associated with the death of all ego-centred processes in the form of communication, needs, experiences, and personality. It is then that the dying person becomes immersed in a particular sphere and in perceptions of an entirely different primordial state of being, which is non-dualistic in nature as reflected through literature related to individuals with N.D.E. (Rohr, 2009). Dying seems to cross a critical, invisible threshold in consciousness which has been reported differently by individuals experiencing N.D.E. (Sanders, 2007; Wills-Brandon, 2000, p. 278). In accordance with the *chakra system* of a human being, the soul is assumed to withdraw from the base upwards. The *Muladhara chakra*, the root plexus, is initially involved which leads to the dissolution of the earth element. This is followed by the *Svadhishthana chakra*, the sacral plexus, where the water element of the body resides. The earth element is believed to be converted to the water element. The body of the being gradually becomes cold. The *Nabhi chakra*, in the region of the solar plexus, above the naval, gets stimulated henceforth and the water element is converted into the fire element. The *Anahata, Hridaya chakra*, the heart plexus, becomes functional where the fire element gets converted into the air element, mixing with the breath of the heart region. This may be manifested by the trembling of the entire body. This is followed by the *Vishuddhi chakra*, the throat plexus becomes operative as air is withdrawn by this chakra to be transformed to ether. The lower portion of the physique is now dead and the *pancha bhutas* (five elements) are dissolved (Patel, 2020). It is after this crossing of the threshold that individuals pass into mystery. The *Brahmtattva* found that the individual soul gets withdrawn and merges back into the *Virat* principle. Yet, immediately before someone reaches that sphere, an anteroom appears to exist. Here, the dying not only hear certain phrases and expressions, but may also engage in symbolic languages (Sanders, 2007; Wooten-Green and Champlin, 2001; Anderson, 2002; Kanzer, 1955). They may help the dying person express their need to make everything fine with a particular individual, a specific situation, or the higher power. These inner experiences hold a profound beauty for the dying, being 'sacred' in nature. Such experiences amount to more than a delirious state. Even if nothing symbolic appears to the dying, they often experience a barely describable presence and intensity. Caregivers can only 'sense,' yet cannot 'know' such experiences. The use of such language helps the dying individual to embrace a 'peaceful death.' Crossing the threshold or going through the transformation of perception occurs from the ego to 'being' and from self-power to connectedness to have the experience of the absolute (Monika, 2015). This transition and gradual transformation of perception appear to be the primary spiritual and emotional processes in dying (Renz, 2000/2008, 2003/2010, 2011/2015; Renz, Schuett Mao, Bueche, Cerny, and Strasser, 2013; Renz et al., 2015). The dying person assumes the role of a spiritual companion – not a leader. A trip does not have to be made alone; the dying person is not responsible for the outcome, as they do not have any control over the timing (Holder and Aldredge-Clanton, 2014).

Transition through primordial fear

Dying persons necessarily need to go through primordial fear, it being a threshold-specific emotion, being an essential aspect of the transition (Kuhl, 2002; Lommel, 2010; Fenwick and Brayne, 2011). The dying individual needs to pass through this emotional 'avalanche.' Many individuals are gripped by the threshold fear, which is defined by death anxiety. Such fears are suffered by the infantile self within all of us. Feelings of being lost, forlorn, and forsaken are self-evident in dying (Renz, 2011/2015). There are often atmospheric experiences related to the process of dying in the form of passing into darkness and the unnamed. Feelings of being overwhelmed and being threatened are common. Individuals are not able to understand themselves and the phenomenon *per se*. This fear comes to the forefront as an invisible experience of the numinous. Numinous connotes to anything which is immeasurably large, boundless, and colossal in qualitative nature, being amorphous, timeless, and thus, incomprehensible. The egoistic 'I' then dies and gets merged into 'Thou' (Monika, 2015; Drewermann, 1987). The ego feels less important, being diminutive and has a sense of being utterly lost. The experience of the numinous Other constitutes the 'threshold experience' of approaching death, which has archetypal origins (Turner, 1969;

Neumann, 1983). The dissolving ego encounters the incalculable One, which may be physically understood as the global whole, of the non-ego, or the world of vibrations, atmosphere, and sounds (energy reservoir).

It becomes important to remind this 'child-self' of the dying person of the presence of a greater refuge in the form of nature, which may be conveyed through silent presence, music, or signs and rituals representing protection (Renz, 2008). Many individuals engage in death bed visions (D.B.V.), mostly of departed loved members, often radiating or being surrounded by an intense light (Sanders, 2007). Such visions are believed to ease the person's transition to the other side, being accompanied by a reduced fear of death and greater inner peace, amidst the wrap of love, which gets blurred into cosmic union (Kubler-Ross, 1991; Wills-Brandon, 2006; Long and Long, 2006). Many individuals are found to experience 'the stare' on the ceiling, usually where their eyes seem to be following a moving object. They may be at a loss of words to express their experience adequately (Kessler, 2000; Sharp and Terbay, 1997). The few who can verbalize their experience are used to report the experience as 'beautiful' (Barrett, 1926). Such death bed visions may be understood at the individual level (Wooten-Green and Champlin, 2001; Atwater, 2005). They may replace the patient having excruciating pain with radiant joy and a sense of tranquillity (Osis and Haraldsson, 1977; Rusnak, 2006). Thus, death may be viewed as a profound process of personal and spiritual discovery in the bon voyage of each individual soul towards enlightenment (Wills-Brandon, 2000).

As such, the dying person appears to enjoy being a witness of 'spiritual scenery.' The raw materials are home and family, culture, religion, heritage, and the experiences and traditions that make his/her life distinctive. No one can presume to know what will refresh the spirit of the weary sojourners. However, it is spiritual scenery of one kind or another which fills a universal need as it lifts beings to the source of strength that can help them through their most difficult times (Holder and Aldredge-Clanton, 2014). Different ways of finding spiritual scenery include life review (through journaling, artistry, ethical wills, fulfilling one's last wishes etc.), reunions and gatherings, rituals (personal rituals, centring prayers, simple rituals), and religious ceremonies.

Struggle with death

Some individuals are observed engaging in a spiritual struggle with their own selves, where they engage in a means of mediation between heaven and earth (Turner, 1969; Rohr, 2011). The struggle involves the discerning of spirits and thereby discernment between Light and Darkness in the form of *Ignatius Loyola*, meaning 'motions of the soul' (Renz, 2011/2015). It is often reported as a triumph amidst capitulation and beyond. The dying individual feels a sort of connectedness with the creator of the universe.

Individuals have to struggle through and endure the whole process to finally attain ultimate inner peace by the coming of the angels (Riedel, 1989). The angels represent the threshold or boundary condition itself, as a bridge across and messenger between two worlds. As such, this struggle is different from the fear of death in the fact that the former is a spiritual endeavour in contrast to an affective process because of some form of fixation at earlier stages. The experience of struggle and hence resistance helps dying individuals maintain the current quality of their relationships as givers and receivers of care and love from others. It governs both dying people and their caregivers to jointly try to combat the ordeal and affirm their relationships, and then to depart when the time is right by reinforcing their long alliance and bonds as significant others. The experience of waiting for some dying individuals also colours their daily experience of reality and their existing relationships (Allan, 2014).

Transition from rebellion to acceptance

Dying involves a transition into an all-encompassing acceptance, where the individual embraces all negations and affirmations. The fundamental decision to be 'free' remains anonymous (Rahner, 1982; Allan, 2014). Many terminally ill or chronically ailing individuals appear at the outset to emotionally bargain for the days and hours that are left for him/her with the Almighty, as their ego seems to perceive the impending transition as similar to a gathering storm. The ego seems to bide some time for the change to be accepted. The dying individual appears to look back, then again forward to the threshold, hesitate, and allow themselves to be lured by the possibilities of prolonging life and of indulging in ego-centred pleasures to some extent. In this to-and-fro journey of the ego, it gradually gets worn out and ceases asking the same questions about destiny and meaning. Thus, during dying, the person either surrenders or fights and defends himself/herself against the loss of love objects (libidinal) or need-fulfilling objects (narcissistic). Many times, the dying person engages in mourning the loss of the external world and the loss of one's own body. During their cathexis, their transference to caregivers and their inner world of fantasy are relatively increased. This gradually increases the level of fantasies on the part of dying individuals. It is often manifested at the end of the dying process in the difficulty of discriminating between fantasy and real communication with the external world (Joffe and Sandler, 1965). The dying person may engage in either pure depression or grief or an admixture and transition of these, which depends on the ability to retain communication with inner objects (Dorpat, 1977; Hagglund, 2006). The dying person experiences narcissistic trauma when he/she comes to terms with the loss of their own body and all external objects including self-objects. This is difficult to grasp as a reality. Freud (1915) opined that our unconscious does not believe in its own death; instead, it behaves as if it were immortal.

The ego comes to the aid here by initially adopting defensive strategies against the threat of death. However, with a gradual increase in awareness of the weakening of the body and feeling the tormenting physical pain, the dying person fails to use denial as a defence mechanism and instead succumbs to an acceptance of the same (Hägglund, 1978). Fear of death may overwhelm the dying person in the form of separation anxiety or a fear of annihilation (Freud, 1925[1926]; Waelder, 1960). Winnicott (1974) conceives fear of death as a childhood fear of total annihilation that threatens the self-system of the individual. When an individual is ailing and on the threshold of death, fear of death at the regressive level can be inferred in the form of fear of losing contact with one's own fantasies, and second, as a fear of losing the possibility of communicating them to other person or inner object. The loss of organized fantasies, being the last link to life, has the meaning of an un-integrated state, symbolizing total annihilation, utmost terror, and endless loneliness. In fact, dying is an experience of aloneness which has an appeal of urgency, acuteness, and devouring nature; it affects the self-system. People with terminal illnesses often experience such disenfranchising moments, owing to severe estrangement, withdrawal, or separation from the world.

The narcissistic conflict of the dying person between the weak and ailing body and the wished-for, ideal state needs to be solved for the person to mourn the weakening, dying body (Hägglund, 1978). It may be overcome by a fantasy of a religious orientation in the form of a fantasy of heaven or returning to flawless nature. The person feels that he/she has, at last, found the way to the universe, an idealized parent, or back to the own idealized self. Survival using one's creativity, through one's children, one's achievements, and the mental image imprinted in the minds of other people appear to be yet another fantasy of the dying individual. It is with this splitting of the self of the dying individual that the loss of one's own body is mourned and de-cathected as the cathexis gets shifted to the fantasy world (Pollock, 1978). This has often been narrated by the dying individual as a peaceful experience (Hägglund, 1978).

It is then that the ego ceases to feel the urge to have different needs and lets it fall if the person surrenders. It is then that the ego mysteriously enters the transition into acceptance. Negative feelings of the person towards himself appears to be gradually dissolved (Rosenthal, 1957). The horizons of the outer world gradually begin to recede, initially at the social level and then in totality. The inner self and its companions naturally begin to sound louder. Hence, the acceptance of the transition can never be deliberately chosen by the self but is given to individuals by life. The acceptance is usually imperceptibly 'breathed' by the individual, always silently (Rohr, 2011; Nouwen, 1998). This enables the individual to engage in the ultimate union with the cosmos. Existentially, death acceptance requires the ailing individual to move beyond self-actualization to self-transcendence as a journey beyond oneself (Tomer, Eliason, and Wong, 2008, Wong, 2008).

It is also to be noted that acceptance involves a spiritual agreement and a vibrational, musical harmony of understanding and being understood. It encompasses all that has been. It means accepting and acknowledging one's own self, existence, illnesses, and limitations of one's own self and the like. This acceptance also engages in acceptance to creation, the creator, and creature, to death and also to suffering since it is real. The acceptance liberates the soul in life as in dying, to experience grace and power, sensuousness, and gratitude for having lived life all these years. It frees life from waiting and entrapment to a spiritual victory in life as in dying (Solle, 1993). The person has now gone beyond pain, tension, and other bodily symptoms.

Reflections of the dying person

It has been realized that suffering, fear, isolation, resistance, or the sadness and anger that dying individuals experience is not one-dimensional in nature. Within even these difficult experiences, humour, positive changes, new and enhanced transitions in relationships, and the birth of other feelings, perceptions or perspectives are observed (Allan, 2014). These journeys make age-worn travellers mould their psyche through reflection, comparison, and contrasts. Hence, the inner life of dying people is enriched with stories, having the major focus of embracing life, particularly in the affirmation and enhancement of personal values and intimacy. Depending on the different circumstances, they become prepared to bid goodbye to their near and dear ones after getting some time to act and reconcile with them.

Dying persons waiting for their final call may also engage in personal choices about what to do with one's remaining time. Some may still be encouraged in new learning and may inculcate a new appreciation of the life that has been taken for granted. Such lessons rebuild or add to the dying individual's inner life. In fact, the review of one's life and reminiscences tend to build bridges of new understanding through realizations. They, in turn, offer others with reflection, insights into mortality, or role modelling for end-of-life conduct and values.

Such experiences of the inner life of dying individuals are life-building in an essential aspect (Allan, 2014). It is their life review that usually offers dying individuals the depth in their understanding that the future is not merely a personal reality but a shared one. This automatically decreases fear of death, issues of vulnerability, and opens up other ideas and possibilities about personal continuity. The transformational experiences of dying people engage them to have greater depth. A new sense of distance to travel along with a new sensation of a timeframe is cultivated as a result. It provides the dying individual with an often-startling realization of the possibility of timelessness as a real, lived experience. As such, paradoxically, people in the transition to death are often found to report feeling better, stronger, happier, more able, and confident than before. They often become surprised by what they had 'become' in the last phase of their lives.

It may help provide the dying individual with spiritual companionship as much as is feasible (Holder and Aldredge-Clanton, 2014; Rohr, 2009). This is because death calls forth the most intense human emotions, both for the dying person and for the spiritual companion. The weary travellers are often compelled to look out for each and every possible spiritual tool that they have collected throughout their life so as to seek help from the higher power when needed. They also concentrate on tapping into every coping mechanism and source of strength than they have ever used before. The spiritual crisis presented by death for both the one who is dying and the companion appears to take some time before consolidation. The acutely painful reality of admitting the unavoidability of death brings forth challenges to the dying person by providing them with an unparalleled opportunity in expanding their spiritual awareness and resources. This helps them constantly seek spiritual adventures and awakenings. Their journey through the rough spiritual terrain needs to accompany some important itineraries, some of which may include those of a sense of wholeness, belongingness, gratitude, humility, reverence, perspective, trust, devotion, and release (letting go). The spiritual companion of the dying person in the form of a caregiver is desirable to be a good 'listener' who engages in acceptance, candour, patience, and a bit of advocacy and humour, and has the courage to face the bad news of the loved one's demise. The companion needs to help the dying individual cross the bridge by coming close and starting the spiritual conversation while helping the person to relax. Comforts for the dying may be provided through touch, sight, sound, taste, and smell. Comfort from a distance may also be applicable in the form of regular telephone calls, letters and encouraging cards, assurance of one's thoughts, and sending care packages to please the different sense modalities of the weary traveller.

Parting ways for the dying person

Parting ways may be accomplished for the dying individual by providing permission to 'go' and reassure him/her that the person will be fine. During the end of one's life, many individuals seem to long for experiencing reconciliation with others as well as their higher power. If that means offering a chance to repent, one needs to listen earnestly and not rush to pardon too quickly. There is healing in earnest repentance. Holy silence may be practised for there will probably be a space of time – hours, days, or weeks – when one's dying loved one is (or appears to be) unresponsive. Spiritual companionship continues in that holy silence. Some theorists think that the dying person turns inward and thereby becomes non-vocal in nature by expending the last little flicker of energy on working with his or her own soul. How good to hold the hand of one who is engaged in that hard work. This is in sync with the Buddhist tradition where the spiritual companion experiences unity with the dying person by rhythmic breathing in the same tune as the ailing individual when they can no longer engage in verbal exchanges. This period of silence may be a time for the companion to reflect on one's own spiritual journey and how he/she has changed and grown from this experience. It may be a time for sitting still, observing oneself, and resting in peace.

Saying or bidding goodbye to the dying person is the hardest part. It is necessary to feel the need for 'closure,' and to progress on to another day. Whether the person who is dying is still interacting or lies in a silent inner world, it is desirable to continue to say the things genuinely one needs to say such as the love for the person, how they will be missed, and how they have been blessed to have the dying person in their life. At the end, the spiritual companion can commit the loved one to their forward journey safely to a destination beyond human understanding. The companion watches on as the real, living person gradually disappears and fades away from physical view. In the end, it is a solitary crossing for the dying person. The spiritual companion turns back to life again, it being a changed one to engage in … A loved one cannot be replaced by anyone else. One goes on, but now carries with him/her own self the memory of one's unique trip and his/her beloved fellow traveller.

This returning to 'normal' life is long and slow. A time almost inevitably comes when the pain of loss diminishes, and life seems to hold energy and hope again. This is not a sign that the one who has died is losing his or her place in one's heart and mind. It is a sign that the spiritual companion is still alive and can reinvent his/her life without that person. Awareness of this ability to go on can bring peace and a sense of renewal. It also affirms that the journey that one was engaging in until that time has ended and the person has returned home to live again with memories of the dead person as narratives or lived experiences in the form of 'stories' to mould their own life journey from then onwards.

Conclusion

The process of dying does not call for the end of life; instead, it is life-affirming in a way, building and enhancing in nature for all life forms. Such processes are active in all of us. It is high time that one needs to look deep into oneself and be intrigued by adaptive processes operant among all of us. Such life-embracing features of the inner dying self tend to make the process more bearable. The anxieties associated with one's impending end therein dissolve to yield a sense of deeper tranquillity. The initial phase of darkness that necessarily accompanies a person's initial sense of the end is usually followed by an insightful reawakening towards life. This imbibes a developmental trajectory, which is experienced differently by different individuals. Hence, it is not that life does end with death, but instead, it continues after life, with death being a mystery. Life and death are two sides of the same coin, with each other forming a synergistic whole.

References

Allan, K. (2014). *The inner life of the dying person.* New York: Columbia University Press.

Anderson, C. (2002). On dying. *Journal of Hospice and Palliative Nursing, 3*(3), 180–183. Retrieved from http://nursingcenter.com/library/JournalArticle.asp?Article_ID=285733

Atwater, P.M.H. (2005). *We live forever: The real truth about death.* Virginia Beach, VA: A.R.E. Press.

Barrett, W. (1926). *Death-bed visions: The psychical experiences of the dying.* London: Psychic Press.

Dhabhar, F.S. (2009). A hassle a day may keep the pathogens away: The fight-or-flight stress response and the augmentation of immune function. *Integrative and Comparative Biology, 49*(3), 215–236.

Dorpat, T.L. (1977). Depressive affect. *Psychoanalytic Study of the Child, 32*, 3–27.

Drewermann, E. (1987). *Das Markusevangelium: Bilder von Erlösung* (2 vols). Olten: Walter Verlag.

Fenwick, P., & Brayne, S. (2011). End-of-life experiences: Reaching out for compassion, communication, and connection-meaning of deathbed visions and coincidences. *American Journal of Hospice and Palliative Care, 28*(1), 7–15.

Freud, S. (1915). Thoughts for the times of war and death. Part II: Our attitude towards death. *S.E., 14*, 289–300.

Freud, S. ([1925]1926). Inhibitions, symptoms and anxiety. *S.E., 20*, 87–172.

Greenberg, J.T. (1996). Programmed cell death: A way of life for plants. *Proceedings of the National Academy of Sciences for the UnitedStates of America, 93*(22), 12094–12097.

Grof, S., & Grof, C. (1984). *Jenseits Des Todes.* Stuttgart: Kösel.

Hägglund, T.B. (1978). *Dying: A psychoanalytical study with special reference to individual creativity and defensive organization.* New York: International Universities Press.

Holder, J.S., & Aldredge-Clanton, J. (2014). *Parting: A handbook for spiritual care near the end of life.* New York: University of North Carolina Press..

Joffe, W.G., & Sandler, J. (1965). Notes on pain, depression, and individuation. *Psychoanalytic Study of the Child, 20*, 394–424.

Hagglund, T.-B. (2006). The final stage of the dying process. In Junkers, G. (Ed.) *Is it too late? Key papers on psychoanalysis and ageing* (pp. 131–140). Taylor & Francis, Oxon.

Kanzer, M. (1955). The communicative function of the dream. *International Journal of Psycho-Analysis, 36*(4–5), 260–266.

Kessler, D. (2000). *The needs of the dying: A guide for bringing hope, comfort, and love to life's final chapter.* New York: HarperCollins.

Kübler-Ross, E. (1991). *On life after death.* Berkeley, CA: Celestial Arts.

Kuhl, D. (2002). *What dying people want: Practical wisdom for the end of life*. Cambridge, MA: Perseus Books.

Lommel, P. van (2010). *Consciousness beyond life: The science of the near-death experience*. New York: HarperOne.

Long, J.A., & Long, J.P. (2006). *Spiritual spectrum stories: Spiritually transforming events, prayer, nearing end of life events*. Out of body Research Foundation. Retrieved from www.oberf.org/ste_prayer_nele.htm

Monika, R. (2015). *Dying: A transition*. New York: Columbia University Press.

Neumann, E. (1983). *Amor und Psyche Deutung eines Märchens: Ein Beitrag zur seelischen Entwicklung Des Weiblichen* (4th ed.). Olten: Walter.

Nouwen, H.J.M. (1998). *Die Innere Stimme der Liebe*. Freiburg: Herder.

Osis, K., & Haraldsson, E. (1977). *At the hour of death*. New York: Avon Books.

Patel, D.K. (2020). Last moments. *Speaking Tree, May*, 9, 1.

Pollock, G.H. (1978). Process and affect: Mourning and grief. *International Journal of Psycho-Analysis*, *59*(2–3), 255–276.

Rahner, K. (1982). *Praxis des Glaubens: Geistliches Lesebuch* (K. Lehmann & A. Raffelt, Eds.). Zurich: Benziger.

Renz, M. (2000/2008). *Zeugnisse Sterbender: Todesnähe als Wandlung und letzte Reifung* (revised 4th ed.). Paderborn: Junfermann.

Renz, M. (2003/2010). *Grenzerfahrung Gott: Spirituelle Erfahrungen in Leid und Krankheit*. Freiburg: Kreuz.

Renz, M. (2008). *Erlösung aus Prägung: Botschaft und Leben Jesu als Überwindung der menschlichen Angst-. Begehrens- und Machtstruktur*. Paderborn: Junfermann.

Renz, M. (2011/2015). *Hinübergehen: Was beim Sterben geschieht: Annäherungen an letzte Wahrheiten unseres Lebens*. Freiburg: Kreuz.

Renz, M., Schuett Mao, M., Bueche, D., Cerny, T., & Strasser, F. (2013). Dying is a transition. *American Journal of Hospice and Palliative Care*, *30*(3), 283–290.

Renz, M., Schuett Mao, M., Omlin, A., Bueche, D., Cerny, T., & Strasser, F. (2015). Spiritual experiences of transcendence in patients with advanced cancer. *American Journal of Hospice and Palliative Medicine*, *32*(2), 178–188.

Riedel, I. (1989). *Die Weise Frau in uralt-neuen Erfahrungen: Der Archetyp der alten Weisen im Märchen und seinem religionsgeschichtlichen Hintergrund*. Olten: Walter.

Rohr, R. (2009). *The naked now: Learning to see as the mystics see*. New York: Crossroad.

Rohr, R. (2011). *Falling upward: A spirituality for the two halves of life*. San Francisco: Jossey-Bass.

Rosenthal, H.R. (1957). Psychotherapy for the dying. In H.M. Ruitenbeek (Ed.), *Death: Interpretations* (pp. 87–95). New York: Dell Publishing, 1969.

Rusnak, K.J. (2006). *The world of the dying*. Retrieved from www.thebrickwall2.com/twotd.htm

Sanders, M.A. (2007). *Nearing death awareness: A guide to the language, Visions and dreams of the dying*. London: Jessica Kingsley Publishers.

Sharp, A.W., & Terbay, S.H. (1997). *Gifts: Two hospice professionals reveal messages from those passing on*. Far Hills, NJ: New Horizon Press.

Sölle, D. (1993). *Leiden*. Freiburg: Herder.

Tomer, A., Eliason, G., & Wong, P.T.P. (Eds.) (2008). *Existential and spiritual issues in death attitudes*. New York: Erlbaum.

Turner, V.W. (1969). *The ritual process: Structure and anti-structure.* London: Routledge and Kegan Paul.

Waelder, R. (1960). *Basic theory of psychoanalysis.* New York: International Universities Press.

Wills-Brandon, C. (2000). *One last hug before I go: The mystery and meaning of deathbed visions.* Deerfield Beach, FL: Health Communications, Inc.

Wills-Brandon, C. (2006). Death bed visions. *Ontario: ParaResearchers of Ontario.* Retrieved from www.pararesearchers.org/Psychic/dbv/dbv.html

Winnicott, D.W. (1974). Fear of breakdown. *International Review of Psychoanalysis, 1*, 103–107.

Wong, P.T.P. (2008). Meaning management theory and death acceptance. In A. Tomer, G. Eliason & P.T.P. Wong (Eds.), *Existential and spiritual issues in death attitudes* (pp. 65–87). New York: Erlbaum.

Wooten-Green, R., & Champlin, J.M. (2001). *When the dying speak: How to listen to and learn from those who face death.* Chicago, IL: Loyola Press.

10

GERIATRIC INTERVENTIONS

The 'eraser' of dark emotionality in the elderly

There has been an explosion of intervention research with older adults, which continues to accelerate growth and development, and the desire to effectively address the needs of elderly people in society. The current mantra of gerontologists appears to be, 'It is good to understand a problem, but even better to show that you can do something about it' (Lawton, 1998). As such, it appears desirable to provide interventions for elderly individuals to aid their development and mental health.

Intervention studies vary in terms of who or what is the target of change amidst other parameters (Smyer and Gatz, 1986). Most commonly, intervention targets the individual to change the psychological and physical health or the social functioning of the older adult. Intervention studies also have a broader focus and are aimed at improving the quality of life of the elderly person in the long run. They highlight how to ease the disorders/ distress(es) that older adults suffer from. Geriatric interventions help treat affective problems of the elderly. Besides, issues of chemical dependency, adjustment to retirement, bereavement, and elder abuse are also dealt with through interventions of different kinds. Investigators have also been interested in examining the benefits of aerobic and anaerobic exercise on the mental and physical functioning of older adults (McAuley and Mihalko, 1998; McAuley and Rudolph, 1995). In addition, the current trend of research studies is to examine the effects of methods such as engaging in reminiscing and life review, participating in intergenerational programmes, and relocating from a long-term care setting to group living. This chapter will sketch the current psychological interventions available to elderly citizens to promote their psychological and physical profiles from a mental health perspective.

Different types of psychotherapeutic interventions for older adults

Cognitive-behavioural therapy

Cognitive-behavioural therapy (C.B.T.) seeks to change thoughts, feelings, and attention by focusing on erroneous perceptions and habitual behaviours which the individual can learn to change. It is directive and symptom-focused or disturbance-focused in nature. It has been found to be effective for certain specific disorders in the elderly such as depression, anxiety, panic attacks, agoraphobia, obsessive-compulsive, and sleep disturbances. The general approach is educational in nature, requiring the help of self-help techniques and homework. The therapist is active, and the sessions are structured and problem-centred, emphasizing the present and future rather than the past. Here the client is psycho-educated to have control over their thought processes that accompany emotional, symptomatic episodes.

Cognitive-behavioural treatment of panic, anxiety, and agoraphobia in late-life takes into consideration psycho-education, cognitive restructuring, respiratory control, relaxation training, and controlled provocation of anxiety and panic states, among others (Sanderson and Wetzler, 1995; Sanderson and McGinn, 1997).

Depression in the elderly is commonly observed in the form of 'depletion syndrome,' characterized by loss of appetite, lack of interest, hopelessness, and thoughts of death (Newman, Engel and Jensel, 1990; 1991a, 1991b). Data from some studies suggest that depressive episodes in late-life may be either a risk factor or an early symptom of Alzheimer's disease (A.D.) (Wetherell, Gatz, Johansson, and Pederson, 1999; Kokmen et al., 1991). A variety of forms of psychotherapy have been used to treat depressive disorders and depressive symptoms in older adults. These include psychodynamic psychotherapy, life review or reminiscence approaches, family therapy, psycho-educational approaches, and various cognitive-behavioural therapies. Several studies to date have compared two or more of these approaches with each other and/or to a no-treatment or placebo group (Scogin, Jamison, and Gochneaur, 1989). Modifications of cognitive-behavioural therapy are also being suggested for the treatment of depression in the chronically ill elderly (Rybarczyk et al., 1992) and post-stroke depression patients (Hibbard, Grober, Wayne, and Aletta, 1990), as well as in dementia patients (Teri and Gallagher-Thompson, 1991).

In sum, treatment studies strongly indicate that certain forms of psychosocial and pharmacological therapy, alone and in combination, can be very effective in treating geriatric depression. At the same time, much remains to be learned regarding which factors account for the efficacy of psychotherapy; the efficacy of combination therapy in initial, continuation, and maintenance phases of treatment; and the best 'match' between types of depression and types of treatment.

Interpersonal psychotherapy

Interpersonal psychotherapy is exploratory in nature and is focused on interpersonal conflict, role change, and deficits (Miller and Markowitz, 1999). It has been successfully modified for use with older adults (Frank et al., 1993). It is used to have a better understanding of distressing thoughts and feelings that may be altered through overall behavioural changes. The focus is on the present interpersonal relations of the individual so that his/her future relationship matrix can be amended (Miller and Markowitz, 1999).

The client's dependency needs and limitations owing to losses of varied kinds are addressed along with his/her lifelong psychopathologies and the existential and practical realities of advanced age. Tele-counselling services may be provided to elders who have difficulty in mobility. Realistic and modest goals are sought for by the therapist.

Short-term psychodynamic therapy

Short-term psychodynamic therapy is problem-focused and does not examine transference relationships, owing to its brevity. It is indicated for older persons with adjustment disorders, grief reactions, and the recent onset of traumatic stress disorders (Lazarus and Sadavoy, 1996). Setting a time limit of 15 sessions avoids excessive dependency. The patient is helped to re-establish a positive sense of self and proficiency. Support is also sought to resolve problems of survivor guilt and negative attitudes towards the self and ageing. Most importantly, patients can achieve insight and successfully terminate treatment without requiring long-term supportive care. Transference and counter-transference issues may surface in the therapeutic process. However, owing to its short-term nature, the scope of interpreting such issues is limited in this therapy.

Life review/reminiscence

Life review involves the recall of personal history to master one's present and future. The therapist encourages a review of the past in an effort to help the patient find meaning in the present through the partial resolution of conflict within the self or with others (Haight, 1992). It might also involve a review of memorabilia, photos, or journals. It may result in the elderly to be reunited with friends or family members or may even prompt him/her to write an autobiography. In addition to solving old problems, the patient may find an increased tolerance for conflict, a lessening of guilt and fears, enhanced creativity and a sense of giving, and acceptance of life circumstances (Butler and Lewis, 1982).

Problem-solving therapy

Problem-solving therapy is focused on change and is narrow and pragmatic in nature. It is directive and brief, usually spanning six sessions. Homework is provided at the end of therapy sessions along with pamphlets or written lists. The client is asked to prioritize his/her problems. Both the client and the therapist attempt to assess the circumstances surrounding the problem. The therapist urges the patient to formulate a feasible approach as well as triage problems with less probability of change to a lower priority. Each problem is identified along with its possible list of solutions. The pros and cons associated with each solution are identified to help the client have a greater clarity and insight into his/her problems. Pessimism and lack of motivation are addressed by taking the problem-solving approach.

Supportive psychotherapy

This type of psychotherapeutic intervention is provided generally to elderly individuals having psychotic problems like schizophrenia, schizophreniform disorders, and the like. This is usually accompanied by pharmacotherapy to enable them to have control over their symptoms.

Dementia-caregiver counselling

Dementia-caregiver counselling is mainly focused on the caregiver role. It combines elements of cognitive-behavioural and interpersonal therapy. A number of studies indicate that the caregiver burden can be reduced and nursing home admission delayed by specific interventions (Mittelman et al., 1995; Whitlatch and Zarit, 1995). With support and training, caregivers can reduce their depressive symptoms and those in their relatives with dementia as well (Teri et al., 1997; Reifler et al., 1981; Zarit et al., 1980).

Conflicts and distorted beliefs over separation-individuation or 'letting go' add to the burden of caregiving (Zarit and Whitlatcht, 1993). Individual counselling and educational support groups have been used to address such issues (Mittelman et al., 1995). Zarit and Zarit (1998) have suggested that assessment and interventions to reduce caregiver burden and improve caregiver skills entail:

1. The characterization of problems emanated directly from the patient's needs and behaviours;
2. Recognition of secondary stressors which add to the caregiver burden but are not client-based. The support available from family, friends, and formal support services are also estimated in such contexts.

A tripartite approach is followed after assessment to offer an intervention to the elderly. It comprises of providing information regarding ailments and the course of illness via counselling and psycho-education, found by specific problem-solving measures which are offered through family meetings and finally providing support at the individual and peer-group level.

Bereavement therapy

Bereavement is a major geriatric issue which is often addressed in the clinical set-up. With advanced age, fewer of the senior's friends and siblings remain. Spousal bereavement is more common among elderly women who are more likely to outlive their husbands, and they have, to a greater extent, disability, solitary living, and institutionalized living. Also, with an increased lifespan, older adults will more frequently live through the loss of an adult child. And the death of a grandchild, particularly in large families, is not entirely remote. Most elderly persons will not perceive bereavement to be a problem that merits professional attention (Shuchter and Zisook, 1993). However, bereavement late in life has been found to correlate with mortality. Bereaved older adults are also more likely to develop a major depressive episode within the year of their loss than younger people (Zisook and Shuchter, 1996). As a result, timely recognition of pathological bereavement is essential. Fatigue, anger issues in relation to the lost person, irritability, insomnia, and social isolation due to the loss are common among the bereaved spouses. Some may even have complicated grief reactions owing to ambivalent past relations with their spouses.

The client is initially offered a session to talk about feelings and coping with the loss. Feelings of self-blame or resentment towards others, associated guilt over the sense of relief at the passing away of a chronically ailing spouse, and anger at the spouse for leaving the widow alone may be some issues which need to be uncovered slowly in the therapeutic process. She may also feel bad to speak ill about the dead person. Bereavement therapy enables in helping the client to work with his/her emotions in a genuine manner.

It is often helpful to ask the client to bring in old photographs of the deceased spouse which are likely to trigger old memories along the lines of a life review system. Regarding behavioural advice, the client should seek to re-establish life's routine and social rhythm. Regular sleep, exercise, attendance of spiritual activities, volunteer organizations, family affairs, and so on should be encouraged. When tears, sleep disturbance, weight loss, and helplessness are severe, persistent, or disabling, medication is indicated. Many elderly individuals have a passive wish for death. However, intrusive thoughts associated with suicide need to be considered as an alarm signal for major depression.

Psychological treatment of late-life insomnia

Insomnia in older adults is more common, especially among women and those who are widowed, separated, or divorced, and is more troublesome than in younger people (Mellinger, Balter, and Uhlenhuth, 1985; Kupfer and Reynolds, 1997). Older adults with insomnia (O.A.W.I.) turn to sleep medication to a disproportionately higher extent, risking addiction, polypharmacy interactions, exacerbation of sleep apnoea, and multiple other side effects (Roth, Zorick, Wittig, and Roehrs, 1982). As one's age crosses the yardstick of 60 years, there is an ascending likelihood of sleep becoming lighter, more fragmented, and highly variable. On average, sleep tends to decline from 7.5 hours per 24-hour period in middle-aged samples to six hours among seniors.

Psychological treatments applied to late-life insomnia include the provision of relaxation, stimulus control (S.C.), sleep restriction (S.R.T.), and sleep compression (S.C.T.) therapies, and C.B.T., as well as sleep education or sleep hygiene.

Progressive relaxation (P.R.) is commonly used for the treatment of insomnia (Lichstein and Fischer, 1985). It requires sequential tensing and relaxation of the body's muscles when the client concentrates on the bodily sensations of tension and relaxation. *Stimulus control* may be particularly well-suited for older adults with insomnia along the lines of maintenance insomnia (Morin, Mimeault, and Gagne, 1999; Bootzin, Epstein, and Wood, 1991; Lawton, 1998). *Cognitive-behaviour therapy* is also used to alleviate insomnia-causing anxiety that arises from undue worrying and exaggerated fears related to sleep (Morin, 1993). Lichstein and Riedel (1994) opine that excessive time in bed perpetuates insomnia. This forms the basis of *S.R.T.* and *S.C.T.* therapies. Moreover, *sleep education* or *sleep hygiene* may have a particular salience for older adults with insomnia who may interpret normal, developmental sleep changes. Sleep hygiene relates to the cumulative effect of daytime activities that may impact sleep (Lichstein and Riedel, 1994). Psychological interventions for O.A.W.I. provide much relief by decreasing the time to fall asleep, increasing total time slept, and improving sleep quality. They also reduce the frequency and duration of nightly awakenings (Morin, Gaulier, Barry, and Kowatch, 1992).

Physical activity interventions in the elderly/ occupational and physical therapy

Research evidence has revealed the efficacy of physical activity interventions among the elderly to enhance both their physical and psychological function (Bokovoy and Blair, 1994; Wagner et al., 1992; McAuley and Rudolph, 1995). Physical activity reduces one's risk of coronary heart disease (Haskell, Leon, and Casperson et al., 1992), cancer (Blair et al., 1989), lowers blood pressure, and protects against non-insulin-dependent diabetes, among other benefits (Helmrick, Ragland, Leung, and Paffenbarger, 1991). It is also found to be accompanied by bringing about arrest in cognitive decline with age (Dustman, Emmerson, and Shearer, 1994), acts as a mood-facilitator by decreasing the elderly individual's level of depression (Mobily, Rubenstein, Lemka, O'Hara and Wallace, 1996), and improves the level of psychological well-being and self-efficacy in the long run (Pierce, Madden, Siegel, and Blumenthal, 1993; Phillips and Haskell, 1995; McAuley, Shaffer, and Rudolph, 1995). Occupational and physical therapy is highly recommended for elderly individuals having different forms of disability for various reasons.

Memory interventions for the elderly

This involves the spontaneous use of memory improvement techniques (Hill, Allen, and Gregory, 1990), mental imagery (Camp, 1996), memory training (Rebok, Rasmussen, and Brandt, 1997), external aids (Smith and Earles, 1996), multi-factorial training (Neely and Backman, 1995), and implicit memory (Squire, 1994) for normal older adults. On the other hand, for pathological older adults, memory interventions comprise initial interventions for cognitive disabilities in dementia (Woods, 1996; Sandman, 1993) (e.g., fading, backwards chaining, cognitive stimulation, pair-association learning), cognitive rehabilitation in the form of spaced retrieval, Montessori-based approaches (Chattin-McNichols, 1992), memory bingo (Camp and Foss, 1997), and the like.

With much evidence showing that older adults with dementia are able to learn and retain new information, the capacity is being utilized to not only put information into memory but also to solve memory deficit problems. Thus, it is of prime necessity to enter into the domain of applied gerontology quickly (Sterns and Camp, 1998).

Speech and language therapy

This therapy is beneficial for elderly individuals having some deficits, especially in the area of speech, owing to different pathological conditions like neurological ailments (e.g., cerebrovascular accident, Parkinson's disease). In addition, focus is provided on issues of communication which are jeopardized in different neurological conditions among the elderly.

Pet therapy/animal-assisted therapy for elderly individuals

The beneficial effect of animal company on people at any age is well known (Ballarini, 2003). Animal company has been found to have a healthy role in individuals having both somatic and mental disorders. This therapeutic process is reported to boost psychological, educational, and physical rehabilitation, and aims to improve the well-being of clients and improve their overall quality of life (Ballarini, 2003). The use of dogs as co-therapists, emotional mediators, and catalysts for socialization began in the 1960s by

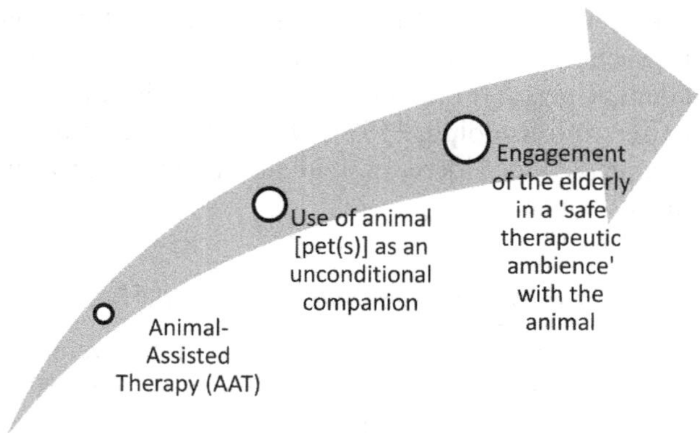

Figure 10.1 The use of animal-assisted therapy (A.A.T.) among the elderly (source: authors).

the psychiatrist Boris Levinson. The favourable role of pet therapy has been observed, particularly among the elderly (Walsh, Mertin, Verlande, and Pollard, 1995; Kanamori, Suzuki, Yamamoto, et al., 2001; Barak, Savorai, Mavashev, and Beni, 2001; Kawamura, Niiyama, and Niiyama, 2007). The frequent co-occurrence of cognitive and mood disorders and psychotic and anxiety symptoms make elderly persons especially suitable for treatments based on affective-emotional motivation and psychological stimulation (Kawamura, Niiyama, Niiyama 2007).

The elderly in our society experience more physical losses, such as mobility, vision, and hearing; psychological losses, such as memory and problem-solving abilities; and social losses, such as support, institutionalization, and the deaths of loved ones (Baun, 1998). How the elderly handle these losses has a large effect on the quality of their remaining years. If the elderly have a companion animal, one that they are attached to, the animal will be a 'moderator in helping the elderly person deal with some of the losses' (Baun, 1998) (Figure 10.1).

Connor writes, 'Most important, animal-assisted therapy (A.A.T.) enhances motivation, the driving force that heals. Animal visitation and therapy in critical care help motivate patients by reminding them that there's a life outside the hospital walls to which, in time, they'll return' (Connor, 2000).

To the elderly, pets provide 'valuable relationships that serve such functions as companionship, tactile stimulation, safety and non-judgmental emotional support' (Graham, 2000). Rogers, Hart and Boltz (1993) report that 'Some elderly people in the United States have no human friends in whom they confide.' Animals step in and 'listen' to all problems passively (Fine, 2000). In some cases, the human–animal relationship may become the necessary ingredient, which alleviates a perceived sense of loneliness and isolation. Improved social interaction, self-esteem, and independence along with the reduction of anxiety and reduced loneliness are some psychological benefits of A.A.T.

Music therapy

Music in synchrony with mood can act as a catalyst in releasing emotions and opening better channels of communication, as it is a cathartic medium (Bailey, 1985). Music has a multi-dimensional nature which allows itself to touch physical, psychological, spiritual, and social levels of consciousness of participants when used therapeutically. This quality of music enables patients with brain deterioration or decreasing ability to communicate effectively to heal therapeutically. It is through musical intervention that meaningful communication to an extent can be re-established with patients. This is particularly true for clients with dementia. Bruscia (1991) proposes that, in this case, music can be helpful in re-orientation, rebuilding social links, and raising moral. He also highlights grief as a common component of dementia.

Palmer (1983) opines that music can improve body-awareness of the elderly through different rhythmic movements which increase their sense of self-esteem, reality orientation, and consequently, increased social awareness. Swallow (1987) argues that music therapy techniques can be used to regularize walking patterns, prevent akinetic freezing, improve posture and control of upper limb movement, and promote relaxation in Parkinson's disease. The use of music therapy in the relief of pain (arising from arthritis or cancer for instance) is relevant to the care of the elderly and therefore merits brief mention. Schorr (1993) investigated the use of music as a unitary-transformative means of altering the perception of pain among women with rheumatoid arthritis and found affirmative findings. Music helps to bring forth relaxation and reduces sleep disturbances in the elderly (Strang, 1970) (Figure 10.2).

Music therapy provides opportunities for bringing about alterations in one's psychological realm by means of the following (Aldridge, 2000; Brotons and Kroger, 2000; Brotons and Marti, 2003; Cevasco and Grant, 2003; Kneafsey, 1997):

- Reinforces reminiscence and overall life satisfaction;
- Brings about positive emotional changes, intensity, and feelings of warmth upon sharing creative music experiences;
- Increases sense of control over life in general;
- Fosters relaxation coupled with stress reduction for older adults and caregivers;
- Brings about non-pharmacological management of pain and discomfort;

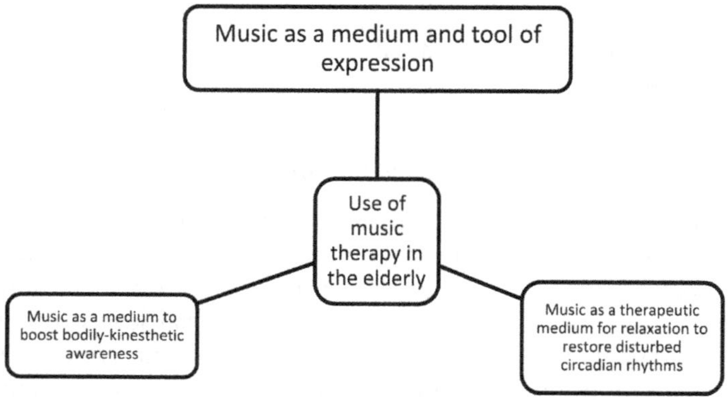

Figure 10.2 Music therapy for the elderly (source: authors).

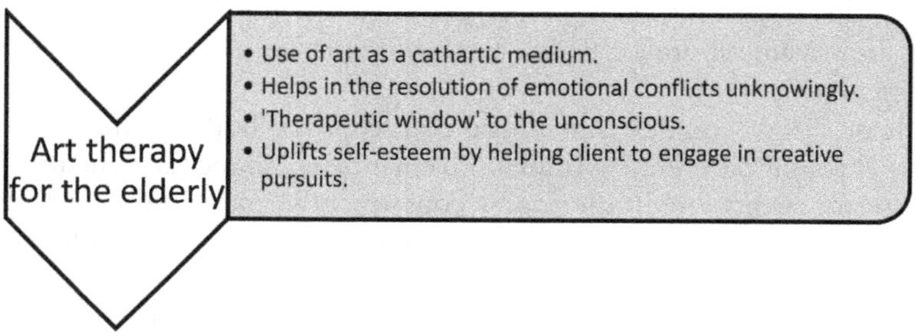

Figure 10.3 The use of art therapy for the elderly (source: authors).

- Provides stimulation that promotes rhythm as an adjunct to physical rehabilitation;
- Encourages social interaction with caregivers and families.

Art therapy

Creating art is cathartic, healing, and life-enhancing in nature. According to Stewart (2004), most elderly adults have little or no experience in using art materials or in expressing themselves visually. Art therapy for the elderly can provide increased involvement of clients along with a sense of pleasure and enhanced opportunities of socialization. It triggers sensory stimulation and self-expression on the part of the clients who are free to choose from a wide range of media to express their repressed thoughts and feelings in relation to emotional conflicts, traumatic experiences, interpersonal relationships, fantasies, dreams, and so on (Figure 10.3).

Art therapy for the elderly helps to deal with the individual's immediate problems, issues pertinent to old age, and provides clients with a sense of dignity (Landgarten, 1981). Drawings provide clients with a tool to engage in self-expression (Oster and Gould, 1987). They may be used in therapeutic modality to creatively portray their feelings, conflicts, wishes, and so on, by allowing clients the freedom of graphic expression (Edwards, 2004). Drawings open the door for the unconscious mind, revealing issues that are often not verbally expressed. The use of drawings is especially beneficial when working with non-verbal, withdrawn, angry, and/or resistant clients (Oster and Gould, 1987). Drawings encourage spontaneity and fantasy in a non-judgemental ambience in the therapeutic set-up.

Leisure education

Leisure education is often used as a therapeutic recreation intervention for the elderly to facilitate the ability to freely choose independent participation in meaningful leisure experiences (Dattilo, 1997). This is accomplished through a process of teaching leisure-related skills, values, and attitudes (Bullock and Morris, 1990). The involvement of elderly individuals in appropriate leisure programmes that are conducive to their social, creative, emotional, psychological, spiritual, and cognitive well-being is welcome (Ingle and Nath, 2008). This not only restores their quality of life but also prevents feelings of loneliness to creep in, thereby making them feel 'meaningful' as far as their life is concerned. It instils personal growth and development by means of individualization of the self and increases the level of satisfaction with life on the whole (Juarbe et al., 2002). Lien (2002) is of the opinion that elderly individuals tend to gain more self-esteem through leisure activities, which, in turn, can calm their moods, increase physical capability, slow down the ageing process, improve quality of life, and reduce medical expenditure. Such activities also promote brain functioning, prevent memory loss, fight off disease-induced disability, and improve nerve conduction.

Dawn–dusk simulation light therapy

Chronic sleep disturbance impairs waking functions (e.g., mood, energy, performance) and life quality (Borkovec, 1982; Morin and Gramling, 1989; Stoller 1994; Simon and Von Korff, 1997). Bright light therapy (Chesson et al., 1999; Montgomery and Dennis, 2002) involves a treatment which is based on reports that many poor sleepers have a disrupted cycle of their circadian rhythms. This suggests that their sleep disorders may be due to a disruption of biological rhythms. Light therapy requires participants to sit in front of a 'lightbox' which emits fluorescent light of a very high intensity

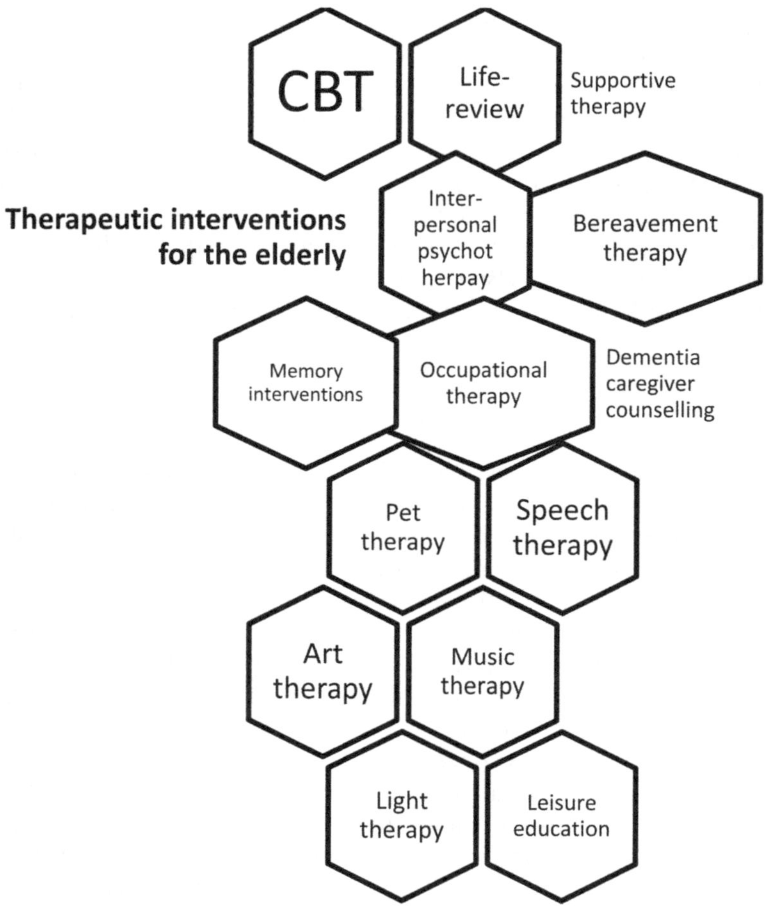

Figure 10.4 Different psychotherapeutic interventions for the elderly (source: authors).

for periods of around two hours daily. This is expected to help restore the disturbed circadian rhythm of the elderly individual.

In addition, dawn–dusk simulation (D.D.S.) is used in mimicking outdoor twilight transitions (Gasioa et al., 2003). It may be considered as a 'naturalistic' light therapy for treating seasonal affective disorder (S.A.D.) (Terman et al., 1989; Partonen and Magnusson, 2001; Avery et al., 2001) and for patients suffering from circadian sleep–wake cycle disorders (Terman and Terman, 2000).

Thus, a number of different therapeutic interventions appear to be available for elderly individuals and they may be tailored for addressing different issues of senior individuals (Figure 10.4).

Policies and programmes tailored for the elderly

It is also worth noting that there are a number of policies and programmes for the aged in India for restoring and maintaining their sense of well-being besides the varied psychotherapeutic interventions previously described. The Indian Constitution has some provisions for the elderly. In fact, in accordance with Article 41 of the Directive Principles of State Policy in the Indian Constitution, the state shall, within the limits of economic capacity, provide assistance to the elderly. The provisions of old-age pensions, social security and social insurance, and economic and social planning are noteworthy steps for the welfare of senior individuals in the country.

Legal measures have also been adopted for the elderly for their security. For instance, according to Section 125 of the Criminal Procedure Code 1973, parents without any means for maintenance have the right to be supported by their children having sufficient means. A bill titled Older Persons (Maintenance, Care and Protection) Bill 2005 was introduced by the central government in parliament for better care of the rapidly growing elderly population in India (Sharma, 2014). It takes consideration of three areas for legislation, namely, maintenance, care, and protection of the elderly. Further, Senior Citizen (Maintenance, Protection and Welfare) Act 2007 enables the protection of life and property of senior citizens and implementing the provisions of the Act by arranging requisite funds.

The National Old Age Pension Scheme, the National Family Benefit Scheme, and the National Maternity Benefit Scheme fall under the jurisdiction of the National Social Assistance Programme (N.S.A.P.). The National Policy on Older Persons (N.P.O.P.) had the chief objective to train geriatric caregivers for the elderly and to create awareness among them to develop into fully independent citizens. Economic security to the elderly to some extent has been provided by the Indira Gandhi National Old Age Pension Scheme (I.G.N.O.A.P.S.), social pensions in various states and union territories, post-retirement benefits for employees of central government, National Pension System (N.P.S.), the Atal Pension Yojana Scheme, Old Age Allowance in Punjab, and so on (Senior Citizens' Guide, 2016).

The Government of India declared the year 2000 as the National Year of Older Persons. The call for the day was for a holistic approach for the elderly by identifying priorities such as health (e.g., Varishtha Mediclaim for Senior Citizens; H.O.P.E. – Health for Privileged Elder; Group Medical Insurance Scheme), shelter, social assistance and security (provision of banking facilities like Senior Citizen Scheme, a personal loan scheme for pensioners, etc.), and freedom from abuse and exploitation, among others. The National Policy on Senior Citizens 2011 (formerly National Policy on Older Persons, 1999) has been in operation in India (Senior Citizens' Guide, 2016). In addition, Vayoshreshtha Samman is a National Award for Senior Citizens provided by the Ministry of Social Justice and Empowerment, which is conferred every year on eminent senior citizens and institutions rendering services for the cause of elderly individuals. The National Institute of Social Defence under the Ministry of Social Justice and Empowerment is actively engaged in giving training to voluntary organizations for the care of senior citizens. Concessions and facilities (health insurance, tax benefits, fare concessions in railways, etc.) are also provided to senior citizens by different ministries/departments of the government.

Internationally, the Madrid International Plan of Action on Ageing may be regarded as a comprehensive and detailed document for restoring the well-being of elderly individuals globally. It takes consideration of elderly individuals with disabilities as well as ensuring enabling and supportive environments in the form of housing and living environments, care and support for caregivers, neglect, abuse and violence, and images of ageing. The significance of eliminating all forms of elder abuse and understanding the risk of potential neglect, abuse, or violence against the elderly has been highlighted in the Madrid Plan. It calls for the 'creation of support services to address elder abuse' while the role of professionals in detecting and preventing abuse is particularly emphasized as well (Political declaration and Madrid international plan of action on ageing, 2003). Furthermore, the United Nations (U.N.) has since 2002 produced a number of additional guidance documents to add impetus to the implementation of the Madrid Plan. This is expected to enable the voices of elderly individuals to be heard and included globally to address their different issues in a non-judgemental manner. Recognizing elderly abuse in the hands of children, other family members, or other individuals in society and taking appropriate action accordingly should be addressed with due immediacy regarding time and pertinence. Reporting and documentation play an important role to develop individual competencies in the long run.

Nevertheless, despite such steps adopted at national and international forums, development and implementation of comprehensive care plans, training for staff, newer policies, and programmes to safeguard the needs of the elderly to bring about an overall improvement in the physical and social environment need to be further addressed.

Conclusion

A number of therapeutic avenues for elderly individuals are available from the desk of the mental health practitioner to understand their specific needs and alter their life-frames along positivistic angles. The overall quality of life is expected to improve consequently by erasing bouts of depression, loneliness, boredom, fatigue, and similar issues as far as practicable. Such therapeutic interventions are likely to help the elderly person move along frames of unconditional acceptance of their selves with their limitations and develop a positive view to enjoy the bliss of life in their remaining days with grace.

References

Aldridge, D. (2000). *Music therapy in dementia care.* London: Jessica Kingsley Publishers.

Avery, D.H., Eder, D.N., Bolte, M.A., Hellekson, K.J., Dunner, D.L., Vitiello, M.V., & Prinz, P.N. (2001). Dawn simulation and bright light in the treatment of SAD: A controlled study. *Biological Psychiatry*, *50*(3), 205–216.

Bailey, L.M. (1985). Music's soothing charms. *American Journal of Nursing*, *85*(11), 1280.

Ballarini, G. (2003). Pet therapy. Animals in human therapy. *Acta biologica et Medica*, *74*(2), 97–100.

Barak, Y., Savorai, O., Mavashev, S., & Beni, A. (2001). Animal-assisted therapy for elderly schizophrenic patients: A one-year controlled trial. *American Journal of Geriatric Psychiatry*, *9*(4), 439–442.

Baun, M.M. (1998). The effect of a therapy dog on socialization and physiological indicators of stress in persons diagnosed with Alzheimer's disease. *Companion Animals in Human Health*, *4*(1), 237–251.

Blair, S.N., Kohl, H.W., III, Paffenbarger, R.S., Jr., Clark, D.G., Cooper, K.H., & Gibbons, L.W. (1989). Physical fitness and all-cause mortality: A prospective study of healthy men and women. *JAMA*, *262*(17), 2395–2401.

Bokovoy, J.L., & Blair, S.N. (1994). Ageing and exercise: A health perspective. *Journal of Ageing and Physical Activity*, *2*(3), 243–260.

Bootzin, R.R., Epstein, D., & Wood, J.M. (1991). Stimulus control instructions. In P.J. Hauri (Ed.), Case studies in insomnia (pp. 19–28). New York: Plenum Press.

Borkovec, T.D. (1982). Insomnia. *Journal of Consulting and Clinical Psychology*, *50*(6), 880–895.

Brotons, M., & Kroger, S.M. (2000). The impact of music therapy on language functioning in dementia. *Journal of Music Therapy*, *37*(3), 183–195.

Brotons, M., & Marti, P. (2003). Music therapy with Alzheimer's patients and their family caregivers: A pilot project. *Journal of Music Therapy*, *40*(2), 138–150.

Bruscia, K. (1991). *Case studies in music therapy* (p. 573). Phoenixville, PA: Barcelona Publishers.

Bullock, C.C., & Morris, L.M. (1990). *The community re-integration program.* Chapel Hill, NC: The University of North Carolina at Chapel Hill.

Butler, R.N., & Lewis, M.I. (1982). *Ageing and mental health: Positive psychosocial and biomedical approaches.* St. Louis, MO: Mosby.

Camp, C.J. (1996). The return of Sherlock Holmes: A pilgrim's progress in memory and ageing research. In M.R. Merrens & G.G. Brannigan (Eds.), *The developmental psychologists* (pp. 217–232). New York: McGraw-Hill.

Camp, C.J., & Foss, J.W. (1997). Designing ecologically valid memory interventions for persons with dementia. In D.G. Payne & F.G. Conrad (Eds.), *Intersections in basic and applied memory research* (pp. 311–325). Mahwah, NJ: Lawrence Erlbaum.

Cevasco, A.M., & Grant, R.E. (2003). Comparison of different methods for eliciting exercise-to-music for clients with Alzheimer's disease. *Journal of Music Therapy*, *40*(1), 41–56.

Chattin-McNichols, J. (1992). *The Montessori controversy.* Albany, NY: Delmar Publishers.

Chesson, A.L., Littner, M., Davila, D., MacDowell Anderson, W., Grigg-Damberger, HartseK., Johnson, S. (1999). Practice parameters for the use of light therapy in the treatment of sleep disorders. *Sleep*, *22*(5), 641–660.

Connor, K. (2000). Help from our animal friends. *Nursing Management*, *3*(1), 317.

Dattilo, K. (1997). *Leisure Education Program planning*. State College, PA: Venture Publishing, Inc.

Dustman, R.E., Emmerson, R., & Shearer, D.E. (1994). Physical activity, age, and cognitive-neuropsychological function. *Journal of Ageing and Physical Activity*, *2*(2), 143–181.

Edwards, D. (2004). *Art therapy*. London: Sage Publications.

Fine, A. (Eds.) (2000). *Handbook of animal-assisted therapy*. San Diego: Academic Press.

Frank, E., Frank, N., Cornes, C. et al. (1993). Interpersonal psychotherapy in the treatment of late-life depression. In G.L. Klerman & M.M. Weissman (Eds.), *New applications in interpersonal psychotherapy* (pp. 167–198). Washington, DC: American Psychiatric Press.

Gasioa, P.F., Kra¨uchia, K., Cajochena, C., Somerenb, E., Amrheina, I., Pachec , M., ... Wirz-Justicea, A. (2003). Dawn–dusk simulation light therapy of disturbed circadian rest–activity cycles in demented elderly. *Experimental Gerontology*, *38*(1–2), 207–216.

Graham, B. (2000). *Creature comfort*. New York: Prometheus Books.

Haight, B.K. (1992). Long-term effects of structured life-review process in homebound elderly subjects. *Journals of Gerontology: Psychological Sciences*, *47*, 312–315.

Haskell, W., Leon, A., Casperson, C., Froelicher, V.F., Hagberg, J.M., Harlan, W., ... Wilson, P.W.F. (1992). Cardiovascular benefits and assessment of physical activity and physical fitness in adults. *Medicine and Science in Sports and Exercise*, *2*(1), 201–220.

Helmrick, S.P., Ragland, J.M., Leung, R.W., & Paffenbarger, R.S., Jr. (1991). Physical activity and reduced occurrence of non-insulin-dependent diabetes mellitus. *New England Journal of Medicine*, *325*(3), 147–152.

Hibbard, M., Grober, S., Wayne, G., & Aletta, E. (1990). Modification of cognitive psychotherapy for the treatment of post-stroke depression. *Behaviour Therapist*, 15–17.

Hill, R.D., Allen, C., & Gregory, K. (1990). Self-generated mnemonics for enhancing free-recall performance in older learners. *Experimental Ageing Research*, *16*(3), 141–145.

Ingle, G.K., & Nath, A. (2008). Geriatric health in India: Concerns and solutions. *Indian Journal of Community Medicine*, *33*(4), 214–228.

Juarbe, T., Turok, X.P., & Perez-Stable, J.E. (2002). Perceived benefits and barriers to physical activity among older Latin women. *Western Journal of Nursing Research*, *24*(8), 868–886.

Kanamori, M., Suzuki, M., Yamamoto, K., Kanda, M., Matsui, Y., Kojima, E., ... Oshiro, H. (2001). A day care program and evaluation of animal-assisted therapy (AAT) for the elderly with senile dementia. *AJADD*, *16*(4), 234–239.

Kawamura, N., Niiyama, M., & Niiyama, H. (2007). Long-term evaluation of animal-assisted therapy for institutionalized elderly people: A preliminary result. *Psichogeriatrics*, *7*(1), 8–13

Kneafsey, R. (1997). The therapeutic use of music in a care of the elderly setting: A literature review. *Journal of Clinical Nursing*, *6*(5), 341–346.

Kokmen, E., Beard, C.M., Chandra, V., Offord, K.P., Schoenberg, B.S., & Ballard, D.J. (1991). Clinical risk factors for Alzheimer's disease: A population-based, case-control study. *Neurology*, *41*(9), 1393–1397.

Kupfer, D.J., & Reynolds, C.F. (1997). Management of insomnia. *New England Journal of Medicine*, *336*(5), 341–345.

Landgarten, H. (1981). *Clinical art therapy*. Bristol, PA: Brunner/Mazel.

Lawton, M.P. (1998). *Annual review of gerontology and geriatrics, 18; focus on intervention research with older adults*. New York: Springer Publishing Company.

Lazarus, L.W., & Sadavoy, J. (1996). Individual psychology. In J. Sadavoy, L.W. Lazarus, L.F. Zarvik et al. (Eds.), *Comprehensive review of geriatric psychiatry – II* (2nd ed., pp. 819–850). Washington, DC: American Psychiatric Press.

Lichstein, K.L., & Fisher, S.M. (1985). Insomnia. In M. Hersen & A.S. Bellack (Eds.), *Handbook of clinical behaviour therapy with adults* (pp. 319–352). New York: Plenum Press.

Lichstein, K.L., & Riedel, B.W. (1994). Behavioral assessment and treatment of insomnia: A review with an emphasis on clinical application. *Behaviour Therapy*, *25*(4), 659–688.

Lien, C.-M. (2002). Unpublished dissertation. Taiwan: Gerontological Research Centre, Yuan Ze University.

McAuley, E., & Mihalko, S. (1998). Measuring exercise-related self-efficacy. In J. Duda (Ed.), *Advancement in measurement in sport and exercise psychology* (pp. 371–390). Morgantown, WV: Fitness Technology Publishers.

McAuley, E., & Rudolph, D. (1995). Physical activity, ageing, and psychological well-being. *Journal of Ageing and Physical Activity*, *3*(1), 67–96.

McAuley, E., Shaffer, S., & Rudolph, D. (1995). Self-efficacy and affective responses to exercise testing in older males. *International Journal of Ageing and Human Development*, *41*(1), 13–27.

Mellinger, G.D., Balter, M.B., & Uhlenhuth, E.H. (1985). Insomnia and its treatment. *Archives of General Psychiatry*, *42*(3), 225–232.

Miller, N.L., & Markowitz, J.C. (1999). Interpersonal psychotherapy of depressed patients. *Journal of Practical Psychiatry and Behavioural Health*, *5*(2), 63–74.

Mittelman, M.S., Ferris, S.H., Shulman, E., Steinberg, G., Ambinder, A., Mackell, J.A., & Cohen, J. (1995). A comprehensive support program: Effect on depression in spouse caregivers of AD patients. *Gerontologist*, *35*(6), 792–802.

Mobily, K.E., Rubenstein, L.M., Lemke, J.H., O'Hara, M.W., & Wallace, R.B. (1996). Walking and depression in a cohort of older adults: The Iowa 65+ rural health study. *Journal of Ageing and Physical Activity*, *4*(2), 119–135.

Montgomery, P., & Dennis, J.A. (2002). Bright light therapy for sleep problems in adults aged 60+. *Cochrane Database of Systematic Reviews*, 2, Art. No.: CD003403.

Morin, C.M. (1993). *Insomnia: Psychological assessment and management*. New York: Guilford.

Morin, C.M., Gaulier, B., Barry, T., & Kowatch, R.A. (1992). Patients' acceptance of psychological and pharmacological therapies for insomnia. *Sleep*, *15*(4), 302–305.

Morin, C.M., & Gramling, S.E. (1989). Sleep patterns and aging: Comparison of older adults with and without insomnia complaints. *Psychology and Aging*, *4*(3), 290–294.

Morin, C.M., Mimeault, V., & Gagne, A. (1999). Non-pharmacological treatment of late-life insomnia. *Journal of Psychosomatic Research*, *46*(2), 103–116.

The National Policy on Older Persons (1999). *Government of India, Ministry of Social Justice and Empowerment*. New Delhi: Shastri Bhawan.

Neely, A.S., & Backman, L. (1995). Effect of multi-factorial training in old age: Generalizability across tasks and individuals. *Journal of Gerontology: Psychological Sciences*, *50B*, 134–140.

Newmann, J.P., Engel, R.L., & Jensen, J. (1990). Depressive symptoms among older women. *Psychology and Ageing*, *5*, 101–118.

Newmann, J.P., Engel, R.J., & Jensen, J. (1991a). Age differences in depressive symptom experiences. *Journal of Gerontology: Psychological Sciences*, *46*(5), 224–235.

Newmann, J.P., Engel, R.J., & Jensen, J. (1991b). Changes in depressive symptom experiences among older women. *Psychology and Ageing*, *6*(2), 212–222.

Oster, G., & Gould, P. (1987). *Using drawings in assessment and therapy*. New York: Brunner/Mazel.

Palmer, M. (1983). Alzheimer's and critical care. *Journal of Gerontological Nursing*, *9*, 86–90.

Partonen, T., & Magnusson, A. (Eds.) (2001). *Seasonal affective disorder. Practice and research*. Oxford: Oxford University Press.

Philips, W.T., & Haskell, W.L. (1995). 'Muscular Fitness': Easing the burden of disability for elderly adults. *Journal of Ageing and Physical Activity*, *3*(3), 261–289.

Pierce, T.W., Madden, D.J., Siegel, W.C., & Blumenthal, J.A. (1993). Effects of aerobic exercise on cognitive and psychosocial functioning in patients with mild hypertension. *Health Psychology*, *12*(4), 286–291.

Rebok, G.W., Rasmusson, D.X., & Brandt, J. (1997). Improving memory in community elderly through group-based and individualized memory training. In D.G. Payne & F.G. Conrad (Eds.), *Intersections in basic and applied memory research* (pp. 327–343). Mahwah, NJ: Lawrence Erlbaum.

Reifler, B.V., Cox, G.B., & Hanley, A.J. (1981). Problems of mentally ill elderly as perceived by patients, families and clinicians. *Gerontologist*, *21*(2), 165–170.

Rogers, J., Hart, L.A., & Boltz, R.P. (1993). The role of pet dogs in casual conversation of elderly adults. *The Journal of Social Psychology*, *133*(3), 265–278.

Roth, T., Zorick, F., Wittig, R., & Roehrs, T. (1982). Pharmacological and medical considerations in hypnotic use. *Sleep*, *5*(Suppl. 1), 46–52.

Rybarczyk, B., Gallgher-Thompson, D., Rodman, J., Zeiss, A., Gantz, F., & Yesavage, J. (1992). Applying cognitive-behavioural psychotherapy to the chronically ill elderly: Treatment issues and case illustration. *International Psychogetriatrics*, *4*(1), 127–140.

Sanderson, W.C., & McGinn, L.A. (1997). Psychological treatment of anxiety disorder patients with comorbidity. In S. Wetzler & W.C. Sanderson (Eds.), *Treatment strategies for patients with psychiatric co-morbidity* (pp. 75–104). New York: Wiley.

Sanderson, W.C., & Wetzler, S. (1995). Cognitive behavioural treatment of panic disorder. In G.M. Asnis & M.H. van Praag (Eds.), *Pathogenetic mechanisms of panic disorder* (pp. 80–98). New York: Brunner/ Mazel.

Sandman, C.A. (1993). Memory rehabilitation in Alzheimer's disease: Preliminary findings. *Clinical Gerontologist, 13*(4), 19–33.

Senior Citizens' Guide (2016). *Fighting isolation, poverty and neglect.* New Delhi: Policy Research and Development Department.

Schorr, A. (1993). Music and pattern change in chronic pain. *Advances in Nursing Science, 15*(4), 27–36.

Scogin, F., Jamison, C., & Gochneaur, K. (1989). Comparative efficacy of cognitive and behavioural biblio-therapy for mildly and moderately depressed older adults. *Journal of Consulting and Clinical Psychology, 57*(3), 403–407.

Sharma, N. (2014). Government policies and programmes for the aged in India. *Paripex- Indian Journal of Research, 3*(7), 207–209.

Shuchter, S.R., & Zisook, S. (1993). The course of normal grief. In M.S. Stroebe, W. Stroebe & R.O. Hansson (Eds.), *Handbook of bereavement: Theory, research and intervention* (pp. 23–43). Cambridge: Cambridge University Press.

Simon, G., & Von Korff, M. (1997). Prevalence, burden and treatment of insomnia in primary care. *American Journal of Psychiatry, 154*(10), 1417–1423.

Smith, A.D., & Earles, J.L.K. (1996). Memory changes in normal ageing. In F. Blanchard-Fields & T.M. Hess (Eds.), *Perspectives on cognitive change in adulthood and ageing* (pp. 192–220). New York: McGraw-Hill.

Smyer, M.A., & Gatz, M. (1986). Intervention research approaches. *Research on Ageing, 8*(4), 536–558.

Squire, L.R. (1994). Declarative and non-declarative memory: Multiple brain systems supporting learning and memory. In D.L. Schachter & E.Tulving (Eds.), *Memory systems* (pp. 203–222). Cambridge, MA: MIT Press.

Sterns, H.L., & Camp, C.J. (1998) Applied gerontology. *Applied Psychology: An International Review, 47*(2), 175–198. .

Stewart, E.G. (2004). Art therapy and neuroscience blend: Working with patients who have dementia. *Journal of the American Art Therapy Association* pp. 148–155.

Stoller, M.K. (1994). The economic effects of insomnia. *Clinical Therapeutics, 16*(5), 873–897.

Strang, C.D. (1970). Music at night: An experiment in a geriatric ward. Journal of the Royal College of Practitioners, *20*(99), 246–247.

Swallow, M. (1987). Can music help? *Current Problems in Neurology, 6*, 109–112.

Teri, L., & Gallagher-Thompson, D. (1991). Cognitive-behavioural interventions for the treatment of depression in Alzheimer's patients. *Gerontologist, 31*(3), 413–416.

Teri, L., Logsdon, R.G., Uomoto, J. et al. (1997). Behavioral treatment of depression in dementia patients: A controlled clinical trial. *Journal of Gerontology: Psychological Sciences, 52B*, 159–166.

Terman, M., Schlager, D., Fairhurst, S., & Perlman, B. (1989). Dawn and dusk simulation as a therapeutic intervention. *Biological Psychiatry, 25*(7), 966–970.

Terman, M., & Terman, J.S. (2000). Light therapy. In M.H. Kryger, T. Roth & W.C. Dement (Eds.), *Principles and practice of sleep medicine* (3rd. ed., pp. 1258–1274). Philadelphia: W.B. Saunders Company.

Political declaration and Madrid international plan of action on ageing (2003). *Second World Assembly on Ageing, Madrid, Spain, 8-12 April, 2012,* United Nations,. New York, p. 43.

Wagner, E.H., LaCroix, A.Z., Buchner, D.M., & Larson, E.B. (1992). Effects of physical activity on health status in older adults: I. Observational studies. *Annual Review of Public Health, 13*, 451–468.

Walsh, P.G., Mertin, P.G., Verlander, D.F., & Pollard, C.F. (1995). The effects of a 'pets as therapy' dog on persons with dementia in a psychiatric ward. *Australian Occupational Therapy Journal, 42*(4), 161–166.

Wetherell, J.L., Gatz, M., Johansson, B., & Pederson, N.L. (1999). History of depression and other psychiatric illness as risk factors for Alzheimer disease in a twin sample. *Alzheimer's Disease and Related Disorders, 13*(1), 47–52.

Whitlatch, C.J., Zarit, S.H., Goodwin, P.E., & von Eye, A. (1995). Influence of the success of psycho-educational interventions on the course of family care. *Clinical Gerontologist, 16*(1), 17–30.

Woods, R.T. (1996). Psychological 'therapies' in dementia. In R.T. Woods (Ed.), *Handbook of the clinical psychology of ageing* (pp. 575–600). Chichester: John Wiley & Sons.

Zarit, S.H., Peterson, K., & Bach-Peterson, K. (1980). Relatives of impaired elderly. Correlates of feelings of burden. *Gerontologist, 20*, 649–655.

Zarit, S.H., & Whitlatcht, C.J. (1993). The effects of placement in nursing homes on family caregivers: Short and long-term consequences. *Irish Journal of Psychology, 14*(1), 25–37.

Zarit, S.H., & Zarit, J.M. (1998*Mental disorders in older adults: Fundamentals of Assessment and Treatment* (pp. 290–319). New York: Guilford Press.

Zisook, S., & Shuchter, S.R. (1996). Grief and bereavement. In J. Sadavoy, L.W. Lazarus, L.F.Zarvik et al. (Eds.), *Comprehensive review of geriatric psychiatry – II* (2nd ed., pp. 529–562). Washington, DC: American Psychiatric Press.

11

END-OF-LIFE CARE IN DEMENTIA

Geriatric burden or elderly blessing?

Extended life expectancy represents a major opportunity to promote and positively manage well-being across the life course. However, the increasing prevalence of cognitive decline with age, particularly due to dementia and other neurodegenerative disorders, poses a critical challenge (Foresight Mental Capital and Wellbeing Project, 2008). Such degenerative disorders serve as dark blotches by transforming the personality of patients. In fact, age is the biggest risk factor for dementia (Knapp et al., 2007). Degenerative processes in different neurological ailments prevent neurons functionally communicating with one another that lead to the breakdown of communication pathways that otherwise anchor a person in their own time and environment. The mind becomes adrift and communication with the self and others is affected. Such an individual regresses to that of an ailing, helpless state regarding his/her functional level (Souren and Franssen, 1994).

Dementia is one such neurodegenerative disorder that is accompanied by a progressive decline in multiple function areas, including memory, reasoning, communication skills, and the skills needed to carry out daily activities (Department of Health, 2009). Individuals may also have associated behavioural and psychological symptoms in the form of depression, psychosis, aggression, and wanderlust (Robinson et al., 2007). Epidemiological studies indicate that about a half of all older people who need personal care have dementia, and about eight out of ten elderly individuals in institutions live with dementia (Prince, Prina, and Guerchet, 2013). An estimated 24 million people in the world live with dementia. It has been predicted that this number will increase to about 81 million by 2040 (Alzheimer's Disease International, 2007). Dementia is not only debilitating for the elderly individuals but also has adverse effects on their friends and family caregiver members. The overall quality of life of the family consequently suffers. Cognitive decline, therefore, presents a major threat to their well-being and urgent action is needed to safeguard and promote well-being for those affected (Prince, Prina, and Guerchet, 2013). The present discourse essentially debates on the psychological bearings of dementia to understand the needed end-of-life care and to weigh the consequent burden and blessings on its caregivers. The necessity to interact with such individuals having neurodegenerative disorders requires mention at this juncture.

Communicating with the 'caged birds' that have dementia

Alzheimer's disease, cerebral attack/stroke/multi-infarct or vascular dementia, Pick's disease, Parkinson's disease, Creutzfeldt-Jakob disease, Huntington's disease, and Lewy body syndrome are considered the primary categories of dementia (McBee, 2008). Dementia is generally not curable, but its rate of progress can be slowed down and managed accordingly. It is challenging, stimulating, frightening, and frustrating to communicate with such individuals. It takes courage and creativity, trial and error, and a willingness to be one's authentic self (McBee, 2008). Myriad emotions paint the affective canvas of people with degenerative disorders, some being depression, humiliation, loneliness, helplessness, embarrassment, frustration, and the sheer aching wretchedness of loss (Wilcock, 2003).

Depression owing to the *loss* of freedom to choose and decide to go out, read, and converse, the loss of personal dignity and privacy, and so on are often the underlying factors in the overwhelming life experience of stroke/vascular dementia patients among others (Wilcock, 2003). Elderly individuals with dementia who need institutionalization may also suffer from pangs of losing their homes. Loss of status and position can also be a source of acute suffering, which is very frightening. They also experience a substantial loss of power, which is important to one's confidence to a sense of self-worth and contentment. Living like this brings the individual into daily companionship with two of the human spirit's most crushing adversaries, namely, helplessness and humiliation.

The *sense of helplessness* in looking at an object across the room, unable to reach or move it, in having food left on the table in front of him/her – not really being able to manage it well – is crushing. An overwhelming *sense of humiliation* and *shame* resulting in *despair* may become associated with one's body image. One may often lose the essential privacy of the bathroom which is humiliating for the senior individual.

Embarrassment has a considerable part to play in such individuals – feeling stupid, being overlooked; what Camus used to describe as *de trop* (Wilcock, 2003). Because of the undermining nature of depression, loss, humiliation, helplessness, isolation, and shame, a further adversary of the spirit that arrives to share life is *fear of further loss and physical vulnerability* – the fear of falling over; the fear of continued pain and discomfort, among others. Such an elderly person often has underlying fears of further strokes, further helplessness, and death.

Loneliness, helplessness, and *boredom* serve as three plagues of institutionalized frail elders (Thomas, 2004). These plagues may also apply to isolated home-bound and bed-bound elders (McBee, 2008). Hence, individuals with neurodegenerative disorders resulting in dementia appear caged and confined emotionally, socially, and physically, thereby posing as chief challenges to caregivers and themselves.

Living well with dementia (Department of Health, 2009) is thus of prime concern which encapsulates the view that people with dementia and their caregivers can and should be able to live well and maintain high levels of well-being. Hence, the dire necessity for raising awareness and understanding, early diagnosis, and ensuring high standards for elderly clients.

Some of the basic tips on communication with demented individuals adapted in part from Alzheimer's Disease International (2007) are as follows:

- Centre oneself and focus fully on the person with dementia with whom one is communicating;
- Consider one's tone, pace, body language, and other non-verbal cues;
- Try to maintain eye contact;
- Use simple language with the elderly;
- Provide simple instructions one-at-a-time;
- Minimize environmental distractions as far as practicable;
- Try to have patience and not correct the person with dementia;
- Use touch to reinforce, but also consider that some touch is not welcome;
- Allow time to respond;
- Listen to verbal and non-verbal communication;
- Accept individuals as they are;
- Try to get connected to the person and respond to his/her feelings as much as practicable.

Family: The important pedestal of providing care to the elderly

The immediate family is regarded as the most important pedestal for the provision of care to senior individuals. Caregiving is found to have a close association with family integrity, which is, in turn, related to ingrained competencies of the family system. Family members often share meaning through legacies across generations in terms of family history, genealogy, and shared characteristics or activities. Older adults gain a sense of satisfaction and inherent feeling of completeness at the individual level owing to family integrity. Further, elderly individuals gain an important sense of meaning, purpose, and connection with others at the familial context because of its integrity. Thus, families have been regarded as universal bedrocks of senior caregiving and economic security, especially in developing countries.

It is to be noted that the extent of family support depends on many important factors – the stage of life of the individual being one of them. Family members are often committed to taking care of their parents and other older members, although exceptions exist as well (Agree and Glaser, 2009; Herlofson, Hagestad, Slagsvold, and Sørensen, 2011). This brings about a plethora of researches related to burdens (and rewards) of family caregiving in the specific field of gerontology (Pinquart and Sörensen, 2003, 2005, 2007). Although many studies have specifically focused on the negative impact of caregiving as far as the psychological well-being of caregivers is concerned, yet, investigations probing into the benefits of the same are also noteworthy. Some of them include engaging in personal growth, defining one's purpose of life, and engaging in greater self-acceptance (Marks et al., 2002).

Thus, it may be said that families serve as central social institutions in different societies, which provide social identity and different roles as well as economic support and physical care to their older members. A sense of belongingness and sustenance for the elderly person are provided by families. However, families sometimes need to take assistance from other agencies like the government and from non-government organizations. The need of the day is to have the feel of a 'global community-family' to provide economic and health support to help supplement the caregiving efforts of family units. In fact, such positive social interactions among elderly individuals and their family members, relatives, friends, and neighbours appear to have protective effects on their physical and psychological health (Seeman et al., 2001; Bowling, 2005).

Spouses as key caregivers amidst the family matrix

Spouses are the first line of caregivers for older married individuals when they encounter any disease or disability. They spend a substantially longer time in caregiving than other family caregivers and engage in various activities, some being tasks of daily living, companionship, providing empathy, supervision, mental stimulation, and so on (Chappell and Kuehne, 1998; Jansson, Norberg, and Grafstrom, 2001). Spouses serve as the most dependable caregivers of each other, which are provided, in some instances, by the marital contract that appears to protect them against institutional placement (Quadagno, 2005). This is perhaps because of love and duty to look after an ill spouse (Miller and Montgomery, 1990; Davidson, Arber, and Ginn, 2000). Studies have revealed that spouses tend to tolerate greater disability for a longer period, often risking their own personal resources due to the presence of few mediating resources (Seltzer and Li, 2000; Burton et al., 1997). The caregiving spouse often has its toll on his/her physical and emotional health (Burton, Zdanuik, Schulz, Jackson, and Hirsch, 2003; Marks, Lambert, and Choi, 2002). This has its repercussions in the care-providing spouse who commonly may have health issues hindering the care-providing process as a result. Mixed results have been obtained by researchers in the context of role conflict and the burden experienced by spouse caregivers, pinpointing the very multi-dimensional nature of the caregiver burden (Young and Kahana, 1989; George and Gwyther, 1986). Meta-analyses have found strong evidence that elderly caregivers, women, and spouses suffer from greater distress than non-caregivers (Pinquart and Sorensen, 2003). They also proposed a common core model for caregiver distress which stressed the importance of the appraisal of caregiving as stressful to trigger distress among elderly caregivers (Pinquart and Sorensen, 2005). This distress may remain stable for a prolonged illness like Alzheimer's disease (Clay et al., 2008; Gwyther, 1990; Rose et al., 1997). Further, social support serves as a mediating factor to buffer the impact of distress on caregivers.

Spouses tend to derive different meanings of caregiving for their spouses. While on the one hand, wives appear to have an *obligation to care* because of the marital contract, husbands tend to perceive more latitude in the assigned role towards their spouses (Davidson, Arber, and Ginn, 2000). Females are likely to have a greater sense of personal responsibility for maintaining their husband's safety, reducing his sufferings, and for bolstering his sense of independence and self-esteem (Jansson et al., 2001). On the contrary, elderly husbands appear to invest in the caregiving role for their wives to a greater extent. This may reflect their perception of caring as a *choice* rather than an *obligation*. They seem to choose the role genuinely because they seem to want to return the years of prior support and nurturance of their wives (Pruchno and Ressch, 1989). This has been referred technically as *delayed quid pro quo reciprocity* (Lobo-Prahbu, Molinari, Arlinghaus, Barr, and Lomax, 2005). This is in contrast to caring by wives which is often regarded as an extension of their daily invisible chore of responding to the different needs of their spouses in the current societal parlance (Davidson et al., 2000).

Illness or disability of a spouse tends to impact socio-emotional, instrumental support networks as well as the financial resources of elderly partners (DiLeonardo, 1992; Szinovacz and Davey, 2004). As far as coping resources are concerned, wives tend to have greater informal networks of social support at the very outset of caregiving in comparison with their husbands, but the picture may gradually change later when caregiving demands escalate (Navaie-Walier et al., 2002). However, other studies have inferred that women tend to use a greater extent of emotion-focused coping strategies at times of crises in contrast with men (Rose, Strauss, Neundorfet, Smyth, and Stuckey, 1997). They are also less likely than husband caregivers to maintain preventive health behaviours (e.g., exercising, taking adequate rest, medication) and appropriate self-care practices (Burton, Newsom, Schulz, Hirsch, and German, 1997). In contrast, husband caregivers rely more on instrumental or problem-solving strategies, which contribute to greater efficacy and positive affect (Kramer, 1997). This prompts them to adopt more task-oriented, care management perspectives by compartmentalizing the 'task' of caregiving and its associated emotions. Hence, husband caregivers appear to enjoy a greater extent of perceived control and self-efficacy and are protected against intense stress and burnout reactions (Szabo and Strang, 1999). Nevertheless, it becomes mandatory to note that the nature of the care recipient's disability, duration of marriage, and age differences between the elderly partners appear to be influential factors in the experience of spousal caregiving (Hooker et al., 2000; Gwyther, 1990; Nijboer et al., 2000).

Apart from spouses, elderly individuals often look up to their adult children whom they have nurtured throughout their lives for their caregiving during the advanced stages of life. The following section narrates the nuances of the new role of these offspring as caregivers for their elderly parents.

Adult offspring as caregivers of the elderly

As elderly parents age together, often both of them suffer from frailty and need to be provided with consistent caregiving. This is often taken up by their adult offspring, who are the next tier of preferred caregivers in the family (Cantor, 1975). Caregiving may take the form of both economic and behavioural health care utilization on the part of elderly parents (Stark, 1995). Multiple adult offspring of an elderly couple may serve as caregivers. There may be five primary parent-care styles (Mathews and Rosner, 1988). Offspring may be engaged in *routine assistance* reflected through regular ongoing assistance of the elderly parent(s). Support and caregiving may also be provided at an intermittent level resulting in *backup assistance.* There may additionally be the availability of *circumscribed assistance*, which has limited scope but is reliable and predictable. Further *sporadic assistance* may also be provided depending on the convenience of a sibling. It is, however, coordinated by support provided by other siblings. *Dissociative assistance* is the last variety in which caregiving assistance to parents is not very reliable and hence unpredictable.

A number of factors have been found to be associated with the style of involvement of adult offspring in terms of caregiving to elderly parent(s). Families with only two daughters have been found to have less prevalence of circumscribed, sporadic, and dissociative styles (Matthews, 1995). The presence of multiple siblings also tends to encourage some to adopt primary roles while others serve more supportive or auxiliary caregiving functions for their parents. Sex differences have also been reported, with sons generally being more likely to exhibit less involved patterns of assistance compared with their sisters, though exceptions are also found to exist (Mathews and Rosner, 1988; Matthews, 1995). If sons are involved, their efforts are usually directed towards fostering independence for their parents to a greater extent than support from daughters and daughters-in-law (Matthews and Heidorn, 1998). Other factors like birth order and family ties also appear

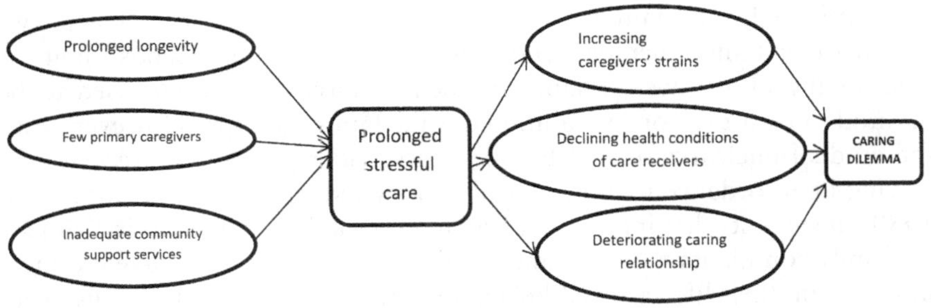

Figure 11.1 The caring dilemma on the part of family caregivers (source: authors).

to be implicated. Furthermore, extra-familial factors appear to influence a sibling's style of assistance, some being geographic proximity of an offspring to enable him/her for hands-on assistance for the parent(s), his/ her employment status, whether married/single or having any other liabilities, individual sibling characteristics, whether biological or step-child, and so on (Ganong and Coleman, 2006).

In the present-day scenario, in Eastern cultures like India, where increasing numbers of nuclear families with single offspring are present, it often becomes imperative for the single offspring to engage in caregiving of his/ her elderly parent(s) not only because of filial obligatory norms but also because of the internalization of values by the offspring during the time of his/her growing up. It is also to be noted that adult offspring are also more likely to be involved in providing assistance to mothers than their fathers since females usually tend to outlive males and women tend to marry men older than their own age as mentioned earlier in the chapter.

It is to be noted that caregivers in the form of spouses, adult offspring, or any other family members also tend to experience *anticipatory grief* about the death of their loved individual and then the death of the person. Though in some cases, they appear to be prepared for the demise of the loved member, yet many studies show that caregivers tend to have 'possessive feelings' for the ailing individual, have complicated grief reactions, and suffer from depression. They often succumb to the caring dilemma of whether to continue stressful family care or send their elderly kin to institutions and thereby suffer from feelings of ambivalence towards the care receiver(s) (Ngan and Kwok, 1992). This is pictorially represented in Figure 11.1.

Studies also pinpoint contradictory findings regarding the psychological and physical health of the caregivers after the death of the care recipient, some indicating a feeling of 'relief' in terms of caregiver burden often followed by a sense of grief, mourning, and bereavement, while others pinpoint a sense of loneliness, depression, and lowered well-being (Robinson-Whelen et al., 2001; Bodnar and Kiecolt-Glaser, 1994).

When single unmarried individuals, issue-less, or separated elder people are considered, their family includes their relatives like nieces or nephews or any other family member whom he/she confides and depends upon for emotional and/or physical support when required. This often used to be naturally taken care of in traditional joint family set-ups. However, with the gradual nuclearization of families, these elder people may receive caregiving in accordance with the social convoy model (Kahn and Antonucci, 1980). It suggests that informal caregiving is usually provided to individuals by family confidants who are emotionally close to them and have a critical influence on their life and well-being. Studies further revealed that disabled, house-bound, and bed-bound elderly individuals have fewer family confidants irrespective of their marital status and that informal support networks decreased with age (Ngan, 1990a, 1990b; Ngan and Kwok, 1992). Litwak (1985) observed in the *theory of shared functions* that immediate emergencies may be handled by neighbours, while long-term care commitment may be taken care of by kin and emotional sharing on the part of the elderly may be done with friends. As such, a *realistic treatment team* composed of informal caregivers may be available by means of networking (Collins and Pancoast, 1978; Lubben, 1988).

With the role of the family been narrated in the context of caregiving, the chief behaviours that accompany dementia are worth mentioning at this juncture.

Behaviours accompanying dementia

Most of our behaviour is an attempt to communicate. Elders with dementia possess the need to feel connected and valued as well as the need to communicate and be stimulated. When other avenues of communication are lost, behaviour, and at times aggressive behaviour can be the only avenue of communication. Thus, persons with dementia who are no longer able to express feelings verbally often evidence physical agitation or difficult behaviours. They may be efforts on the part of the individual to express their inner cry of distress. Stress-reduction skills can offer relief and repose to agitated persons in a non-judgemental format.

Hence is the need to be willing to individualize treatment, use trial and error, and tolerate feelings of helplessness, confusion, and vulnerability of the elderly clients on the part of the caregivers as far as practicable. One must take responsibility for communication, and not merely blame the person with dementia. The implementation of dementia-friendly communities is of significance at this crucial juncture.

Dementia-friendly communities

The notion of a dementia-friendly community is a multi-faceted concept and involves tackling a wide range of issues at national, regional, and local levels. An early diagnosis of dementia, training of staff in businesses and other organizations, raising awareness of dementia, and addressing the design of the physical environment are noteworthy to improve quality of life and well-being and support people with dementia.

A key tenet of dementia-friendly communities concerns challenging stigma, increasing understanding, and awareness about dementia and how to support individuals in the long run. The time is ripe to re-think old age and its different issues by adopting an accommodative stance rather than having a negative orientation. The issue of gerontophobia needs to be addressed proactively (Coleman, 2000). Thus, the notion of cognitive decline in dementia as having few positive features for which they have been denied cognitive citizenship (Graham, 2004) remains a major threat to well-being.

Generally, relationships of people with dementia with their family and friends, social contacts, leisure activities, their physical health, and having a sense of independence and choice over their lives appear to be key factors in shaping their quality of life in advanced years (Sclai, Trimble, Rosser, and Harvey, 2000). Other factors such as self-esteem, a sense of self and identity, and a sense of control remain fundamental concepts for well-being and are extremely important for the ability of people with cognitive decline to continue to manage their lives with support and adapt to changes, and the impact of these on their day-to-day experiences with friends and family. However, when autonomy, choice, and control are threatened for the elderly, it becomes detrimental to their well-being. Thus, it becomes necessary for dementia-friendly communities to have adequate support to help maintain a reasonable life.

It is essential to well-being that people with dementia feel included and valued (Bond, Corner, Lilley, and Ellwood, 2002). Responding to the challenge of dementia and creating truly dementia-friendly communities is a long process, demanding innovative thinking, creative responses, and fresh approaches to the re-shaping of our public services and design of our environments. Supporting people to be included in their communities and ensuring high-quality care provision with a motivated and skilled workforce are cornerstones of ensuring high well-being at all stages of the dementia journey.

Complementary and alternative interventions for dementia

People with advanced dementia suffer a range of symptoms comparable with those dying with cancer, with 64% of people dying with dementia experiencing pain and 57% loss of appetite (McCarthy et al., 1997). Evidence has revealed that people with advanced dementia experience suboptimal care in the form of increased hospitalization, worse pain control, and fewer palliative care interventions compared with those dying with cancer (Aminoff and

Adunsky, 2004; Evers, Purohit, Perl, Khan, and Martin, 2002; McCarthy et al., 1997; Mitchell, Kicly, and Hamel, 2004; Sampson, Gould, Lee, and Blanchard, 2006; Scherder et al., 2005). Professionals often experience many difficulties in meeting the palliative care needs of people with advanced dementia (Birch and Draper, 2008). Many of these physical symptoms are poorly detected and untreated (Shega, Hougham, Stocking, Cos-Hayley, and Sachs, 2006); assessment and management of pain are particularly difficult as patients cannot verbalize their symptoms and there is currently no single assessment tool deemed useful for widespread use in practice (Herr, Bjoro, and Decker, 2006; Zwakhalen, Hamers, Abu-Saad, and Pberger, 2006). Hence, the utmost necessity of providing complementary and alternative interventions for patients suffering from dementia.

Breathing exercises

They offer persons with dementia a stress-reduction activity that can be easily understood, imitated, and accomplished (Erikson, 1950; Tornstam, 2011).

Aromatherapy

Provision of aromatherapy can provide a soothing, cost-effective means of relaxation to elderly individuals with dementia as well as their caregivers. Lavender oil, jojoba oil, cypress, tea tree, and so on may be used for aromatherapy (Robinson et al., 2007).

Hand massage and reflexology

The soft, gentle, repetitive stroking is non-invasive and connects the massage-giver and massage-receiver through touch which, at times, is the only remaining avenue of communication available. Hand massage may be provided at an individual or group level.

Reflexology may also be used with individuals with dementia to stimulate their different reflex points appropriately so as to have adequate sensations in the brain. However, reflexology needs to be applied with caution for stroke victims having a history of haemorrhages because reflexology may stimulate circulation and hence the movement of small clots within the system, which can result in the development of emergencies (Crane, 2010, 1998).

Warm touches: Verbal and non-verbal

Persons with dementia can be especially sensitive to unspoken affect and emotion, and the practitioner's demeanour may speak louder than his/her words. In addition, using simple, concrete language and repetition can assist persons with cognitive deficits to understand the message given to them (McBee, 2008; Shega et al., 2006).

Yoga stretches

Guided yoga stretches in the form of chair stretches and stretches in all direction are helpful to elderly people suffering from dementia (McBee, 2008). Progression of the symptoms of dementia may be delayed and function and independence can be maximized by means of guided yoga stretches (Fjellman-Wiklund, Nordin, Skelton, and Lundin-Olsson, 2016).

Social activities and inclusion: A necessity for terminal care in dementia

Social inclusion in any form by fostering interaction as far as practicable has been found to demonstrate positive mood, reduce feelings of isolation and distress, and reduce the emergence of behavioural symptoms in the form of wandering, agitation, and aggression (Ballard et al., 2002). Opportunities to participate in arts and cultural activity have also been demonstrated to have a beneficial effect on the well-being of people with dementia (Mittleman and Epstein, 2009). In addition, the provision of therapeutic activities, such as art or music therapy, may be useful in enabling a positive social environment and give opportunities for self-expression where the individuality of the person is recognized and respected (Department of Health, 2009).

Dementia-friendly communities highlight a focus on solutions rather than problems, and a focus on what can be achieved and maintained rather than what is lost. This is a significant shift in addressing the issues that contribute to positive well-being and the challenge of living well with dementia (Kirkwood and Cooper, 2014). The practitioners do not have a magic wand that can dispel life's difficulties, and no caregiver can lift from a patient's shoulders the responsibility for his or her own path in life. Nevertheless, everyone can help and come forward to uplift the quality of life of individuals with dementia. Certain salient points that need to be followed in handling dementia cases are as follows:

Adequate use of time

As mental health professionals, practising empathy adequately with individuals suffering from dementia is noteworthy to bring about a change in their state of well-being. Wilcock (2003) suggests that even *two minutes is adequate and five minutes is a lot* in offering quality nursing care to such individuals. For instance, the task of washing a patient in the evening after tea can be achieved very economically, wasting no time at all. But the minute it takes at the end of it to squeeze his/her hand, or give him/her a goodnight kiss on the forehead, or just stop and look into his/her eyes and say what a wonderful person s/he is to nurse and spend time with is genuinely transformative. It invites a perspective to *look deeply* on the part of the caregiver. The caregiver needs to have authenticity in his/her temperament.

Respect

Moreover, offering *respect* serves as a crucial feature in palliative care. This can be imparted by providing such an individual with *a choice*. Even when someone can no longer speak or has a severe disability owing to dementia that can impede expression, there are many ways of discovering preferences. Offering someone a choice is a form of respect which helps to rebuild self-esteem damaged by disability and can restore hope.

Respect also means at *all times* remembering the presence of the individual in conversation as well as in body language. Respect for a person who requires intimate care means meticulous attention to modesty, both in ensuring privacy and in the way one speaks to them (Wilcock, 2003). Respect involves acknowledging the disabled person *as a person*. This may be practised by the caregivers to restore a sense of dignity and identity of the elderly individual with dementia.

Coming to terms with one's own vulnerability

Keeping company with the long-term ill and disabled, as well as the dying, can only be comfortable and sustainable if one comes to terms with one's own helplessness and inadequacy through identification. We do not have all the answers of the cosmos, do not have endless resources of unconditional love, and cannot always be there. Everything cannot be done, but at least some steps may be adopted for the senior individuals suffering from dementia. The humbling thing is that so often we come away from an encounter with someone struggling with suffering, feeling irritable, useless, and ashamed, only to learn later that just our going and spending time with him/her and caring for him/her restored a level of meaning and hope. Thus, according to Thera and Bodhi (1999), growing old, falling sick, and dying are obvious events of life. There is no need to 'control' the cork amidst the gushing currents of a flowing river; instead, observing the cork to ride with the tide calls forth self-realization and wisdom in abundance.

Equanimity

It is essential for the caregiver of the dementia patient to maintain a peaceful awareness regarding the attitude one has chosen so that they do not interfere with the indignities and infirmities of impairment offered by dementia of various kinds (McBee, 2008).

Honesty

It is often helpful to acknowledge the level of difficulty and disability someone is experiencing rather than suffering in silence and being acknowledged by nobody. Catharsis in any form is needed on the part of the caregiver to lessen the burnout effect.

Acknowledging dread

Many people living with dementia carry the draining and debilitating experience of dread. This may be associated with deep existential questions in the form of fear of death, loss of faith, or an overwhelming sense of meaninglessness at one's end. At the other end, it may be associated with the fear of mundane distress.

It is helpful if one is able, without being intrusive, to enable the person with dementia and consequent impairment to express and explore the worst: to find, sometimes protected under feelings and thoughts related to denial and avoidance, what it is about dread and where does it reside (Kirkwood and Cooper, 2014).

Facing anger

Many individuals with dementia have pent-up emotions of hidden anger which need to come out or have 'underlying aggression' (Wilcock, 2003). Anger and aggression are secondary emotions that present when a wound is still sore and raw or when festering is being protected. Such issues may often have a physical basis in the form of painful misery of pressure sores and the like.

Humour

Humour involves not belittling but softening – that which one can laugh at – with amusement, not bitterness – one has accepted and overcome the crisis. The day one can laugh about some of the indignities of life offered by dementia on the part of the patient and the caregiver himself/herself is a healing milestone in the palliative journey of the elderly. Gibson (1998) is of the opinion that dementia rips apart individuals to the essence of their being and makes them in greater direct touch with their emotions. They tend to communicate with greater authenticity than controlled emotions that are customarily expressed.

In fact, dementia attacks intellectual capacity and semantic memory but leaves feelings and those memories linked to strong emotions largely untouched (Killick, 2003). This may be because of the losses in some areas, a person tends to put greater emphasis on other areas to compensate, making the affective component of such an individual strongly developed. Hence, individuals with dementia who use humour as a mature defence appear to transcend over the limitations of various kinds.

Caring for the caregivers of dementia

It is often stressful for family caregivers of people with dementia as they are more likely to experience depressed mood, report burnout, and have worse general health compared with caregivers of chronic conditions (Brodaty et al., 2002). In dementia, caregivers may grieve or experience loss as their relative loses functional and cognitive abilities and the tangible benefits of companionship, affection, and intimacy (Zarit and Zarit, 2008). Caregivers may suffer from pangs of a 'living death' in the family due to dementia of their loved one (Woods, 1989). It may also prompt the shift of the senior person with dementia to residential care (Grasel, 2002). As such, primary care physicians should endeavour to provide proactive caregiver support and monitor their health and well-being, in addition to caring for the person with dementia (Cameron, Aggar, Robinson and Kurrle, 2011). They should get adequate time and space to touch upon their lives with respite being offered by others. Their personal care seems to be others' responsibility to help them in the care and concern for the person with dementia.

The mental and physical health of caregivers is of importance for the realistic, long-term possibility of community care. Psychosomatic interventions for caregivers of people with dementia can reduce psychological morbidity for caregivers and help their relatives stay at home longer (Brodaty, Green, and Koschera, 2003; Smits et al., 2007). Besides, family caregivers of people with advanced dementia require more emotional support and respite care prior to the person's death than afterwards (Albinsson and Strang, 2003). There is some evidence that advance care planning may improve the 'quality of dying' in people with dementia, largely through reducing unnecessary hospital admissions (Harrison-Dening, Jones, and Sampson, 2011; Robinson, Dickinson et al., 2011).

Seeking the spiritual dimension in dementia

Theorists have often linked spirituality with the notion of personhood and identified emotion as an essential element of the concept. It is difficult to be sure that a person with dementia who has lost speech is on an inward journey. However, sitting with someone in silence or holding their hand or looking along the prolonged scrutiny of their gaze has proved memorable and fulfilling to many caregivers, taking the caregiver out of the context of the ordinary and into a new realm of 'being,' thereby confirming a qualitative leap in the spiritual journey (Killick, 2003; McKinlay, 1998; 2002).

Hence, amidst the mixed bag of varied emotional upheavals of caregivers for their elderly care recipients, a spiritual dimension of caregiving behaviour

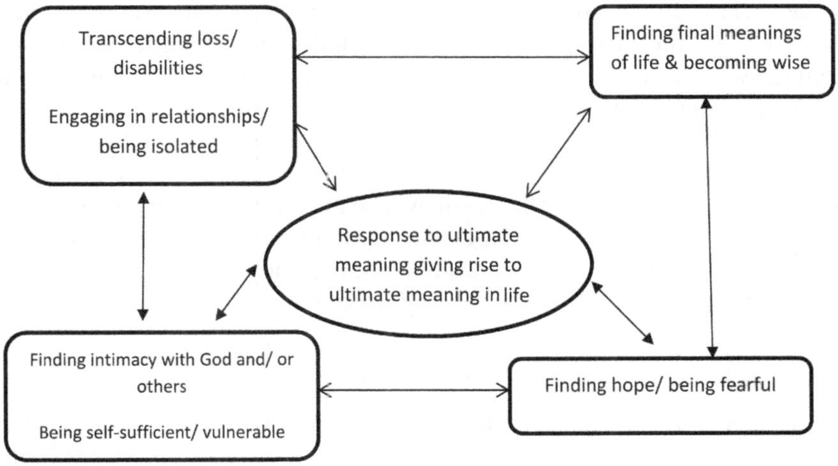

Figure 11.2 Themes of ageing associated with spirituality among caregivers of elderly individuals (source: authors).

is noteworthy. It accounts for fuelling one's meaning in life on the part of care providers. This spectrum ranges from attempts to seek ultimate meaning in life, understanding the nuances of self-sufficiency versus vulnerability, relationship versus isolation, hope versus despair, unfurling the specific responses to understand meaning in life, and the attainment of wisdom (MacKinley, 2000). This is underlined by concern and love for the elderly person and acknowledging the contributions of the senior individual in the immediate family as well as society at large in an indirect manner. The caregiver often comes to terms with issues of transcendence by spontaneously serving the *soul* of the other person, and hence the *cosmic power* – understanding him/her in entirety as much as possible, cherishing the lived moments together, engaging in empathy, 'letting go' of hidden pains, and even the individual when s/he is about to leave the world and thereby engaging in personal growth. S/he may also attain meaning in life by feeling 'close' to the *supreme power* through the very act of caregiving. Issues of vulnerabilities, fear, and isolation of the elderly individual are addressed by the 'soft, caressing and healing hands' of caregivers who enable the former to have some sense of self-sufficiency, hope, a feeling of 'connectedness,' and sense of wisdom as far as practicable. This is further elaborated diagrammatically in Figure 11.2.

Perhaps the most remarkable statement of the gifts people with dementia can bring to us in the spiritual realm is reflected from Everett's (1996) view that people suffering from dementia are similar to 'magic mirrors' where one can see the plight of the human condition, and can repudiate the commonly held societal values, some being those of power and prestige, that are unreal and shallow. People with dementia have their unconscious very close to the surface, owing to the ego being stripped apart. They, thereby, show the caregivers the masks behind which we hide our authentic personhood from the world. They reflect their authentic selves and enable 'life lessons' to be given to their caregivers as 'gifts.' It is in the offering to care and nurture persons with dementia that one arrives very near to nature which has the unique opportunity to serve the Almighty. The spiritual chord is hit accordingly. It is a supreme irony that those whose personhood we have the temerity to question may be the very people to teach us to see our personhood in a fresh light and to lead us to re-evaluate human possibility. Thus, can they be burdens or blissful sources of energy for us?

Conclusion

It is only our society and communities together, drawing on all resources of the able-bodied and those not as able-bodied, that can face up hopefully and realistically to the challenge of an ageing society. We can do so by discovering and encouraging the positive wisdom and resources of those growing older. Unless we discover our capacity for elderly blessing, we shall be less and less able to positively bear our burdens – and even worse, ignore some blessings in them. Hence, to reap the harvest offered by the elderly, one needs to acknowledge their positivity, transcendence, and personhood to understand and realize life in its myriad vistas to the utmost level. It is only then that elderly blessings can be realized in the serene ambience of life to enable us to move forward in our voyage.

References

Agree, E.M., & Glaser, K. (2009). Demography of informal caregiving. In P. Uhlenberg (Ed.), *International handbook of population aging* (vol. 1). (pp. 647–668). Dordrecht: Springer Science.

Albinsson, L., & Strang, P. (2003). Differences in supporting families of dementia patients and cancer patients: A palliative perspective. *Palliative Medicine*, *17*(4), 359–367.

Alzheimer's Disease International (2007). *The global impact of dementia*. Retrieved from http://www.alz.co.uk/media/demntia.html

Aminoff, B.Z., & Adunsky, A. (2004). Dying dementia patients: Too much suffering, too little palliation. *American Journal of Alzheimer's Disease and Other Dementias*, *19*(4), 243–247.

Ballard, C., Powell, I., James, I., Reichelt, K., Myint, P., Potkins, D., ... Barber, R. (2002). Can psychiatric liaison reduce neuroleptic use and reduce health service utilization for dementia patients residing in care facilities? *International Journal of Geriatric Psychiatry*, *17*(2), 140–145.

Birch, D., & Draper, J. (2008). A critical literature review exploring the challenges of delivering effective palliative care to older people with dementia. *Journal of Clinical Nursing*, *17*(9), 1144–1163.

Bodnar, J.C., & Kiecolt-Glaser, J.K. (1994).Caregiver depression after bereavement: Chronic stress isn't over when it's over. *Psychology and Aging*, *9*(3), 372–380.

Bond, J., Corner, L., Lilley, A., & Ellwood, C. (2002). Medicalization of insight and caregivers' response to risk in dementia. *Dementia*, *1*(3), 313–328.

Bowling, A. (2005). *Ageing well: Quality of life in old age*. Maidenhead: Open University Press.

Brodaty, H., Green, A., & Koschera, A. (2003). Meta-analysis of psychosocial interventions for caregivers of people with dementia. *Journal of the American Geriatrics Society*, *51*(5), 657–664.

Burton, L.C., Newsom, J.T., Schulz, R., Hirsch, C.H., & German, P. (1997). Preventive health behaviors among spousal caregivers. *Preventive Medicine*, *26*(2), 162–169.

Burton, L.C., Zdaniuk, B., Schulz, R., Jackson, S., & Hirsch, C. (2003). Transitions in spousal caregiving. *Gerontologist*, *43*(2), 230–241.

Cameron, I.D., Aggar, C., Robinson, A.L., & Kurrle, S.E. (2011). Assessing and helping carers of older people. *British Medical Journal Clinical Review*, *343*(5202), 1–5.

Cantor, M.H. (1975). Life space and the social support system of the inner city elderly of New York. *Gerontologist*, *15*(1 Pt 1), 23–27.

Chappell, N.L., & Kuehne, V.K. (1998). Congruence among husband and wife caregivers. *Journal of Aging Studies*, *12*(3), 239–254.

Clay, O.J., Roth, D.L., Wadley, V.G. , & Haley, W.E. (2008). Changes in social support and their impact on psychosocial outcome over a 5-year period for African American and White dementia caregivers. *International Journal of Geriatric Psychiatry*, *23*(8), 857–862.

Coleman, P.G. (2000). Aging and the satisfaction of psychological needs. *Psychological Inquiry*, *11*(4), 291–293.

Collins, A.H., & Pancoast, D.L. (1978). *Natural helping networks: A strategy for prevention*. Washington, DC: National Publishing.

Crane, B. (1998). *The complete illustrated guide to reflexology: Massage your way to health and well-being*. London: Harper Collins.

Crane, B. (2010). *Reflexology: Therapies & techniques for well-being*. London: Duncan Baird Publishers.

Davidson, K., Arber, S., & Ginn, J. (2000). Gendered meanings of care work within late life marital relationships. *Canadian Journal on Aging*, *29*(4), 536–553.

Department of Health (2009). *Living well with dementia: A national strategy*. Retrieved from http://webarchive.nationalarchives.gov.uk/20130107105354/http://www.dh.gov.uk/prod_consum_dh/groups/dh_digitalassets/@dh/@cn/documents/digitalasset/dh_094051.pdf

DiLeonardo, M. (1992). The female world of cards and holidays: Women and families and work of kinship. In B. Thorne & M. Yalom (Eds.), *Rethinking the family*. (pp. 246–261). Boston: Northeastern University Press.

Erikson, E.H. (1950). *Childhood and society*. New York: W.W. Norton.

Everett, D. (1996). *Forget me not: The spiritual care of people with Alzheimer's disease*. Edmonton: Inkwell Press.

Evers, M.M., Purohit, D., Perl, D., Khan, K., & Martin, D.B. (2002). Palliative care and aggressive end of life care for patients with dementia. *Psychiatric Services*, *5395*, 609–661.

Fjellman-Wiklund, A., Nordin, E., Skelton, D.A., & Lundin-Olsson, L. (2016). Reach the person behind the dementia physical therapists' reflections and strategies when composing physical training. *PLOS ONE*, *11*(12), 1–15.

Foresight Mental Capital and Wellbeing Project (2008). *Final project report – executive summary*. London: Government Office for Science.

Ganong, L.H., & Coleman, M. (2006). Obligations to stepparents acquired in later life: Relationship quality and acuity of needs. *Journals of Gerontology: Social Sciences*, *61B*, 80–88.

George, L.K., & Gwyther, L.P. (1986). Caregivers for dementia patients: Complex determinants of well-Being and burden. *Gerontologist*, *26*(3), 253–259.

Gibson, F. (1998). Unmasking dementia. *Community Care Suppl*, 'Inside dementia,' 29 Oct.–4 Nov.

Graham, R. (2004). Cognitive citizenship: Access to hip surgery for people with dementia. *Health: An Interdisciplinary Journal for the Social Study of Health, Illness and Medicine*, *8*(3), 295–310.

Grasel, E. (2002). When home care ends – changes in the physical health of informal caregivers caring for dementia patients: A longitudinal study. *Journal of the American Geriatric Society*, *50*(5), 843–849.

Gwyther, L.P. (1990). Letting-Go: Separation-Individuation in a wife of an Alzheimer's patient. *Gerontologist*, *30*(5), 698–702.

Harrison-Dening, K., Jones, L., & Sampson, E.L. (2011). Advance care planning for people with dementia: A review. *International Psychogeriatrics*, *23*(10), 1535–1551.

Herlofson, K., Hagestad, G., Slagsvold, B., & Sørensen, A.M. (2011). *Intergenerational family responsibility and solidarity in Europe*. Oslo: Norwegian Social Research (NOVA). Retrieved from http://www .multilinks-project.eu/ uploads/ papers/0000/0038/ herlofson_deliverable.pdf

Herr, K., Bjoro, K., & Decker, S. (2006). Tools for assessment of pain in non-verbal older adults with dementia: A state-of-the-science review. *Journal of Pain and Symptom Management*, *31*(2), 170–192.

Hooker, K., Manoogian-O'Dell, M., Monahan, D.J., Frazier, L.D., & Shifren, K. (2000). Does type of disease matter? Gender differences among Alzheimer's and Parkinson's disease spouse caregivers. *Gerontologist*, *40*(5), 568–573.

Jansson, W., Norberg, G., & Grafstrom, M. (2001). Patterns of elderly spousal caregiving in dementia care: An observational study. *Journal of Advanced Nursing*, *34*(6), 804–812.

Kahn, R.L., & Antonucci, T.C. (1980). Convoys over the life course: Attachment, roles and social support. In P.B. Baltes & O. Brim (Eds.), *Life-span development and behaviour* (vol. 4, pp. 253–286). New York: Academic Press.

Killick, J. (2003). Magic mirrors: What people with dementia show us about ourselves. In Jewell, A. (Ed.) *Ageing, spirituality, and well-being* (pp. 143–152). London: Jessica Kingsley Publishers.

Kirkwood, T.B.L., & Cooper, C.L. (Eds.) (2014). Wiley clinical psychology handbooks. *Wellbeing: A Complete Reference Guide, Well-being in Later Life, IV*. Wiley-Blackwell.

Knapp, M., Prince, M., Albanese, E., Banerjee, S., Dhanasiri, S., Fernandez, J.L., & Stewart, R. (2007). *Dementia UK: The full report*. London: Alzheimer's Society.

Kramer, B.J. (1997). Differential predictors of strain and gain among husbands caring for wives with dementia. *Gerontologist, 37*(2), 239–249.

Litwak, E. (1985). *Helping the elderly: The complementary roles of informal networks and formal systems*. New York: Guilford Press.

Lobo-Prahbu, S., Molinari, V., Arlinghaus, K., Barr, E., & Lomax, J. (2005). Spouses of patients with dementia: How do they stay together 'till death do us part'? *Journal of Gerontological Social Work, 44*(3–4), 161–174.

Lubben, J.E. (1988). Assessing social networks among elderly populations. *Family and Community Health, 11*(3), 42–52.

MacKinlay, E. (2001). The spiritual dimension of caring: Applying a model of spiritual tasks of ageing. In E. MacKinlay, J.W. Ellor and S. Pickard (Eds.), *Ageing, spirituality and pastoral care: A multi-national perspective* (pp.151–166). New York: The Hawarth Press, Inc.

MacKinlay E. (2002). The spiritual dimension of caring: Applying a model for spiritual tasks of ageing. *Journal of Religious Gerontology, 12*:151–166.

Marks, N.F., Lambert, J.D., & Choi, H. (2002). Transitions to caregiving, gender, and psychological well-being: A prospective U.S. national study. *Journal of Marriage and Family, 64*(3), 657–667.

Matthews, S.H. (1995). Gender and the division of filial responsibility between lone sisters and their brothers. *Journals of Gerontology: Social Sciences, 50B*, 312–320.

Matthews, S.H., & Heidorn, J. (1998). Meeting filial responsibilities in brothers-only sibling groups. *Journals of Gerontology: Social Sciences, 50B*, 278–286.

Matthews, S.H., & Rosner, T.T. (1988). Shared filial responsibility: The family as the primary caregiver. *Journal of Marriage and the Family, 50*(1), 185–195.

McBee, L. (2008). *Mindfulness-based elder care: A CAM model for frail elders and their caregivers*. New York: Springer Publishing Company.

McCarthy, M., Addington-Hall, J., & Altmann, D. (1997). The experience of dying with dementia: A retrospective study. *International Journal of Geriatric Psychiatry, 12*(3), 404–409.

McKinlay, E.B. (1998). *The spiritual dimension of ageing: Meaning in life, response to meaning, and well-being in ageing*. Doctoral Dissertation. La Trobe University, Melbourne.

Miller, B., & Montgomery, A. (1990). Family caregivers and limitations in social activities. *Research on Aging, 12*(1), 72–93.

Mitchell, S.L., Kicly, D., & Hamel, M.B. (2004). Dying with advanced dementia in the nursing home. *Archives of Internal Medicine, 164*(3), 321–326.

Mittleman, M., & Epstein, C. (2009). *The MoMA Alzheimer's project: Making art accessible to people with dementia, made possible by MetLife Foundation*. Retrieved from http://www.moma.org/meetme/about/index

Navaie-Walier, M., Spriggs, A., & Feldman, P.H. (2002). Informal caregiving: Differential experiences by gender. *Medical Care, 40*(12), 1249–1259.

Ngan, R. (1990a). *The informal caring networks among Chinese families in Hong Kong*. Ph.D. Thesis. Department of Social Work, University of Hong Kong.

Ngan, R. (1990b). The availability of informal support networks to the Chinese elderly in Hong Kong and its implications for practice. *Hong Kong. Journal of Gerontology, 4*(2), 19–25.

Ngan, R., & Kwok, J. (1992). Informal caring networks among Chinese elderly with disabilities in Hong Kong. *International Journal of Rehabilitation Research*, *15*(3), 199–207.

Nijboer, C., Triemstra, M., Tempelaar, R., Mulder, M., Sanderman, R., & van den Bos, G. (2000). Patterns of caregiver experiences among partners of cancer patients. *Gerontologist*, *40*(6), 738–746.

Pinquart, M., & Sörensen, S. (2003). Associations of stressors and uplifts of caregiving with caregiver burden and depressive mood: A meta-analysis. *Journal of Gerontology: Psychological Sciences*, *58B*, 112–128.

Pinquart, M., & Sörensen, S. (2005). Ethnic differences in stressors, resources, and psychological outcomes of family caregiving: A meta-analysis. *Gerontologist*, *45*(1), 90–106.

Pinquart, M., & Sörensen, S. (2007). Correlates of physical health of informal caregivers: A meta-analysis. *Journal of Gerontology, Series B: Psychological Sciences and Social Sciences*, *62*(2), 126–137.

Prince, M., Prina, M., & Guerchet, M. (2013). *World Alzheimer report 2013: Journey of caring: An analysis of long-term care for dementia*. London: Alzheimer's Disease International. Retrieved from http://www.alz.co.uk/ research/world-report-2013

Pruchno, R.A., & Resch, N.L. (1989). Husbands and wives as caregivers: Antecedents of depression and burden. *Gerontologist*, *29*(2), 159–165.

Quadagno, J. (2005). *Aging and the life course* (3rd ed.). Boston: McGraw-Hill.

Robinson, L., Dickinson, C., Rousseau, N., Beyer, F., Clark, A., Hughes, J.,...Exley, C. (2011). A systematic review of the effectiveness of advance care planning interventions for people with cognitive impairment and dementia. *Age and Ageing*, *41*(2), 263–269.

Robinson, L., Hutchings, D., Dickinson, H.O., Corner, L., Beyer, F., Finch, T., ... Bond, J. (2007). Effectiveness and acceptability of non-pharmacological interventions to reduce wandering in dementia: A systematic review. *International Journal of Geriatric Psychiatry*, *22*(1), 9–22.

Robinson-Whelen, S., Tada, Y., MacCallum, R.C., McGuire, L., & Kiecolt-Glaser, J.K. (2001).Long-term caregiving: What happens when it ends? *Journal of Abnormal Psychology*, *110*(4), 573–584.

Rose, S.K., Strauss, M.E., Neundorfer, M.M., Smyth, K.A., & Stuckey, J.C. (1997). The relationship of self-Restraint and distress to coping among spouses caring for persons with Alzheimer's disease. *Journal of Applied Gerontology*, *16*(1), 91–103.

Sampson, E.L., Gould, V., Lee, D., & Blanchard, M.R. (2006). Differences in care received by patients with and without dementia who died during acute hospital admission: A retrospective case note study. *Age and Ageing*, *35*(2), 187–189.

Scherder, E., Oosterman, J., Swaab, D., Herr, K., Ooms, M., Ribble, M.,... Benedetti, F. (2005). Recent developments in pain in dementia. *British Medical Journal*, *330*(7489), 461–464.

Sclai, C.E., Trimble, M.R., Rosser, M.N., & Harvey, R.J. (2000). The Quality of Life Assessment Schedule (QOLAS) – A new method for assessing quality of life in dementia. In S.M. Albert & R.G. Logsdon (Eds.), *Assessing quality of life in Alzheimer's disease* (pp. 31–48). New York: Springer Publishing Company.

Seeman, T.E., Lusignolo, T.M., Albert, M., & Berkman, L. (2001). Social relationships, social support and patterns of cognitive ageing in healthy, high-functioning older adults. MacArther studies of successful ageing. *Health Psychology*, *20*(4), 243–255.

Seltzer, M.M., & Li, L.W. (2000). The dynamics of caregiving: Transitions during a three- year prospective study. *Gerontologist*, *40*(2), 165–178.

Shega,J.W., Hougham, G.W., Stocking, C.B., Cos-Hayley, D., & Sachs, G.A. (2006). Management of non-cancer pain in community-dwelling persons with dementia. *Journal of American Geriatric Society*, *54*(12), 1892–1897.

Smits, C.H., deLange, J., Drocs, R.M., Mciland, F., Vernooji-Dassen, M., & Pot, A.M. (2007). Effects of combined intervention programmes for people with dementia living at homes and their caregivers: A systematic review. *International Journal of Geriatric Psychiatry*, 22(12), 1181–1193.

Souren, L., & Franssen, E. (1994). *Broken connections: Alzheimer's disease. Part 1 Origin and course* (p. 14). Lisse: Swets and Zeitlinger Publishers

Stark, O. (1995). *Altruism and beyond: An economic analysis of transfers and exchanges within families and groups*. Cambridge: Cambridge University Press.

Szabo, V., & Strang, V. (1999). Experiencing control in caregiving. *Image: -the Journal of Nursing Scholarship*, *31*(1), 71–75.

Szinovacz, M.E., & Davey, A. (2004). Retirement transitions and spouse's disability: Effects on depressive symptoms. *Journal of Gerontology: Social Sciences*, *59B*, S333–S342.

Thera, N., & Bodhi, B. (Trans & Eds.) (1999). *Numerical discourses of the Buddha: An anthology of Suttas from the Anguttara Nikaya*. Walnut Creek, CA: AltaMira.

Thomas, W.H. (2004). *What are old people for? How elders will save the world*. Acton, MA: VanderWyk & Burnham.

Tornstam, L. (2011). Maturing into gero-transcendence. *The Journal of Transpersonal Psychology*, *43*(2), 166–180.

Wilcock, P. (2003). The caged bird: Thoughts on the challenge of living with stroke. In Jewell, A. (Ed.), *Ageing, spirituality and well-being* (pp. 58–72). London: Jessica Kingsley Publishers.

Woods, R.T. (1989). *Alzheimer's disease: Coping with a living death*. London: Souvenir Press.

Young, R.F., & Kahana, E. (1989). Specifying caregiver outcomes: Gender and relationship aspects of caregiving strain. *Gerontologist*, *29*(5), 660–666.

Zarit, S.H., & Zarit, J.M. (2008). Flexibility and change: The fundamentals for families coping with dementia. In M. Downs & B. Bowers (Eds.), *Excellence in dementia care* (pp. 85–102). Milton Keynes: Open University Press and McGraw Hill.

Zwakhalen, S.M.G., Hamers, J.P.H., Abu-Saad, H.H., & Pberger, M.P.F. (2006). Pain in elderly people with severe dementia: A systematic review of behavioural pain assessment tools. *BMC Geriatrics*, 6, 1–15.

12

MINDFULNESS PRACTICES

The essential alchemy of meaningful ageing

> There is greater power in quietness and stillness…
>
> Be still and know that you are just not a 'Being'
>
> You are a 'Spirit'…
>
> You are a vibrating energy reservoir…

The declining conditions of old age in general show reduced alertness, unmindfulness, and forgetfulness as common features. But it is not just the frail body, but an uninterested, self-occupied, and complaining mind that stays de-focused and unmindful. The process makes them looser in fact. As long as we live, if we have sufficient interest in our surrounding world of people, events, and happenings – the mind stays active being alert and healthy. Even in old age, when we can breathe normally, we can see things around us and smell the aroma of food, fruits, and flowers – we seem to be blessed. Life demands its acknowledgements; these are givens of life and we need to declare the state for us to feel happy and be mindful. Hence, mindfulness seems to be an important concept to take account of in our extended years of life. In fact, mindfulness practices have demonstrated acceptability with the elderly and their caregivers (Smith, 2004, 2006; McBee, 2004). As an adopted process, mindfulness seems to engage one into non-materialistic yet intrinsically satisfying subjective perceptive experiences (Olendzki, 2012) and self-pursuits (Brown and Kasser, 2005). It enables an enriching of the elder-self as regard to different aspects of his/her personality and helps one to be more centred and integrated in totality. Mindfulness is just self-awareness. People miss all the joy of the inner spirit by being disconnected from within life's roots. It is only when one is in the present and is aware of one's inner and outer world and act with empathy, love, or other positive features of the mind that one is bound to feel blessed and at peace. Mindfulness practice seems to be the only way to it. To bring pause between two acts and thoughts is the art of mindfulness. When one practices this, the spontaneous result is the clarity of thoughts and feelings.

In its fold, the self-system calms down and in this calmness, true love feelings turn into generative-ness, with more to give rather than demand from life. The state seems very much matched with positive ageing. Ageing does not stand there as decay; it spreads the web of fulfilment and happiness. The present chapter showcases the use of mindfulness-based practices for elderly participants to improve their overall quality of life by embracing positivity in general.

Mindfulness: Its conceptual overview

Mindfulness, being a unique quality of consciousness, involves a receptive awareness of ongoing internal states, behaviour, and external realities (Brown et al., 2007). It is accompanied by an open and distortion-free perception of what is present right at the moment (Brown and Kasser, 2005). It thus relates to the existential paradigm of the self. The practice of mindfulness entails an unconditional presence and unconditional openness on the part of the individual (Brown et al., 2007). It is a simple, yet very powerful practice of training one's attention. It involves paying attention to sensations, thoughts, and emotions that are occurring at the present moment in a non-judgemental manner. It enables in loosening one's rigid sense of morality which otherwise tends to tighten up the self-system, making individuals fail in touching the present 'bliss' components of the self. Mindfulness practice is powerful since it interrupts the habit of getting lost in thoughts, mostly about the future or past, which are often stressful in nature. Mindfulness training helps individuals to place their attention where they want it to be and to sustain the same for longer periods of time (Jha, Krompinger, and Baime, 2007)

There are a total of 12 *mindfulness qualities*, of which seven were initially defined by Kabat Zinn (1990), with an additional five been offered by Shapiro and Schwartz (2000) to explicitly address the affective qualities of the mindfulness construct. They may be described as follows:

a. *Non-judging*: Involves being aware of judgemental qualities and the reaction to inner and outer experiences without censoring or blocking them;
b. *Non-striving*: Prompts one to be non-goal-oriented and to remain unattached to the outcome or achievement. It helps one in realizing that being one's own self to the genuine extent is more important than achieving any goal in life;
c. *Acceptance*: Relates to accepting things as they are at present;
d. *Patience*: Involves understanding and accepting that sometimes things must be given their own time to be unfolded;
e. *Trust*: Makes the individual take responsibilities for being him/her own self and learning to listen and trust his/her own being;

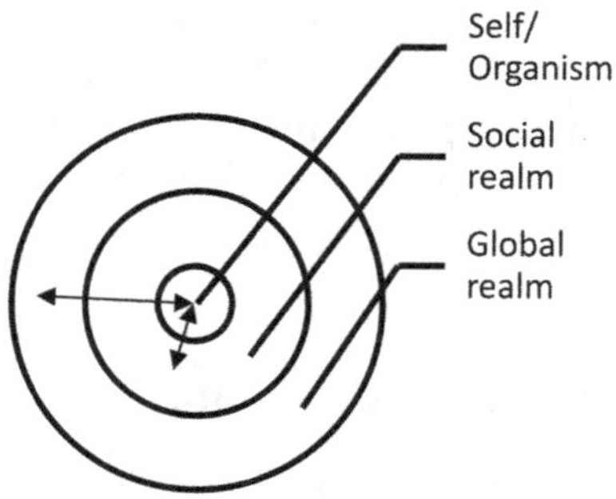

Figure 12.1 Interactions among the different realms with regard to the self in accordance with intentional systemic mindfulness (source: authors).

f. *Beginner's mind* leading to *openness*: Involves seeing, feeling, and perceiving everything as if for the first time;
g. *Letting go*: Relates to forgiving self and others by releasing thoughts, feelings, and situations that the mind seems to want to hold on to;
h. *Gentleness*: Its characteristic features are being soft, considerate, and tender;
i. *Generosity*: Enables an individual to give in the present moment within an ambience of love as well as compassion without any thought of return;
j. *Empathy*: Relates to feeling and understanding others' perspective in the present moment and communicating this with the individual;
k. *Gratitude*: Relates to reverence, appreciation, and being thankful for the present moment;
l. *Loving kindness*: Involves embodying benevolence, compassion, and cherishing the present moment by the individual to bring about a merging of forgiveness with unconditional love.

Within the periphery of mindfulness qualities, intentional systemic mindfulness (I.S.M.) seems to be another concept that needs inclusion to attain positive psychological qualities in the individual in an enhanced form (Shapiro, Schwartz, and Santerre, 2002). It addresses both how individuals attend as well as why they attend to different stimuli. This may be charted in the form of a model (Shapiro, Schwartz, and Santerre, 2002) (Figure 12.1).

It relates to the intentional directing of the energy component in the different layers of the self, some being biophysical and others psychobiological or individual. It emanates to the social or familial level to gradually emerge itself with the global and universal cosmos, it being the reservoir of all our resources and energy. Mindfulness training encourages individuals to bring an attitude of warmth and kind curiosity to whatever they experience in terms of thoughts, feelings, and body sensations – from moment-to-moment. It thus helps individuals to let what *is* the case *be* the case (Chaskalson, 2011).

Pillars of mindfulness practice

The practice of mindfulness is based on four different foundations (McCown et al., 2010):

- *Mindfulness of the body* – Here, attention is provided to the breath, then to the calming of the body, and finally to the awareness of the physique in sensation, posture, and movement (Kabat-Zinn, 2013; McCown et al., 2010). This is expected to help increase one's sense of body-space awareness.
- *Mindfulness of feelings* – Here, attention is focused on the feeling that accompanies the experiences of each moment (Grabovac, Lau, and Willett, 2011; McCown et al., 2010). It comprises feelings of both pleasant and unpleasant as well as neutral nature, which are noticed as they arise and pass away like the waves of the sea.
- *Mindfulness of the mind* – Here, the individual focuses his attention on the activity, or processing of the mind, noticing shifts in states of awareness, concentration, and distraction (Kabat-Zinn, 2013). The mind appears to be a crystal-clear mirror at this junction where certain subtle changes in psychological functioning are 'sensed,' having their repercussions in the crystal-clear waters of the psyche.
- *Mindfulness of mind-objects* – Here, attention is brought to the things the mind is thinking about. Such stimuli may emanate from both within the self-system or may be external in nature. The mind tries to notice the stimulus which is being focused in a non-judgemental manner.

Mindfulness in Buddhism

Mindfulness is also based on the Four Noble Truths which form the essence of Buddhism (Gunaratana, 2001; McCown et al., 2010). The first two truths are aimed at the identification of the problem followed by the diagnosis, while the other two truths are targeted towards the resolution of the problem. Understanding what *suffering is* acknowledges the very notion that dissatisfaction is unavoidable (Gunaratana, 2001). Kabat-Zinn (2013) notes that it is the relationship of individuals with their universal feelings of pain that tends to create or enhance their sense of suffering. It is to be noted that everything in the world has the potential to create suffering owing to cravings and vain attempts to grasp 'objects' on the part of individuals (Wallace, 2011). For instance, for many elderly people, their physical body discernibly gives way to the gradual ravages of time as a result of one's state of well-being and narcissistic equilibrium being compromised. The elderly individual often has to come to terms with the radical inconsistency of the imagined and/or wished-for body of the earlier days with a robust and hardy psychosexual self-concept (Milne, 2013), and the real, diminished body that one inhabits. It is often associated with grave humiliation, lowered self-esteem, self-concept, and a sense of depression with a feeling of helplessness, hopelessness, and worthlessness (Marcus, 2013, 2017; Rorty, 1989). This consequently makes such individuals have a sense of suffering. Hence, letting go of such cravings appears to be a critical aspect of freedom or liberation of the individual from suffering of multiple kinds (McCown et al., 2010). The third truth relates to the possibility of the cessation of cravings and one's freedom from suffering. The Fourth Noble Truth showcases the Eightfold Path of Buddhism to liberation. This involves developing a positivity-laden lifestyle which is conducive to end suffering on the part of individuals (Bien, 2006).

Realization of the impermanence of life through mindfulness practice

It is the rhythm of life and nature in the broader sense that calls forth impermanence in each and every aspect. Everything changes and nothing remains still (Kabat-Zinn, 2013; Shapiro and Carlson, 2009; Bien, 2006; Grabovac et al., 2011). There are movement and dynamicity in life at every juncture. It is only when individuals resist or tend to forget this fact that they end up in suffering. Individuals often appear to cling on to wonderful experiences and wish them to be relatively permanent (which is just a utopia).

This very truth of life is palpably felt by the individual through the practice of mindfulness. It is during mindfulness that one becomes aware of different thoughts or stimuli that are present at the current moment – those which are perceptively important for the individual at the moment but cease to be significant at some later point. When the elderly person is engaged in the practice of mindfully noticing his thoughts, feelings, bodily sensations, and the like, he/she gradually realizes the enormous gush (torrent) of stimuli that bombards the self-system at any point of time, which are essentially transient. The elderly individual engaged in mindfulness practice develops patience, self-compassion, unconditional acceptance, and regard for the self as an authentic system as a consequence.

The practice of non-attachment through mindfulness

Individuals use their sensorium to have a feeling of the stimulus in the internal or external environment. Each sense impression gets reflexively paired with a feeling tone, being positive, negative, or neutral. It is often observed that habitual reactions such as attachment and aversion to feelings of a sense impression or mental event, as well as a lack of awareness of the process, may lead to suffering (Grabovac et al., 2011). Non-attachment comes to the rescue here. It is the process of not attaching to or attempting to avoid thoughts, feelings, people, things, and so forth since it originates at the most basic levels. When an individual is mindfully focusing on his/her breath/body/posture/movement/thoughts, he/she is noticing them from the perspective of a neutral, objective observer who is detached from materialistic cravings for the time being. It involves a style of *accepting* what is present in the 'form' as it is. Acceptance is intended to mean an acknowledgement of or a cessation of resistance to something. This practice also has a reverberatory impact on the self-system, thereby making the individual engage in a non-materialistic endeavour.

Mindfulness in relation to physiology

Mindful practices have been found to have an intricate relationship with neurophysiology. They are believed to reinforce the functioning of the pre-frontal orbital cortex (P.F.C.), known for its executive control, inhibition, decision making, and purposeful intention (Hanson and Mendius, 2009). These practices strengthen access to the parasympathetic nervous system, which is recognized for calming the body and mind (Hanson and Mendius, 2009). Positive emotional experiences are cultivated from the limbic system which is the emotional centre of the brain (Hanson and Mendius, 2009). Finally, such practices create neurological integration within the brain, allowing for increased feelings of inner and outer harmony, attunement, and integrity (Siegel, 2010). This neurological integration of the circuits in the brain is responsible for instilling a sense of peace and inner calm which persists within the system as a reverberation.

Tailoring mindfulness-based practices for elderly individuals

Mindfulness practices are often taught to elderly individuals with a variety of conditions and in a variety of settings. They along with their caregivers are even found to report benefit from adaptations to the model (Lynch, Morse, Mendelson, and Robins, 2003; McBee, 2004; McBee, Westreich, and Likourezos, 2004; Smith, 2004, 2006). Amidst the frailty of elderly individuals, mindfulness practices adopted for them need to take into consideration the following points:

- Elders are often less emotionally expressive;
- Mindfulness practices need to be designed for single individuals;
- Elders may have difficulty participating in groups equally due to physical, cognitive, and communicative frailties. This calls forth tailoring mindfulness practices according to their suitability;

- Frail elders are more responsive to directives or clear questions rather than open-ended questions due to their sense of overall lowered confidence and sometimes comprehensibility;
- Some frail elders engage in passive involvement;
- Mindfulness practices in groups (if participants have at least some degree of mobility) can provide a safe and non-threatening environment to connect with others;
- Elders may not be able to exhibit consistent attendance in groups, owing to illness, frailty, transportation problems, or forgetfulness. This may affect group cohesion in the long run.
- Elders experience a decrease in stamina and a slowing down of reaction time. Big groups may be too tiring and defeat the benefits of mindfulness-based elder care;
- Psycho-educational groups may require reinforcement of skills and techniques (Hooyman and Kiyak, 1988; Toseland, 1995).

It is to be noted that mindfulness classes may be offered to elderly individuals residing in institutions like nursing homes. Such practices provide skills, support, and solace for residents and caregivers. Mindfulness teaches informal and formal skills that, if practised regularly, may reduce suffering and may lead to profound life changes in individuals. It may be practised in daily living in the form of ***mindful eating***. For instance, in the practice mode, group members may be given a few raisins and asked to eat them slowly while observing their physical sensations, thoughts, and feelings. The exercise may be for about 10–15 minutes where participants are asked to give their full attention to holding the raisin(s), looking at them, touching, seeing, smelling, placing them, tasting, chewing, swallowing, and finishing them. This can offer a new relationship to the experience of eating as well as a new way of experiencing other routine events.

Mindfulness meditation: An essential tool of a mindfulness manifesto for the elderly

Mindfulness meditation is yet another practice which may be applicable for the elderly. It is not about only paying attention to the concept of breathing. Rather, it is about following the physical breath with great curiosity as to its texture, temperature, and other sensation. These may include the cool flow of air at the nostrils or the rising and falling of the belly or chest. Mindfulness meditation is also termed opening-up meditation practice. It is often observed that initially, instead of paying attention to each breath, the mind swerves off during mindfulness meditation. It reaches into the future, worries about the past, or judges meditation as a waste of time. Observing the wandering mind is the first track of mindfulness practice. Mindfulness allows individuals to relate more fully to experience – to absorb the world

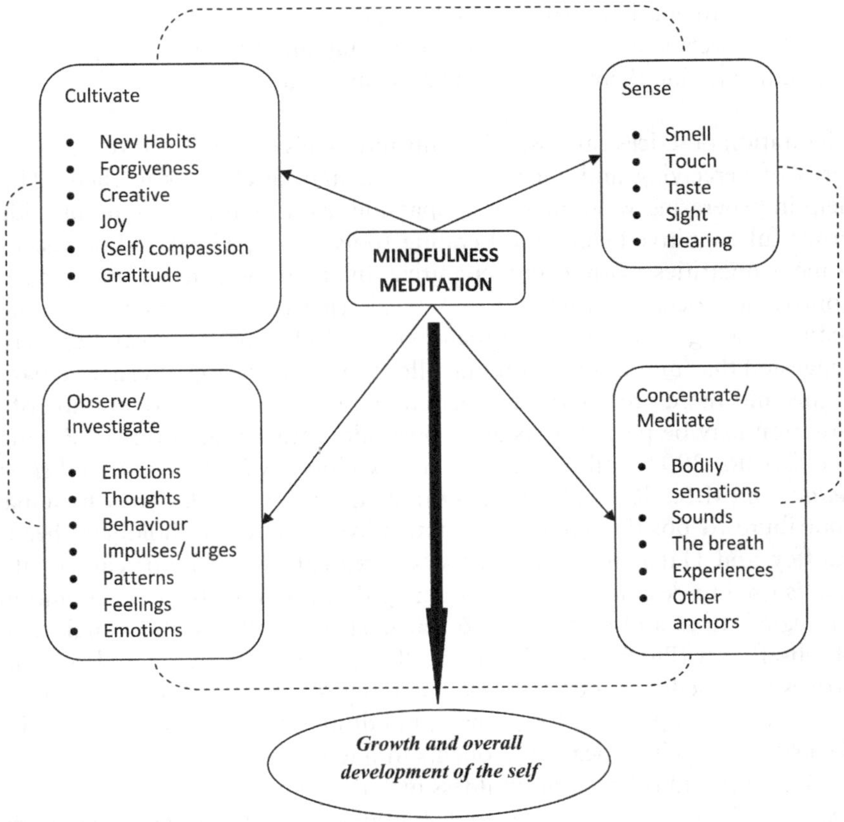

Figure 12.2 Mindfulness meditation (source: authors).

and to see the superficial appearance of things and the conditioned ideas one has about them. This may be represented by the schematic representation in Figure 12.2.

The chief characteristics of mindfulness meditation are as follows (Heaversedge and Halliwell, 2010):

1. True compassion, being the gift of mindfulness meditation;
2. Helping to 'learn to *be*' – doing less and noticing more, paving the ground for wisdom;
3. Practising gently, being an approach to life – how one relates to their own selves and the world around them;
4. Acknowledging the mind-body connection;
5. Being in our bodies;
6. Having support in pain management;

7. Encouraging body mindfulness to bring about greater acceptance and commitment, letting go, and taking action;
8. Reinforcement of individuals in enjoying mindful relationships;
9. Encouraging them to engage in a positive way of 'being.'

Meditation practices can foster insights into one's habitual and reactive patterns of perceiving and behaving, thus facilitating changes in them. They help in generating wisdom and compassion. Mindfulness training provides powerful cognitive-behavioural coping tools (Astin, 1997). While sharing some similarities with other cognitive interventions, mindfulness-based approaches focus on attending to and altering cognitive processes rather than changing their content (Orsillo et al., 2004). Some researchers have suggested that mindfulness training allows one to develop alternative paradigms and therefore interpret experiences in new ways, so that a stressful situation may be perceived as an opportunity rather than a threat. Roemer and Orsillo (2002) call this 'cognitive flexibility.' *Mindfulness-based stress reduction* (M.B.S.R.) is also thought to cultivate self-regulation, which may contribute to positive changes in both physical and psychological health (Coffey and Hartman, 2008). This 'self-regulated' psychological orientation is used to describe a kind of learning that is guided by meta-cognition, strategic action, and motivation to learn. They usually exhibit a high sense of self-efficacy (Pintrinch and Schunk, 2002). Thus, research-based evidence proves that meditation techniques, including M.B.S.R., can cultivate qualities such as compassion, forgiveness, mindfulness, and spirituality inviting the positive psychological components in one's behavioural frame.

Other ground rules of mindfulness include the presence of *here and now*, *being kind to one's own self*, and *commitment*. Mindfulness makes the individual adopt an attitude of compassion towards himself/herself. It also involves making a commitment to both meditating and practising mindfulness as a way of living/being (Frey and Totton, 2015).

Deep breathing may be used as an example of how one can stretch a little further each day with regular practice. This calls forth the elderly individual to engage in body-transcendence leading to ego-integrity (Erikson, 1950; Tornstam, 2011). A new awareness is developed of how to take good care of the body without being obsessed. For instance, this may be practised by the elderly individual by picking two colours. With his/her eyes closed, he/she may imagine breathing in one colour and breathing out with the other. This can be repeated with different colours and may be weaved all together by drawing on a page. One may also draw the waves of his/her breath and notice the intrinsic nature of them carefully.

In addition, ***body scan*** is a helpful technique whereby elderly individuals often see their bodies through the lens of their ageist society. They see wrinkles, disability, and illness to define themselves. It is body scan which neutralizes this self-view by encouraging participants to observe their bodies slowly, part by part, without judgement or criticism. It can offer an opportunity to be grateful for those parts of the body that are still operative and functional. Many individuals describe the experience as relaxing. There is an increased awareness of the body as a whole, more than a series of conditions and problems accompanied by a decrease in self-centredness (Tornstam, 2003). The physical body is confronted by the individual along the self-dimension of gero-transcendence (Tornstam, 2011).

Gentle yoga further provides an opportunity for senior individuals to experience physical pleasure and abilities. It follows the principles of mindfulness in the body. Many individuals may have disabilities preventing them from joining in all of the stretches, but all can partake in some way after a mild alteration of the exercises. Chair yoga may be appropriate for some who are unable to engage in other difficult poses (McBee, 2008).

Mindfulness teaches individuals to be with what is, accepting life as it presents itself. ***Guided imagery*** could be perceived as a way to escape life as it is, or it can provide a powerful metaphor to illuminate the process of shifting to a mindful awareness. One needs to be sensitive to the emotionality of the client while engaging him/her in guided imagery techniques. Guided imagery exercises of being a flower may be practised to inculcate positivity in the self. The senior participant attempts to comprehend that the flower is a part of himself, and he/she is also a part of the flower simultaneously (which is similar to the perception of the micro- and the macrocosm). The participant is encouraged to feel how the separateness of himself and the flower is transcended and replaced with a feeling of a wholeness and togetherness. He/she then experiences the joy and pleasure of the comprehension of being himself as well as the flower together. This may be represented by the steps as follows:

- Buy or pick a flower;
- See it with open eyes;
- Smell it with closed eyes;
- Feel it with closed eyes;
- Visualize it with closed eyes;
- Try to feel the 'flower in you';
- Water the flower and feel the sensations;
- Try to realize that the 'flower in you' and your own self as an entity are separate and at the same time connected;
- Try to enjoy this feeling of connectedness.

Standing and walking meditation is another traditional mindfulness practice. Here, participants are asked to stand or walk with an awareness of physical sensations, feelings, and thoughts. Elderly individuals in wheelchairs or those who walk with walkers or canes can also participate using such devices. Such meditations are used when participants can generally tolerate the exercise for short periods of time.

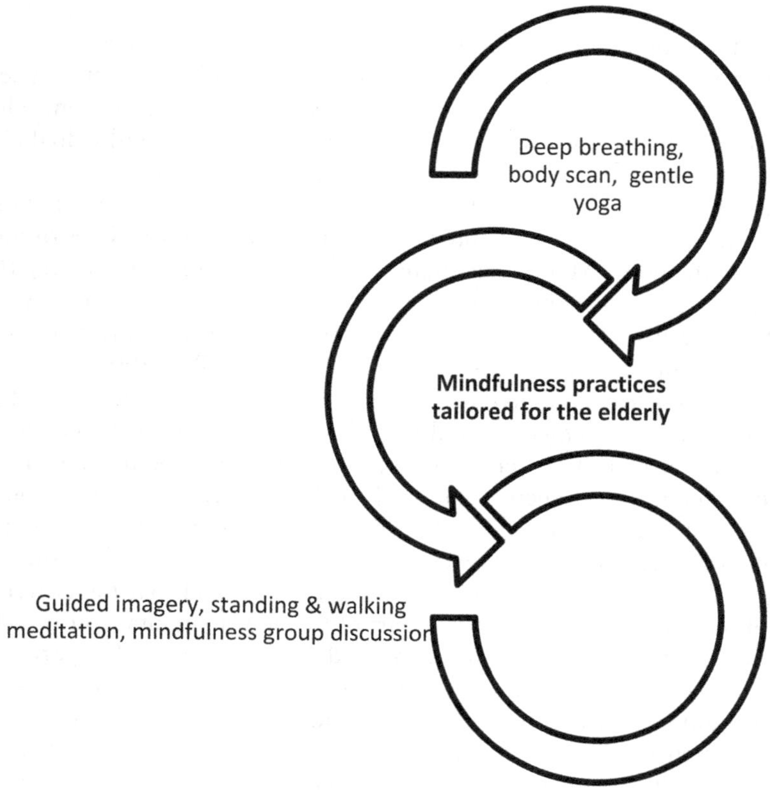

Figure 12.3 Some mindfulness exercises for the elderly (source: authors).

Mindfulness group discussions may be encouraged among the elderly. Such groups not only connect individuals to others in the group but may also create a sense of connection to the larger whole beyond time and place. The elderly person comes to terms with the temporal continuum. The subtle borderline between now and then gets transcended and this may also include a return to and re-configuration of childhood (Tornstam, 2011). An increased awareness of being a part of the flow of generations is palpably felt by the senior individual (Tornstam, 2003, 2005; Chinen, 1989). The essence of the continuation of life as such is understood as being much more significant than the mere importance of individual life (Figure 12.3).

Outcomes of mindfulness practice

Research studies indicate that mindfulness has been associated with well-being and voluntary simplicity, a lifestyle shaped around intrinsically satisfying pursuits and expressions of the self and away from material goods as mentioned earlier (Brown and Kasser, 2005). Awareness of the individual is associated with conscious registration of stimuli with different sense modalities and functions of the mind (Brown et al., 2007). It is essential that the individual uses all the sensations to the fullest extent and understands their pure richness in a non-judgemental manner as mentioned earlier. Mindfulness leads to a clarity of awareness of both inner and outer worlds on the part of the individual (Brown, Ryan, and Creswell, 2007). This includes thought processes, emotions, and behavioural actions as well as one's surroundings as they exist moment-to-moment (Brown et al., 2007), as such individuals have a better understanding of their thoughts, emotions, and behaviour, and the external context. Thus, mindfulness involves 'the skillful attention to both your inner and outer worlds' (Hanson and Mendius, 2009). It is during mindfulness that individuals work towards bare attention (Brown et al., 2007). Here, individuals work to de-couple the nearly automatic tendency to intertwine attention and cognition (Brown et al., 2007). When the mind engages in mindfulness practice, it does not compare, judge, categorize, evaluate, contemplate, reflect, introspect, or ruminate on experiences based on what is known (Brown et al., 2007). Rather, it is open and present with bare attention to any input manifested by simply noticing what is happening in the current moment. In other words, it inculcates moment-to-moment awareness of the individual (Brown et al., 2007). It is able to segregate attention from cognition and helps the individual to notice streamlined thoughts that intrude the self-system from time to time. Mindfulness is a fundamental way of being, of inhabiting one's body and moment-by-moment experiences (Shapiro and Carlson, 2009; Shapiro, 1980). It is a practice of the mind, body, and heart (McBee, 2008).

Mindfulness practices are associated with many positive outcomes, including increased ability to self-regulate one's emotions, having an increased sense of well-being, greater awareness and understanding of emotions, and an increased ability to adjust unpleasant mood states by monitoring one's emotional control and associated intelligence (Brown and Ryan, 2003; Duckworth, Grant, Loew, Oettingen, and Gollwitzer, 2011; Shapiro and Carlson, 2009; Siegel, 2010). Brown and Ryan (2003) found that more mindful individuals show a stronger relationship between implicit and explicit affect than those who are less dispositionally mindful. Knowing oneself in this way is a key aspect to self-regulation and is critical for the maintenance of a healthy, authentic representation of the self.

Clarity and objectivity appear to be the key outcome of mindfulness. The net result of mindfulness is '*re-perceiving*' by means of which there is a subtle turning about in the consciousness of individuals as what was previously 'subject' now becomes 'object' (Shapiro, Carlson, Astin, and Freedman, 2006). It is to be noted that from proper object-relations and attainment of object-constancy, individuals gradually develop the *ability to* '*re-perceive*.' This brings about *empathy* within individuals giving rise to a gradual *widening of the self*. The ultimate result is increased objectivity of the self (Chaskalson, 2011). The experience of mindful re-perceiving helps in a deeper knowing of the self, which mingles greater intimacy with whatever arises moment-by-moment. The practice of re-perceiving, in turn, gives rise to a profound, penetrative, non-conceptual seeing into the nature of the mind as well as the world (Kabat-Zinn, 2003). The shift from unmindfulness to mindfulness is almost alchemical in quality, as it involves transmutation to take place in the individual system, making it more tolerant, manageable, interesting, and vital. Its aim is thereby to develop empathy, compassion, self-compassion, forgiveness, and spiritual orientation to the individual. It also helps to reduce burnout reactions and compassion-fatigue in caregiving services.

Conclusion

Mindfulness is being grounded in stark reality. Being lost in vagueness, in fear of death, or in apprehensions of countless things are associated with old age. With effort and awareness, if the mind is trained to be not only practical but taking the true philosophy within the mind's own strengths by being mindful and acknowledging the tiniest sources of happiness in life, the old age canvas would not be so gloomy. It would offer elderly individuals a wide arena of understanding of their own selves from a spiritual perspective. They are likely to become more resourceful to embrace life with all its challenges and enjoy their remaining days with grace, joy, and happiness. They are expected to have greater clarity of thought and emotions that would keep them rooted in life. The vague apprehensive layer of thought would not wrap them; rather, the moment-to-moment experience in the general form of 'being-in-the-present' would help them enjoy life as it exists for them. The fear of the unknown – if not present prominently in the self but having a general mindfulness orientation – simple happenings, or things in life would be extra special and meaningful, and life would seem to radiate colours, touching the fringes of mindfulness.

References

Astin, J.A. (1997). Stress reduction through mindfulness meditation: Effects on psychological symptomatology, sense of control and spiritual experiences. *Psychotherapy and Psychosomatics*, *66*(2), 97–106.

Bien, T. (2006). *Mindful therapy: A guide for therapists and helping professionals*. Boston, MA: Wisdom Publications.

Brown, K.W., & Kasser, T. (2005). Are psychological and ecological well-being compatible? The role of values, mindfulness, and life style. *Social Indicators Research*, *74*(2), 349–368.

Brown, K.W., & Ryan, R.M. (2003). The benefits of being present: Mindfulness and its role in psychological well-being. *Journal of Personality and Psychological Well-Being*, *84*(4), 822–848.

Brown, K.W., Ryan, R.M., & Creswell, J.D. (2007). Addressing fundamental questions about mindfulness. *Psychological Inquiry: An International Journal for the Advancement of Psychological Theory*, *18*(4), 272–281.

Chaskalson, M. (2011). *The mindful workplace: Developing resilient individuals and resultant organizations with MBSR* (1st ed.). Chichester: John Wiley & Sons, Ltd.

Chinen, A.B. (1989). From quantitative to qualitative reasoning: A developmental perspective. In E.E. Thomas (Ed.), *Research on adulthood and ageing: The human science approach* (pp. 37–64). Albany, NY: State University of New York Press.

Coffey, K.A., & Hartman, M. (2008). Mechanisms of action in the inverse relationship between mindfulness and psychological distress. *Complementary Health Practice Review*, *13*(2), 79–91.

Duckworth, A.L., Grant, H., Loew, B., Oettingen, G., & Gollwitzer, P.M. (2011). Self-regulation strategies improve self-discipline in adolescents. Benefits of mental contrasting and implementation intentions. *Educational Psychology: An International Journal of Experimental Educational Psychology*, *31*(1), 17–26.

Erikson, E.H. (1950). *Childhood and society*. New York: W.W. Norton.

Frey, A., & Totton, A. (2015). I am here now: A creative mindfulness guide and journal. In *The mindfulness project*. London: Ebury Press.

Grabovac, A.D., Lau, M.A., & Willett, B.R. (2011). Mechanisms of mindfulness: A Buddhist psychological model. *Mindfulness*. doi:10.1007/s12671-011-0054-5

Gunaratana, B.H. (2001). *Eight mindful steps to happiness: Walking the Buddha's path*. Boston, MA: Wisdom Publications.

Hanson, R., & Mendius, R. (2009). *Buddha's brain: The practical neuroscience of happiness, love and wisdom*. Oakland, CA: New Harbinger Publications.

Heaversedge, J., & Halliwell, E. (2010). The mindful manifesto: How doing less and noticing more can help us thrive in a stressed-out world. Australia: Hay House.

Hooyman, N.R., & Kiyak, H.A. (1988). *Social gerontology: A multidisciplinary perspective*. Boston: Allen and Bacon.

Jha, A.P., Krompinger, J., & Baime, M.J. (2007). Mindfulness training modifies subsystems of attention. *Cognitive, Affective and Behavioural Neuroscience*, *7*(2), 109–119.

Kabat-Zinn, J. (1990). *Full catastrophe living*. New York: Delta Books.

Kabat-Zinn, J. (2003). Mindfulness-based interventions in context: Past, present and future. *Clinical Psychology: Science and Practice*, *10*(2), 144–156.

Kabat-Zinn, J. (2013). *Full catastrophe living, revisited edition: How to cope with stress, pain and illness using mindfulness meditation*. New York: Bantam Press Books.

Lynch, T.R., Morse, J., Mendelson, T., & Robins, C. (2003). Dialectical behaviour therapy for depressed older adults: A randomized pilot study. *American Journal of Geriatric Psychiatry*, *11*(1), 33–45.

Marcus, P. (2013). In *Search of the spiritual: Gabriel Marcel, psychoanalysis, and the sacred*. London: Karnac.

Marcus, P. (2017). *The psychoanalysis of career choice, job performance, and satisfaction: How to flourish in the workplace.* London: Routledge: Taylor and Francis Group.

McBee, L. (2004). Mindfulness practice with the frail elderly and their caregivers. Changing the practitioner-patient relationship. *Topics in Geriatric Rehabilitation, 19*(4), 257–264.

McBee, L. (2008). *Mindfulness-based elder care: A CAM model for frail elders and their caregivers.* New York: Springer Publishing Company.

McBee, L., Westreich, L., & Likourezos, A. (2004). A psycho-educational relational group for pain and stress management in the nursing home. *Journal of Social Work in Long-Term Care, 3*(1), 15–28.

McCown, D., Reibel, D., & Micozzi, M.S. (2010). *Teaching mindfulness: A practical guide for clinicians and educators.* New York: Springer.

Milne, D. (2013). *The psychology of retirement: Coping with the transition from work.* West Sussex: Wiley-Blackwell.

Olendzki, A. (2012). Wisdom in Buddhist psychology. In C.K. Germer & R.D. Siegel (Eds.), *Wisdom and compassion in psychotherapy: Deepening mindfulness in clinical practice.* New York: Guilford Press.

Orsillo, S.M., Roemer, L., Block-Lerner, J., & Tull, M.T. (2004). Acceptance, mindfulness and cognitive-behaviour therapy: Comparisons, contrasts and applications to anxiety. In S. Hayes, M. Linchan & V. Folette (Eds.), *Mindfulness and acceptance: Expanding the cognitive-behavioural tradition* (pp. 66–95). New York: Guildford.

Pintrich, P.R., & Schunk, D. (2002). *Motivation in education: Theory, research and applications* (2nd ed.). Upper Saddle River, NJ: Merrill Prentice Hall.

Roemer, L., & Orsillo, S.M. (2002). Expanding our conceptualization of and treatment for generalized anxiety disorder: Integrating mindfulness/ acceptance-based approaches with existing cognitive-behavioural models. *Clinical Psychology: Science and Practice, 9*(1), 54–68.

Rorty, R. (1989). *Contingency, irony, and solidarity.* Cambridge: Cambridge University Press.

Shapiro, D.H. (1980). *Meditation: Self-regulation strategy and altered state of consciousness.* New York: Aldine.

Shapiro, S.L., & Carlson, L.E. (2009). *The art and science of mindfulness: Integrating mindfulness into psychology and the helping professions.* Washington, DC: American Psychological Association.

Shapiro, S.L., Carlson, L.E., Astin, J.A., & Freedman, B. (2006). Mechanisms of mindfulness. *Journal of Clinical Psychology, 62*(3), 373–386.

Shapiro, S.L., & Schwartz, G.E.R. (2000). The role of intention in self-regulation: Toward intentional systemic mindfulness. In M. Boekaerts, P.R. Pintrich, & M. Zeidner (Eds.), *Handbook of self-regulation* (pp. 253–273). New York: Academic Press.

Shapiro, S.L., Schwartz, G.E.R., & Santerre, C. (2002). Meditation and positive psychology. In C.R. Snyder & S.J. Lopez (Eds.), *Handbook of positive psychology* (pp. 632–645). Oxford: Oxford University Press.

Siegel, D. (2010). *The mindful therapist: A clinician's guide to mind-sight and neural integration.* New York: W.W. Norton.

Smith, A. (2004). Clinical uses of mindfulness training for older people. *Behavioural and Cognitive Psychotherapy*, *32*(4), 423–430.

Smith, A. (2006). 'Like waking up from a dream': Mindfulness training for older people with anxiety and depression. In R.A. Baer (Ed.), *Mindfulness-based treatment approaches* (pp. 191–212). Burlington, MA: Elsevier.

Tornstam, L. (2003). *Gero-transcendence from young old age to old old age.* Online publication retrieved from the Social Gerontology Group. Uppsala. Retrieved from http://www.soc.uu.se/download.aspx?id = %2fY51QkWQkn0%3d

Tornstam, L. (2005). *Gero-transcendence – A developmental theory of positive ageing*. New York: Springer.

Tornstam, L. (2011). Maturing into gero-transcendence. *The Journal of Transpersonal Psychology*, *43*(2), 166–180.

Toseland, R.W. (1995). *Group work with the elderly and family caregivers*. New York: Springer.

Wallace, B.A. (2011). *Minding closely: The four applications of mindfulness*. Ithaca, NY: Snow Lion Publications.

13

THE LIFE-STORY MATRIX

The retrospective wisdom forum

Life review is a normal aspect of human ageing, especially for the aged, who are said to belong to the *age of the memoir* (Butler, 2005). In fact, it was Butler (1955/1963) who coined the term *life review*, indicating that it is very natural for elderly individuals to want to put their experiences in perspective to resolve past conflicts, grieve losses and changes in their life, forgive themselves and others, celebrate successes, and have a 'feel' of a sense of completion within. This is made possible as older adults watch their children and grandchildren grow through the same stage(s) of life as themselves. It helps them to appreciate their own lives in a better manner. Being emotionally more mature, they realize the necessity to integrate their life experiences and tie up loose ends to feel content and fulfilled within. This often produces the increasing realization that they are passing through the final stages of life. The wisdom reaped through living life's different phases appears to help in the development of strengths, knowledge, and understanding among the elderly, which have been culturally revered for centuries. It has been observed that the memories of elderly individuals from the distant past become more distinct as an individual enters into the 80s and beyond (Kunz and Soltys, 2007). This may be related to new brain development in old age past the age of 65 as suggested by Cohen (2005), leading to accompanying psychosocial development at such an advanced age contrary to expectations. Narrating stories about one's life tends to bring about a metaphysical presence and provides a natural, intuitive, and spiritual order to communication (Crazy Bull, 1997). Stories tend to get woven into the threads of life's fabric as far as individual life is concerned (Barton, 2004).

The life-story matrix may be understood as a framework for understanding different dimensions of life-story work, some of them being a continuum from reminiscence to life review, from private to public expression, and from a focus on content to an emphasis on process (Kunz, 2002). Reminiscence and life review activities essentially enable in helping elderly individuals to find meaning in life, improve problem-solving skills, assist with grief process(es), increase emotional support, strengthen self-esteem, decrease negative emotions like depression and anxiety, and develop therapeutic interventions for individuals with neurodegenerative disorders such as those suffering from dementia (Kunz, 1991). They help to provide a connection to other individuals, render a sense of connection between life events, unlock an opportunity for healing to occur, help to achieve the fullness of human potential, and lead to an integrated sense of the self (Sandelowski, 1994). The elderly individual gains perception about time through storytelling leading to alterations in his/her sense of place, stimulation by strong emotions, and to facilitate changes and gain a forum for personal introspection to assess, understand, and change health-related behaviours (Banks-Wallace, 2002; Hodge, Pasqua, Marquez, and Geishirt-Cantrell, 2002; Sandelowski, 1991; Snyder, 1992). This is because elderly individuals engage in a healing environment when they get involved in storytelling or reminiscing their own life stories (Lindesmith and McWeeny, 1994). Other features inherent in the storytelling perspective, namely, non-judgement, and the very fact that others listen to their story makes them feel that they are valued as an individual by both the self and others (Clark et al., 2003; Koch, 1998). There are spontaneity and creativity ingrained in the process as well (Heiney, 1995; Kuhrik, 1995). Reminiscing also allows natural healing to flow by helping the person to be consciously present in the moment (Dossey, Keegan, and Guzzetta, 2000). Empathy and a sense of caring are often a few consequences of the process through which it is difficult to distinguish between the speakers and listeners for they dwell within the 'lived experiences' of each other (Heinrich, 1992; Diekelmann, 1994/1995). As such, reminiscence and life review approaches may be adopted for myriad reasons for engaging in fun, group connection, individual growth, historical purposes, social and therapeutic goals, and in dealing with human grief and loss at the end of life (Kunz and Soltys, 2007).

Belief in elementality as an outcome in the retrospection of life narratives

Retrospections of one's life engage the person in spontaneously returning to life's earlier phases with their pleasures, associated memories, and emotions to develop inner strength and a sense of peace to embrace 'life.' It enables the individual to have freedom from existential anxiety and instead to embrace life to its fullest in a moment-by-moment manner (Butler, 2005). Cohen (2005) offered four phases to the second half of one's life as follows:

1. *Midlife re-evaluation*;
2. *Liberation;*
3. *Summing up*;
4. *Encore phase.*

Life narratives in the form of midlife re-evaluation are characterized by re-assessment, exploration, and transition. Brain changes during this period account for developmental intelligence which serves as the basis of one's wisdom-frame (Cohen, 2005). The liberation phase brings forth relative freedom, experimentation, and innovation. This may be underlined by the formation of new neuronal associations in the information processing portion of the brain resulting in a desire for novelty. The following phase of summing up is reinforced by bilateral involvement of the hippocampus that, in turn, contributes to the capacity for autobiographical memory (Cohen, 2005; Kunz, 2005). The ageing brain creates a type of back-up copy of lifelong memories in the less dominant hemisphere of the brain so that they may be protected from injuries and decay. Summing up involves a phase where the elderly individual comes to terms with his/her self as regards integrity and overall harmony. The final phase of encore helps the aged individual to embrace the concept of elementalism by attempting to live well to the very end of life as much as feasible. This is brought about by further changes in the amygdalae that seem to promote positive emotions and boost one's overall morale (Cohen, 2005; Kunz and Soltys, 2007). Thus, the brain has the capacity to 're-model' itself with age to develop reserves of strength and agility that tend to compensate for the effects of ageing in other areas. It is also to be noted that elderly individuals may revisit these phases time and again as per their individualistic needs. Reminiscence and life review activities thereby become more significant as people gradually age.

Reminiscence from the functional perspective

Webster (1997), Webster and McCall (1999), and Gibson (2004) summarize the different functions of reminiscence that seem to apply for individuals across all age groups as follows:

- Boredom-reduction;
- Death-preparation by means of valuing the life lived so far;
- Seeking one's own identity;
- Engaging in problem solving;
- Involving in conversation with self and others;
- Engaging with personally significant individuals and thereby in intimacy maintenance;
- Sustaining memories associated with bitterness revival;
- Teaching/informing others about values and history.

Such functions have prompted the development of Webster's Reminiscence Function Scale (Webster, 1997). They have also helped to design different theoretical models associated with reminiscence. The SolCos model (Soltys and Coats, 1994) is one among them which also offers specific methods to facilitate different functions. Its foundations are looked at in the following section.

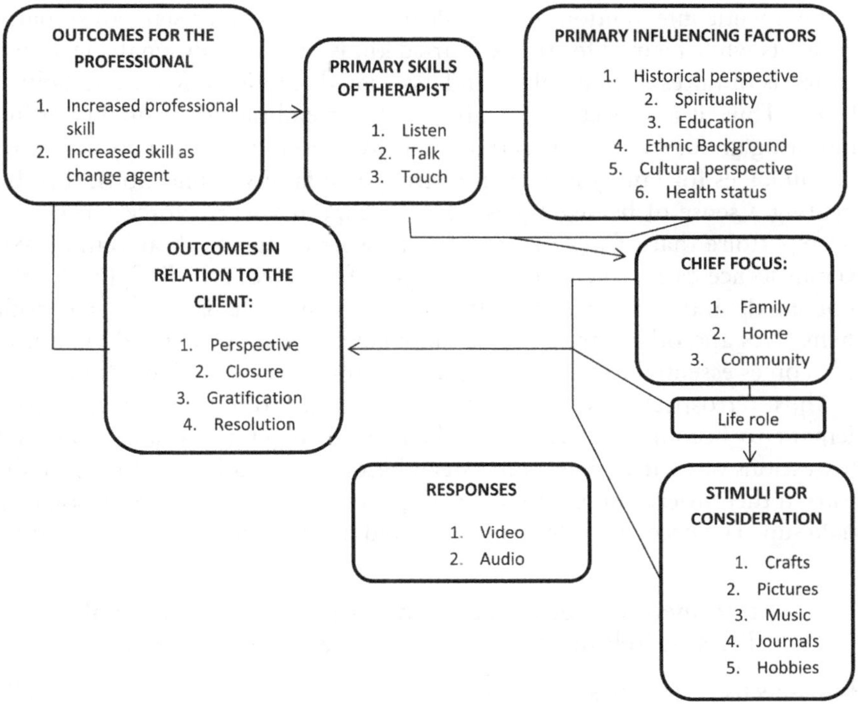

Figure 13.1 Facilitator and client outcomes in accordance with the SolCos model (source: authors).

Art of reminiscence in the SolCos model

The model has three chief elements, namely, processes, items, and outcomes. Primary skills, primary influencing factors, and focus comprise the processes components. Moreover, the items component has two subcomponents, namely, stimuli and responses. Finally, the outcome category has two subcomponents – client outcomes and interviewer outcomes. Client outcomes may be defined as benefits to the interviewee as a result of the reminiscence process. This is schematically represented in a flowchart (Soltys and Coats, 1994) (Figure 13.1).

Reminiscence may be used for a number of reasons. It may inform and help evaluate life or may even be a symptom of guilt in unhealthy conditions (LoGerfo, 1980). It may take up different forms such as those of storytelling (Molinari and Rechlin, 1984–1985). It may also offer information and appreciation to an individual's life by gathering information concerning psychological factors, underlying health beliefs, coping skills, and cultural perspectives. Reminiscence may boost one's self-esteem and energize oneself including elderly individuals suffering from dementia. It may further be used in therapeutic interventions to provide inner strength and a sense of stability to clients while facing life crises of varied kinds. It may additionally lead to a catharsis of unresolved conflicts and associated emotions (Kunz and Soltys, 2007). Thus, it is expected to enable clients to embrace their quality of life and bring about overall integrity in their lives. Reminiscence may also provide linkages for family history and strengthen family connections, thereby creating a sense of belongingness. This is expected to reinforce one's coping repertoire that relates to different stressors of ageing (Franklin, 2005). Reminiscence can create thinking that is self-directed, self-disciplined, self-motivated, and self-corrective. It also helps individuals to forgive both themselves and others and become more flexible and open-ended in nature. It becomes essential for self-healing and attaining peace with one's life.

Thus, retrospection seems to play an important role for the elderly participant to become relatively 'detached' from materialistic and relational possessions of varied kinds, and instead become more adaptive to life conditions. It thereby encourages them to adopt wisdom-flares in their personality make-up. The necessity is felt to understand its different theoretical notions.

Attainment of 'retrospective wisdom' as an outcome of life storytelling from varied theoretical perspectives

Retrospective wisdom is the virtue to be reaped from the harvest of storytelling one's own life-matrix to both the self and others. It not only makes the individual look back at life from a more emotionally mature perspective but also helps one to realize the errors that one had committed earlier in a non-judgemental manner. In a healthy mental context, reminiscence allows him/her to acknowledge the givens in life and to understand the deeper meanings that life has to offer. It provides a tranquil ambience to 'mirror' one's own self from an emotionally intelligent perspective. The process is bound to provide the 'gift' of wisdom as a harvest. Characteristically, wisdom includes openness, reflectiveness, empathy, fairness and sound judgement, serenity, humour, self-knowledge, humility, and a transpersonal perspective. Wisdom is thus the fulcrum of all emotive-cognitive-conative actions of the elderly. Attaining wisdom and getting equipped to face the end of life, ageing proves resourcefulness and establishes positivity in life. This may be understood through glancing back at one's life stages in a seemingly spontaneous manner, to have a feel of life's *narrative analysis*.

Recall of personal history enables the elderly to master one's present and future by enabling the search of meaning in the present through the partial resolution of conflict within the self or with others (Haight, 1992). It might also involve the review of memorabilia, photos, or journals. Some of the life-story activities that older adults may engage in include recording and/or writing life stories, participating in spiritual and religious group activities, engaging in club activities, having regular meetings with members of the same cohort hailing from one's family, peer group, or neighbourhood, engaging in storytelling, writing stories or music, attending or leading reminiscence groups, volunteering others in such activities, establishing memorials to ensure that history is remembered, and so on (Kunz and Soltys, 2007). In addition to solving old problems, the elderly may find an increased tolerance for conflict, a lessening of guilt and fears, enhanced creativity and a sense of giving, and acceptance of life circumstances (Butler and Lewis, 1982). This has a therapeutic notion as mentioned earlier which may be referred to as 'album therapy' as it stimulates different personal relatedness and interlinks with distinct episodes in life and triggers the elder adult's autobiographical and flashbulb memories to be reinforced. The mature elderly person ultimately gets ready with realization-laden filters to decipher the deeper meanings of life perspectives that are inked in cosmic colours.

The Berlin wisdom model is a theoretical model which requires highlighting at this juncture.

- ***Berlin wisdom model*** (Baltes and Smith, 2008)
  Older adults, owing to the attainment of 'retrospective wisdom,' are adorned with *rich factual knowledge*, thereby having a deep understanding of human nature, lifelong development, social norms and their implications, variations in developmental processes and outcomes, interpersonal and intergenerational relations, and identity issues (Baltes and Smith, 2008). Such individuals also have *rich procedural knowledge* for which they are able to know how and when to apply one's knowledge to review past life decisions, give advice about different dilemmas in life, and design a plan for the future. It requires the optimal use of three meta-criteria, namely, lifespan contextualism, value relativism, and the recognition and management of the fundamental uncertainty of life matters (Baltes and Staudinger, 1998, 2000). Lifespan contextualism refers to knowledge about the normative and non-normative influences on an individual's life. Value relativism refers to acknowledging the differences in values, goals, and priorities. Such knowledge is often manifested in the expression of tolerance and respect for beliefs and actions that may be unfamiliar or contrary to one's own. Third, knowledge about life's uncertainty refers to accepting limitations in one's own knowledge and being comfortable with uncertainty. This is diagrammatically represented in Figure 13.2.

  Further, other theoretical perspectives view wisdom, attained through retrospection, from a slightly different angle.
- ***Balance theory of wisdom*** (Ryle, 1984; Laub and Auerhahn, 2017)
  In accordance to the balance theory of wisdom (Ryle, 1984; Laub and Auerhahn, 2017), wisdom attained by elderly individuals requires tacit knowledge and practical intelligence as mediated by values in order to

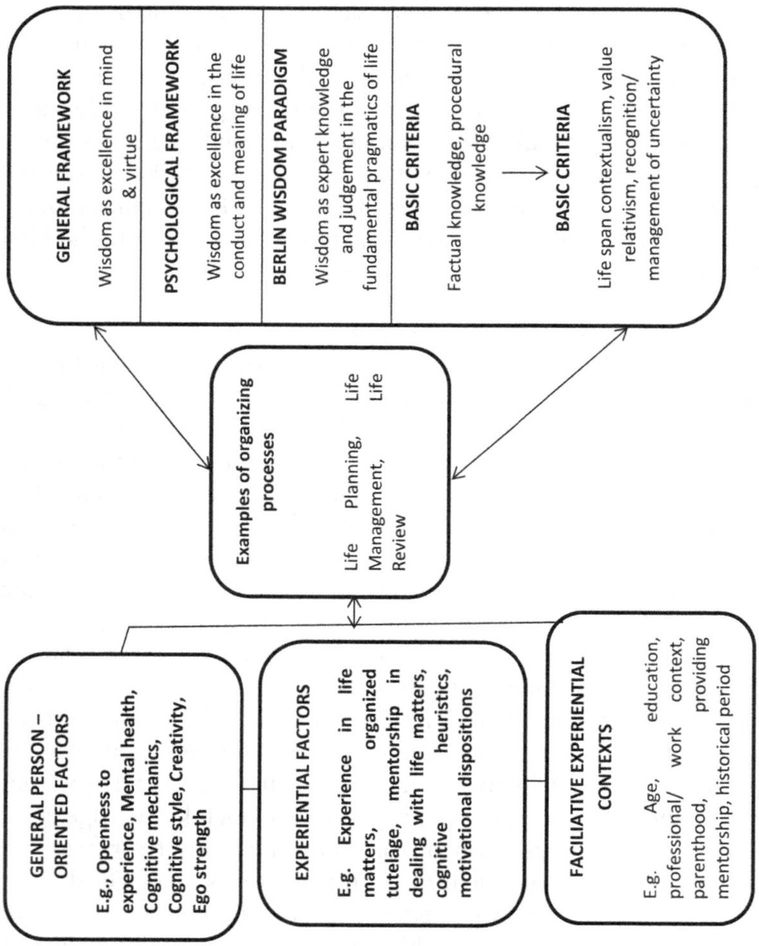

Figure 13.2 Schematic representation of wisdom (source: authors).

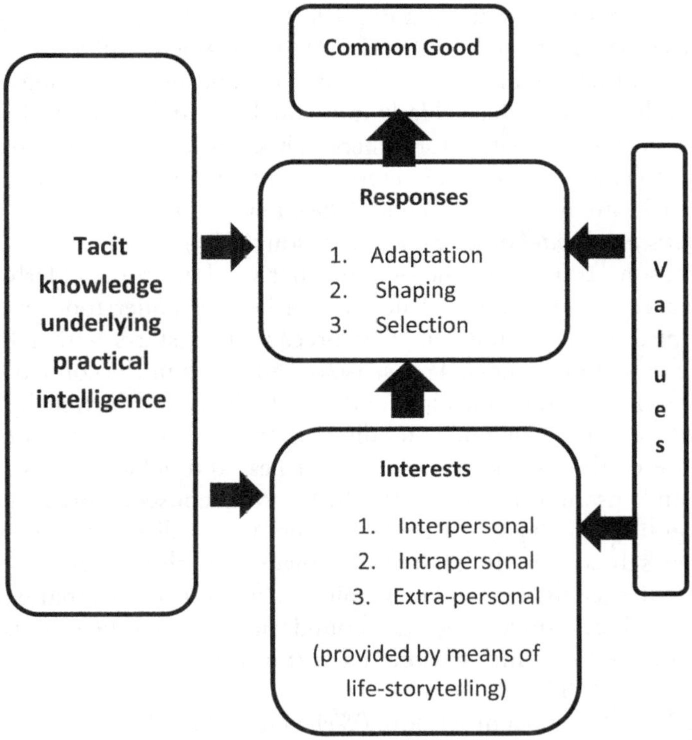

Figure 13.3 Balance theory of wisdom (source: authors).

achieve common good through the balancing of ***interpersonal*** (interests of others), ***intrapersonal*** (self-interests), and ***extra-personal interests*** (interests of the society as a whole). It further involves balancing three courses of action: ***adaptation of oneself*** **or** ***others to existing environments***, ***shaping of environments*** to render them more compatible with oneself or others, and ***selection of new environments*** (Sternberg, 2001, 2003). Storytelling about one's life events appears to be one important avenue to help engage elderly individuals in wisdom-associated processes. This is represented in Figure 13.3.

- ***Three-dimensional model of wisdom*** (Ardelt, 2003)
  Ardelt (2003) highlighted the presence of tripartite components of wisdom, namely, cognitive, affective, and reflective elements. Life as such is better understood by elderly individuals who are then able to comprehend the significance and deeper meaning of phenomena and events, particularly with regard to intrapersonal and interpersonal matters (Chandler and Holliday, 1990; Blanchard-Fields and Norris, 1995, Ardelt, 2000). They appear to be self-aware, have self-insight, and

look at phenomena from different perspectives (Garland and Garland, 2004; Clayton, 1982; Taranto, 1989; Chandler and Holliday, 1990; Csikszentmihalyi and Rathunde, 1990; Kramer, 1990). As a consequence of having an insightful awareness and understanding of events and other people, wise elderly individuals naturally tend to have compassion and sympathy for others. They are characterized by having positive emotions, with an absence of indifference or negative emotions towards others (Pascual-Leone, 1990; Levitt, 1999).

- ***Levenson's model of wisdom*** (Levenson, 2009)
  Levenson (2009) is of the opinion that wisdom in the elderly may be regarded as self-transcendence. It can be best understood in terms of the phases of development that precede it. It starts with self-knowledge or self-awareness. This sense of self arises in the context of roles, achievements, relationships, and beliefs. This is followed by detachment, which is an understanding of the transience and provisional nature of the things, relationships, roles, and achievements that create and sustain one's sense of self. It would consequently result in the integration of the system, which refers to the dissolution of separate 'inner selves.' The individual no longer feels threatened by issues of existential crisis. Lastly, being able to detach from external definitions of the self and dissolving rigid boundaries between the self and others allows one the manifestation of self-transcendent wisdom (Loy, 1996; Levenson, 2009).
- **H.E.R.O.(E) model of wisdom** (Webster, 2003, 2007)
  Webster proposed five components of wisdom, namely, humour, emotional regulation, life experiences, openness, and reflection as interacting with one another to comprise wisdom (Figure 13.4).

Wise elderly individuals use humour as a strategy to cope with serious life circumstances and to uplift others and oneself during times of stress (Randall, 2012). They are able to experience a wide array of complex emotions with adequate understanding and detachment (Webster, 2003). They are able to reflect upon critical life experiences and derive meaningful lessons of life (Webster, 2007). Wise elderly individuals are open to new experiences, novel facts, and are high on exploration. This may also be explained in terms of Brown's wisdom development model (Brown, 2002, 2004), which is schematically represented in Figure 13.5.

The much-revered experiential flavour of wisdom among elderly individuals may be understood from different theoretical angles. However, elderly individuals are always on the quest and upward journey for wisdom as, ideally, the attainment of absolute wisdom is a utopia, which is seldom completely reached. This indicates that mapping the future of reminiscence has eminence in research and practice, especially in gerontology (Webster and Haight, 2002). For instance, taking an extensive autobiography may help older adults

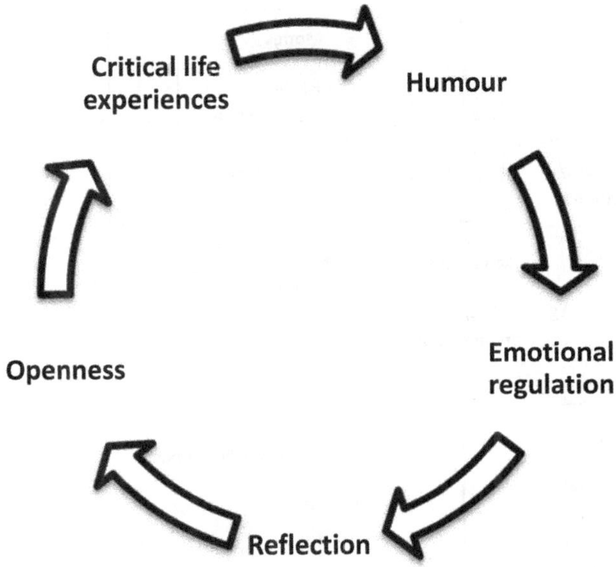

Figure 13.4 H.E.R.O.(E) model of wisdom (source: authors).

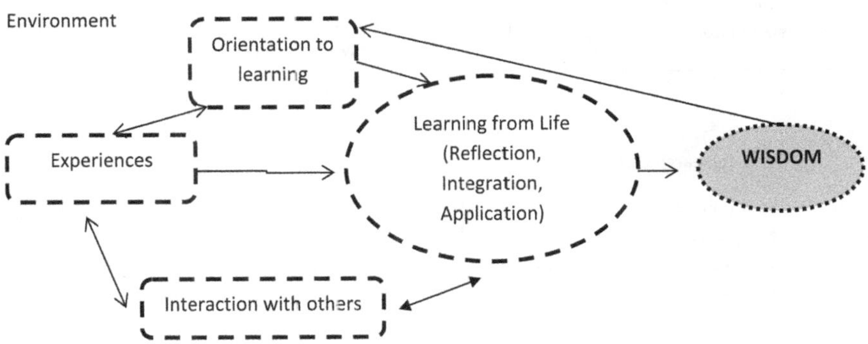

Figure 13.5 Brown's wisdom development model.

to clarify, deepen, and understand the varied learning and realizations of one's life (Butler, 1974). Relationships between reminiscing and measures of adaptation have been explored (McMahon and Rhudick, 1964; Havighurst and Glasser, 1972; Boylin, Gordon, and Nehrke, 1976; Lowenthal, Thurnher, and Chiriboga, 1975; Coleman, 1974; Lewis, 1971). Consequently, it is expected to reduce depression, uplift self-esteem, and life satisfaction in the long run (Lappe, 1987; Perrotta and Meacham, 1981). In fact, reminiscence components may be depicted in a heuristic model as shown in Figure 13.6.

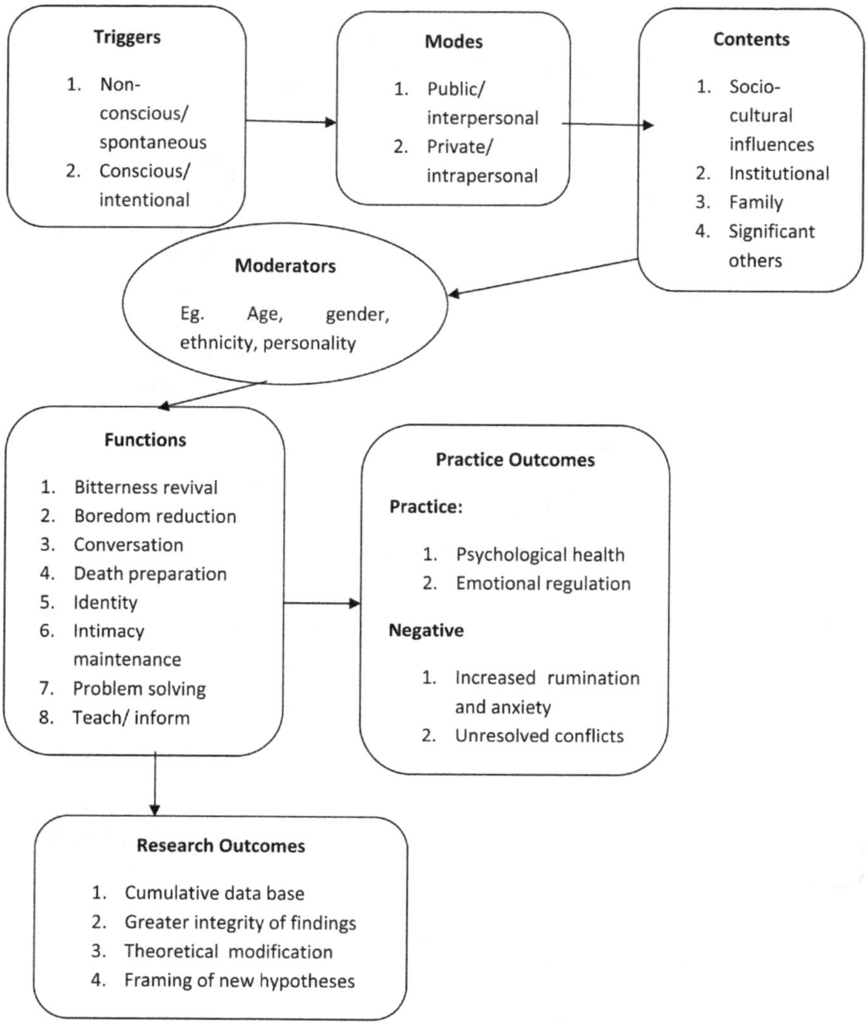

Figure 13.6 Reminiscence components in accordance with the heuristic model (source: authors).

Hence, therapists need to caution that reminiscence interventions can have negative effects (Westerhof et al., in press). Thus, careful planning and testing of reminiscence protocols are crucial (Goldfriend and Wolfe, 1996; Bluck and Levine, 1998). Such interventions need to take account of factors like the context, goals of intervention, psychological and developmental theory, characteristics of the target group, expertise of the therapist, and so on (Lin et al., 2005). Reminiscence interventions may be of three different types (Westerhof, Bohmeijer, and Webster, in press):

- Simple/ unstructured reminiscence;
- Structured reminiscence/life review;
- Life-review therapy.

Simple reminiscence is mainly unstructured and involves autobiographic storytelling and spontaneous reminiscence which often may take place within a relational context, for example, family get-togethers, reunions, and among friends. Structured reminiscence in the form of life review focuses on the integration of both positive and negative life events and is evaluative in nature (Haight and Dias, 1992; Webster and Young, 1998). Such interventions help elderly individuals to focus on successful past coping repertoires and values that have guided them in their lives so as to adapt successfully to changes and life events in their present lives. Finally, life-review therapy is highly structured in nature and is usually aimed at individuals having severe levels of depression or anxiety. Its focus is on diminishing reminiscence functions of bitterness revival and boredom-reduction (Cappeliez, 2002; Kropf and Tandy, 1998). Thus, the three different types of reminiscence interventions may be seen as three levels of intensity of reminiscence against which specific reminiscence protocols may be developed (Garland and Garland, 2002).

Conclusion

Retrospection is an integral part of all individuals irrespective of age and sex. Glancing back at life with a 'narrative lens' is common among older adults. This practice helps to have a non-judgemental and neutral outlook towards life in general, which appears to offer inner serenity to individuals as a consequence. The ripened years of life offer golden 'harvests' of wisdom-rimmed experiences that are a treasure for members of younger generations. Hence, it is the appropriate time for storytelling in different forms with elderly individuals being the focus, which may restore quality of life for everybody in general. Therapeutic benefits are expected to be boundless as a result of this process.

References

Ardelt, M. (2000). Antecedents and effects of wisdom in old age: A longitudinal perspective on ageing well. *Research on Ageing*, 22(4), 360–394.

Ardelt, M. (2003). Empirical assessment of a three-dimensional wisdom scale. *Research on Ageing*, 25(3), 275–324.

Baltes, P.B., & Smith, J. (2008). The fascination of wisdom: Its nature, ontogeny and function. *Perspectives on Psychological Science, 3*(1), 56–64.

Baltes, P.B., & Staudinger, U.M. (1998). Wisdom. In H. Friedman (Ed.), *Encyclopedia of mental health* (pp. 699–706). New York: Academic Press.

Baltes, P.B., & Staudinger, U.M. (2000). Wisdom: A meta-heuristic (pragmatic) to orchestrate mind and virtue toward excellence. *American Psychologist, 55*(1), 122–142.

Banks-Wallace, J. (2002). Talk that talk: Storytelling and analysis rooted in African American oral tradition. *Qualitative Health Research, 12*(3), 410–426.

Barton, S.S. (2004). Narrative inquiry: Locating aboriginal epistemology in a relational methodology. *Journal of Advanced Nursing, 45*(5), 519–526.

Blanchard-Fields, F., & Norris, L. (1995).The development of wisdom. In M.A. Kimble, S.H. McFadden, J.W. Ellor, & J.J. Seeber (Eds.), *Ageing, spirituality, and religion: A handbook* (pp. 102–118). Minneapolis, MN: Fortress Press.

Bluck, S., & Levine, L.J. (1998). Reminiscence as autobiographical memory: A catalyst for reminiscence theory development. *Ageing and Society, 18*(2), 185–208.

Boylin, W., Gordon, S.K., & Nehrke, M.F. (1976). Reminiscing and ego integrity in institutionalized elderly males. *Gerontologist, 16*(2), 118–124.

Brown, S.C. (2002). A model for wisdom development – and its place in career services. *Journal of Career Planning and Employment, 62*(4), 29–36.

Brown, S.C. (2004). Learning across the campus: How college facilitates the development of wisdom. *Journal of College Student Development, 45*(2), 134–148.

Butler, R.N. (1955/1963). The life review: An interpretation of reminiscence in old age. *Psychiatry Journal for the Study of Interpersonal Processes, 26*, 65–76.

Butler, R.N. (1974). Successful aging and the role of the life review. *Journal of the American Geriatrics Society, 22*(12), 529–535.

Butler, R.N. (2005). The nature of memory, life review, and elementality. In *International reminiscence and life review conference 2005, selected conference papers and proceedings* (pp. 9–18). Superior: University of Wisconsin-Superior.

Butler, R.N., & Lewis, M.I. (1982). *Ageing and mental health: Positive psychosocial and biomedical approaches*. St. Louis, MO: Mosby.

Cappeliez, P. (2002). Cognitive-reminiscence therapy for depressed older adults in day hospital and long-term care. In J.D. Webster & B.K. Haight (Eds.), *Critical advances in reminiscence work: From theory to application* (pp. 300–313). New York: Springer Publishing.

Chandler, M.L., & Holliday, S. (1990). Wisdom in a post-apocalyptic age. In R.J. Sternberg (Ed.), *Wisdom: Its nature, origins and development* (pp. 121–141). Cambridge, UK: Cambridge University Press.

Clark, A., Hanson, E.J., & Ross, H. (2003). Seeing the person behind the patient: Enhancing the care of older people using a biographical approach. *Journal of Clinical Nursing, 12*(5), 697–706.

Clayton, V. (1982). Wisdom and intelligence: The nature and function of knowledge in the later years. *The International Journal of Ageing and Human Development, 15*(4), 315–323.

Cohen, G. (2005). *The mature mind*. New York: Basic Books.

Coleman, P.G. (1974). Measuring reminiscence characteristics from conversation as adaptive features of old age. *International Journal of Aging and Human Development*, *5*(3), 281–294.

Crazy Bull, C. (1997). A native conversation about research and scholarship. *Tribal College: Journal of American Indian Higher Education*, *9*(1), 17–23.

Csikszentmihalyi, M., & Rathunde, K. (1990). The psychology of wisdom: N evolutionary interpretation. In R.J. Sternberg (Ed.), *Wisdom: Its nature, origins, and development* (pp. 25–51). Cambridge: Cambridge University Press.

Diekelmann, N. (1994/1995). Sharing nursing work through stories. *Nursing New Zealand*, *2*(11), 8.

Dossey, B.M., Keegan, L., & Guzzetta, C.E. (2000). *Holistic nursing: A handbook for practice* (3rd ed.). Gaithersburg, MD: Aspen Publishers.

Franklin, J.H. (2005). *Mirror to America.* New York: Farrat, Straus & Giroux.

Garland, J., & Garland, C. (2004). *Life review in health and social care: A practitioner's guide.* Hove: Brunner-Routledge, Hove, UK. .

Gibson, F. (2004).*The past in the present.* Baltimore, MD: Health Professions Press.

Goldfried, M.R., & Wolfe, B.E. (1996).Psychotherapy practice and research: Repairing a strained relationship. *American Psychologist*, *51*(10), 1007–1016.

Haight, B.K. (1992). Long-term effects of structured life-review process in homebound elderly subjects. *Journals of Gerontology: Psychological Sciences*, *47*, 312–315.

Haight, B.K., & Dias, J.K. (1992). Examining key variables in selected reminiscing modalities. *International Psychogeriatrics*, *4*, 279–290.

Havighurst, R.J., & Glasser, R. (1972). An exploratory study of reminiscence. *Journal of Gerontology*, *27*(2), 245–253.

Heiney, S.P. (1995). The healing power of story. *Oncology Nursing Forum*, *22*(6), 899–904.

Heinrich, K.L. (1992). Create a tradition: Teach nurses to share stories. *Journal of Nursing Education*, *31*(3), 141–143.

Hodge, F.S., Pasqua, A., Marquez, C.A., & Geishirt-Cantrell, B. (2002).Utilizing traditional storytelling to promote wellness in American Indian communities. *Journal of Transcultural Nursing*, *13*(1), 6–11.

Koch, T. (1998). Story telling: Is it really research? *Journal of Advanced Nursing*, *28*(6), 1182–1190.

Kramer, D.A. (1990). Conceptualizing wisdom: The primacy of affect-cognition relations. In R.J. Sternberg (Ed.), *Wisdom: Its nature, origins, and development* (pp. 279–290). New York: Cambridge University Press.

Kropf, N.P., & Tandy, C. (1998). Narrative therapy with older clients: The use of a 'meaning-making' approach. *Clinical Gerontologist*, *18*(4), 3–16.

Kuhrik, M. (1995). Telling stories in the classroom. *Nurse Educator*, *20*(5), 4–5.

Kunz, J. (1991). Case reports: Counseling approaches for disoriented older adults. *Illness, Crisis and Loss*, *1*(2), 91–96.

Kunz, J. (2002). *The joys and surprises of telling your life story.* Superior: Center for Continuing Education/ Extension: University of Wisconsin-Superior.

Kunz, J. (2005). *We'll have these moments to remember: The life and spirit of Evelyn Bedore* [Video]. Superior: Center for Continuing Education/ Extension University of Wisconsin-Superior.

Kunz, J.A., & Soltys, F.G. (2007). *Transformational reminiscence: Life story work*. Springer Publishing Company.

Lappe, J.M. (1987). Reminiscing: The life review therapy. *Journal of Gerontological Nursing*, *13*(4), 12–16.

Laub, D., & Auerhahn, N.C. (2017). Knowing and not-knowing massive psychic trauma: Forms of traumatic memory. *The International Journal of Psycho-Analysis*, *74*(2), 287–302.

Levenson, M.R. (2009). Gender and wisdom: The roles of compassion and moral development. *Research in Human Development*, *6*(1), 45–59.

Levitt, H.M. (1999). The development of wisdom: An analysis of Tibetan Buddhist experience. *Journal of Humanistic Psychology*, *39*(2), 86–105.

Lewis, C.N. (1971). Reminiscing and self-concept in old age. *Journal of Gerontology*, *26*(2), 240–243.

Lin, Y.C., Dai, Y.T., & Hwang, S.L. (2005). The effect of reminiscence on the elderly population: A systematic review. *Public Health Nursing*, *20*(4), 297–306.

Lindesmith, K.A., & McWeeny, M. (1994). The power of storytelling. *The Journal of Continuing Education in Nursing*, *25*(4), 186–187.

LoGerfo, M. (1980).Three ways to reminiscence in theory and practice. *International Journal of Human Development*, *12*(1), 63–65.

Lowenthal, M.F., Thurnher, M., & Chiriboga, D. (1975). *Four stages of life: A comparative study of women and men facing transitions*. San Francisco: Jossey-Bass.

Loy, D. (1996). *Lack and transcendence: The problem of death and life in psychotherapy, existentialism and Buddhism*. Amherst, NY: Prometheus Books.

McMahon, A.W., & Rhudick, P.J. (1964). Reminiscing: Adaptational significance in the aged. *Archives of General Psychiatry*, *10*, 292–298.

Molinari, V., & Rechlin, R.E. (1984–1985). Life review and reminiscence in the elderly. A review of the literature. *International Journal of Ageing and Human Development*, *202*(2), 81–92.

Pascual-Leone, J. (1990). An essay on wisdom: Toward organismic processes that make it possible. In R.J. Sternberg (Ed.), *Wisdom: Its nature, origins, and development* (pp. 244–278). Cambridge: Cambridge University Press.

Perotta, P., & Meacham, J.A. (1981). Can a reminiscing intervention alter depression and self-esteem? *International Journal of Aging and Human Development*, *14*(1), 23–29.

Randall, W.L. (2012). The importance of being ironic: Narrative openness and personal resilience in later life. *Gerontologist*, *53*(1), 9–16.

Ryle, G. (1984). *The concept of mind*. London: Hutchinson.

Sandelowski, M. (1991). Telling stories: Narrative approaches in qualitative research. *Image: The Journal of Nursing Scholarship*, *23*(3), 161–166.

Sandelowski, M. (1994).We are the stories we tell: Narrative knowing in nursing practice. *Journal of Holistic Nursing*, *12*(1), 23–33.

Snyder, M. (1992). *Independent nursing interventions* (2nd ed.). Albany, NY: Delmar Publishers.

Soltys, F.G., & Coats, L. (1994). The SolCos model: Facilitating reminiscence therapy. *Journal of Gerontological Nursing*, *20*(11), 11–16.

Sternberg, R.J. (2001). What is the common thread of creativity? Its dialectical relation to intelligence and wisdom. *American Psychologist*, *56*(4), 360–362.

Sternberg, R.J. (2003). *Wisdom, intelligence, and creativity synthesized*. New York: Cambridge University Press.

Taranto, M.A. (1989). Facets of wisdom: A theoretical synthesis. *The International Journal of Ageing and Human Development*, *29*(1), 1–21.

Webster, J.D. (1997). The reminiscence functions scale. *International Journal of Ageing and Human Development*, *44*(2), 137–262.

Webster, J.D. (2003). An exploratory analysis of a self-assessed wisdom scale. *Journal of Adult Development*, *10*(1), 13–22.

Webster, J.D. (2007). Measuring the character strength of wisdom. *International Journal of Ageing and Human Development*, *65*(2), 163–183.

Webster, J.D., & Haight, B.K. (Eds.) (2002). *Critical advances in reminiscence work: From theory to application*. New York: Springer Publishing.

Webster, J.D., & McCall, M.F. (1999). Reminiscence functions across adulthood: A replication and extension. *Journal of Adult Development*, *6*(1), 73–85.

Webster, J.D., & Young, R.A. (1988). Process variables of the life review: Counseling implications. *International Journal of Aging and Human Development*, 26(4), 315–323.

Westerhof, G.J., Bohlmeijer, E., & Webster, J.D. (2010). Reminiscence and mental health: A review of recent progress in theory, research, and intervention. *Ageing and Society*, *30*(4), 697–721.

14

HEALTH PROMOTION AND WELL-BEING IN AGEING

With the advent of technology and the bombardment of environmental stimuli, the well-being of individuals is currently at stake and is gradually withering. The constant push to succeed and 'achieve' creates spiralling expectations and exhausts one's life in a panic-stricken manner rather than living in the moment. It is an irony to comprehend the fact that technology has offered humanity 'speed and power' to move forwards. However, civilization is stepping backwards in spirituality and value-orientation (Tarkington, 1994). The issue of health is of crucial significance here because while science and technology have offered us myriad avenues to lengthen our longevity, it is taking a toll on the 'quality of life' of elderly people in the background. In fact, health may be looked at from the vantage of the lifespan developmental perspective at the level of the species in an evolutionary context, at the level of the population in a socio-historical context, and at the individual level in an ontogenetic context (Finch and Crimmins, 2004; Fogel, 2003; Aldwin et al., 2006; Gluckman and Hanson, 2004). Lalonde (1981) recognized the importance of environment and lifestyle in playing significant roles in determining health. It becomes pertinent at this juncture to understand the promotion of health for elderly individuals for uplifting their sense of well-being. This is expected to enable them to inculcate tools for personal growth to experience the fleeting joy of 'becoming' and to be a channel of life-force (Hammarskjold, 1964). The present chapter addresses the well-being of such individuals from the mental health point of view primarily though the importance of physical and spiritual health is intertwined with it as well.

It is to be comprehended that health promotion adheres to both personal and collective achievement on the part of the individual. It requires developing a repertoire of good health habits on his/her part early in life so as to carry them forwards throughout adulthood and old age (Sanyal, 2019). *Health behaviours* are of importance at this juncture. They refer to behaviours undertaken by people to enhance or maintain their health. Poor health behaviours appear to accumulate junk in the body and contribute to illness. A *health habit* is a health-related behaviour that is often internalized on the part of the individual, without his/ her own awareness. These habits, such as brushing teeth, eating a healthy diet, running playfully, or having a lot of physical movement, usually develop in childhood and begin to stabilize around the age of 11 or 12 (Cohen et al., 1993). The habits are generally introduced by caregivers. Hence, health awareness is an epitome of the mature 'elder-mind.'

Mental well-being is essentially brought forth by means of building positive psychological and personal resources that enable individuals to be satisfied with their lives by balancing one's emotionality, having unconditional acceptance of oneself, and finding purpose and meaning in life; seeking personal growth, autonomy, and competence; and having a sense of personal control and generally experiencing optimism on the whole (ODPHP, 2016). As such, individuals with sound well-being are likely to transmogrify life's myriad problems into moderate and beneficial challenges through their coping skills (Szabo, Tache, and Somogyi, 2012). It is to be noted that a certain base level of physical well-being is needed to attain mental well-being. Different parameters appear to play roles in this process to help provide individualized health resources, which will be discussed in this chapter.

Developing healthy habits in life (lifestyle determinants)

Maintaining good sleep hygiene: A 'must' for restoring health

Good sleep is absolutely critical to the well-being and health promotion of individuals (Cohen et al., 2010). It is reported to restore psychological functioning by facilitating the removal of toxic waste substances (Xie et al., 2013) and restoring the resources of an individual which can predict how they feel, think, or behave (Cropanzano, Rupp, and Byrne, 2003). In fact, sleep deprivation is found to be associated with increased vulnerability of individuals to depression, anxiety, and other associated disorders (Breslau, Roth, Rosenthal, and Andreski, 1996; Harvey, 2000, 2002; Harvey and Greenhall, 2003). Chronic insomnia may jeopardize the ability of an individual to secrete and respond to the hormone insulin, which can heighten the risk of developing detrimental ailments like coronary heart disease (Bonner and Arand, 1998; Center for the Advancement of Health, 2004; Weintraub, 2004). A chronic lack of sleep increases one's risk of obesity, diabetes, cardiovascular disease, and infections. Thus, the maintenance of a healthy sleep routine becomes imperative.

It is to be noted that as people get older, the pattern of sleep also changes – especially the amount of time spent in deep sleep. Across the lifespan, older adults tend to go to bed earlier and wake earlier. Non-R.E.M. sleep also has a qualitative change with age, becoming gradually lighter. People awaken more throughout the night from midlife through late life, thereby resulting in their sleep being disturbed. A healthy sleep may be fostered by creating a comfortable sleep environment, relaxing well, having good physical exercise throughout the day to make the body fatigued by the end of the day, setting a consistent bedtime routine including a regular time for sleep and awakening, sleeping only when sleepy, having control of one's negative thoughts and compartmentalizing them away from the bedroom, avoiding smoking, caffeine, and alcohol before bed, and so on.

Eating balanced meals

The foundation of subjective well-being is laid down by maintaining a balanced diet which involves not only having food in the right combination and amount but also having sufficient fluid intake for the metabolism of the congested food and the interaction between different organ systems. It is water which carries needed minerals and nutrients to the body and complements a good diet. It is to be noted that for maximal objective well-being, even mild dehydration can impair cognitive performance (Riebl and Davy, 2013).

Balanced food helps in acquiring 'good gut' bacteria, a process which starts right from birth (Jakobsson et al., 2013). The intake of food helps to develop a profile of micro-flora which affects our body functions, immune systems, and our thoughts (O'Mahony, Clarke, Borre, Dinan, and Cryan, 2014). Biopsychosocial factors tend to influence one's eating habits. Hence, the necessity of making mindful decisions regarding diet to have a personal and thoughtful review of 'needs' versus 'wants.' The goal of a great diet is balanced biochemistry which provides optimal energy efficiency for a specific body and situation (van Praag, Fleshner, Schwartz, and Mattson, 2014). This is highly applicable for an elderly individual who has special needs as per his/her bodily requirements.

Thus, a balanced meal combines mindful consumption of food with positive psychosocial elements. It must be recognized that food and drink are powerful social tools in the current society; therefore, mindful consumption of them in a personally meaningful environment is expected to lead to enhancement in well-being. It becomes relevant to explore environmental (e.g., availability of sources, cost, quality) and psychosocial influences (e.g., busy schedules, sedentary lifestyles, social pressures) on water and food intake to help individuals take control of their personal health and to improve their personal hydration status.

Engaging in daily exercises

Both physical and mental activities help to enhance the well-being of individuals. Physical exercise helps in uplifting one's mood, promoting physical health, and sharpening cognitive function. It further aids individuals in developing resilience and insulation against stressors of different kinds (van Praag et al., 2014).

In addition, engaging in meaningful mental exercise provides context and meaning in our lives. Both activities perpetuate a sense of forward momentum and build excitement and optimism among individuals (Brooks, 2013). It is useful to combine a range of low energy exercises like tai chi, meditation, walking, and reading, along with high energy exercises like aerobics and so on, as far as possible keeping in consideration the limitations of the elderly person. Aerobic exercise improves the body's utilization of oxygen over a prolonged period of time, for example, jogging, cycling, and swimming. Exercise has been found to accompany a number of benefits as follows (Center for the Advancement of Health, 2004; Lee and King, 2003; Sanyal, 2019):

- *Increases maximum oxygen consumption on the part of the body*;
- *Improves the strength of cardiac muscles*;
- *Decreases use of energy sources*;
- *Increases slow-wave sleep and thereby the restorative function of sleep*;
- *Increases high-density lipoprotein – unchanged total cholesterol*;
- *Decreases cardiovascular diseases*;
- *Decreases obesity*;
- *Increases immune system functions*;
- *Decreases negative mood*;
- *Increases longevity*.

The variation in the exercise regimen of elderly individuals directly enhances well-being by combating boredom and melancholy (Martin, Sadlo, and Stew, 2006). As such, it increases energy including vigour and vitality and serves as a positive and protective psychological resource of an individual.

Keeping body weight in control

Weight needs to be regulated by maintaining a proper diet and getting enough exercise. The emerging problem of obesity in the general population has brought about the concern for maintaining body weight in individuals. Obesity, being the excessive accumulation of body fat, appears to be a risk factor for many disorders, both in its own right and because it affects other risk factors (Kopelman, 2000). Protective factors against obesity have been considered by Swinburn, Caterson, Seidell, and James (2004) to be regular physical activity; a high intake of dietary non-starch polysaccharides (N.S.P.)/fibre which appear to be convincing factors; as well as probable factors in the form of supportive home and school environments for children and breastfeeding. On the contrary, risk factors for obesity were considered to be sedentary lifestyles (convincing); a high intake of energy-dense, micronutrient-poor foods (convincing); heavy marketing of energy-dense food including fast food; soft drinks, and fruit juices being sweetened with sugar (probable); and adverse social and economic conditions. The rates of disability (which has a positive association with obesity) have also increased in the last few decades. Hence, maintaining optimal weight for an individual by regulating one's dietary habits essentially serves as an important health-promoting behaviour. Snacking and the frequency of such eating behaviour have been found to be associated with overweight conditions of the body. Thus, keeping body weight in control requires de-cluttering the body with adequate self-control measures (Sanyal, 2019).

Investing in rest, renewal, and savouring

An important set of health behaviours that are only beginning to be understood involves processes of relaxation and renewal, the restorative activities that help people reduce and restore their personal balance. The ability to savour positive aspects of life may provide enormous health benefits (Gump and Metthews, 1998; Steptoe, Roy, and Evans, 1996). Health psychologists are of the opinion that rest, renewal, and savouring – involving activities such as going on holidays, relaxing, enjoying nature, and similar activities – are of help in promoting the health of the individual. This is pertinent for elderly individuals since a greater ability to savour positive experiences and higher resilience are found to be associated and are reported to predict greater happiness, lower depression, and greater satisfaction with life (i.e., greater psychological well-being) (Smith and Smith, 2014).

It is worth mentioning at this juncture that interacting with plants and animals as well as observing nature, even through windows, accounts for enormous human health benefits like reducing both physical and mental stress, helping patients recover more quickly, and calming prisoners and improving their behaviour (Maller, Townsend, Pryor, Brown, and St. Leger, 2006). Humans look up to nature in different forms in order to seek a sense of well-being. This is because exposure to nature has a soothing impact on individuals. Gardening, being with a pet, and other such activities are thereby 'healing' in nature. In fact, the touch and feel experience of earth, air, smells, and the soothing sights of greenery in different shades can make one extra energetic in body and mind. Nature and living things, it seems, tend to make most people feel good (Kellert and Wilson, 1993; Maller et al., 2002). Many psychologists recognize that exposure to green space is useful as a means of boosting well-being (Gable and Haidt, 2005). 'Find nearby nature' (p. 177) has been regarded as a proven strategy to increase one's level of positivity (Fredrickson, 2009). American naturalist and writer Burroughs (1837–1921) commented 'I go to nature to be soothed and healed, and to have my senses put in tune once more' (Eliades, 2013; Sanyal, 2017)

Reframing oneself from the clutches of health-compromising behaviours

Health promotion among the elderly can be fostered by keeping them in control of health-compromising activities such as substance dependence, alcoholism, problem drinking, smoking, and so on. *Physical dependence* on a substance often ends up in producing a state of *tolerance* on the part of the individual concerned. Further, alcohol consumption has been linked to a number of disorders, including high blood pressure, stroke, cirrhosis of the liver, some forms of cancer, and foetal alcohol syndrome, a condition of retardation and physiological abnormalities that arises in the offspring of heavy drinking mothers (Higgins-Biddle, Babor, Mullahyl, Daniels, and McRee, 1997). Excessive drinking may also lead to substantial cognitive impairments, many being irreversible in nature (Goldman, 1983; McGuire, 1982). Smoking has been regarded as one of the single greatest causes of preventable death (McGinnis et al., 1992). In addition to the risks for heart disease and lung cancer, smoking increases the risk of chronic bronchitis, emphysema, respiratory disorders, and damage and injuries due to fires and accidents, among others (Center for the Advancement of Health, 2000).

Thus, it is of dire necessity to curb such health-compromising behaviours and reinforce the health-promoting ones to improve the overall quality of life of elderly individuals in general.

Making the environment elder-friendly (environmental determinants)

Physical environment

Air and water

Clean air and water are basic requirements of sound health. Industrial and urban settings having high levels of particulates, nitrogen oxides, sulphur dioxide, carbon monoxide, volatile organic compounds (V.O.C.), and other substances are likely to impair the health of individuals residing nearby. Hence, residential settings that have facilities of clean air and water are good for elderly residents in maintaining sound health. According to the World Health Organization (W.H.O.), reducing air and water pollution is crucial for saving human lives and to reducing climate change. Nature (especially trees) also plays an important role in purifying the ambience of the neighbourhood in this regard and helps elderly individuals breathe in purified air.

Housing

Housing further plays a pertinent role in the mental health and well-being of individuals, especially senior members (Lee, 2007; Department of Transport and Department of Health, 2011). In fact, cold, damp, noisy, and insecure houses affect the physical and mental health of residents, making them vulnerable to different respiratory and other illnesses and an increased risk of accidental injuries (Lee, 2007). Housing is understood to play an increasingly important role in meeting older people's health and differential needs (Minter, 2011; Moriarty, 2005). In fact, a number of studies have related housing, health, and well-being of individuals (Housing Corporation, 2006; Blackman and Harvey, 2001). Housing, its location and allied factors like the degree of comfort and security associated with it appear to be crucial for laying the foundation of a good quality of life. Supportive housing options (e.g., extra care housing, home improvement agencies) and technologies to support the links of elderly individuals with their family and their communities is a pertinent issue. However, there is a long way to go to satisfy this in the Indian scenario.

In addition to the home, other aspects of the built environment like access to leisure facilities, shops, and other services make it easier to keep individuals healthy. Furthermore, access to green space and safe areas where elderly individuals can relax and see younger members of the community are useful for maintaining optimal health. The built environment needs to be especially accommodative for the elderly so that their differential demands can be met adequately.

Transport

Transport facilities need to be easily available for the elderly. Public transport (buses and trains) allows people to visit friends and relatives and thereby have a feel of 'connectedness,' and also access medical and other services. However, the means of transport need to be accommodative to the different physical challenges of the elderly. Such services need to be within easy walking distance of people's homes as well as be reasonably frequent and reliable. If required, provisions of wheelchairs, stretchers, ambulances, and so on must be available depending on the individual needs of the elderly person. Changes in physiology and cognition associated with later life may demand the necessity of curtailing longer journeys. Thus, frequent senior-friendly transportation facilities are needed (Kerschner and Silverstein, 2017).

Built and natural environments

Ecological psychology suggests that both built and natural environments influence the mental health of residents. Social interaction is encouraged by open places in towns and cities. Besides, pleasant environments encourage people to go out and be physically active. Well-designed environments are good for mental health. In warm weather, shade helps people avoid too much exposure to the sun, and in bad weather, shelter helps protect them against cold and wet conditions (St Leger, 2003; Lee and Maheswaren, 2011). Further, in accordance with the biophilia hypothesis, humans feel good when they are in contact with other forms of animal life and vegetation.

Socio-economic environment

The socio-economic environment of an elderly person relates primarily to one's absolute as well as relative income from different sources like pensions, other investments, and the like. They are pertinent for maintaining a sense of personal control and autonomy for the senior individual to make his/her different ends meet. It has been noted that social, economic, and environmental factors tend to interact among each other, which, in turn, appear to influence population ageing in the long run (Xu, Zhao, Zhang, and Xia, 2018). Swaminathan (1996) is of the opinion that family background, health condition, economic status, and living arrangements are some factors which tend to influence the socio-economic environment of the elderly.

Personal and relational environment

This involves enriching the self-system of the elderly individual in terms of different personal and social resources/potentials as follows:

Developing a sense of gratitude and reflecting on positive events

Gratitude has been regarded as an 'empathic emotion' by Lazarus and Lazarus (1994) which reflects recognition or appreciation of an altruistic gift. Similarly, Emmons and Crumpler (2000) are of the opinion that gratitude is an emotional response to a gift. The word originated from the Latin word 'gratia' meaning graciousness, grace, or gratefulness (Pruyser, 1976). Fitzgerald (1998) mentioned three important components of gratitude including:

a. *A sense of warm appreciative concern for something or somebody*;
b. *A sense of goodwill towards that thing or person*;
c. *A tendency to act positively because of the inherent sense of appreciation.*

It becomes imperative that a sense of gratitude, if inculcated by elderly individuals for the different 'givens' of one's life, is likely to result in:

a. *A sense of abundance*;
b. *A sense of appreciation of the contribution of others to their well-being*;
c. *A tendency to appreciate simple pleasures, the ones readily available to most people*;
d. *Open acknowledgement of experiencing and expressing gratitude.*

In addition, reflecting on good events/things in life helps individuals to counter the tendency to focus more on negative events, combats hedonic adaptations by compelling them to focus on the positive events that may remain unnoticed, makes such events more accessible to memory, and makes oneself more mindful of available resources (Bono et al., 2013; Gander, Proyer, Ruch, and Wyss, 2013). Such an elderly person is likely to be contented in life and enjoy life to the fullest. Health promotion is expected to be at the epitome for such an individual, thereby instilling a sense of well-being.

Inculcating a forgiving stance

Kearns and Fincham (2004) emphasize that the act of forgiveness is a *journey* or *process* of releasing anger and fear, which reduces the desire to retaliate. Binau (2007) also agrees that forgiveness is more of a *process of discovery* which comes from having a transcendent experience or a connection with a higher being. The ability of the individual to forgive others essentiates the ability to forgive one's own self from different imperfections. It consequently eliminates oneself from feelings of anger, hurt, shame, and guilt and releases an emotional burden that created an incapacity to love others. It helps individuals move towards freedom. Forgiveness is thus about freedom, the freedom to 'hold on' and 'let go' at will (Binau, 2007). When people realize this, their hearts move away from hardness caused by resentment. Instead, the individuals' behaviour changes to accepting other's imperfections when they accept their own flaws. Forgiveness is a virtue that when inculcated by elderly individuals can enable them to have a mature and embracing perspective towards life in general. Consequently, selfless compassion will develop.

Hence, forgiveness is indispensably related to psychological adjustment and well-being (Berry and Worthington, 2001). It helps to deal with closure, reduces anger, and increases a sense of well-being among individuals by enhancing close relationships (Orcutt, 2006; Berry, Worthington, O'Connor, Parrott, and Wade, 2005).

Focusing on deep breathing

Rather than slouching, it is recommended to sit up straight to allow more room for the lungs to take in oxygen. One needs to understand the tense body areas, mentally 'breathe into' such areas, and see them relax as one breathes in. One also needs to be conscious of breathing through one's nose rather than mouth.

During the time of inhalation, it is desirable to use abdominal breathing by gently pushing one's stomach outwards and breathing as though one's filling the stomach. On the contrary, it is during exhalation that the individual requires to slowly breathe out, which allows the stomach to return to its normal position. The difference between shallow breathing (which stops at the chest) and abdominal or diaphragmatic breathing (which fills the lower lobes of the lungs and encourages full oxygen exchange) needs to be understood. Abdominal breathing helps to massage the internal organs through the movements of the diaphragm.

Slow, deep, rhythmic breathing helps an individual to detach from negative thoughts and gain control over one's mind. This, in turn, stimulates the parasympathetic nervous system, which further reduces heart rate, relaxes muscles, calms the mind, and normalizes brain function. For the elderly individual, this practice can be regularized to inculcate a sense of acceptance and inner tranquillity.

Developing self-care practices

Self-care practices need to be developed by elderly individuals to help maintain good physical and mental health so as to have adequate control of life with competence, autonomy, and self-reliance as much as possible. The first and foremost dimension of self-care for senior individuals involves adaptation to functional limitations of various kinds (Konrad, 1998). Self-care activities may be broadly categorized as follows:

a. Use of *assistive devices* if needed (Centers for Disease Control, 1992; DeWitt, 1991): They may range from simple homemade tools to sophisticated and expensive equipment (e.g., motorized wheelchairs) which may be adopted by senior individuals.
b. *Modification of a person's living environment*: Structural alterations of an individual's home to facilitate mobility (e.g., constructing a ramp) or physically relocating to a more accommodative residence with elevators, an accommodation having a door wide enough to allow passage of a wheelchair, etc.
c. *Intra-individual factors*: Activity accommodations (e.g., doing things more slowly or less often, avoiding lifting heavy objects, and avoiding bending/stooping as per the different demands of the elderly), psychosocial coping to the varied restrictions in one's routine, and other lifestyle or behaviour changes may be incorporated by elderly individuals to tailor to their special requirements.

In addition, medical diagnostic and therapeutic tools and techniques may also be kept readily available for the needs of elderly individuals (e.g., thermometer, hot water bag, first aid kit).

Developing sound intrapersonal and interpersonal relationships (social capital)

Well-being can be fostered and maintained by engaging in healthy intrapersonal as well as interpersonal interactions and thereby increasing one's

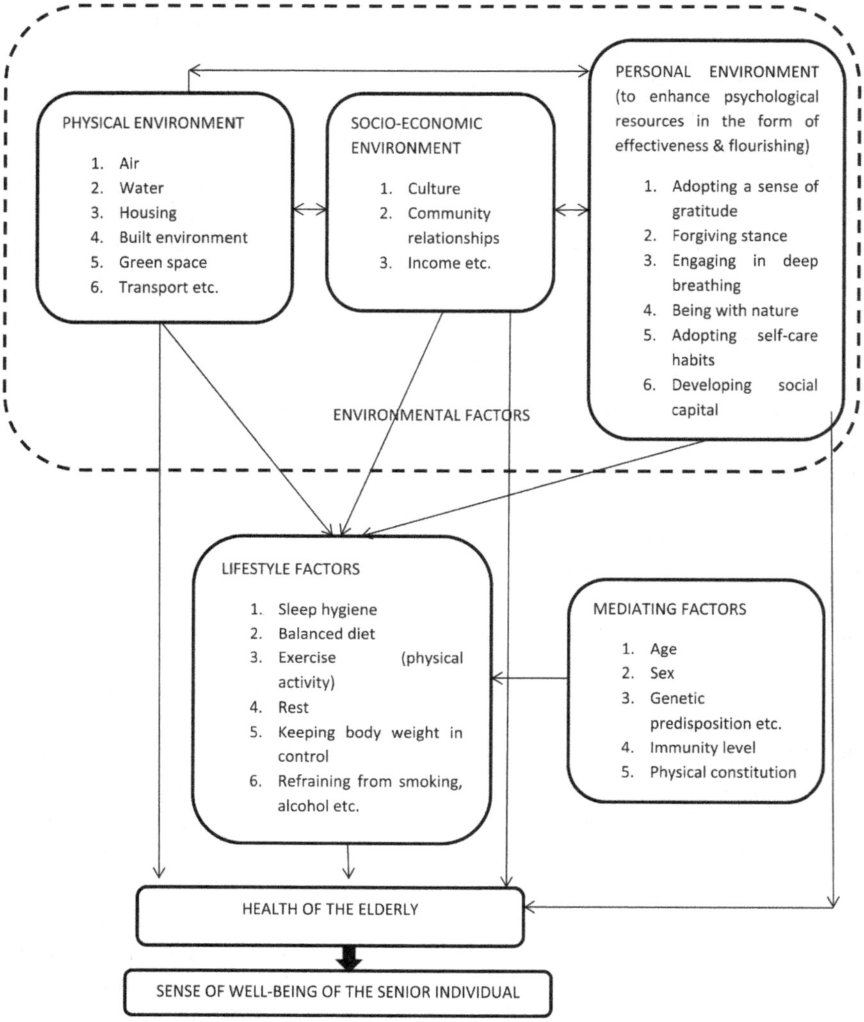

Figure 14.1 Factors influencing health among the elderly (source: authors).

social capital. Intrapersonal well-being can be maintained by senior individuals if they are able to engage in intentional activities on the cognitive, behavioural, and volitional levels (Lyubomirsky et al., 2005). Such activities must be initiated, which requires self-regulatory effort and will, and sustenance on the part of the elderly person.

Sense of well-being and good health also depends on the degree of our connectivity with others and the extent of social support an individual has. Relationships with other people in the community, including one's own family and neighbourhood, appear to be crucial for the interpersonal well-being of individuals. This may be traced to the anthropological beginnings of human beings to live in groups and feel 'at home' for universal purposes of protection, food, and nurturance.

For the elderly individual, resource-building throughout his/her life makes him/her happy as they enhance themselves with skills, knowledge, and abilities of different kinds in later years. Both intrinsic and extrinsic rewards play an important role in influencing the well-being of an individual. On the one hand, while intrinsic rewards include a sense of competence and autonomy (Gagne and Deci, 2005), combining with a sense of relatedness or connectivity with others helps individuals to feel 'related' (Deci et al., 2001).

Hence, health promotion among the elderly can be understood by means of a schematic representation as shown in Figure 14.1.

Conclusion

To wrap up the discussion, it may be said that health promotion among the elderly is dependent on a number of lifestyle and environmental factors. It is by fostering personal resources that the psychological/mental capital of the elderly is enhanced. This may involve the development of virtues such as forgiveness, gratitude, kindness, humour, and having greater experiences with nature, among others, which serve as a foundation from which meaningful directions may be launched towards a greater sense of well-being. Inculcating healthy habits in life such as maintaining regular sleep hygiene, a dietary regimen, and so on also serve as external determinants to take the upper hand in this regard. The senior but decapacitated individual is thus expected to enjoy life to its fullest, encouraging him/her to reap the harvests of an enriched journey of experiences in a satisfactory manner.

References

Aldwin, C.M., Spiro, A. III, & Park, C.L. (2006). Health, behavior, and optimal aging: A life span developmental perspective. In J.E. Birren & K.W. Schaie (Eds.), *Handbook of the psychology of aging* (6th ed., pp. 85–104). Burlington, MA: Elsevier.

Berry, J.W., & Worthington, E.L. (2001). Forgivingness, relationship quality, stress while imagining relationship events, and physical and mental health. *Journal of Counseling Psychology*, *48*(4), 447–455.

Berry, J.W., Worthington, E.L., O'Connor, L.E., Parrott, L., & Wade, N.G. (2005). Forgivingness, vengeful rumination, and affective traits. *Journal of Personality*, *73*(1), 183–225.

Binau, B.A. (2007). 'Holding On' and 'letting go': The dynamics of forgiveness. *Word and World*, *27*(1), 23–31.

Blackman, T., & Harvey, J. (2001). Housing renewal and mental health: A case study. *Journal of Mental Health*, *10*(5), 571–583.

Bonner, M.H., & Arand, D.L. (1998). Heart-rate variability in insomniacs and matched normal sleepers. *Psychosomatic Medicine*, *60*(5), 610–615.

Bono, J., Glomb, T., Shen, W., Kim, E., & Koch, A. (2013). Building positive resources: Effects of positive events and positive reflection on work stress and health. *Academy of Management Journal*, *56*(6), 1601–1627.

Breslau, N., Roth, T., Rosenthal, L., & Andreski, P. (1996). Sleep disturbance and psychiatric disorders: A longitudinal epidemiological study of young adults. *Biological Psychiatry*, *39*(6), 411–418.

Brooks, K. (2013). New program reduces agitation in dementia patients. *Johns Hopkins Magazine*, Winter. Retrieved from http://hub.jhu.edu/magazine/2013/winter/dementia-agitation-activities-program

Burroughs, J. (1837–1921). *Accepting the universe: Essays in naturalism*. Boston: Houghton Mifflin Company. (page images at HathiTrust).

Center for the Advancement of Health (2000). *Selected evidence for behavioural approaches to chronic disease management in clinical settings: Dietary practices*. Washington, DC: Author.

Center for the Advancement of Health (2004). *What we do*. Retrieved from http://www.cfah.org/about/ what_we.cfm

Centers for Disease Control (1992). *Advance data: Assistive technology devices and home accessibility features: Prevalence, payment, need and trends (United States public health service,* 217). National Center for Health Statistics.

Cohen, D., Wang, W., Wyatt, J., Kronauer, R., Dijk, D., Czeisler, C., & Klerman, E. (2010). Uncovering residual effects of chronic sleep loss on human performance. *Science Translational Medicine*, *2*(14), 14ra3.

Cohen, S., Tyrrell, D.A.J., & Smith, A.P. (1993). Negative life events, perceived stress, negative affect, and susceptibility to the common cold. *Journal of Personality and Social Psychology*, *64*(1), 131–140.

Cropanzano, R., Rupp, D., & Byrne, Z. (2003). The relationship of emotional exhaustion to work attitudes, job performance, and organizational citizenship behaviors. *Journal of Applied Psychology*, *88*(1), 160–189.

Deci, E.L., Ryan, R.M., Gagn´e, M., Leone, D.R., Usunov, J., & Kornazheva, B.P. (2001). Need satisfaction, motivation, and well-being in the work organizations of a former Eastern Bloc country. *Personality and Social Psychology Bulletin*, *27*(8), 930–942.

Department of Transport and Department of Health (2011). *Transport and health: Delivering healthy local transport plans*. London: Department of Health.

DeWitt, J.C. (1991). The role of technology in removing barriers. *Milbank Quarterly*, *69*(Suppl. 1–2), 332.

Eliades, A. (2013). *Well-being gardening. Gardening for the body, mind and spirit*. Posted June 5, filed under General Health and Disease.

Emmons, R.A., & Crumpler, C.A. (2000). Gratitude as human strength: Appraising the evidence. *Journal of Social and Clinical Psychology*, *19*(1), 56–69.

Finch, C.E., & Crimmins, E.M. (2004). Inflammatory exposure and historical changes in human life-spans. *Science*, *305*(5691), 1736–1739.

Fitzgerald, P. (1998). Gratitude and justice. *Ethics*, *109*(1), 119–153.

Fogel, R.W. (2003). Secular trends in physiological capital: Implications for equity in health care. *Perspectives in Biology and Medicine*, *46*(3), S24–S38.

Fredrickson, B. (2009). *Positivity*. New York: Random House Inc.

Gable, S.L., & Haidt, J. (2005). What (and Why) is positive psychology? *Review of General Psychology*, *9*(2), 103–110.

Gagn´e, M., & Deci, E.L. (2005). Self-determination theory and work motivation. *Journal of Organizational Behavior*, *26*(4), 331–362. doi:10.1002/job.322

Gander, F., Proyer, R.T., Ruch, W., & Wyss, T. (2013). Strength-based positive interventions: Further evidence for their potential in enhancing well-being and alleviating depression. *Journal of Happiness Studies*, *14*(4), 1241–1259.

Gluckman, P.D., & Hanson, M.A. (2004). Living with the past: Evolution, development, and patterns of disease. *Science*, *305*(5691), 1733–1736.

Goldman, M.S. (1983). Cognitive impairment in chronic alcoholics: Some cause for optimism. *American Psychologist*, *38*(10), 1045–1054.

Gump, B.B., & Metthews, K.A. (1998). Vigilance and cardio-vascular reactivity to subsequent stressors in men: A preliminary study. *Health Psychology*, *17*(1), 93–96.

Hammarskjold, D. (1964). *Markings* (L. Sjoberg & W.H. Auden, Trans.). London: Faber & Faber.

Harvey, A.G. (2000). Pre-sleep cognitive activity: A comparison of sleep-onset insomniacs and good sleepers. *British Journal of Clinical Psychology*, *39*(3), 275–286.

Harvey, A.G. (2002). A cognitive model of insomnia. *Behavioral Research and Therapy*, *40*(8), 869–893.

Harvey, A.G., & Greenhall, E. (2003). Catastrophic worry in primary insomnia. *Journal of Behavior Therapy and Experimental Psychiatry*, *34*(1)1, 11–23.

Higgins-Biddle, J.C., Babor, T.E., Mullahyl, J., Daniels, J., & McRee, B. (1997). Alcohol screening and brief intervention: Where research meets practice. *Connecticut Medicine*, *61(9)*, *565–575*.

Housing Corporation (2006). *Good housing and good health sector study*. London: Housing Corporation/CSIP.

Jakobsson, H.E., Abrahamsson, T.R., Jenmalm, M.C., Harris, K., Quince, C., Jernberg, C.,...Andersson, A.F. (2013). Decreased gut microbiota diversity, delayed Bacteroidetes colonisation and reduced the responses in infants delivered by caesarean section. *Gut*, *63*(4), 559–566. doi:10.1136/gutjnl-2012-303249

Kearns, J.N., & Fincham, F.D. (2004). A prototype analysis of forgiveness. *Personal Sociology & Psychology Bulletin*, *30*(7), 838–855.

Kellert, S.R., & Wilson, S.O. (Eds.) (1993). *The biophilia hypothesis*. Washington DC: Island Press.

Kerschner, H., & Silverstein, N.M. (2017). Senior transportation: Importance to healthy aging. *Journal of Gerontology and Geriatric Research*, 6(1), 381. doi:10.4172/2167-7182.1000381

Konrad, T.R. (1998). The patterns of self-care among older adults in western industrialized societies. In M.G. Ory& G.H. DeFriese (Eds.,). *Self-care in later life: Research program, and policy issues*. (pp. 1-23). New York: Springer Publishing Company, Inc .

Kopelman, P.G. (2000). Obesity as a medical problem. *Nature*, *404*(6778), 635–643.

Lalonde, M. (1981). *A new perspective on the health of Canadians*. Ottawa: Ministry of Supply and Services. Retrieved from http://www.phac-aspc.gc.ca/ph-sp/pdf/per spect-eng. pdf

Lazarus, R.S., & Lazarus, B.N. (1994). *Passions and reason: Making sense of our emotions*. New York: Oxford University Press.

Lee, A.C.K., & Maheswaren, R. (2011). The health benefits of urban green space: A review of the evidence. *Journal of Public Health*, *33*(2), 212–222.

Lee, M. (2007). *Improving services and support for older people with mental health problems. The second report from the UK enquiry into mental health in later life.* London: Age Concern England.

Lee, R.E., & King, A.C. (2003). Discretionary time among older adults: How do physical activity promotion interventions affect sedentary and active behaviours? *Annals of Behavioural Medicine*, *25*(2), 112–119.

Lyubomirsky, S., Sheldon, K.M., & Schkade, D. (2005). Pursuing happiness: The architecture of sustainable change. *Review of General Psychology*, *9*(2). Retrieved from http://escholarship.org/uc/item/4v03h9gv

Maller, C., Townsend, M., Brown, P., & St. Leger, L. (2002). *Healthy parks healthy people.* Melbourne: Deakin University and Parks Victoria.

Maller, C., Townsend, M., Pryor, A., Brown, P., & St. Leger, L. (2006). Healthy nature, healthy people: 'Contact with nature' as an upstream health promotion intervention for populations. *Health Promotion International*, *21*(1), 45–54. Retrieved from http://heapro.oxfordjournals.org/content/21/1/45.long

Martin, M., Sadlo, G., & Stew, G. (2006). The phenomenon of boredom. *Qualitative Research in Psychology*, *3*(3), 193–211. doi:10.1191/1478088706qrp066oa

McGinnis, M., Richmond, J.B., Brandt, E.N., Windom, R.E., & Mason, J.O. (1992). Health progress in the United States: Results of 1990 objectives for the nation. *JAMA*, *268*(18), 2545–2552.

McGuire, F.L. (1982). Treatment of the drinking driver. *Health Psychology*, *1*(2), 137–152.

Minter, J. (2011). Housing: The backdrop to good mental health and well-being in later life. In T. Williamson (Ed.), *Older People's mental health today: A handbook.* Brighton: Pavilion Publishing. Ltd.

Moriarty, J. (2005). *Update for SCIE best practice guide on assessing the mental health needs of older people.* London: King's College London.

OFFICE of disease prevention and health promotion (Office of Disease Prevention and Health Promotion) (2016). *Health-related quality of life and well-being.* Rockville, MD: ODPHP. Retrieved July 2016, from http://www. Healthy people. gov /2020/topics-objectives/topic/health-related-quality-oflife- well-being

O'Mahony, S.M., Clarke, G., Borre, Y.E., Dinan, T.G., & Cryan, J.F. (2014). Serotonin, tryptophan metabolism and the brain-gut-microbiome axis. *Behavioral Brain Research*, *277*, 32–48. Epub ahead of print. doi:10.1016/ j.bbr.2014.07.027

Orcutt, H.K. (2006). The prospective relationship of interpersonal forgiveness and psychological distress symptoms among college women. *Journal of Counseling Psychology*, *53*(3), 350–336.

Pruyser, P.W. (1976). *The minister as diagnostician: Personal problems in pastoral perspectives.* Philadelphia, PA: Westminster Press.

Riebl, S.K., & Davy, B.M. (2013). The hydration equation: Update on water balance and cognitive performance. *ACSM's Health and Fitness Journal*, *17*(6), 21–28. doi:10.1249/FIT.0b013e3182a9570f

Sanyal, N. (2017). *Pebbles of positivism, positive psychology and spirituality: Contents and approaches.* Kolkata: Ramakrishna Mission Institute of Culture, Golpark.

Sanyal, N. (2019). De-cluttering of lifestyle through self-control: The most needed track to health attainment. *Journal of Health Studies (JHS)*, *1*(1), 21–39.

Smith, J.L., & Smith, L.H. (2014). Savoring, resilience, and psychological well-being in older adults. *Aging and Mental Health*, *19*(3), 1–9.

Steptoe, A., Roy, M.P., & Evans, O. (1996). Psychosocial influences on ambulatory blood pressure over working and non-working days. *Journal of Psychophysiology*, *19*, 218–227.

St Leger, L. (2003). Health and nature: New challenges for health promotion. *Health Promotion International*, *18*(3), 173–175.

Swaminathan, D. (1996). Integration of the aged into the development process in India. *Help Age India Research & Development Journal*, 2(2), 3–8.

Swinburn, B.A., Caterson, I., Seidell, J.C., & James, W.P.T. (2004). Diet, nutrition and the prevention of excess weight gain and obesity. *Public Health Nutrition*, 7(1A), 123–146.

Szabo, S., Tache, Y., & Somogyi, A. (2012).The legacy of Hans Selye and the origins of stress research: A retrospective 75 years after his landmark brief 'letter' to the editor of nature. *Stress*, *15*(5), 472–478. doi:10.3109/10253890. 2012.710919

Tarkington, B. (1994). *The magnificent Ambersons*. New York: Bantam Press Books. Originally published 1918.

van Praag, H., Fleshner, M., Schwartz, M.W., & Mattson, M.P. (2014). Exercise, energy intake, glucose homeostasis, and the brain. *Journal of Neuroscience*, *34*(46), 15139–15149. doi:10.1523/JNEUROSCI.2814-14.2014

Weintraub, A. (2004). I can't sleep. *Business Week*, *67–70*, 72, 74.

Xie, L., Kang, H., Xu, Q., Chen, M.J., Liao, Y., Thiyagarajan, M.,...Nedergaard, M. (2013). Sleep drives metabolite clearance from the adult brain. *Science*, *342*(6156), 373–377.

Xu, X., Zhao, Y., Zhang, X., & Xia, S. (2018). Identifying the impacts of social, economic, and environmental factors on population aging in the Yangtze River delta using the geographical detector technique. *Sustainability*, *10*(5), 1528–1543. doi:10.3390/su10051528

15

REFLECTIVE RIPPLES OF GERIATRIC LIFE

The flow of life is a journey led by everyone. The life that starts with birth does not have a definite length to move on. Experience and advanced life-space in that context are akin to a spontaneously achieved 'gift' from life itself. Acknowledgement of this value and positivity that can be brought in as an added flavour in life are merged in this concluding chapter, which enumerates different folds of realization in the context of ageing along a positive psychological route. These have been provided in the form of meditative observations to create a resonance of rich experiential wisdom in the elderly. The essence of transcendence has been explored. The story of loss and challenges posed by ageing is comprehended in the light of personal maturity of senior individuals to accept different givens of life gracefully and look back in a mode of reminiscence to locate the stories of happiness and contentment. This naturally deconstructs the stereotypes associated with ageing. A 'counting-up' strategy is consequently cultivated in terms of experiential treasures instead of a countdown perspective. The formula to positive ageing is inscribed by living in the present, with 'senescence-identity wrath' serving as an inner light to gero-transcendence (Baltes et al., 2005; Sanyal, 2014). The self no longer remains truncated and egoistic; instead, it broadens with a horizon of 'contemplative imagination' resting with Mother Nature (Schultz, 2010). The phase of a second childhood in the form of old age is adorned with not only maturity but selfless compassion for members of the younger generation. The winter façade of life calls forth serenity in the spiritual space and reverence from others in society towards the senior individual. The rich experiences of the elderly serve as a 'treasure trove' for both themselves and younger individuals. The culmination of a wide experiential matrix in the context of ageing has been summarily depicted in different sections in the form of certain observations and meditative notes as follows.

Life narratives of the elderly

The toothless smile of a granny resembles that of a toothless smile of a child. Both need tender care and love. They need compassionate bonds and warm hands around them to accommodate failing lights in life. The stretched hours of forlorn timespan need more sleep and cosy comforts in passing moments. Authentic warmth is the first emotional need of a child at birth. It paints the growing mind with positivity. Ageing is the crown of life. The wrinkled skin, grey hair, slow movements, toothless smiles ... there are umpteen numbers of stories to tell. If one has the patience to listen to such stories, it makes lives only richer in experience. Old age should be grace personified to narrate the stories of life satisfaction without any stagnation feelings. Ageing also involves bathing in the reservoir of pain. Its pain-based realizations of life, ripples are 'swimming towards wisdom.' The wisdom-laden ageing mind carries crystals of compassion; hence, they are priceless assets in one's life.

Cellular and organismal senescence is bound to occur in human beings following the principles of nature (Waters, 2007; Floyd, Hensley, Forster, Kelleher-Andersson, and Wood, 2002). However, ageing requires looking back at one's life and taking a glimpse at different narratives in a retrospective manner. This runs parallel with the discussion in Chapter 13 of this book on a life-story matrix to attain wisdom. The increase in measures of crystallized intelligence among the elderly supplants the experiential wisdom attained by them (Surprenant and Neath, 2007). This is reflected in their expertise and deliberate cognitive and fitness training which may even be nurtured through creative pursuits discussed as in Chapter 5 (Kramer et al., 2003; Colcombe et al., 2003). Storytelling is associated with health-related behaviours such as being mindful and non-judgemental (Banks-Wallace, 2002; Hodge, Pasqua, Marquez, and Geishirt-Cantrell, 2002). Its efficacy has been supported by different theoretical models (Soltys and Coats, 1994). This further needs to be taken into special consideration in the therapeutic intervention of life review that is specifically meant for the elderly (Cappeliez, 2002; Garland and Garland, 2004).

Personality features of the matured elderly person

The fragile bodies with sparkling eyes are full of experientiality layers. Touching these layers enrich the younger ones. The fallen resources bend the aged, painting grace lines of wisdom on them. The man in senescence does not have a sparkling identity but has lines of sombreness and depth creating the crater of solitude. Aged individuals are thus storehouses of experience resources and absorbed realizational folds. Advanced age is the hallmark of attainment of advancement in all respects and regards. The veil of ageing is 'maturity' and just not longevity. The quality of resilience that is observed in the matured aged is a ready model in life education.

> *The aged person is a prolific source of guidance and advice treading the paths of life picking up its varied vicissitudes. The countdown is not the tune of ageing; it is rather the 'count-up.' The wide range of experientiality and attained wisdom of the aged person becomes the repertoire of resources for generations to come. One should never underestimate it. The elderly may not bring materialistic ease and pleasure in life, but their guidance alone is priceless. Hence, major developments of a nation depend a lot on the shoulders of knowledgeable aged people. One may have a fruitless tree in the garden, but at least it provides shade ... You will not cut it off, will you? It is the fragrance of wisdom and sapience which wraps old age. This age throws open the windows of knowledge and rests on an all-encompassing vision. Should we not salute it?*

Socio-emotional aspects of ageing have gathered much scholarly interest. This is because of the matured personality frame of the elderly person who has sublimated his/her narcissistic orientation and has adopted a generative stance for younger members. It has its obvious ripples in the rich relationship matrices that integrated seniors enjoy with others owing to their sound cognitive-emotional regulation and decreases in negative interactions (Fingerman and Baker, 2007; Carstensen, Fung, and Charles, 2003; Birditt and Fingerman, 2003). Strategies such as putting into perspective, focusing on planning, and positive reappraisal appear to be better among matured elderly individuals. Looking after the elderly thus should be looked upon as a blessing. Well-being coupled with a sound meaning in life, wisdom flare and experientiality are expected to be fostered, accompanied by mellowed, golden-hued emotional rewards of advanced age (Cole and Sierpina, 2007; Sanyal, Dasgupta, and Sinha, 2011; Dasgupta and Dasgupta, 2014).

Spiritualistic orientation in the elderly

> *Ageing is inevitable but growing old positively is a choice of basic temperament. Less involvement with life is a needed habit for the aged to get ready to shake off worn-out life and be in bliss. Less external items in life and less handling of money prepare them for non-materialistic transcendental peace. Human beings usually cling to narcissism to have self-glory. This is 'non-generative' ageing where inward freedom is missed in the worldly experience of suffocation. Post-narcissistic orientation in senescence etches marks of spirituality to create freedom of narcissism in the mind. In the end-span of ageing, if one is matured enough, the 'no-self' existence, being free of mundane materialistic desires and demands, is the acquisition point. It meets life-sensations without fragmentation of*

> *mind and enjoys the experience of the fullness of the moment. Here, one is completely ready to face death. In the younger days of life, 'identity-search' is a stepping-stone for creating chains of progression in life. 'Senescence-identity wrath' is the inner light to paths of transcendence. Ageing is a multi-layered story of happiness and so much unhappiness. Senescence to transcendence is a collage of realized philosophies of life (Kalam and Tiwari, 2015).*

It is detachment from worldly endeavours which allows the self to engage in an interior journey and be a witness of divinity in the self and others that enables the elderly person to attain bliss. This offers parallels to the discussion in Chapter 8 on detachment. The silence that is thus inculcated engages one in personal growth and transcendence (Palmquist, 2006). Solitude helps the individual to have a clearer and mindful perspective of life as elaborated in Chapter 12 on mindfulness (Zielinski and Bassuk, 2005; Heaversedge and Halliwell, 2010). Practices such as yoga, pranayama, prayers, and meditation are the epitome of the daily regimen of senior individuals as shown in Chapter 1. Virtues of humility and forgiveness develop consequently, resulting in spiritual awakening (Eggers and Hensley, 2005). Obviously, it calls forth decreased anxiety in relation to one's demise. Aged life then shines with 'contemplative realization.' Life is a given gift of God, nature, or any supreme power. In the old-age canvas, counting so many positive experiences of ours, could we write it as a formula?

Ageing in sync with nature

> *The more aged one is, the more life-travelled is he/she. Travel is the platter of spending in life that has made them only rich. In life, the natural gift is our very 'existence.' Ageing is the span to enjoy this gift. Ageing is also the winter facade of life, with fallen leaves and bare structures, with dim lights to paint serenity and reverence. The fallen leaves in winter make a nature carpet. Old age is like rain in the mountain. One cannot take a stroll but can observe nature with its full grace/freshness. Old age is the sunshine after heavy rain. The sufferings persist, but their smile of wisdom is a priceless gem.*

These lines remind us of the discussion in Chapter 6 where nature was seen as a companion and philosopher in advanced age. The instructions of the cosmos are inscribed in nature, with human ageing following its norms as well (Cox and Cohen, 2013; Sanyal, 2017). Mindful attention to different structural features of nature can serve as an emotional-spiritual anchor to the elderly to attain tranquillity (Maller et al., 2002; Eliades, 2013). The principles associated with it may be used in horticulture therapy as well as eco-therapy, specifically for senior individuals (Trellis, 2013; Burls, 2007).

It may be specifically tailored for the elderly ailing from neurodegenerative disorders. In the present era of digitalization, with an upsurge of smart technology, including the 'internet of things,' the need for a connection to nature becomes ever more pertinent (Chopra, 2016; Baers, 2010).

Conclusion

As we draw the curtain close, the theme of this book, namely, ageing, may be viewed as not solely a phase of challenges and losses, but the maker of new design layouts. Experiencing pain does not earn the licence to inflict pain on others. In fact, a frequent expression of mental pain in late age is a regressive attention demand. Paranoia in ageing reflects an unfulfilled life. Lack of trust and faith in earlier stages paves the way to insecurity in the aged state. This book offers a positivistic perspective to the process not only for the senior individual but also for others who come in close physical, social, emotional, and spiritual contact. Its aim of touching upon applied aspects of geriatrics has been cogently exercised along multiple facets. If the messages in the chapters are well-received and create ripples in the minds of the readers, our lives and thought processes are thanked profusely. We end with a thread to hold to understand positive ageing: *In ageing, the being is not the child of parents anymore but that of the cosmos itself.*

References

Baars, J. (2010). Philosophy of aging, time, and finitude. In T.R. Cole, R. Ray, & R. Kastenbaum (Eds.), *A guide to humanistic studies in aging* (pp. 105–120). Baltimore: Johns Hopkins University Press.

Baltes, P.B., Freund, A.M., & Li, S.C. (2005). The psychological science of human ageing. In M.L. Johnson (Ed.), *The Cambridge handbook of age and ageing* (pp. 47–71). Cambridge: Cambridge University Press.

Banks-Wallace, J. (2002). Talk that talk: Storytelling and analysis rooted in African American oral tradition. *Qualitative Health Research*, *12*(3), 410–426.

Birditt, K.S., & Fingerman, K.L. (2003). Age and gender differences in adults' emotional reactions to interpersonal tensions. *Journal of Gerontology: Psychological Sciences*, *58B*, 237–245.

Burls, A. (2007). People and green spaces: Promoting public health and mental well-being through eco-therapy. *Journal of Public Mental Health*, *6*(3), 24–39.

Cappeliez, P. (2002). Cognitive-reminiscence therapy for depressed older adults in day hospital and long-term care. In J.D. Webster & B.K. Haight (Eds.), *Critical advances in reminiscence work: From theory to application* (pp. 300–313). New York: Springer Publishing.

Carstensen, L.L., Fung, H.H., & Charles, S.T. (2003). Socioemotional selectivity theory and the regulation of emotion in the second half of life. *Motivation and Emotion*, *27*(2), 103–124.

Chopra, R. (2016). Environmental degradation in India: Causes and consequences. *International Journal of Applied Environmental Sciences*, *11*(6), 1593–1601.

Colcombe, S.J., Erickson, K.I., Raz, N., Webb, A.G., Cohen, N.J., McAuley, E., & Kramer, A.F. (2003). Aerobic fitness reduced brain tissue loss in aging humans. *Journal of Gerontology: Medical Sciences*, *58*(2), 176–180.

Cole, & Sierpina (2007). Humanistic gerontology and the meaning(s) of ageing. In K.F. Ferraro & J.M. Wilmoth (Eds.), *Gerontology: Perspectives and issues* (3rd ed., pp. 245–263). New York: Springer Publishing Company.

Cox, B., & Cohen, A. (2013). *Wonders of life*. London: HarperCollins Publisher.

Dasgupta, C., & Dasgupta, M. (2014). Maturity of the evolving self: Is it a function of age? – A quest through the positive lenses of psychology. *Journal of Positive Psychology*, *11*, 77–102.

Eggers, S.J., & Hensley, B.H. (2005). Empowering spirituality and generativity through intergenerational connections. In B. Mark & H. Deborah (Eds.), *Spiritual assessment and intervention with older adults: Current directions and applications* (pp. 87–108). New York: Taylor & Francis Group.

Eliades, A. (2013). *Well-being gardening. Gardening for the body, mind and spirit.* Posted June 5, filed under General Health and Disease.

Fingerman, K.L., & Baker, B.N. (2007).Socioemotional aspects of ageing. In K.F. Ferraro & J.M. Wilmoth (Eds.), *Gerontology: Perspectives and issues* (3rd ed., pp. 183–202). New York: Springer Publishing Company.

Floyd, R.A., Hensley, K., Forster, M.J., Kelleher-Andersson, J.A., & Wood, P.L. (2002). Nitrones, their value as therapeutics and probes to understand aging. *Mechanisms of Ageing and Development*, *123*(8), 1021–1031.

Garland, J., & Garland, C. (2004). *Life review in health and social care: A practitioner's guide*. Hove: Brunner-Routledge.

Heaversedge, J., & Halliwell, E. (2010). The mindful manifesto: How doing less and noticing more can help us thrive in a stressed-out world. Australia: Hay House.

Hodge, F.S., Pasqua, A., Marquez, C.A., & Geishirt-Cantrell, B. (2002).Utilizing traditional storytelling to promote wellness in American Indian communities. *Journal of Transcultural Nursing*, *13*(1), 6–11.

Kalam, A.P.J., & Tiwari, A. (2015). *Transcendence: My spiritual experiences with Pramukh Swamiji*. Noida: Harper Element.

Kramer, A., Colcombe, S., McAuley, E., Eriksen, K., Scalf, P., Jerome, G., … Webb, A.G. (2003). Enhancing brain and cognitive function of older adults through fitness training. *Journal of Molecular Neuroscience*, *20*(3), 213–222.

Maller, C., Townsend, M., Brown, P., & St. Leger, L. (2002). *Healthy parks healthy people*. Melbourne: Deakin University and Parks Victoria.

Palmquist, S. (2006). Ontology and the wonder of silence. *Journal of Wisdom and Philosophy*, *6*, 67–76.

Sanyal, N. (2014). Gerotranscendence: The contemplative dimension of positive ageing with wisdom at the core. *Journal of Positive Psychology*, *11*, 28–39

Sanyal, N. (2017). *Pebbles of positivism, positive psychology and spirituality: Contents and approaches*. Kolkata: Ramakrishna Mission Institute of Culture, Golpark.

Sanyal, N., Dasgupta, M., & Sinha, S. (2011). Generativity, attachment style, personal meaning in life and related psychosocial variables across the developmental trajectory: An exploratory study. *Indian Journal of Psychology and Education (IJPE)*, *1*(1), 41–57.

Schultz, N. (2010). Nurture nature. *New Scientist*, *208*(2785), 35–37.

Soltys, F.G., & Coats, L. (1994). The SolCos model: Facilitating reminiscence therapy. *Journal of Gerontological Nursing*, *20*(11), 11–16.

Surprenant, A.M., & Neath, I. (2007). Cognitive ageing. In K.F. Ferraro & J.M. Wilmoth (Eds.), *Gerontology: Perspectives and issues* (3rd ed., pp. 89–109). New York: Springer Publishing Company.

Trellis, S. (2013). *Therapeutic horticulture: Theory and evidence*. Retrieved from www.trellisscotland.org.uk

Waters, D.J. (2007). Cellular and organismal aspects of senescence and longevity. In K.F. Ferraro & J.M. Wilmoth (Eds.), *Gerontology: Perspectives and issues* (3rd ed., pp.59–87). Springer Publishing Company.

Zielinski, S., & Bassuk, D. (Eds.) (2005). *Psychology and silence*. Wallingford, PA: Pendle Hill Publications.

GLOSSARY

Activity theory A theory of ageing that emphasizes increased activities and taking active roles as mandatory for having healthy ageing.

Amàtra The 'measureless' and 'limitless' reality.

Anahata, Hridaya chakra The heart plexus.

Animal-assisted therapy (A.A.T.) Therapeutic intervention with the help of animals (often pets) and aims at improving the well-being of clients and overall quality of life. Also known as pet therapy.

Anticipatory grief Grief in anticipation of the death of the loved individual.

Aromatherapy An alternative therapeutic modality involving the use of aromatic, soothing, and a cost-effective means of relaxation like lavender oil, jojoba oil, cypress, or tea tree.

Art therapy A therapeutic intervention where art is used as a cathartic medium for healing by triggering sensory stimulation and self-expression.

Authenticity Relating to being in touch with one's inner self, knowing the self, having a sense of one's own identity, and then living in accordance. Self-identity, individuality, and meaning-making are associated terms.

Backup assistance Assistance to elderly parents in the form of support and caregiving provided at an intermittent level.

Balance theory of wisdom Theoretical position according to which wisdom attained by elderly individuals requires tacit knowledge and practical intelligence as mediated by values in order to achieve common good through the balancing of interpersonal, intrapersonal, and extra-personal interests.

Bereavement therapy Therapeutic intervention meant for bereavement issues for spouses, offspring, siblings, and other near acquaintances, often applicable for the elderly.

Berlin wisdom model Model of wisdom which emphasizes rich factual and procedural knowledge. It requires the optimal use of three meta-criteria, namely, lifespan contextualism, value relativism, and the recognition and management of the fundamental uncertainty of life matters.

Bibliotherapy Spiritual reading that involves the use of literature to help gain insight into feelings and behaviours and to assist with positive coping.

Body-transcendence Involves awareness of different bodily changes to the optimal extent by not putting one's self or the body in focus. It is a sign of maturity and enables a form of detachment in old age.

Brahmacharya Ashrama The first stage of life involving childhood having character-building and learning duty to others according to Hindu scriptures.

Brahman The Eternal.

Brain plasticity The ability of the brain to induce the sprouting of new dendrites, thereby enhancing brain reserves at the physiological level to take over the function of the part which is affected by disease or degeneration. Challenging activities in the form of engaging in creative endeavours are reported to be associated with brain plasticity.

Bridge employment Transitional work of a shorter duration that occurs between full-time employment in a career and complete labour force withdrawal.

Cabin fever Having to stay 'all alone,' often experienced by retired older male partners of women who are still working.

Circumscribed assistance Assistance to elderly parents which has limited scope but is reliable and predictable.

Cognitive-behavioural therapy An approach to psychotherapy that involves extension of the modification and re-learning procedures to cognitive processes like imagery, fantasy, thought, self-image, and so on. Often useful for depression.

Conscious ageing Ageing which is regarded as a developmental phase by integrating divergent elements of the self into increased awareness and living consciously in later life. It supports values of autonomy, individuality, expressiveness, and self-transcendence.

Contemplative ageing Has the theme of 'Being' where older persons attempt to resolve troubling past issues and arrive at a better understanding of one's self and determine the meaning of one's life.

Continuity theory A theory that states that individuals develop preferences to be spiritual in their traditions as old age approaches. It also emphasizes the role of spiritual practices in the experiential process of dying.

Cosmic consciousness A consciousness that develops when individuals spend more time in meditation.

Cosmic dimension A dimension of emotional detachment which gets reflected by means of the gradual shift from egoism to altruism. It is important for the development of a generative self.

Dawn–dusk simulation light therapy A therapeutic intervention requiring the mimicking of outdoor twilight transitions to help restore disturbed circadian rhythm of the elderly individual.

Dementia-caregiver counselling Mainly focuses on the caregiver role of individuals with dementia which combines elements of cognitive-behavioural and interpersonal therapy.

Dementia-friendly community A multi-faceted concept which concerns challenging stigma, increasing understanding, and awareness about dementia and how to support individuals with dementia.

Disengagement theory A theory of ageing which assumes that societal benefit is the result of adults' withdrawal from all roles and activities to be filled up by the youth.

Dissociative assistance Assistance to elderly parents in which caregiving assistance is not very reliable and hence unpredictable.

Eco-therapy Therapeutic intervention involving the relationship between a healthy environment and the individual.

Ego-integrity Characterized by the feeling that one's life is worth living and is the major developmental task in old age.

Empty-nest syndrome A common syndrome experienced by senior individuals when they realize that the 'nest' that they had invested so deeply throughout their lives suddenly becomes empty due to varied reasons like children getting married, settling down elsewhere, and so on, often resulting in pangs of loneliness.

Encore career options Involves pursuing a 'new phase of work' after the departure from career employment, is usually deeply personal and characterized by purpose, passion, and meaningful contribution.

Finitization The perspective of having the underlying idea that the inevitability of change can inspire individuals to appreciate the uniqueness of people and where situations are finite as they are changing over time.

Forgiveness Letting go of negative emotions or associated pain at will.

Generativity Selfless concern for the members of the next generation.

Geographical gerontology Subdomain of gerontology which studies not only the nature of how and where people age but also the qualitative nuances of the same process taking into consideration diversity and access to supportive care, especially in rural and remote areas, etc.

Gerontophobia Fear of age-related self-degeneration.

Gero-transcendence Phase of intrinsic development that surpasses beyond the egoistic self in old age. It refers to the capacity to transcend time and space of the present world by transporting oneself to the future. It connects the self with the universe implying re-defining time, death, and the self.

Gratitude A sense of graciousness, grace, or gratefulness.

Green exercise Doing exercise amidst nature to achieve good physical and mental health.

Garhastha Ashrama The second stage of life beginning at marriage according to Hindu scriptures.

Guided imagery Process of imaging, often with the help of instructions, meant for relaxation.

H.E.R.O.(E) model of wisdom Model of wisdom having five components of wisdom, namely, humour, emotional regulation, life experiences, openness, and reflection

Hand massage Involves the use of soft, gentle, repetitive stroking. It is non-invasive and connects the massage-giver and massage-receiver through touch.

Horticulture therapy Garden-cultivation as a mode of therapeutic intervention, especially for the elderly.

Ich-Tod Refers to the death of the ego-centered processes in the form of communication, needs, experiences, and personality, which is claimed to precede death. It is often observed among individuals suffering from chronic illnesses of various kinds and having the realization that their days are limited.

Ignatius Loyola Motions of the soul.

Impact bias Emotionally tinged event because of retirement.

Interpersonal therapy A therapeutic intervention that is exploratory in nature and is focused on interpersonal conflict, role change, and deficits, i.e., on the present interpersonal relations of the individual.

Jivatma Individual self.

Kaivalya Freedom/liberation.

Kumbhaka The retention of energy or realizing the very core of one's body.

Leisure education A therapeutic recreation intervention, often used for the elderly to facilitate the ability to freely choose independent participation in meaningful leisure experiences.

Leisure 'Non-work' time, regarded as a way of life marked by a sense of freedom and independent choice and as an opportunity for earning self-actualization. It enriches people with a sense of identity and personal autonomy, thereby adding meaning to life and encouraging personal growth and self-expression. Refers to free and unbounded time where chosen activities are adopted to feel good rather than doing perfunctory activities as a daily routine.

Levenson's model of wisdom Model which stresses that wisdom in the elderly is regarded as self-transcendence best understood in terms of different phases of development that precede it. It starts with self-knowledge or self-awareness, followed by detachment, and finally the manifestation of self-transcendent wisdom.

Life review/reminiscence A therapeutic intervention which involves the recall of one's personal history to master the present and future by finding meaning in the present through a partial resolution of conflict within the self or with others.

Mindfulness group discussions Group discussions with mindfulness practice in focus.

Muladhara chakra The root plexus.

Music therapy A therapeutic intervention where music in synchrony with mood is used as a cathartic medium to release emotions and open better channels of communication.

Nabhi chakra The solar plexus.

Niruddha The highest state of mind and being – a controlled, restrained mind to attain peaks of self-actualization. According to Patanjali, persistent practice of yoga helps in the attainment of *niruddha*.

Pancha bhutas Five elements – earth, water, fire, air, and ether.

Paramatma The Universal Self.

Post-formal rationality Ability to enter into the thoughts and expressions of others, the capacity to deal with problems creatively by using various approaches, and adopting a flexible view.

Problem-solving therapy Is a therapeutic intervention which is focused on change and is directive and brief where the client is asked to prioritize his/her problems.

Psychological age A person's age in terms of the level of adaptive capacities on the basis of learning, memory, intelligence, emotional control, motivational strength, coping styles, and so on.

Reflexology An alternative therapeutic modality which involves stimulation of different reflex points appropriately so as to have adequate sensations in the brain.

Routine assistance Assistance reflected through regular ongoing assistance of elderly parent(s).

Sannyasa Ashrama The final stage of life when one mentally renounces all worldly ties in accordance with Hindu scriptures. The elderly person entering this stage spends all his/her time in meditation and contemplation, pondering the mysteries of life.

Short-term psychodynamic therapy A brief therapeutic intervention which is problem-focused in nature and does not examine transference relationships; often indicated for older persons with adjustment disorders, grief reactions, and a recent onset of traumatic stress disorder.

Socio-emotional selectivity theory A theory of ageing which has a greater emphasis on emotional goals as individuals become aware of the brevity of life.

SolCos model Model of reminiscence having three chief elements, namely, processes, items, and outcomes.

Spiritual age A person's age in terms of developmental changes on the spiritual dimension including a preoccupation with intergenerational relationships, the meaning of life, and death.

Sporadic assistance Assistance to elderly parents which may be provided depending on the convenience of a sibling, however, it is not coordinated by support provided by other siblings.

Successful ageing Involves the ability to maintain a low risk of disease and disease-related disability; intact mental and physical function, and active engagement with life.

Sunyata The highest meditative state or experience.

Supportive psychotherapy A type of psychotherapeutic intervention which is provided generally to elderly individuals having psychotic problems, usually accompanied by pharmacotherapy as well to have control over florid symptoms.

Svadhishthana chakra The sacral plexus.

Theory of developmental intelligence Theory that emphasizes a more flexible and sophisticated thought process in the form of post-formal thought and wisdom in the second half of life. It is supported by evidence of continuing interaction of myelin and axons in the brain.

Theory of shared functions Theoretical proposition that opines that immediate emergencies of elderly individuals may be handled by neighbours, long-term care commitments may be taken care of by kin, and emotional sharing may be done with friends.

Three-dimensional model of wisdom Model that states three components of wisdom – cognitive, affective, and reflective elements.

Transcendent wisdom Re-orientation towards spiritual perspectives in old age to feel connection and concern for things larger than oneself.

Transpersonal gerontology Subdomain of gerontology which focuses on a contemplative perspective.

Turiya Realization of the self in association with the whole universe.

Vanaprastha Ashrama The third stage of life which involves leaving home when children have reached adulthood in accordance with Hindu scriptures.

Vishuddhi chakra The throat plexus.

Vrittis Agitating thoughts of the mind in the form of waves.

Zazen Meditation (which is the epitome of spirituality) according to Zen Buddhism.

INDEX

activity theory 8, 110
adulthood 52
ageing 3, 23–24, 38–39; authentic 28–32; autumn of life 5; conscious 39–40; contemplative 41–42; creativity in 67–71; dementia and 157–172; detachment and 110–118; dying person, reflective mind of 125–134; emotional detachment and 111–114; as finitization 28–30; health promotion in 210–221; inter-human vulnerability and 24–25; leisure in relation to 54–62; by living in different times 27–28; as loss 3–5; with nature 229–230; panorama of 53–54; as personal challenge 33–34; positive 52–62; psychological 6; as sadness 3–5; social engagement and 110–111; spiritual 6; spirituality and 5–9, 42–45; well-being in 210–221; and wisdom, connection between 25–27; yoga and 11–17
Alcoholic Anonymous (A.A.) 10
Alzheimer's disease 82
amàtra 16
Anahata, Hridaya chakra 126
animal-assisted therapy (A.A.T.) 143–145
anticipatory grief 163
aromatherapy 166
art therapy 146–147
attachments 110
authentic ageing 28–32
authenticity 28–32
autumn of life 5
awakening, by means of detachment 114–118; humility 117; life review 117–118; meditative mind 114–115; silence 115–116; solitude 116; withdrawal 115

backup assistance 162
balance theory of wisdom 199–201
bereavement therapy, for elderly people 141–148
Berlin wisdom model 199
Bhagavad Gita 10, 112
bibliotherapy 10
body-transcendence 114, 186
Brahmacharya Ashrama 3
Brahman 16
Brahmtattva 127
brain plasticity 74–75
breathing exercises 166
breath meditation 14–15
bridge employment 99–100
Brown's wisdom development model 202–203
Buddhism, mindfulness practices in 181–182

cabin fever 103
calm judgement 117–118
catharsis 169
circumscribed assistance 162
cognitive-behavioural therapy (C.B.T.) 138–139
collective unconscious 112
connective faith 5
conscious ageing (C.A.) 39–40; late-life developmental tasks as precursor of 40–42
contemplative ageing 41–42
continuity theory 9, 114
cosmic consciousness 42, 46
cosmic dimension 113
counting-up strategy 226
creativity, in ageing 67–71; alleviating illness(es), activities against backdrop of 75; brain plasticity 74–75;

outcomes of 75–76; sense-of-control mechanism 71–72; social engagement 72–74

dawn–dusk simulation light therapy 147–148
death 125–134; anxiety 24–26; fear of 130–131
death bed visions (D.B.V.) 128
de Beauvoir, Simone 94
deep breathing 218–219
dementia in elderly people 157–172; acknowledging dread in 169; adequate use of time for 167–168; adult offspring as caregivers 162–164; aromatherapy 166; behaviours accompanying 164; breathing exercises for 166; caregiver counselling 140–141; caring for caregivers of 170; categories of 158–159; complementary and alternative interventions for 165–167; depression 158; embarrassment 158; equanimity for 168; facing anger in 169; family role in 159–160; friendly community 164–165; hand massage and reflexology in 166; honesty for 169; humbleness for 168; humour in 169–170; living well with 159; loneliness, helplessness, and boredom 158–159; respect and 168; sense of helplessness 158; social activities/inclusion for 167–170; spiritual dimension in 170–172; spouses as key caregivers 160–162; warm touches in 166–167; yoga stretches for 166–167
depression 158
detachment 110–118; awakening 114–118; emotional 111–114; old age 113–114; orientations 112–113
developmental intelligence 25
dharma 114
disengagement theory 8
dissociative assistance 162
dying 125–126, 133–134; person, parting ways for 132–133; person, reflections of 131–132; primordial fear, transition through 127–128; as process of transition 126–127; rebellion to acceptance, transition from 129–131; struggle with death 128–129

Earth 80–81
eco-therapy 82
ego 126, 129–130; *see also Ich-Tod*
ego-integrity 33
elderly people: autumn of life 5; bereavement therapy for 141–148; creativity in 67–76; dementia in 157–172; detachment and 110–118; emotional detachment 111–114; etching existential/personal meaning among 32–33; in Indian subcontinent 82; leisure activities among 55–56; life narratives of 226–227; meditation among 15–16; mindfulness practices for 183–188; nature and 81–82, 84–89; OM utterance, spiritual significance of 16–17; personality features of 227–228; policies and programmes for 149–150; pranayama among 16–17; psychotherapeutic interventions for 138–141; recreation for 56–60; reminiscence as therapy for 17; social engagement 110–111; spiritual interventions in 9–11, 17–18; spiritualistic orientation in 228–229; spirituality and 5–9; yoga among 11–15
embarrassment 158
emotional correctness 4
emotional detachment 111–114
empty nest syndrome 98
encore career options 100
environmental determinants, elder-friendly: air 215; built and natural environments 216–217; deep breathing 218–219; forgiveness 218; gratitude 217–218; housing 215–216; intrapersonal/interpersonal relationships 219–221; personal and relational environment 217–221; self-care practices 219; socio-economic environment 217; transport 216; water 215
Erikson, Joan 4

faith 5–6; connective 5; individuation-reflective 5; intuitive-projective 5; mythic-literal 5; synthetic-conventional 5; universalizing 6
fears 127–128
finitization, ageing as 28–30
forgiveness 10, 116–117, 218
freedom 31

Garhastha Ashrama 3
generativity 4
geriatric interventions, for older adults 137–150; art therapy 146–147; bereavement therapy 141–148; cognitive-behavioural therapy 138–139; dawn–dusk simulation light therapy 147–148; dementia-caregiver counselling 140–141; insomnia, psychological treatment of 141–142; interpersonal psychotherapy 139; leisure education 147; life review/reminiscence 139; memory interventions 143; music therapy 145–146; occupational and physical therapy 142–143; pet therapy/animal-assisted therapy 143–145; problem-solving therapy 140; psychotherapeutic interventions 138–141; short-term psychodynamic therapy 139; speech and language therapy 143; supportive psychotherapy 140
gerontology: geographical 85; transpersonality in 45–47
gerontophobia 165
gero-transcendence 4, 9, 40–42, 45, 111–113
gratitude 217–218
green exercise 81
group prayer 10
guided imagery 187
guided meditation 14

hand massage 166
health behaviours 210
health habits 210–211; body weight in control 213–214; daily exercises, engaging in 212–213; eating balanced meals 212; health-compromising behaviours, reframing oneself from 215; rest, renewal, and savouring 214; sleep hygiene 211–212
H.E.R.O.(E) model of wisdom 202–203
horticulture therapy 82
humility 117

Ich-Tod 126
Ignatius Loyola 128
impact bias 95–96
individuation-reflective faith 5
insomnia, psychological treatment of 141–142
intentional systemic mindfulness (I.S.M.) 180
inter-human vulnerability 24–25
interpersonal psychotherapy 139
intrapersonal/interpersonal relationships 219–221
intuitive-projective faith 5
Iyengar, B.K.S. 12

jivatma 10

kaivalya 10
kumbhaka 16

leisure: activities 55–56, 60–61; and ageing 54–62; benefits 55; in conceptual frame 56–58; education 147; in late-life context 61–62
Levenson's model of wisdom 202
life review 117–118, 139, 194
life-story matrix 194–205; reminiscence 196–198, 204–205; retrospections 195–196; retrospective wisdom 198–205; SolCos model 197–198

Madrid International Plan of Action on Ageing 150
mantra 14
meditation 13–17; breath 14–15; guided 14; mindfulness practices 184–188; OM utterance 16–17; pranayama 16–17; transcendental 14; as treatment 15–16; yoga 13–17
memory interventions 143
mental well-being 211
mindfulness group discussions 188
mindfulness practices 178–190; of body 181; in Buddhism 181–182; conceptual overview 179–181; for elderly individuals 183–188; of feelings 181; impermanence of life, realization of 182; meditation 184–188; of mind 181; of mind-objects 181; of non-attachment 182–183; outcomes of 188–190; in physiology 183; pillars of 181; qualities 179–180; training 179–180
Muladhara chakra 126
music therapy 145–146
mythic-literal faith 5

Nabhi chakra 126
National Policy on Older Persons (N.P.O.P.) 149

National Social Assistance Programme (N.S.A.P.) 149
nature 80–89; aesthetic beauty of 80; ageing with 229–230; body and mind and 81; elderly people and 81–82, 84–89; as friends of *Homo sapiens* 87; and human life 80; as means of connection 83–84; observe and care, passion to 80–81; as relaxer and healer in life 87–88; as spiritual connection for the elderly 84–87; 'touch and feel' experiences of 81
naturopathy treatment 81
near-death experiences (N.D.E.) 125–126
niruddha 10

OM utterance 16–17

pancha bhutas 126
paramatma 10
Parkinson's disease 82
pet therapy 143–145
policies/programmes for elderly people 149–150
positive ageing 52–62; concept 52–53; leisure in relation to 54–62; panorama of 53–54; recreation in 56–60
positivism 52–53
post-formal rationality 25
pranayama 16–17
prefrontal orbital cortex (P.F.C.) 183
problem-solving therapy 140
psychological ageing 6

recreation: benefits of 60; in conceptual frame 56–58; for elderly 58–60
reflexology 166
religion 39
reminiscence 17, 139, 196–198, 204–205
repentance 10
retirement identity 94–95, 107; associated trust *vs.* mistrust 99–100; autonomy *vs.* shame/doubt 100; dilemma, choice 97–98; domestic responsibilities 98; emotional changes and 100–101; generativity *vs.* stagnation 104–107; grieving, phase of 97–98; with impact bias 95–96; individuation in 94–95, 98–107; industry *vs.* inferiority 101–102; initiative *vs.* guilt 100–102; intimacy *vs.* isolation 103–104; looking back 97; looking forward 97; losing world, issues of 99–100; narcissistic injury feeling in 96–97; *vs.* role confusion 102–103; routinization 95; transition to 96, 98
retrospections 195–205
retrospective wisdom 198–205; balance theory of wisdom 199–201; Berlin wisdom model 199; Brown's wisdom development model 202–203; H.E.R.O.(E) model of wisdom 202–203; Levenson's model of wisdom 202; three-dimensional model of wisdom 201–202
routine assistance 162

Sacred Song 112
Sannyasa Ashrama 3
second maturity 40
self-care practices 219
Senior Citizen (Maintenance, Protection and Welfare) Act 2007 149
sense-of-control mechanism 71–72
sense of helplessness 158
short-term psychodynamic therapy 139
silence 115–116
social detachment 111
social engagement 72–74, 110–111
socio-emotional selectivity theory 8
SolCos model 197–198
solitary prayer 10
solitude 116
speech and language therapy 143
spirituality 6; activity theory 8; ageing and 5–9, 42–45; continuity theory 9; and dementia in elderly people 170–172; with diminishments 47–49; disengagement theory 8; as expected tune in ageing 43–45; generic dimension 7; gero-transcendence, concept of 9; interventions 9–11, 17–18; journey 42–43; late-life developmental tasks as precursor of 40–42; practices 10; reminiscence 17; search for life 9; socio-emotional selectivity theory 8; specific dimension 8; tasks 6–7; theme 7–8
spiritual reading/bibliotherapy 10
spiritual well-being 9

sporadic assistance 162
successful ageing (S.A.) 39–40
Sunyata 14
supportive psychotherapy 140
Svadhishthana chakra 126
synthetic-conventional faith 5

theory of disengagement 39
theory of shared functions 164
three-dimensional model of wisdom 201–202
transcendence 4, 31
transcendental meditation (T.M.) 14
transcendent wisdom 45
transpersonal gerontology 38–39, 46–47, 49
turiya 16

universalizing faith 6

Vanaprastha Ashrama 3
Virat principle 127
Vishuddhi chakra 126
Vishwatmananda, Swami 13
vrittis 14

warm touches 166–167
wisdom 117–118
withdrawal 115

yoga 10–17; among elderly 11–15, 167; meditation 13–17; stretches 167

zazen 14
Zen Buddhism 112

Taylor & Francis Group
an **informa** business

Taylor & Francis eBooks

www.taylorfrancis.com

A single destination for eBooks from Taylor & Francis with increased functionality and an improved user experience to meet the needs of our customers.

90,000+ eBooks of award-winning academic content in Humanities, Social Science, Science, Technology, Engineering, and Medical written by a global network of editors and authors.

TAYLOR & FRANCIS EBOOKS OFFERS:

- A streamlined experience for our library customers
- A single point of discovery for all of our eBook content
- Improved search and discovery of content at both book and chapter level

REQUEST A FREE TRIAL

support@taylorfrancis.com

Routledge
Taylor & Francis Group

CRC Press
Taylor & Francis Group